T0243368

AMERICAN APOCALYPSE

AMERICAN APOCALYPSE

THE SIX FAR-RIGHT GROUPS WAGING WAR ON DEMOCRACY

RENA STEINZOR

STANFORD UNIVERSITY PRESS
Stanford, California

Stanford University Press
Stanford, California

Printed in the United States of America on acid-free, archival-quality paper

Cataloging-in-Publication Data available upon request.
Library of Congress Control Number: 2023041526
ISBN: 9781503634596 (cloth), 9781503639324 (ebook)

Cover design and art: Michel Vrana / Black Eye Design

CONTENTS

ONE

ORIGIN STORIES

A CONSTELLATION OF ARMIES

Intractable polarization, a steady drift toward autocracy, and chronic discontent with government have provoked widespread concern over the stability of American democracy. Where the gridlock and polarization will end is hard to see. Scientists warn that another global pandemic is inevitable and climate change is not only getting worse but happening faster. Without an effective national government, people will die or become disabled for no reason except our inability to agree on what we need government to do. People have died or been injured before for this reason—the slow journey out of slavery was not that long ago. But our big challenges move faster now, powered by the buildup of industrial pollution, the downsides of globalization, and the destructive use of technology.

Most participants in conversations about the stability of American democracy focus on the demographics and attitudes of the American people. They explore the revolt of angry white people fearful of racial diversity.[1] They consider an expanding cultural devotion to the preservation of individual rights and prerogatives over community needs.[2] Some concentrate on the emerging brands of right-wing populism that attract the disaffected.[3] Others emphasize the yawning wealth gap that has created a permanent underclass.[4]

These analyses are valid, but they focus on outcomes, not causes. Such a corrosive state of affairs did not rise, bottom up, from the people but instead was pushed, top down, by private-sector special interest groups. Viewed from this perspective, starkly different diagnoses emerge.

For decades, what I will call "the six" have waged an unrelenting, intense, and successful war on government. In the order they are discussed in this book, they include big business; the Tea Party and the Freedom Caucus, its descendant in the House of Representatives; the Federalist Society; Fox News; white evangelicals; and militia members. Power, money, and fame are their leaders' central motivations, as well as the conviction that living in a country led by left-leaning politicians is intolerable.

The six have achieved victories in a surprisingly wide range of political deployments because they are the backbone of today's Republican party. They have produced razor-thin margins in both houses of Congress and a conservative supermajority on the Supreme Court. The presidency boomerangs back and forth between Republicans and Democrats, imposing conflicting goals that further destabilize government work.

Evidence has yet to emerge that the six coordinate their attacks on government in any conscious or methodical way. On occasion, their short-term goals conflict. But their priorities fall within a surprisingly tight bull's-eye: the size and power of the administrative state, especially agencies that protect public health, worker and consumer safety, and the environment.

Cumulatively, the six are a deconstructive force of awe-inspiring power, all the more so because they have avoided recognition for what they plainly are: a constellation of armies fighting along parallel paths. The damage they cause could be devastating in the near term if it results in the ascension of another autocratic, right-wing leader to the presidency. Over the long term, an incapacitated national government will harm our children and their children in ways we can barely imagine.

COMPLICATED AGENDAS

Each of the six exists to implement complicated agendas extending far beyond the war on government. Big business is preoccupied with besting competitors around the world. The Tea Party began as a taxpayer revolt against corporate bailouts after the 2008 market crash but evolved into a crusade against big government in any form. The Federalist Society presents itself as a professional association of conservative lawyers, but its animating purpose is to host, indoctrinate, cull, and seat potential judicial nominees. Fox News's top priority is to retain, and, if at all possible, expand its loyal audience of Trump supporters. White evangelicals follow the calling of converting non-believers to Christianity by preaching the gospel. Militia members are preoccupied with guns—buying them, displaying them, and using them.

As this broader context shows, the six have plenty on their plates. Why, then, did they become involved in prosecuting a war against government? Because, as they grew stronger, they got to the point that they refused to tolerate government interference with pursuit of their overriding goals. The war on government became a matter of great importance, fueled by the Republican Party's drift rightward, away from an affirmative agenda and toward the negative one of dismantling the federal government. As former president Ronald Reagan famously said when he was inaugurated for the first time, "Government is not the solution to our problem; government is the problem."[5] Unwise appointments and Democratic resistance pushed Reagan into compromising this bold statement, but a crucial ideological marker was thrown down.

RALLYING CRIES

In line with Reagan ideology, the six have converged on a handful of common themes:

—Government is bloated, inefficient, and wasteful.

—Taxes support the bloat and should be cut, especially for "producers," defined as corporations and their owners and operators that make prosperity possible for everyone else.

—Overregulation is undermining the nation's economy and global competitiveness.

—The civil service is composed of about 2.1 million employees who are incompetent, power hungry, or both.

—Misguided federal and state officials mandated extreme and unnecessary measures to control the COVID-19 pandemic, in the process trampling on individual freedom.

—Assessments of the severity of climate change are exaggerated. Efforts to reduce greenhouse gas emissions are too expensive. The United States should not take these expensive steps until the largest emitters—countries like China and India—step up too. Or, alternatively, white evangelicals believe that God has plans for the human race that include climate change, portending the End of Days, the Second Coming of Christ, and the saving of the faithful.

—The January 6, 2021, insurrection arose for understandable reasons and could happen again if the next election is stolen.

Not every corporate executive, Tea Party adherent, Federalist Society member, Fox News host, white evangelical, or militia member agrees with all of these statements. At any given time, some of the six might focus on only one or two. Yet their steady repetition has heightened disdain for government not just among traditional conservatives, but across a full spectrum of disaffected Americans.

Six decades ago, when John F. Kennedy was president, 73 percent of Americans trusted government to do the right thing all or most of the time. Its overall approval rating now hovers around 20 percent.[6] The downward trend has endured, with only one notable but brief spike in the immediate aftermath of the September 11, 2001, terrorist attacks. Thirteen percent of respondents to a Gallup poll released in October 2023 approved of the way Congress was doing its job.[7] A second Gallup poll released at the same time found that President Biden's overall approval rating had fallen from forty percent, the same number as the approval rating during the Trump presidency, to thirty-seven percent, a record low. In an unusual change likely tied to its decision to overturn a five-decade precedent granting a constitutional right to abortion, 58 percent disapproved of the Supreme Court's performance in September 2023, a record low.[8]

SHATTERED NORMS AND DESTRUCTIVE BLOCKADES

Four characteristics have proved essential to the success of the six and are worth making explicit as guideposts to the rest of the book. All six have access to enough money to wage the war against government. Each group is organized hierarchically and produces internal discipline and charismatic leaders. The six break fundamental economic, political, and social norms. Some threaten blockades and other forms of extreme action. Much of this behavior would have been unthinkable just a few years ago. It has made the growth of MAGA possible as an intense base that reliably supports Trump's reelection.

Unprecedented amounts of money flood the electoral system, preoccupying candidates full time. Overall, according to the invaluable OpenSecrets website run by the Center for Responsive Politics, the 2020 national election cost $14.4 billion, more than doubling the amount spent on what had been the record-breaking 2016 cycle.[9] The average senator up for reelection in 2020 raised an average of $19,100 per day, and the typical House member raised $2,400 per day.[10]

Lobbying is an equally important expense, especially for big business. The nation's largest corporations began to expand their presence in Washington, D.C., in the early 1970s, opening individual offices and sponsoring trade associations for entire industries that are supplemented by private lobbying firms fielding former members of Congress and their top staff. In 2022, business groups spent 86.9 percent of the money devoted to lobbying at the federal level, for a total of $3.1 billion.[11] Some 12,609 registered lobbyists plied their trade, or about twenty-three for each member of Congress.[12] This high tide dwarfs environmental and consumer groups, civil rights organizations, and advocates for children and social service organizations.

Families that made or inherited a great deal of money in business have established their own distinct sources of funding. The best-known are the Koch brothers, immortalized in Jane Mayer's bestseller *Dark Money: The Hidden History of the Billionaires behind the Rise of the Radical Right*. The Kochs led the way but were soon followed by the Scaife Foundations, the Mercer Family Foundation, and a dozen others. They have donated hundreds of millions of dollars to right-wing think tanks, professional associations, and grassroots groups. The money is "dark" because loopholes in the tax code mean the funding sources remain anonymous.

From a norm-breaking perspective, the most powerful one of the six is the House Freedom Caucus, a well-organized group of forty-five to fifty representatives from many of the most conservative districts in the country. When Republicans control the House, party leaders will not bring legislation to the floor unless they can persuade a majority of their own members to vote in favor. When Freedom Caucus members threaten to defect, they wield enormous power, especially when the margin between the parties is close and Democrats oppose the legislation.

Dating back to 2011, when the members affiliated with the Tea Party first joined Congress and a Democrat was president, decisions to raise the debt ceiling became the favorite target of conservative representatives, along with the passage of continuing resolutions to fund the government. Their standard strategy was to threaten to vote against raising the limit or appropriate the money unless the Democratic president agreed to drastic cuts in government spending. Approval of debt-ceiling increases do not authorize the government to spend more money. Instead, a higher ceiling enables the payment of *past* bills for goods and services. If the country defaults on existing debts, the consequences would be devastating, crashing America's credit rating and causing global financial system losses. Failures to pass continuing resolutions shut down the government, an expensive and disruptive outcome that can send the lowest paid employees to soup kitchens, including enlisted members of the military. The money is eventually paid, but the trauma is real at the time. Such battles not only weaken the national government but, not incidentally, make the job of leading a Republican House majority during Democratic administrations close to unmanageable. Former Republican Speaker of the House John Boehner (R-OH) once called members of the Freedom Caucus "legislative terrorists."[13] Moderate or weak-kneed Boehner is not. He became a top lieutenant for Newt Gingrich (R-GA) soon after he joined the House, helping to achieve the political miracle of flipping the House to the Republicans in 1994 for the first time in four decades. Boehner resigned from Congress in 2015.

The dysfunction within the Republican House membership was on incredulous display during the first months of the 118th Congress, when the House cast an unprecedented fifteen ballots to elect Speaker Kevin McCarthy (R-CA) only to have a handful of far-right members depose him months later after nearly causing the shutdown of the government. The hunt for a replacement took weeks more as Republicans considered and discarded three prominent candidates only to settle on Mike Johnson (R-LA), a white evangelical with impeccable conservative credentials but no experience in a leadership role. As this book goes to press, the future stability of the House remains in alarming doubt, a government shutdown is looming, and failures to extend the debt ceiling remain real possibilities.

According to itself, the Federalist Society is a nonprofit, tax-exempt membership organization composed of conservative lawyers who meet, develop contacts, talk about their objections to liberal legal doctrines, and formulate alternatives. The group sponsors numerous conferences across the country. Panels include liberals to spice up the debate. But this benign description of enthusiastic debate and helpful networking among like-minded lawyers is misleading. In fact, securing judicial appointments is the group's primary mission. Leonard Leo, its former vice president and current co-chair of its board of directors, was a powerhouse among lobbyists and is widely credited with securing the confirmation of conservative

Supreme Court justices John Roberts, Samuel Alito, Neil Gorsuch, Brett Kavanaugh, and Amy Coney Barrett.

The backstory of Leonard Leo's success in populating the federal bench with conservatives during the Trump administration illustrates political norm breaking at its most effective. Nine months before the end of his second term, President Obama nominated then D.C. Circuit Court of Appeals judge Merrick Garland to the Supreme Court. Senate majority leader Mitch McConnell (R-KY) refused to bring the nomination to the floor, arguing that the privilege of nominating the next justice should be reserved for the president elected in 2016, a startling departure from the practice of considering a sitting president's choice. When McConnell started thinking about this strategy, his first call was to Leo.

Democrats thought Republicans had stolen the seat but were mistakenly confident that Hillary Clinton would be elected president so no harm, no foul. Instead, Trump was elected and made the nomination of Federalist Society–approved judges his top affirmative priority, solidifying a conservative supermajority on the Supreme Court. The sixth conservative justice, Amy Coney Barrett, was confirmed a handful of days before the 2020 election. During his single term, Trump accomplished the placement of 231 additional judges on federal and appellate courts and securing more seats than any recent two-term president, Democrat or Republican. The Federalist Society was largely responsible for this achievement, choosing the nominees and lobbying for their appointment successfully.

Leo's well-funded campaigns will continue. In 2021, Barre Seid, an electronic components manufacturer, donated $1.6 billion to the Marble Freedom Trust, a new group founded by Leo that is committed to waging battles over abortion rights, voting rules, and climate change policy. Seid avoided taxes by donating all the shares in his company, Tripp Lite, to Leo before it was sold to an Irish conglomerate for $1.65 billion.

A final example of norm breaking is provided by Fox News, a multi-billion dollar international media conglomerate founded and controlled by Rupert and Lachlan Murdoch, entrepreneurs who live in Australia. Rupert Murdoch founded what became the Fox Corporation in 1976. In 2023, at the age of ninety-two, he announced that he was stepping back from daily involvement with the multi-billion dollar media empire, turning full responsibility over to Lachlan, his eldest son, although he is likely to retain considerable influence behind the scenes.

The Murdochs insist on ironclad loyalty and obedience from even their biggest stars, as illustrated by the abrupt dismissal Tucker Carlson, the most popular commentator on Fox News, who was fired in April 2023 for texting obscenities about other hosts. At the time, all the network's commentators were engaged in helping to debunk the soundness of the 2020 election results, hosting controversial Trump advisers who, among other falsehoods, defamed two companies that provided voting machines to the states. Lachlan reportedly made the decision regarding Carlson, although Rupert was almost certainly consulted. Carlson is attempting to raise money to support his own media outlet, but other deposed Fox News hosts have had great difficulty without the network's imprimatur and resources.

Regardless of his departure, Carlson set the tone and content necessary to maintain a loyal and sizeable audience, and these extremes are bound to be duplicated in some form by other Fox hosts. The most poisonous of Carlson's monologues advances the conspiracy theory of white replacement. It holds that America has a ruling class (or elite) consisting of white people from upper-middle-class backgrounds who grew up on the coasts and are well-educated. (Although he never mentions it, Carlson has the same background.) He claims that this elite is determined to accomplish the replacement of the white American majority by importing undesirable people of color from poor countries. Over time, immigrants of color will outnumber white people and, because they are docile and easily led, they will elect Democrats, an obvious catastrophe for the country. Carlson also claims that the national government is biased toward people of color and discriminates against white people. A final thread charges that independent career women emasculate men.

In 2022, a few months before he was fired, Carlson sat for an interview with Ben Smith, the top editor of the streaming service Semafor. Smith asked whether he believes that whites are superior to other races. Carlson laughed and said,

> No, of course not. . . . You would find no instance where I'm like, "I'm mad at Black people." One hundred percent of the people that I'm mad at are well-educated white liberals. In my mind, the sort of archetype of person I don't like is, like, a 38-year-old female white lawyer with a barren personal life.[14]

Replacement theory is widespread among extremists. During the torch-carrying demonstration that opened the violent Unite the Right rally in Charlottesville, Virginia, in August 2017, demonstrators shouted "Jews will not replace us" and carried Nazi banners.[15] Or, in other words, by purveying white replacement theory, Carlson helped to revive a fascist creed that had resulted in the most extensive genocide the world has ever known.

When Jonathan Greenblatt, the head of the Anti-Defamation League, wrote Fox News to protest this content, Lachlan Murdoch responded that Carlson was merely talking about voting rights issues.[16] Murdoch never responded to a letter from Senate Majority Leader Chuck Schumer (D-NY) making similar points.

White evangelicals have the best turnout of any group active in electoral activities, a characteristic that has compensated for their slowly dwindling numbers. In 2020, white evangelicals were 15 percent of the population but 28 percent of the electorate. The reason is that in an age of mega-churches, with congregations in the tens of thousands and large campuses, devout white evangelicals attend more than one church service weekly and are active in a range of bible study and political education groups. Their role in the war on government is supported by old-fashioned sweat equity.

The largest association of white evangelical churches is the Southern Baptist Convention, now engaged in a series of destructive internal battles. The conference is knee-deep in its own sexual abuse scandal involving allegations that women were victimized by pastors and other elders. When an ultraconservative pastor ran for the presidency of the organization, the group's small Black minority openly considered resigning. Revolts by MAGA parishioners against their pastors' insufficient fealty to Trump have rocked evangelical congregations across the country. And in the summer of 2023, a majority of members voted to exclude churches that admit women pastors. These disagreements are likely to erode white evangelism over time because they will prove unacceptable to young people already drifting away from the church. But in the short run, the movement will remain loyal to the Republican Party and its nominee for president in 2024 and beyond.

Militia are organized at the state and the national level. Members pay modest dues to state and national organizations. Demographic details and economic circumstances of individual members are unclear. What members definitely have is a fanatic interest in guns and the time to arm themselves and engage in weapons training. Summoned by social media, they appear with their guns at demonstrations when unarmed people of like mind need help.

All militia members are ferociously opposed to any impingement on what they consider their constitutional right to bear arms. In the lead-up to January 6, 2021, they provided an armed presence to support unarmed people demonstrating for causes they approved. When hundreds marched through Lansing, Michigan, to protest pandemic restrictions imposed by Democratic governor Gretchen Whitmer, armed militia were out in force, brandishing semiautomatic weapons. They traveled to Ferguson, Missouri, with long guns, ostensibly to guard the stores of small business owners during Black Lives Matter demonstrations that followed the fatal shooting of Michael Brown. They were well-represented at the Unite the Right weekend in Charlottesville.

The most recognizable national militia leader was Stewart Rhodes, founder of the Oath Keepers in 2009. The group focuses on recruiting former or serving members of the military and the police. Most reporting about Rhodes mentioned that he is a graduate of Yale Law School. The stories do not mention that Rhodes was disbarred for abandoning his clients. He wears an eye patch because he dropped a loaded gun on the floor, shooting himself in the eye. When Trump began to gather steam with his stolen election campaign, Rhodes joined up enthusiastically, exhorting Oath Keepers to travel to Washington to take the country back.

Ironically, Rhodes never went inside the Capitol and did not interact violently with the hard-pressed Capitol police. But on his way to Washington from his home in Texas, he accumulated a small arsenal of weapons that he stored in a Virginia motel to be used when Trump invoked the Insurrection Act, as Rhodes kept exhorting him to do. The act authorizes the president to deploy armed units—specifically, "state militia" and the military—against Americans if necessary to suppress rebellion or domestic violence.[17] Rhodes thought the Oath Keepers qualified as state militia under the act and that if Trump invoked it, they could enter the District of Columbia with their guns and fight alongside other insurgents and—hopefully—members of the military ordered to take the field by the commander in chief.

The Department of Justice prosecuted Rhodes and other militia members on a slew of charges after January 6, the most prominent of which was seditious conspiracy, a felony carrying a potential sentence of two decades defined as colluding (with others) to "overthrow, put down, or to destroy by force the Government of the United States [including] to prevent, hinder, or delay the execution of any law."[18] In the first militia case to go to trial, the jury found Rhodes guilty of seditious conspiracy, among other charges, and the judge sentenced him to eighteen years in prison. Enrique Tarrio, the leader of the equally prominent Proud Boys, was sentenced to twenty-two years. The key to these verdicts was the elaborate planning to attack the Capitol done by the two men and senior members of both militias.

THE MEANING OF LEGALITY

Almost all the activities explained above other than the January 6 insurrection are legal, however objectionable opponents might find them. They are deeply embedded in the normal state of operation of American politics and policymaking. Yet that status camouflages the radical implications of what the six do by ignoring the cumulative and destabilizing impact these activities have on the national government.

The purpose of the criminal justice system is to forbid bad behavior or acts that most people would agree should be punished. Many argue that criminal law is too inclusive, allowing prosecutors to "indict a ham sandwich."[19] Others think the laws are enforced in a discriminatory and overly stringent manner, leading to mass incarceration, among other evils. (The United States has 5 percent of the world's population but 25 percent of its prisoners.) Accepting actual criminality as the ceiling for judging the behavior of the most privileged participants in our politics has grave implications for the stability of American democracy.

No one who has studied American history or is familiar with the legal system could endorse the notion that just because an activity is legal, it is desirable, acceptable, fair, or in the public interest. To mention just a few examples, Congress has not raised the federal minimum wage since July 2009, when it was capped at $7.25 per hour. Most large corporations and the country's richest people manipulate the tax system to avoid paying taxes.[20] Despite the Civil War, segregation in the public schools was legal until 1954, and many public schools have relapsed into that state.[21] In 2010, the Supreme Court granted corporations First Amendment rights, triggering the tsunami of money that has flooded electoral politics and destabilized Congress.[22] All these conditions are legal, wrong, and weaken the country.

People who strongly disagree with this perspective would say that the correct approach is not to stand outside the system waving your arms and declaring disaster but to become part of it, fighting individual battles for change. Most activists—right- or left-leaning—have followed that advice. But for all the reasons explained in the following pages, this book was written at a dangerous time and has different goals.

The first is to drive out into the open the dangerously weakened state of the federal government, especially with respect to the protection of public health and worker and consumer safety, and the implications that follow from that condition. The second is to explain how the nation got into such trouble, focusing on the six interest groups primarily responsible for the damage. The cumulative effect of their activities have pushed American government to the brink of failure. Conditions are so bad that the country does not have time to engage in long, slow, and exhausting reexamination of specific laws, increment by increment. Instead, broader, more far-reaching solutions are necessary. Again, a few examples bring these points home.

Oil and coal companies launch incessant and costly litigation that bog down the EPA's regulatory efforts to curb the emission of greenhouse gases causing climate change. Yet the agency has such a stunning shortage of funding that it operates with roughly the same resources it had in the mid-1980s before we understood the existential threat climate change poses to life on the planet.

The pressures on Congress are intense, and it has become dysfunctional. The amount of money needed to win election has had the practical effect of changing the congressional schedule to the point that members spend as much as thirty hours a week raising money, diminishing the amount of time left to do their official work to three days a week. To compensate, the Senate and the House have drifted far from the "regular order" followed throughout the twentieth century. Especially when Republicans are in charge, legislation is crafted in the leadership's office in close consultation with industry lobbyists instead of being written at the subcommittee level by members and staff who have expertise in the subject matter. Members vote without adequate notice of what bills contain. The shrinking professional press has little chance to vet their content. As veteran congressional experts Thomas Mann and Norman Ornstein have written, both parties have engaged in these practices, but Republicans have relied on them more often and with far worse effect.[23]

The following chapters consider the six in the order of their place on a spectrum from most embedded in the legal system to least. Chapter 2 looks at corporations and their construction of an overpowering lobby that does business on Capitol Hill and the White House. The third chapter is focused on the Freedom Caucus, which wields influence far beyond its numbers within Congress, now the weakest branch of government. Chapter 4 examines the success of the Federalist Society in populating the judiciary with conservative judges, including every one of the six justices who control the Supreme Court. The fifth chapter concentrates on the media, specifically Fox News and its parent, the Fox Corporation. Chapter 6 explains the political role of white evangelicals, the most reliable constituency of the Republican Party. Chapter 7 considers American militias and the undercurrent of violence they bring to American politics. Chapter 8 examines why center/left groups have been ineffective in opposing the six. Chapter 9 presents one solution that would go a long way to resolving the core of the problem, congressional paralysis: campaign finance reform.

INSURRECTION

Chapters 2–7 end with a section that explains how the six were connected to the January 6, 2021, insurrection at the Capitol that resulted in the deaths of seven people, injuries to dozens of others, and the most serious threat to the stability of national government since the Civil War. The day was a momentous turning point because the invasion of Congress transformed perceptions that the federal government might be unstable to the conviction that it is. The sight of congressional staffers crawling under desks and hoping the door locks would hold was sickening. The revelations about what former president Trump was doing at the time were mind-boggling, from watching televised reports of the violence to throwing a plate at the wall. The six pushed aside the implications of the insurrection with remarkable speed, as did Republicans in general.

Right after the insurrection, many of the largest corporations in the country announced that they would suspend contributions to Republicans, especially those who voted against the certification of President Biden's victory. They reversed the decision within weeks. As Trump continued his claims of election fraud and the House investigative committee finished its work, then House Speaker Kevin McCarthy (R-CA) turned over 41,000 hours of tapes assembled by law enforcement to Tucker Carlson, who was still working at Fox News. Carlson's staff found small sections on the tapes showing demonstrators standing around peacefully outside the Capitol, which he used to claim that the insurrection was instead a peaceful demonstration of loyal Americans and any evidence to the contrary was a "false flag" operation masterminded by dissident elements at the FBI and the military.

Fox News hosts invited Trump lawyers Rudolph Giuliani and Sidney Powell on air and they concocted conspiracy theories around two companies that manufactured and sold vote-counting equipment to the states. Both sued Fox News, and the Murdochs paid $787.5 million to settle the first case to go to trial, paying Dominion Voting Systems. A second case, alleging that several of its commentators promoted the falsehood that the company rigged its voting machines, stealing votes from Trump and transferring them to Biden, sought recovery of $2 billion in damages and was pending as this book goes to press.

High-profile members of the Federalist Society supported President Trump before, during, and after the January 6 insurrection. Senators Ted Cruz (R-TX) and Josh Hawley (R-MO), graduates of Harvard and Yale law schools, respectively, both voted against certifying the election. Two other active members, John Eastman and Jeffrey Clark, also played key roles in Trump's campaign to overturn the election. Eastman developed the untenable legal theory that Vice President Mike Pence could unilaterally overturn the results of the election. Clark offered to take over the Justice Department and steer it into supporting Trump's claims.

Christian nationalists were active participants in the insurrection, erecting a cross in front of the Capitol and carrying placards picturing Jesus in a MAGA hat. The extreme right wing of the evangelical movement, Chistian nationalists believe that the U.S. constitution was divinely inspired and that the separation of church and state should be abolished.

WHEN THE WAR BEGAN

Any effort to trace the history of social movements and their assaults on government must pick a place to begin. This book begins five decades ago, at the end of Lyndon Johnson's presidency and the beginning of President Richard Nixon's first term, when the modern regulatory state was born.

It focuses on the protection of public health, consumer and worker safety, and the environment.

Historians often overlook the early 1970s in their accounts of the two heydays of progressive government—the New Deal and the Great Society—yet the period was no less momentous.[24] In an astonishingly brief time, Congress passed unprecedented laws designed to prevent the harm caused by industrialization. The goal was to substitute prevention of injury for inadequate compensation of victims after the fact. This idea was framed as the "precautionary principle," which means taking every possible action to forestall adverse effects. The commitment to precaution represented a decision to sweep aside the laissez-faire assumption that damage to public health, worker and consumer safety, and the environment are acceptable by-products of industrial activities.

The new laws promised safety in virtually every aspect of American life, from the food we eat to the water we drink, to the pills we take when ill. Regulators would be on patrol, ensuring the purity and efficacy of drugs, mandating antilock brakes, and reducing the air pollution that keeps children indoors on code red pollution days. When the flurry of activity ended, Congress had given unprecedented power to a slew of new and strengthened agencies, including the Environmental Protection Agency, the Consumer Product Safety Commission, the Department of the Interior, the Food and Drug Administration, the National Highway Traffic Safety Administration, and the Occupational Safety and Health Administration, mandating them to write rules that would cost billions of dollars. These aspirations were naïve in important respects and no one who understood the American political system should have expected that their implementation would go smoothly. But they captured the public imagination and inspired enthusiastic support.

Today, as wildfires, hurricanes, drought, and heat worsen and a global pandemic caused almost seven million deaths worldwide, one-seventh in the United States, that optimism has largely dissipated. Over a period of three decades, members of Congress from both parties cut funding for agencies throughout the government, with the exception of the military, to the point that they have the same resources as they possessed in the mid-eighties. Controversial agencies like the EPA that attract fervent attention from the corporate lobby are in especially bad shape. Compounding these attacks, constant "bureaucracy bashing," especially by members of Congress, has demoralized the civil service to the point that it has lost courage, independence, determination, and creativity.[25]

By setting up the health, safety, and environmental agencies to fail and continuing to attack government in general terms, the six have depressed the public's confidence in this vital enterprise to historic lows. Yet public disaffection is not even the worst problem the country faces. However Americans feel about the national government, we need it more than at any other point in country's relatively short history.

TWO

CORPORATIONS

CORPORATIONS AT THE FOUNDING

The British statesmen and entrepreneurs responsible for colonizing America financed their ventures through business corporations. The Virginia Company founded Jamestown, leveraging its economic potential by introducing tobacco as a crop. The Massachusetts Bay Company was chartered in 1629 by British king Charles I to colonize parts of New England. Although the ordinary business corporation was common in Europe, only a few existed in the developing American colonies. The framers were among the wealthiest men in the colonies, and many relied on corporate investments to increase their resources. But they reacted with hostility to the possibility that the corporate form would take root in their new country.

As law professor Adam Winkler writes in his excellent book *We the Corporations: How American Businesses Won Their Civil Rights,* Thomas Jefferson and James Madison, among others, said that corporations were just another threat to the individual freedom they were intent on protecting.[1] Jefferson wrote: "I hope we shall . . . crush in its birth the aristocracy of our monied corporations which dare already to challenge our government to a trial of strength, and to bid defiance to the laws of their country."[2] Madison wrote that "the indefinite accumulation of property from the capacity of holding it in perpetuity by ecclesiastical Corporations" was an "evil" that must be resisted because "the growing wealth acquired by them never fails to be a source of abuses."[3]

Regardless, Winkler adds, the framers borrowed heavily from the "extraordinary and exceptional" corporations that "heavily influenced their understanding of limited government, individual rights, and constitutionalism."[4] The Virginia Company provided "the first taste of democracy to America."[5] The Massachusetts Bay Company provided "a model for limited government based on a written constitution."[6] The East India Company provoked the excessive taxation that was a catalyst for the Revolutionary War and the Constitution.[7]

Unfortunately, perhaps because corporations' influence and future role in the development of the country were not explicitly acknowledged as the framers wrote the Constitution, they never considered whether and how to treat the corporation in the document. The Constitution used the noun *person*, as did the ten amendments added by the Bill of Rights shortly after its ratification. Given their suspicions about the influence and the uncontrolled growth of corporations, the framers must have used the word to connote individual white men. Slaves and women were promoted much later, along with the massive influx of immigrants who made the country's expansion possible. But no mention of a corporation operating outside the government was included in the document.

As in so many areas, the framers' fears were overrun by the wildly successful growth of corporations in America. Without any doubt and with due respect to the framers, America's economic spine was built by big businesses. Native corporations caught up with the Industrial Revolution in Europe. They employed millions of people, providing economic security and educational advancement. They made it possible to fight in two world wars and many smaller conflicts.

Large corporations accomplished two more changes that confirmed Madison and Jefferson's deepest fears. They built the most successful lobbying operation in American history, developing enough political muscle to exert control over domestic policymaking almost whenever they wished. And they fought a two-hundred-year, ultimately successful battle to broaden the constitutional meaning of the word *person* to include corporations so that they had the same constitutional rights as individual citizens, including in the arena of campaign contributions.[8]

The following analysis of how big business became an overpowering political force makes no effort to cope with globalization. Industrial sectors are not considered individually. The root causes of economic successes and failures are left unexamined. Instead, the terms *big business* or *large corporations* are used to connote size—somewhere in the vicinity of Fortune 500—and the analysis examines how members of that elite group brought government agencies to heel. In the end, most agencies, especially those created in the congressional optimism in the early 1970s, were no match for the corporate lobby.

Recent polling by Gallup and the Pew Research Center reports that on a bipartisan basis, Americans have lost a significant amount of confidence in big business. Gallup does an annual poll that measures confidence in what it calls "major U.S. institutions." Results in 2021–2022 show that confidence in big business dropped from 18 percent to 14 percent.[9] Overall, the poll showed a downturn in confidence across the board. For example, the top two institutions ranked by respondents—small business and the military—dropped from 70 percent to 68 percent and from 69 percent to 64 percent, respectively. Big business ranked at the bottom of the list, with only television news (16 percent to 11 percent) and Congress (12 percent to 7 percent) ranking lower. The Pew poll had similar results, showing that the public's views of banks, other financial institutions, and large corporations have become "much more negative in recent years."[10] Respondents' reaction by party converged. For once, Republicans' reaction was not polarized by party, with confidence in large corporations standing at 26 percent for Republicans and 25 percent for Democrats.

A CALL TO ARMS

Like many crucial turning points, historians understood only in retrospect the event that catalyzed the building of the nation's most powerful lobby.[11] The catalyst took the form of a confidential, thirty-four-page memorandum addressed to the Chamber of Commerce in August 1971 by Lewis Powell, then a highly successful corporate lawyer in Richmond, Virginia, only months away from joining the Supreme Court.[12] Muckraking newspaper columnist Jack Anderson got his hands on a copy and made it public, using it to accuse Justice Powell of misrepresenting himself as a moderate during his confirmation hearings.[13] Ironically, the publicity generated by the Anderson column widened the Powell memo's circulation throughout the business community.

Powell styled the memorandum, entitled "The Attack on the American Free Enterprise System," in the harsh cadence of a general mustering the troops:

> No thoughtful person can question that the American economic system is under broad attack. . . . We are not dealing with sporadic or isolated attacks from a relatively few extremists or even from the minority socialist cadre. . . . The most disquieting voices joining the chorus of criticism come from perfectly respectable elements of society: from the college campus, the pulpit, the media, the intellectual and literary journals, the arts and sciences, and from politicians. . . . One of the bewildering paradoxes of our time is the extent to which the enterprise system tolerates, if not participates in, its own destruction. . . .
>
> What has been the response of business to this massive assault upon its fundamental economics, upon its philosophy, upon its right to continue to manage its own affairs, and indeed upon its integrity? The painfully sad truth is that business, including the boards of directors and the top executives of corporations great and small and business organizations at all levels, often have responded—if at all—by appeasement, ineptitude and ignoring the problem.[14]

Powell argued that seditious, left-wing forces had infiltrated vital institutions delivering everything from secondary education to the nightly news. The business community had a civic duty to defend free enterprise against what could become a full-fledged takeover of education, media, and government. He warned that his recommendations should be subject to "thorough study" but that "this would be an exercise in futility unless the Board of Directors of the Chamber accepts the fundamental premise of this paper, namely, that business and the enterprise system are in deep trouble, and the hour is late."[15]

The memorandum explained at length why the drift to the left was so dangerous. As evidence, Powell culled clippings from conservative commentators published in mainstream media. A central example was a column by conservative *Newsweek* columnist Stewart Alsop giving "a chilling description of what is being taught on many of our campuses."[16] Alsop wrote: "Yale, like every other major college, is graduating scores of bright young men who are practitioners of 'the politics of despair.' These young men despise the American political and economic system . . . [their] minds seem to be wholly closed. They live, not by rational discussion, but by mindless slogans."[17]

Powell wrote, "Perhaps the single most effective antagonist of American business is Ralph Nader, who—thanks largely to the media—has become a legend in his own time and an idol of millions of Americans."[18] His authority for this characterization was an article in the business magazine *Fortune* that described Nader as a "passionate man" intent on "smashing utterly the target of his hatred, which is corporate power. He thinks, and says quite bluntly, that a great many corporate executives belong in prison—for defrauding the consumer with shoddy merchandise, poisoning the food supply with chemical additives, and willfully manufacturing unsafe products that will maim or kill the buyer."[19]

Nader has spent his life engaged in passionate criticism of corporate power. But he did not become famous for advocating the demise of the free enterprise system, much less nationalizing key industries. At the beginning of his career, newly graduated from the Harvard Law School, he wrote *Unsafe at Any Speed: The Designed-In Dangers of the American Automobile.*[20] General Motors was so threatened by this charismatic and handsome young man, who wore a suit and surveyed the world with intense brown eyes, that it made the colossal mistake of hiring private investigators to go through his trash and find information that would discredit Nader. The gambit failed, propelling forward Nader's effort to coax Congress into passing legislation that would create a government agency to regulate safety in the auto industry.[21] Congress passed the 1970 Highway Safety Act, creating the National Highway Traffic Safety Administration. Nader knew that Americans would not stop buying cars from some of the world's largest corporations. He just wanted them to be safe, and he wanted the government to take care of the problem.

Powell prescribed an elaborate agenda of concrete steps the business community should take to increase its political influence. Every major corporation should create the position of "executive vice president" whose "responsibility" should be "to counter—on the broadest front—the attack on the enterprise system."[22] Businesses should devote 10 percent of their annual advertising budgets to the promotion of free enterprise. The Chamber of Commerce should lead efforts to demand "equal time" for "attractive, articulate, and well-informed speakers" who can explain the vital importance of the free enterprise system on college campuses.[23] Popular news shows should be monitored constantly for bias.

Before continuing the story of how businesses across the full spectrum of manufacturing sectors embraced the Powell memorandum, it is worth considering how this wealthy, privileged, genteel, and conservative man reached the agitated state of high dudgeon. Did he believe that capitalism and the American economy could collapse because a generation of college students were demonstrating against the Vietnam War and some professors were joining them? Or was he being overly dramatic to motivate people he saw as naïve and passive? The tone of the memorandum was out of character for a man who would gain a reputation for moderation in word and deed when he served on the Supreme Court. In an obituary when Powell died in 1998, Linda Greenhouse, the influential Supreme Court reporter for *The New York Times*, wrote that he was "the *Supreme* Court Justice who brought a voice of moderation and civility to an increasingly polarized Court during his 15-year tenure."[24] Moderation and civility do not characterize the memorandum that became one of the most important accomplishments of Powell's life.

No doubt the times were challenging, even by today's standards. The civil rights movement had provoked horrific violence by white nationalists. Theophilus "Bull" Connor unleashed firehoses and attack dogs on thousands of peaceful demonstrators in Birmingham, Alabama, in 1963. A year later, three civil rights organizers were run off the road and murdered in Mississippi. Peaceful demonstrators were viciously beaten as they crossed the Edmund Pettus Bridge on the march from Selma to Montgomery, Alabama, in 1965. Martin Luther King Jr. fell to an assassin's bullet in April 1968.

The war in Vietnam was stalemated, with generals demanding more troops and President Johnson enmeshed in political and military quagmires he recognized but believed he could not escape. As casualties rose, military leaders insisted that the war could be won if more troops were thrown into battle. Galvanized by the draft and an increasingly unpopular war, students were protesting on college campuses across the country, sometimes violently. An estimated two million people participated in the first Moratorium to End the War in Vietnam in October 1969, the largest demonstration in American history up to that point. Johnson announced he would not run for president again in March 1968. His most feared rival, Robert Kennedy, was assassinated that June, just two months after King.

Any one or all of these developments could have propelled Powell to write his cri de coeur. Yet he ignored the civil rights movement, the Vietnam War, the assassinations, and Nixon's reelection campaign, focusing only on the "massive" assault on American capitalism. Given the contrast between the memorandum and Powell's demeanor as a justice, the likely conclusion is that he was not posturing but actually believed that students, the civil rights movement, and other activist groups were attacking free enterprise and had a realistic chance of toppling American capitalism. This belief seems odd in the context of the times and with the benefit of historical hindsight.

Regardless, the timing of the Powell memorandum was propitious. As historian Kim Phillips-Fein observes in her insightful analysis of growing business activism during the period, it "crystallized a set of concerns shared by business conservatives in the early 1970s."[25] With the cooperation of President Nixon, who was worried about a challenge from Senator Ed Muskie (D-ME), frenetic congressional activity produced a raft of progressive laws that created half a dozen new agencies to carry them out and strengthened the authority of the agencies that already existed.

As the agencies wrote regulations to implement these far-reaching and expensive programs, corporate managers grew increasingly restless. When President Reagan was elected, they expected some reprieve. But Reagan appointed extremists in two key positions—the administrator of the Environmental Protection Agency (Ann Gorsuch Burford, Justice Neil Gorsuch's mother) and the secretary of the Department of the Interior (James Watt)—and they got in so much trouble with the press and Democrats in Congress that he was forced to fire them and find more moderate alternatives. Reagan was also confronted by a bipartisan group of environmentalists in Congress. The result was a second round of legislation that expanded and strengthened environmental laws, which Reagan believed he had no choice but to sign, exacerbating business dread.

FRENETIC GROWTH, DETERMINED ACTIVISM

As the agencies began to implement the new precautionary laws, business leaders upped their game in Washington by orders of magnitude. In a remarkably short period of time, the largest corporations built an unprecedented infrastructure for the advocacy of business interests. This framework has two distinct components: the institutions and personnel needed to lobby Congress, the White House, and the agencies; and the think tanks that churn out bigger-picture policy papers, op-eds, and briefing books.

Phillips-Fein reports that in 1970, most *Fortune* 500 companies lacked offices to deal with "public affairs," but a decade later, 80 percent had them.[26] The number of individual companies with registered lobbyists jumped from 175 to 650 during the same period. By 1978, two thousand corporate trade associations representing specific industrial sectors were able to field large staffs to influence Congress and the executive branch.

In his pathbreaking book on the history of the political power of American business, political scientist David Vogel writes that "during the second half of the 1960s, the political defeats experienced by business were confined to individual industries. But from 1969 through 1972, virtually the entire American business community experienced a series of political setbacks without parallel in the postwar period."[27] Vogel adds that by 1980, business forces in Washington included "12,000 lawyers representing business before federal regulatory agencies and the federal courts, 9,000 business lobbyists, 50,000 trade-association personnel, 8,000 public relations specialists, [and] 1,300 public-affairs consultants."[28]

Today, the database kept by OpenSecrets, the nonprofit organization that assembles such information, shows that in 2022, spending on lobbying was $4.1 billion, and 12,609 lobbyists were in the field. OpenSecrets bases its data analysis on mandatory reports submitted to the Senate's Office of Public Records.[29] Because the reporting rules do not include the large staffs that back up those who register as lobbyists, even these numbers substantially undercount those resources.[30]

The preeminent business group is the Chamber of Commerce. Conceived in 1912 by President William Howard Taft, who was determined to counter the growing power of organized labor, the chamber describes itself as "the world's largest business organization representing the interests of more than three million businesses of all sizes, sectors, and regions. Our members range from mom-and-pop shops and local chambers to leading industry associations and large corporations."[31] The chamber's diverse membership means that it must juggle conflicting interests, and corporate executives soon established other organizations to sidestep this problem.

Backfilling the chamber are hundreds of other trade associations representing every industry. Association lobbyists are ubiquitous on Capitol Hill and equally active at the agencies, anticipating new rules and bird-dogging their development throughout the rulemaking process. But even specialty trade associations can end up with internal conflicts among their members. To further hedge their bets, the largest companies have opened their own branch offices in Washington or hired individual firms to represent them. In 2022, the five largest independent lobbying firms earned $234 million in fees.[32]

The concern generated by Powell's memorandum was not confined to hands-on lobbying of Congress and the White House. In 1973, a group of wealthy businessmen agreed that they needed to create a nonprofit think tank that would frame and develop conservative ideas. Donors to the Heritage Foundation have included beer magnate Joseph Coors; Richard Scaife, heir to the Mellon banking fortune; and Charles and David Koch, founders of a massive industrial conglomerate based in oil and gas production. Heritage, and then the Cato Institute in 1977, joined the older American Enterprise Institute to write scores of white papers, op-eds, and briefing memos.

By 1980, Heritage had a $5.3 million budget, the equivalent of $17 million today. It provided the incoming Reagan administration with a *Mandate for Leadership*, containing "more than 2,000 policy suggestions" that the *Washington Post* said were "a bible of sorts for many in the Reagan White House."[33] Thirty-six years later, as Trump ran for president, it prepared a six-volume series "calculated to help the next president 'Make America Great Again,'" later boasting that

> by the time we closed the book on 2017, the Trump Administration had embraced 64 percent of our 321 recommendations. Congress embraced many of them too: enacting once-in-a-generation tax reform, rolling back onerous regulations, and starting the long haul toward rebuilding our dangerously depleted military. And once again, Washington observers referred to Heritage as 'the president's think tank.'[34]

Battles over legislation are hard fought and very important, but they are only the first stage in the development of what business groups claim is an excessively onerous regulatory system. The agencies spend years writing implementing regulations to resolve the crucial details of legislative mandates. They do not toil in isolation. Instead, the few available empirical studies indicate that business lobbyists dominate the rulemaking process.

Political scientists Jason and Susan Yackee found that by the mid-2000s, business interests contributed 57 percent of the comments in forty rulemakings conducted by four agencies, and only 6 percent of that total was expended by public interest organizations.[35] A team of researchers led by law professor Wendy Wagner examined ninety rulemakings mandated by the Clean Air Act to control emissions of hazardous air pollutants.[36] They found that corporate interests had an average of eighty-four contacts before a rule was even proposed, while public interest groups averaged 0.7 contacts per rule. These early, pre-rule contacts, which typically include meetings, phone calls, and letters, often determine the content of a rule before a public comment period has begun.

Rulemaking has become arduous, complex, and lengthy. Many agencies shy away from it because they lack the resources to keep up with interested industries. Unless a rule is mandated by law with a set deadline, no matter how crucial its content, it does not get proposed, much less done. A classic example is binding limits on how high temperatures can get before people must stop working outside. Climate change makes the omission not just harmful but deadly. As just one example, UPS drivers have measured temperatures as high as 140 degrees in the cargo bay areas where they unload their trucks.

One key element of rulemaking delays is the requirement that agencies do elaborate cost-benefit analyses and submit them for White House review, a feature that was built into the system from the beginning.

WHITE HOUSE RESCUE

Congressional support for precautionary laws was bipartisan, and the legislation passed by strikingly wide margins. The new laws stressed the protection of public health, worker and consumer safety, and the environment and de-emphasized consideration of regulated industries' compliance costs. For example, a core provision of the Clean Air Act instructs the EPA to protect public health from exposure to six priority pollutants with "an adequate margin of safety."[37] In an opinion written by Justice Antonin Scalia for a unanimous Supreme Court bench, this language was interpreted to prohibit the consideration of compliance costs when the EPA set limits for the six pollutants.[38] The act requires the EPA to review the adequacy of the limits every five years and, like every other pollutant the agency regulates, scientific research has driven these numbers steadily downward to make them more protective. But emissions of some of the six—most notably the smog that exacerbates respiratory illness—still plague cities like Los Angeles where car and truck exhaust are not under adequate control. It turns out that stringent provisions in the law only deliver if responsible agencies enforce them aggressively, which is where below the radar interference by the White House comes in.

As the legislation sped through Congress, business groups avoided the limelight, wary of the negative publicity they would generate if they tried to block the bills. But as the staff of the new agencies assembled and studied their new legal authority, business groups demanded that the White House strengthen its oversight to rein in costly regulatory initiatives. The strategy was successful because it leveraged a powerful trend toward expanding presidential power, the White House staff was business-oriented and conservative, and extensive White House transactions with the business lobby escaped notice.

Maurice Stans, the secretary of Commerce, persuaded chief domestic policy advisor John Ehrlichman to set up an industry task force to help White House staff oversee the EPA. The agency, once characterized by former EPA administrator William Ruckelshaus as suffering from "battered agency syndrome," has always been the leading target of industry opposition because severe pollution problems are expensive to remedy.[39] Stans' National Industrial Pollution Control Council included sixty-three executives from the most prominent corporations, as well as two hundred more tapped to serve on the council's thirty separate sub-councils. "Here is a very large part of the industrial might of the country," Stans bragged at one meeting.[40] The council gave business lobbyists a perpetually open, backdoor channel to the president, his immediate staff, and sympathetic cabinet members.

As a second fail-safe, the White House instructed the EPA to submit regulatory proposals to the Office of Management and Budget (OMB) for prepublication review. The OMB is accountable only to the president. Most of the staff conducting the reviews were economists. Their first question was whether intervention in the operations of the "free" market was justified or whether the market would resolve the problem on its own. In theory, of course, the laws passed by Congress had already made that decision.

In 1980, Congress passed a "good government" law called the Paperwork Reduction Act. Its ostensible goal was to reduce the burden on business of government requests for information from the private sector.[41] The act established a new unit at the OMB called the Office of Information and Regulatory Affairs (OIRA) to implement the act. President Reagan issued an executive order directing *all* executive branch agencies, not just the EPA, to prepare a "regulatory impact analysis" containing cost-benefit analyses for any "major" rule having an "annual effect on the economy of $100 million or more."[42] No agency could propose or finalize such a rule without submitting it to the OIRA for approval. Environmentalists, other public interest groups, and organized labor soon realized that OIRA review involved bargaining between agency staff who wrote the rule and economists concerned that the rules were too strict. The negotiations were bad enough, but they were not the end of the story. The agencies internalized what OIRA staff were likely to say and started to self-censor.

The framework of the Reagan executive order was changed by President Clinton. A broad coalition of public interest groups implored him to cut back the OIRA's power, but they won only modest concessions. Clinton issued a new executive order setting up deadlines to avoid having rules get stuck at the OIRA indefinitely. The order also required more extensive disclosure of what was going on between the agencies and the OIRA reviewers.[43] But the order did not reduce the influence of the reviewers, and the deadlines were frequently violated. The Clinton order has remained in effect through the George W. Bush, Obama, and Trump administrations, although changes that do not eliminate cost benefit analysis but modulate its impact to a small degree were adopted in 2023 by the Biden administration.

"KNOWING THE COST OF EVERYTHING AND THE VALUE OF NOTHING"

Supporters of cost-benefit analysis compare the methodology to household budgeting.[44] Just like the average person, the government figures out how much it will cost to achieve a goal and decides whether the expenditure is worthwhile. People make the same kind of financial decisions all the time goes this argument. We figure out how much it costs to heat our houses and decide whether we are willing to pay more to turn the thermostat higher on a cold night. Or we consider how much more it will cost to drive to work rather than take public transportation and whether we are willing to assume the extra expense.

The problem with this analogy is that for health, safety, and environmental policymaking, the interests of the people who are causing the problem and those who are benefiting from abating it are not the same, raising the severe equity problems that precautionary laws were intended to eliminate. An asthmatic child gasps for breath in an inner-city hospital emergency room on a code red pollution day. The EPA proposes a rule requiring the installation of equipment on power plants to reduce the harmful emissions that exacerbate the disease. But electric utilities do everything they can to kill the rule, from lobbying Congress to importuning the White

House, to suing the agency. If the regulation is adopted, utility lobbyists warn, the costs imposed on electricity utilities will be egregious. Should protecting the child's health be overridden for the economic benefit of the company's stockholders?

Cost-benefit analysis has three important advantages for big business. Costs imposed by a regulation are justified by the benefits the regulation would deliver to the public, with both ends of the equation expressed in dollars. In one stupendously astute stroke, the methodology put those harmed by industrial practices—the victims—on the same footing as the businesses that caused the harm. The overriding goal of precautionary laws—to protect public health from pollution or multiple other harms—was deep-sixed without further notice.

A second advantage is that all the number crunching is complex and confusing, obscuring the myriad value judgments made along the way. The EPA and its sister agencies hire economists to write regulatory review analyses. These documents typically run into hundreds of pages, full of mathematical formulae that actually depend on a raft of hidden assumptions. To get to them, you must dig through a crowded docket without knowing exactly where to look, much less how to interpret what you find.

Third, the numbers generated by the economists' estimates look quite precise and, in a society obsessed with numbers, they are assumed to be reliable. The calculations can be manipulated to make health and safety rules look very expensive. The use of this methodology not only departs from the laws but makes rulemaking choices inaccessible to any group or individual that does not have the resources to critically analyze these copious materials. The vast majority of Americans have no idea that such values are even at play in decisions about public health and the environment.

On the benefits side of the equation, regulators undertake the job of translating into dollars the harm that a regulation could avoid. Their fundamental building block is the monetary value of a life *before* the life is lost. The economists label potential, future fatalities as "statistical lives." The going rate for such a life is $10.1 million. To derive the $10.1 million figure, economists travel down a counterintuitive path. They try to determine what "wage premium" people might earn if they took a higher-risk job. The assumption is that workers are willing to take on more risk in exchange for more money. Calculations are based on studies that measure the amounts workers earn if they accept employment in a non-dangerous occupation (for example, office worker) versus a more hazardous one (for example, production line worker at a refinery). The economists do not ask any actual workers whether they are aware of the hazards present in the more dangerous workplace but instead assume they have such knowledge.

Another approach is to determine people's "willingness to pay" money to avoid the risk. These numbers are derived from opinion surveys. If the risk of becoming cancer-ridden and dying is 10 percent, would a survey respondent spend $2 million to avoid the risk? More? Less? No amount of money? Unsurprisingly, answers to these questions depend on the financial status of the people surveyed. Young people with less money are likely to be more hesitant about spending to avoid risk, and their parents or grandparents probably are willing to pay more. Poorer people have less money overall and cannot imagine spending large amounts.

Calculating benefits also requires placing a monetary value on nonfatal injuries. For example, the EPA is in charge of reducing industrial discharges of lead and mercury, two highly toxic heavy metals. When ingested by children under six, including infants in utero, very small amounts of lead cause irreversible damage to the development of the brain, kidneys, and nervous systems. The children do not die, but they lose intellectual capacity measured in IQ points. EPA economists estimate that the value of each IQ point lost by a child exposed to environmental sources of lead (for example, chipping or peeling lead paint) is $8,800. One factor the economists considered when developing this low estimate is that the education of children with lower IQs is generally less expensive, saving money for society as a whole regardless of the harm caused to the individual child. The assumption is as heartless as it is obscure, lost in the shuffle of assumptions.

One final ground rule applies to the calculation of benefits. If a benefit accrues at some point in the future, the monetized figure is subject to discounting. Discounting is based on the idea that avoiding long-term risk is analogous to an investment. The question becomes how much money must be invested today to deliver the amount necessary when the result occurs. The most important problem caused by discounting is to lower the benefits of taking steps to prevent climate change by cutting emissions of greenhouse gases. To calculate whether the expense of reducing emissions is justified by the benefits, economists must estimate how many lives would be saved in 2050, when emissions released decades earlier cause droughts, floods, and heat waves. If the value of future lives is discounted too much, people alive today have little economic incentive to spend money to protect their children's children, at least according to the economists at the White House.

For many years, the applicable rates were dictated by an OMB memorandum written during the George W. Bush administration and they were steep, demanding discounting at rates of 3 and 7 percent. In October 2023, the Biden administration revamped the memorandum to soften impact of discounting by making it more flexible, although the revisions preserve the practice and could be subject to manipulation.

On the cost side of the equation, affected companies estimate how much they will be compelled to spend to comply with regulatory mandates, and they often inflate these amounts.[45] To eliminate hazardous air pollutants, for example, the EPA has required the installation of scrubbers on industrial smokestacks to catch toxic gases and fine particles before they are released into the ambient air. If the equipment is already available for sale, cost estimates are grounded in reality. But if the technology is new, determining how much it will cost is guesswork at best. Regulations have the effect of creating a market for required equipment. As potential suppliers compete, prices drop. This possibility is often ignored in the calculations.

Economists also try to quantify the "indirect" or "ancillary" economic effects of the regulation. Conservative economist Jerry Ellig defines such effects as the "value lost when people cut back purchases in response to regulation-induced price increases, reductions in quality or convenience caused by regulation, and risk/risk tradeoffs. . . . Like an iceberg largely submerged below the surface, indirect costs are hidden—but dangerous to ignore."[46] This definition would expand the analysis to the point that an agency must determine how a regulation's requirements will ripple through the economy. Verifying that a regulatory action is the only—or even the primary—reason people cut back on spending and jobs are lost, as opposed to all the other factors that affect employment, is fraught with uncertainty. Conservative House Republicans have talked about moving legislation to impose this new burden on regulators but so far it has little chance of passing both houses when a president is in office who would be willing to sign it.

Left-leaning activists and commentators are the most prominent critics of cost-benefit assumptions. But at one point, the far right end of the political spectrum joined liberals inadvertently. In August 2009, as Congress was debating health care reform proposals supported by the Obama administration, Sarah Palin and other right-wing Republicans attacked Democrats for contemplating the inclusion of "death panels" that would decide whether to grant limited health care resources to the elderly and disabled. Former House Speaker and conservative activist Newt Gingrich published an op-ed in the *Los Angeles Times* entitled "Healthcare Rationing: Real Scary" reiterating the claim that the legislation would authorize "bureaucrats" to limit access to scarce medical treatments like organ transplants by considering a patient's overall health and probable life expectancy.[47] Gingrich added, "What we see at town hall meetings are Americans who legitimately believe it would be fundamentally unjust for government panels to make these kinds of ethical decisions instead of individuals, loved ones and doctors."[48] Palin and Gingrich scored a few points, but number-crunching at the agencies continued.

What happened next was a shrewd escalation in the battle to vilify regulation and the agencies that produce it. As President Obama settled into office and the Tea Party movement emerged, conservatives dropped references to benefits and talked only about costs. Cost-only analyses make the federal government's attempts to protect public health and the environment look like agencies are determined to sweep massive amounts of money into a big pile and set the pile on fire for no apparent reason.

COSTS WITHOUT BENEFITS

In 2010, the federal Small Business Administration's Office of Advocacy unveiled an analysis asserting that federal regulations cost Americans $1.75 trillion annually, almost half a trillion more than the budget deficit for that year.[49] The report claimed that "had every U.S. household paid an equal share of the federal regulatory burden, each would have owed $15,586 in 2008."[50] Its authors were Nicole and W. Mark Crain, married economists teaching at Lafayette College in Easton, Pennsylvania. They reached the $1.75 trillion figure by combining estimates of the annual compliance costs imposed by "economic" regulations, environmental regulations, the federal tax code, occupational safety and health regulations, and homeland security regulations. These calculations and the assumptions behind them were replete with leaps beyond logic, but the figure stuck.

The largest category of spending was economic regulations, which accounted for $1.24 trillion of the $1.75 trillion total. The category included "burdensome" rules "such as import restrictions, antitrust policies, telecommunications policies, product safety laws, and *many other restraints* on business activities . . . implemented outside of the OMB regulatory review process."[51] Even without the catch-all phrase "many other restraints," this definition is so broad and vague that verifying these huge sums was impossible.

Instead of scaling back the definition or developing an actual list of what regulations they intended to include, the Crains turned in a different direction. They focused on a World Bank report that tried to analyze regulatory policies in two hundred countries.[52] The World Bank researchers developed a "regulatory quality index" as one of six "governance indicators" they considered to describe each country's economy. To derive a single number as the regulatory index for each country, the World Bank researchers consulted a variety of sources, including opinion surveys of local business leaders, commercial business information providers, and nonprofit organizations. In 2008, the Crains concluded that the regulatory quality index for the United States was 1.579. From there, they set up a regression analysis that calculated the monetary value, as expressed by an increase in gross domestic product (GDP), that would result if the United States improved its regulatory quality index score from 1.579 to 2.5. Once again, the rationale for the leap in logic was faulty because the World Bank researchers never intended the opinion survey to be used to calculate the costs and benefits of specific rules.

In addition to the World Bank's regulatory quality index, the Crains' calculations incorporated other variables, such as "foreign trade as a share of GDP, total population, primary school enrollment as a share of the eligible population and broadband subscribers as a share of the population."[53] The upshot of the calculations showed that GDP per capita was positively related to the regulatory quality index, as well as the share of foreign trade and the proportion of broadband subscribers in the population. But, inexplicably, the fraction of the population that had access to a primary education was a *negative* influence on GDP. As law professor Lisa Heinzerling and economist Frank Ackerman wrote in their critique of the analysis: "If this regression were accurate, and if correlation always implied causation, GDP per capita could be increased by *raising* the [regulatory quality index], the dependence on foreign trade, or the number of broadband subscribers, or by *decreasing* enrollment in primary education."[54] Further confounding these errors, the Crains divided the costs of environmental regulation into two groups: pre-1988 and post-1988. Their post-1988 count includes rules that were never implemented because the agency pulled them back or the courts overturned them. Heinzerling and Ackerman conclude that "the mistakes are so many, cut in only one direction so thoroughly, and could have been discovered by the authors so easily, that one is pressed to conclude that the study was *designed* to produce a really big number. The number is a rhetorical device, a talking point, a trope; it is not the product of sound analysis."[55]

Members of Congress used the $1.75 trillion figure to justify regulatory reform legislation, and some proposed a bill to establish a government office to calculate "total regulatory costs and benefits."[56] Because it had garnered such attention on Capitol Hill, the nonpartisan Congressional

Research Service examined the Crains' work. Analyst Curtis Copeland reported that the Crains omitted the monetary value of the benefits achieved by rules because their report "was not meant to be a decision-making tool for lawmakers or federal regulatory agencies to use in choosing the 'right' level of regulation."[57] Left unsaid was how the report helped lawmakers seeking to eliminate regulations altogether.

The Crains reemerged in 2014 with new cost figures, this time under the auspices of the National Association of Manufacturers.[58] The price tag had increased to $2.03 trillion, "an amount equal to twelve percent of GDP."[59] This time, the Crains relied on information developed by the World Economic Forum, a private sector nonprofit famous for sponsoring an annual conference in Davos, Switzerland. The forum compiles the annual Global Competitiveness Index that ranks the overall competitiveness of 148 countries based on their score on 114 criteria grouped into twelve "pillars," or characteristics such as infrastructure, labor market, financial system, and overall market size. The evaluation of each country's performance within the pillars depends on two sources: specific, verifiable facts and the results of an opinion poll administered to an average of ninety-five business employees from each country regarding their perceptions of various economic conditions on home ground.[60]

The opinion poll includes seventy-six criteria and asks one question about each. The Crains ignored all but three. Those questions asked respondents to rate their countries' regulatory systems. The first question read: "In your country how burdensome is it for businesses to comply with governmental administrative requirements (e.g., permits, regulations, reporting?) (1 = extremely burdensome; 7 = not burdensome at all)."[61] The second and third questions asked for ratings regarding the efficiency of legal frameworks available to challenge regulations and whether regulations governing securities exchanges were effective.

The Crains used these highly subjective responses to construct an "economic regulation index," ranking the countries according to overall score. They said they used these scores to run a regression analysis that included controls for other economic and demographic variables, such as foreign trade as a share of GDP. These calculations showed that the average score of the five highest ranked countries was 26 percent higher than the score for the United States. From there, the Crains concluded that if the United States were not burdened by economic regulations, its GDP would be 36 percent, or $1.439 trillion, higher. Because they never defined economic regulations, used less than 3 percent of the questions asked by the forum, and added controls haphazardly, the number is mysterious at best.

In 2023, as this book went to press, the Crains were back with yet another study, again sponsored by the National Association of Manufacturers (NAM), that claimed regulatory costs were $3.079 trillion, or 12 percent of GDP, a $465 billion increase since 2012.[62] The Crains claimed that these costs fall disproportionately on small businesses, costing $12,800 per employee at all firms but $14,700 at firms with less than fifty employees. Tax compliance was included, at $1.3 million per firm, as was a counterintuitive mix of Occupational Health and Safety and Homeland Security regulations, at $900,000 per firm. The Crains said their 2023 report depended on the same methodology as its 2014 predecessor so that regulatory costs could be compared over time. But this time around, NAM conducted its own survey of American manufacturers. Asked to identify challenges affecting business, 78 percent named inflation, 73 percent identified attracting and retaining employees, and 72 percent selected supply-chain disruption. Federal regulations came in fourth, at 58 percent.

The Crain reports are supplemented by analyses produced at the Competitive Enterprise Institute (CEI), a think tank founded in 1984 to advance business interests from a libertarian perspective. The most important is a series of reports entitled "The Ten Thousand Commandments: An Annual Snapshot of the Federal Regulatory State." The reports are authored by Clyde Wayne Crews, vice president for policy, whose website biography announces that "he can do a handstand on a skateboard and loves motorcycles."[63]

The 2021 CEI report concluded that the "regulatory compliance and economic effects of federal intervention" were $1.9 trillion annually.[64] Crews described this figure as a "placeholder estimate" made necessary by the poor job the federal government does when calculating cost figures.[65] He asserted that $1.9 trillion "rivals" federal individual and corporate income tax receipts combined.[66] Crews's list titled "Unmeasured Costs of the Administrative State and Intervention" was somewhat more detailed than the Crains' definition, but many of the listed categories were even more unknowable. For example, Crews claimed that the report quantified the costs of "abandoning property rights," "over-licensing," and "permanent bureaucracy."[67]

In a pie chart titled "Annual Cost of Federal Regulation and Intervention, 2021 Placeholder Estimate, $1.9 Trillion," Crews allocated $196 billion to "health" (presumably health care costs) and $316 billion to "tax compliance" (the time it takes all taxpayers to complete their tax returns), but omitted the costs imposed by the Department of Defense entirely.[68] "If it were a country," he wrote, "U.S. regulation would be the world's eighth-largest economy."[69] Yet consistency was a hobgoblin for Crews, who declared thirty-seven pages later: "Regulatory costs are unknowable in an elemental sense. They are not observable or calculable—and many of the economic calculations necessary to enable central economic planning are impossible."[70]

The studies—the Crains in 2010, 2014, and 2023 and Crews on an annual basis—have attracted attention outside Congress. Mitt Romney's presidential campaign used them as the basis for a figure depicting "the hidden cost of red tape" in his "Plan for Jobs and Economic Growth."[71] Presidential candidate Donald Trump told a cheering crowd in Toledo, Ohio, "My economic agenda can be summed up in three very beautiful words. Jobs. Jobs. Jobs. We have to bring our jobs back. . . . Excessive regulation costs our economy two trillion dollars a year. Can you believe that? Two trillion dollars per year."[72] Nationally recognized outlets that reach tens of millions, including Fox News, Newsmax, Breitbart, *Forbes*, the *Wall Street Journal*, and *USA Today*, have featured the studies in news reports and political commentary.[73]

Americans' attitudes toward government are as riven by partisanship as their views on most other high-profile domestic policy issues.[74] Republicans are more upbeat when their party controls the presidency, and vice versa for Democrats.[75] But when asked whether government in general is doing too much, not even the Trump presidency improved Republican voters' outlook. In 2019, 71 percent of Republicans told the Pew Research Center that government is doing too much, compared to 78 percent of Democrats who said it should do more.[76] Sixty-eight percent of Republicans agreed with the statement that government was "wasteful and inefficient" compared to forty-seven percent of Democrats.[77] Proving a causal relationship between cost-only claims and partisan attitudes toward government is impossible. Yet repetition of such claims in the right-wing press and in Congress made them a prominent tool to demean government.

A CAR STORY

When it chooses to engage with an issue, the business lobby dominates every aspect of policymaking in Washington, D.C. It does not always win, but it is successful much of the time. It is the most nimble, adroit, and well-funded force among the six groups featured here and by far the most powerful. Members of the group cover every industry in America and reside in every state. As a whole, they are not a monolith except in one crucial respect: they strongly oppose health and safety regulation. When compelled to cut a deal because the law requires a rule, they push for the weakest standard.

In 2016, the future for big business looked bright, despite occasional threats by far-right members of Congress that they would not increase the nation's debt ceiling. The prospect terrified business because of its sobering implications for credit ratings, the stability of the stock market, and global trade.[78] Then, to the considerable amazement of CEOs, politicians, commentators, and most Americans, Donald Trump was elected president, and fixed expectations about how the government would operate began to change.

The business lobby was delighted with the Trump administration's widely publicized pledges to stop regulating and begin deregulating, even as the new president provoked upheaval in international relations and exacerbated racial tensions at home. The Trump administration made rapid progress in issuing deregulatory initiatives at agencies like the EPA, although it often lost public-interest-group challenges to those decisions in court.[79] On the other hand, many business leaders did not care what the rule books said if violations were never prosecuted, and the Trump administration slowed that aspect of agency activities to a crawl.[80]

The Trump White House chose political appointees determined to stop and reverse their agencies' regulatory activities but lacking in management experience. They distrusted professional staff, excluding them from these activities, and provoking a brain drain among seasoned mid-level managers and other experts, especially scientists.[81] The White House staff, which normally supervises controversial initiatives, was plagued by turnover and the difficulty of working with Trump.[82] On notable occasions, the zealotry of Trump political appointees and the instability and incompetence of the White House staff made a big mess of vital regulatory issues. Fuel economy standards proposed by the Department of Transportation and the EPA are a revelatory example.

Days after his inauguration, President Trump held a photo op with the CEOs of the American "Big Three"—General Motors, Ford Motor, and Fiat Chrysler (now known as Stellantis). They asked him to roll back the Obama administration's fuel economy standards, a cornerstone of efforts to reduce the emissions that cause climate change. The carmakers had agreed to the Obama rule because at the time, soon after the 2008 market crash, GM and Chrysler were on the cusp of bankruptcy and needed government bailouts. Ford was solvent but took a federal loan so its competitors would not get an unfair advantage. Escaping the Obama deal by substituting much weaker standards was an attractive option for the carmakers. Trump promised: "I'm sure you've all heard the big news that we're going to work on the CAFE [corporate average fuel economy] standards so you can make cars in America again. We want to be the car capital of the world again. We will be, and it won't be long."[83] Tightening or loosening the fuel economy standards—more mileage per gallon of gas is the overall goal—does not affect whether American car companies can manufacture their products at home. Fuel economy does affect the design of the cars that every manufacturer is allowed to sell in the country. As for driving American companies offshore, those big and expensive decisions are prompted by labor and energy costs, and tax policy, not air pollution regulations.

Trump's regulators and their White House supervisors set to work, but they immediately faced one big problem. The state of California, the fifth largest economy in the world, has the legal right to impose more stringent fuel economy standards if it can prove that "compelling and extraordinary circumstances" demand tighter controls.[84] Severe smog conditions in Los Angeles have justified these "California car rules" for decades. Sixteen states and the District of Columbia have laws that adopt California car standards automatically, further fracturing the potential market unless federal and state regulators agree on unified standards.[85] One big incentive for the carmakers to cut a deal with the Obama administration was that California and the EPA had agreed on the same requirements. They needed the same arrangement with the state for a weaker Trump administration rule.

But Trump could not have cared less about California, a blue state that he attacked often, in word and deed.[86] Conversely, California and its aggressive environmental regulators could not have cared less about him. Trump's political appointees responsible for the new fuel efficiency rules were Elaine Chao, secretary of the Department of Transportation and the wife of Senate majority leader McConnell (R-KY), and Andrew Wheeler, administrator of the EPA and a former oil industry lobbyist. Chao and Wheeler told their staff to get a deal the carmakers would like. But the negotiations with the carmakers and California dragged on.

In December 2018, *New York Times* reporter Hiroko Tabuchi reported that Trump had been lobbied by Marathon Petroleum Corporation, the largest American refinery company, and Americans for Prosperity, the conservative group funded by Charles and David Koch, who made much of their fortune producing oil and gas. Operating on the simple principle that they wanted to sell as much gasoline as they could without government interference, Marathon and the Kochs demanded even more drastic changes than the carmakers had requested. The White House, Chao, and Wheeler agreed to what the oil companies requested, California walked out of the negotiations, and the carmakers were beside themselves at the prospect of dealing with two rules: the more stringent California version and the more lenient Trump administration version.

A regulatory system run by marginally competent political appointees lacks the vital stability that the business lobby must have to prosper. Partnered with a president unconcerned about how his government performs, perilous outcomes were possible: two standards, a strict California rule applicable to a large share of the American economy, and a weaker national rule that satisfied the oil companies. Making and selling two different cars was unthinkable. Repealing the Clean Air Act and other popular statutes would impose too high a price. The oil companies had intervened and the carmakers were left in a big jam. Or, in other words, mindless deregulation can be worse than thoughtful rules.

INSURRECTION

The events of January 6, 2021, when President Trump summoned militia to the Capitol to "stop the steal," marked a radical turning point in the nation's history. The mob breached the Capitol's defenses, ran through the halls looking for Vice President Mike Pence and Speaker Nancy Pelosi with the shouted intent of doing them grave harm, and kept multiple members of Congress and their staff huddled in locked rooms for hours. The rioters overwhelmed the Capitol police force, and several officers were seriously injured as they struggled to beat back the mob without backup from a superior force. At least seven people died.[87] Much later that night, power was transferred peacefully, but for the first time in modern American history, certainty over the achievement of that outcome was cast in doubt.

As events at the Capitol escalated, some prominent business leaders condemned what happened, although most remained silent. To its credit, the most notable exception was the National Association of Manufacturers. Its CEO, Jay Timmons, released a statement calling on "armed violent protestors" to stand down: "Throughout this whole disgusting episode, Trump has been cheered on by members of his own party, adding fuel to the distrust that has enflamed violent anger. This is not law and order. This is chaos. It is mob rule. It is dangerous."[88]

On January 8, 2021, in an article on the business community's reaction to the insurrection, the *Washington Post* reported:

> The bargain with the business world worked like this: They mostly tolerated President Trump's sometimes outrageous behavior in exchange for business-friendly corporate tax cuts and regulatory rollbacks, deals they celebrated over Oval Office handshakes. . . . Business groups big and small largely stuck by Trump as he broke one norm after another over the past four years. . . . The once-comfortable alliance between Trump and corporate America has shown unprecedented strain since Wednesday's attack, forcing a reexamination of everything that businesses had won over the last four years from a White House now thrown into chaos.[89]

Six months after the Capitol riot, Gerald Seib, an executive editor at the *Wall Street Journal*, made the following observation in an essay entitled "How Corporate America Became a Political Orphan":

> Like other institutions, the U.S. business community is being buffeted by the angry partisan winds coursing through the country. But this rapid-fire series of hits illustrates an even deeper problem for corporate leaders: The Republican and Democratic parties are both undergoing a historic transformation, which increasingly makes the business community a political orphan, without a comfortable home in either party. Corporate leaders still have suitors in Washington, to be sure, but it's not as easy as it used to be to get a date to the prom. One prominent business figure privately refers to his community's place in the current political landscape as a "small and shrinking island."[90]

Seib surely oversimplifies. His analysis and the sources he consulted in the business community are overly pessimistic. Big business continues to have huge influence over Congress and the White House. However alarming CEOs found the events of January 6, 2021, most returned to regular business within weeks. According to the nonprofit Citizens for Responsibility and Ethics in Washington, 249 corporations pledged to stop their political contributions to the 147 Republicans who had opposed certification of the election. Only 85 ended up keeping the pledge. The Chamber of Commerce announced that it would not pull support for members of Congress on the basis of how they voted on the certification.

Leaders of the country's largest corporations are not monolithic; they affiliate with and contribute to both parties. Yet their antipathy to government regulation compels them to hedge their bets by supporting Republican members of Congress no matter what. They seem convinced that they can continue to win the support of Democrats and Republicans on a range of issues from climate change to more aggressive regulation of the financial services industry. Big business thwarted the implementation of controls on the financial system required by the Dodd-Frank Wall Street Reform and Consumer Protection Act.[91] Think tanks funded by the biggest family foundations that earn money from their multinational corporations have even gotten into the suppression of Democratic voters in purple states.

In May 2021, *Mother Jones* reported on a leaked tape of a presentation by a representative of Heritage Action, an affiliate of the Heritage Foundation, which lobbies state legislators. Speaking to donors about the organization's effort to encourage the passage of laws that make it more difficult for people perceived as Democratic supporters to vote, Jessica Anderson, the executive director of Heritage Action, stated: "In some cases, we actually draft [the bills] for them, or we have a sentinel on our behalf give them the model legislation so it has that grassroots, from-the-bottom-up type of vibe."[92] One of the efforts she highlighted was enactment of legislation in Georgia that would curtail ballot access for voters in Democratic counties, make it a crime to offer food or water to voters waiting in lines, and ban mobile early voting centers.

In response, African American business executives organized a statement proclaiming support for voting rights that was signed by hundreds of companies, including Amazon, American Express, BlackRock, GM, Google, and Merck. Entitled "We Stand for Democracy," the statement appeared as an ad in the *New York Times*, the *Washington Post,* and other major newspapers.[93] The *New York Times* called it "the biggest show of solidarity so far by the business community as companies around the country try to navigate the partisan uproar over Republican efforts to enact new election rules in almost every state."[94] But hundreds of the largest companies, including the oil and gas industry, were conspicuously missing from the list. Trump and McConnell responded by warning companies to stay out of politics.

When the 2024 election arrives, a replay of the January 6 insurrection is a real threat. Of all the institutions that affect the American future, few are as dependent on a stable, rational, constitution-honoring government as major corporations and their senior managers. While walking both sides of the street has always seemed beneficial, corporate silence on these disturbing events could impose financial reverses that would make the costs of most regulations look modest.

THREE

TEA PARTY

THE MOVEMENT THAT BROKE CONGRESS

The event that incited the Tea Party movement happened one month after Barack Obama was inaugurated for the first time. Rick Santelli, a typically raucous host on the CNBC Business News network show *Squawk on the Street*, was broadcasting live from the floor of the Chicago Mercantile Exchange. In the midst of his monologue, he attacked the administration's plans to provide relief for homeowners with underwater mortgages. Santelli challenged the Obama administration to put up a website where people could vote on whether they wanted to "subsidize the losers' mortgages" as opposed to those assets being foreclosed on and auctioned off to those who could "carry the water instead of drink the water."[1] Turning to traders sitting behind him, Santelli shouted, "This is America. How many of you people want to pay for your neighbor's mortgage that has an extra bathroom and can't pay their bills? Raise their hand."[2] His audience was happy to provide him with lusty boos and groans. What we need, declared Santelli, is a "Chicago tea party" to protest President Obama's misguided policies. The name Tea Party became, all at once, a reference to the 1773 demonstration when colonists dumped imported tea into the Boston Harbor, an intimation that a new political party should be formed, and the acronym for one of the movement's rallying cries: "Taxed Enough Already."

Santelli hit a nerve because the times were churning with financial angst. The stock market's spectacular crash in 2008 wiped out the retirement savings of millions. The George W. Bush administration had initiated bailouts of Wall Street valued in the hundreds of billions of dollars. The Obama administration supported the bailouts and advocated a stimulus package that would cost even more. The country was deeply in debt because of the wars in Iraq and Afghanistan. White, middle-class, conservative people were enraged by their perception that the nation would get deeper in the hole to help people who did not work as hard as they did.

The movement blossomed quickly, producing hundreds of disorganized grassroots groups scattered across the country. Veteran Democratic pollster and commentator Stanley Greenberg estimates that somewhere between 400,000 and 810,000 people joined 542 rallies across the country during this period, and about 250,000 joined one of the loosely organized national Tea Party networks, including the Tea Party Patriots, ResistNet, Tea Party Express, Tea Party Nation, FreedomWorks Tea Party, and 1776 Tea Party. Supported by money and expertise from Americans for Prosperity and FreedomWorks, two sophisticated national groups funded by the family foundations of billionaire industrialists, local activists were taught how to run meetings, attract members, organize demonstrations, develop policy statements, interview political candidates who wanted their support, and participate effectively in federal, state, and local elections. A final component of the movement's growth was conservative media, especially Fox News and its leading conspiracy theorist, Glenn Beck. Greenberg estimated that three out of five Tea Party supporters watched Fox News. Beck devoted his show to lessons about the many enemies of his viewers, replete with a blackboard where he drew elaborate diagrams of how those enemies planned to win.

In 2012, several dozen Tea Party–affiliated candidates ran for Congress and had remarkable success. Their agenda was a negative one: eliminate, reduce, and curtail. They came to Washington with the explicit goals of thwarting the Obama presidency. They would fight a guerilla war for much smaller government, far less regulation, deep cuts to social safety net programs, and strict limits on immigration. Living to fight another day, going along to get along, and bringing home money for local public works projects were not part of this agenda. They were novice politicians determined to get attention. If their goals and tactics upset mainstream Republicans or Wall Street, so be it.

Rolling Stone political reporter Tim Dickinson wrote that to understand the Tea Party class of politicians, it was necessary to

> focus less on personality than on political circumstance. They serve blood-red districts—"homogenous echo chambers," says Norman Ornstein, the American Enterprise Institute scholar who [co]wrote the book on congressional dysfunction, *It's Even Worse Than It Looks.*
>
> Their districts are typically composed of far-flung suburbs, exurbs and rural communities, sometimes a third- or fourth-tier city—Grand Rapids, Michigan—thrown in. Economically these districts fare slightly better than average: Their voters are just hanging on in the middle class but hardly thriving, with a median household income of $54,000, just $1,000 above average. . . .
>
> When election season rolls around, these politicians don't fear moderate Democrats—they are only threatened by more right-wing Republicans in a primary fight. Instead of seeking to make inroads with Hispanics or independent women, their political imperative is to serve up red meat to furious constituents who say they want "their country back."[3]

The clash between this new breed and traditional Republicans was tumultuous and important. It continues to wreak havoc in the House of Representatives, especially when Republicans control that body. In those early days, mainstream members of Congress on both sides of the aisle assumed that they were sent to Washington, D.C., to figure out what the federal government should do and to oversee presidential performance, especially when the president was from the other party. Regardless of ideology, professional politicians did not run for election with the goal of sabotaging the government's operations. Instead, they were preoccupied with legislative "wins" they could use to campaign for reelection, and they were sensitive to the charge that sessions of Congress were "do-nothing."[4] The Tea Party class collided with incumbents like a blizzard in May.

In 2015, with two election cycles under their belts, members of the House aligned with the Tea Party created the Freedom Caucus. Special interest caucuses are common in the House, giving members an opportunity to meet like-minded representatives to discuss the issues, strategize how to accomplish their mutual goals, and operate as a voting block when controversial legislation comes to the floor. The Freedom Caucus became one of the most successful groups because it is well-organized and disciplined, with members who enjoy the limelight. It has become especially adept at manipulating Speakers of the House who drift toward what Freedom Caucus members perceive as the middle.

During the Trump administration, three of its founders would go on to bigger jobs, have more influence, and continue to disrupt Congress. Former representatives Mick Mulvaney (R-SC) and Mark Meadows (R-NC) both served as White House chiefs of staff under Trump—Mulvaney in acting status during the penultimate year of the Trump presidency and Meadows during the months leading up to the 2020 election until the end of the administration. Ron DeSantis (R-FL) left the House in 2018 to run for governor of Florida. He made a name for himself by opposing pandemic restrictions and is running as a candidate for president in 2024.

As they settled themselves more deeply into their new jobs, especially in the House, these members achieved a goal few thought possible: they broke Congress.

THE DEATH OF DEALS

The genius of the Constitution is the separation of powers. The framers set up three distinct branches: the legislature, the executive, and the judiciary. Unlike the parliamentary systems common in Europe, the three branches have independent memberships that do not overlap. Members of Congress never serve in the executive branch at the same time. The framers' goal was to guarantee that the branches would check and balance each other, forestalling the tyranny of the English empire the revolution overthrew.

The Constitution established Congress in its first article and assigned the House and Senate the indispensable power to make laws. Based on colonial-era conceptions of what was needed to run a country, Congress was explicitly authorized to impose taxes, mint money, build roads and post offices, and raise armies. A catch-all appeared at the end of the list, granting the power to "regulate Commerce with foreign Nations, and among the several States."[5] Regulatory programs are based on this "commerce clause." Obviously, the federal government has grown far beyond the initial short list, and this outcome is at the core of what animates members of the Freedom Caucus.

For well over two centuries, the House and Senate managed to get the people's legislative business done, making slow but steady progress through periods of tremendous stress, including one civil and several foreign wars; two global pandemics (1919 and 2020); economic upheavals, including two stock market crashes; government expansions and contractions; and other challenging domestic and international problems. Congress created a stable banking system, set up a complicated system to collect taxes, assembled and structured the military, built interstate highways, preserved civil rights, launched the New Deal and the Great Society, and passed precautionary laws, among many other accomplishments. Republicans and Democrats fought zealous battles in the House and Senate. When either party was in the majority, it did its best to control the congressional agenda and reduce the influence of the minority party. Legislating was not a peaceful process, but Congress managed to pass laws that met the needs of a rapidly growing country with a diverse population.

Somewhere along the line between 1994, when Representative Newt Gingrich (R-GA) became Speaker of the House, and 2012, when the first Tea Party class was elected, a critical mass of Republican members developed such hostility to government that legislating through bipartisan compromise became impossible. This outcome damaged American democracy as much as any other challenge the country has ever faced with the exception of the Civil War. Long-standing procedural rules became weapons used to compel paralysis.

The filibuster ties the Senate in knots, requiring a supermajority of sixty votes to close debate and vote on legislation that before was passed by simple majority vote. The sixty votes needed to achieve cloture spell the death knell for any bill the Senate minority leader decides to oppose after consulting with the Republican conference. (Conferences are formal meetings with every member from the same party.) Some two thousand filibusters have occurred in Congress since 1917, when the Senate first adopted the cloture rule. Half this number have happened in just the last twelve years.[6] The only exception to filibusters and gridlock—or, in other words, a return to the commonsense approach of allowing a simple majority to settle an issue—is confirmations of presidentially appointed senior executive branch officials and federal judges.

Senator Mitch McConnell (R-KY), the skilled and relentless chief of Senate Republicans, and Representative John Boehner (R-OH), his House counterpart, were particularly determined to undermine the Obama administration. Shortly before the 2010 midterms, McConnell told the *National Journal*: "The single most important thing we want to achieve is for President Obama to be a one-term president."[7] *Politico* reporter Andy Barr asked minority leader John Boehner (R-OH) how he would respond to the Obama legislative agenda. Boehner, who was about to become Speaker of the House, said, "We're going to do everything—and I mean everything we can do—to kill it, stop it, slow it down, whatever we can."[8] The Obama administration lost many legislative confrontations; the swing to the far right cost Boehner his job; and McConnell engineered the appropriation of a Supreme Court seat that rightly belonged to the Democrats.

Ironically, despite the enthusiasm of Republicans for the original intent of the Constitution, its framers rejected supermajority requirements as a prerequisite for routine congressional lawmaking. As Alexander Hamilton wrote in the *Federalist Papers*:

> The necessity of unanimity in public bodies, or of something approaching towards it, has been founded upon a supposition that it would contribute to security. But its real operation is to embarrass the administration, to destroy the energy of the government, and to substitute the pleasure, caprice, or artifices of an insignificant, turbulent, or corrupt junto, to the regular deliberations and decisions of a respectable majority.[9]

The filibuster first became a recognized practice in the Senate in 1806, when senators approved what they thought was a housekeeping rule eliminating a simple majority vote to end debate, allowing individual senators who felt strongly about an issue to talk as long as they could in opposition to a motion before the body.[10] The first version of a cloture rule imposed a requirement of two-thirds of the senators present to stop debate. It was adopted in 1917. In 1975, the Senate lowered the number to sixty.

Until relatively recently, senators wishing to filibuster had to stand up and talk as long as they could without yielding the floor to opposing senators. When southern Democrats tried to block passage of the 1964 Civil Rights Act, they talked for seventy-five hours and cloture was imposed for only the second time since 1927. These days, senators may threaten to filibuster without going to such lengths. The taint of opposition to civil rights has never left the rule, and when former president Barack Obama spoke at the funeral for congressman and civil rights hero John Lewis (D-GA), he said the filibuster was a "Jim Crow relic" and called for its elimination if it was used to block voting reforms badly needed to protect civil rights.[11]

Senators have the further privilege of placing indefinite holds on nominations, most often to achieve concessions from the reigning administration regarding problems that have nothing to do with the nominee's credentials or suitability for the job. The majority leader of the Senate must recognize the hold for it to be effective, but when the president is of one party and the Senate dominated by the other party, the practice becomes routine. Negotiations typically end the hold, but they can drag on for months, even years. In the meantime, the government must operate without the president's chosen senior managers, undermining agencies' ability to formulate policy and take action.

House rules are also problematic. When Republicans control the House, their leadership follows the unfortunate "Hastert rule," named after Dennis Hastert (R-IL), who was elected to replace Newt Gingrich (R-GA) as Speaker. Under this informal "majority of the majority" rule, Republican leaders refuse to bring legislation to the floor unless it has the support of a majority of Republican members.

Beginning in 2010, somewhere between forty-five and fifty members of the House adopted the Tea Party ideology and tactics. Gradually, they realized the power they could wield if they operated as a unified voting bloc, especially in a closely divided House. They learned how to leverage their minority status by threatening to upend some of the most important but ordinarily routine pieces of congressional business—from extending the debt ceiling to funding the government. In an amazingly short period of time, Congress became the "broken branch," the vivid label coined by political scientists Thomas Mann and Norman Ornstein.[12] One leg of the three-legged stool of American government buckled, leaving the government listing dangerously to one side.

The vacuum left by congressional dysfunction is dangerous because the other two branches have stepped boldly into the void. As will be discussed further in chapter 4, the conservative majority on the Supreme Court is engaged in a determined campaign to reduce the federal government's legal authority. Holding the Constitution up as both a shield and a weapon, the conservative justices insist that they are just trying to preserve congressional prerogatives to make laws, knowing, of course, that today's Congress cannot. As disturbing, a conservative president willing to curb the rule of law is left an open field.

The genesis of congressional Republicans' conversion from mainstream members to anti-government champions began in 1978, when a talented, determined, and relentless politician with a huge appetite for power arrived as a freshman member of the 95th Congress.

THE METEOR THAT FLAMED OUT

Newt Gingrich (R-GA), a history professor and political novice, was elected as the first Republican representative in the history of Georgia's sixth district when Jimmy Carter was president. Between 1979, when he was sworn in, until the 1994 midterm elections, Gingrich waged a single-minded battle to win back the House after forty years of Democratic control. The centerpiece of Gingrich's crusade was the claim that the House was mired in corruption and the Democrats were to blame. No evidence exists that Congress was in better or worse shape from an ethical perspective than at any other time in its history. But Gingrich figured out how to fan the embers of alleged misconduct into blazes, assisted along the way by ineffective Democratic defenses.

His most imposing target was Jim Wright (D-TX), who succeeded the legendary Tip O'Neill (D-MA) as Speaker of the House. Gingrich charged that Wright used bulk sales of his autobiography to increase speaking fees in excess of legal limits. These allegations were relatively minor, but they were exacerbated by reports that Wright's top staffer, John Mack, whose brother was married to Wright's daughter, had served a prison term for attacking a woman with a hammer and a knife and leaving her for dead. Wright mishandled the allegations and in the end was forced to resign in disgrace.

Gingrich and his lieutenants hunted other prey, continuing to paint Democrats as corrupt. When the 1994 midterms arrived, with the Clinton presidency weakened by the collapse of its signature healthcare reform plan, Gingrich was ready. He persuaded Republicans to run on domestic issues, as set forth in the brilliantly titled Contract *with* America that called for welfare cuts, tax cuts, and a balanced budget. Republicans picked up fifty-four seats, one of the great upsets in American electoral history, and Gingrich became Speaker. Democrats did not retake the House until the 110th Congress (2007–2009), when George W. Bush's low approval ratings undermined Republican incumbents.

With both houses in Republican hands, their leaders thought they had a good chance to pass bills the president would not like and then override his vetoes. The strategy would present a dilemma for Clinton. If he vetoed too many bills, he would look like he had lost control of the national agenda. One of the most talented politicians ever to hold the office, Clinton moved briskly to the political center and won reelection in 1996, to Gingrich's great disappointment.

In the throes of extravagant and, as it turned out, misguided self-confidence, Gingrich made a big mistake. Misreading the mood of the country as well as members of both parties in the Senate, he attempted to impeach President Bill Clinton. The scandal of the president's relationship with Monica Lewinsky and subsequent efforts to deny it had undermined Clinton's reputation, but not to the point where even a Republican-majority Senate was willing to convict him. Gingrich deftly guided articles of impeachment out of the House, but the Senate could not muster even a bare majority for a negative verdict, much less the two-thirds vote required by the Constitution.

Republicans lost five seats in the 1998 midterms but retained control. Hoisting Gingrich on his own petard of scandalmongering, the House reprimanded him on a relatively minor ethics charge. Under pressure from Republican colleagues, Gingrich resigned from the speakership in 1998 and relinquished his seat in 1999.

Atlantic staff writer McKay Coppins gives Gingrich credit for "pioneer[ing] a style of partisan combat—replete with name-calling, conspiracy theories, and strategic obstructionism—that poisoned America's political culture and plunged Washington into permanent dysfunction."[13] Historian Julian Zelizer, author of *Burning Down the House: Newt Gingrich, the Fall of the Speaker, and the Rise of the New Republican Party*, agrees:

> Too often, we treat partisan polarization in our recent history as an inexorable force that nothing could stop. Because of large-scale forces of history, the social scientists say, voters have been sorted into "red" and "blue" states. . . . But this view of polarization as inevitable denies agency to the politicians and leaders who pushed partisan combat into a deeper

> abyss at very specific moments. . . . The battle over Speaker Wright in 1989 was one such turning point, a crucial event, from which Washington never recovered.[14]

Gingrich created a poisonous atmosphere that certainly undermined bipartisanship. He did not last long in a leadership position and, once he was gone, the Senate and especially the House were more angry, suspicious, and divided institutions. But true gridlock was yet to come.

THE RISE AND FALL OF JOHN BOEHNER

John Boehner (R-OH) arrived in Congress at the height of the Gingrich years. Like Gingrich, he was a political novice and a dark horse candidate. A successful small-business owner conscious of how banks compete through interest rates and free checking, he was irritated to discover that House rules required direct deposit of his paycheck into the House bank. He discovered a Government Accountability Office report noting that more than eight thousand checks had bounced. This fact suggested that the institution was, at the least, poorly run or, at the worst, corrupt.

Boehner realized that Minority Leader Gingrich would be quite interested in pursuing a potential House bank scandal as yet another verification of his accusations that Democrats were ethically challenged. Boehner assembled and led a group of his fellow Republican freshmen to pursue his suspicions. Known as the Gang of Seven (and sometimes the Young Turks), the group discovered that members of Congress could write checks without adequate funds in their accounts and the bank covered the deficits until members deposited more money. Some members left their accounts overdrawn for months. Most of the offenders identified in an audit of accounts were Democrats.

Gingrich was delighted with these revelations and publicized them enthusiastically. A related investigation of corruption in the House post office resulted in the resignation and criminal conviction of Dan Rostenkowski (D-IL), the powerful chairman of the House Ways and Means Committee, reenforcing the perception that Republicans were out for big game and usually bagged their prey. Media coverage not only helped Republicans to flip the House but provoked multiple resignations.

Boehner's role in exposing the scandals propelled him to the core of House leadership. From 1995 to 1999, he served as the House Republican Conference chairman, making him the fourth-ranking Republican behind Speaker Gingrich (R-GA), Majority Leader Dick Armey (R-TX), and Majority Whip Tom DeLay (R-TX). When Gingrich resigned in 1998, Boehner lost his position as conference chair to another member. Some members thought Boehner might quit Congress. Instead, he soldiered on, telling reporter Tim Alberta, who wrote a profile of him for *Politico Magazine*, that he told Barry Jackson, his chief of staff, "I'm never going to let 'em see me sweat. They're never going to see an ounce of disappointment on my face. We're just going to earn our way back."[15]

Thanks to a strong relationship with President George W. Bush, unusual patience, and cultivation of relationships within the Republican caucus, Boehner did make a comeback and was elected House minority leader in 2007. When Republicans regained the House in 2011, he became Speaker. Boehner was a seasoned practitioner of the tough brand of intra-party politics necessary to keep restless Republicans in line. But he was unprepared for the new breed of Tea Party members who marched into Washington convinced that this time Congress must be different.

Displaying the bravado that arises from an explosive mixture of hubris and single-mindedness, the group decided that the best opportunity to flex its muscles was to rebel against the routine business of voting to raise the federal debt ceiling. Refusing to raise it would have no effect on the activities Congress had already authorized the government to undertake in the appropriations process. Rather, a higher debt ceiling is necessary to pay bills for past activities already authorized by Congress. The rebels thought that a negative vote would reassure the base that they were on track to curb government spending. They downplayed the potentially disastrous consequences. Refusing to raise the debt ceiling would throw the government into default on its debts, tank the nation's credit rating, and cause upheaval in international financial markets.

Under pressure from Wall Street and big business, the Tea Partyers decided to rally around a plan called Cut, Cap, and Balance. It said that in exchange for raising the debt ceiling, Obama and the Democrats should agree to cut federal expenditures, put a cap on future levels of spending, and amend the Constitution to require Congress to balance the budget forevermore. Boehner privately lampooned the proposal, calling it "Snap, Crackle, and Pop," and when Republicans in the House approved the legislation in mid-July, Obama and the Democratic Senate rejected it out of hand.[16]

Boehner tried to appease the rebels by promising that every new dollar of debt incurred would be offset by the same amount of spending cuts. They were not mollified. The crisis continued for weeks as Wall Street and big business became increasingly hysterical. The ratings agency Standard & Poor's downgraded the nation's credit rating for the first time, and the stock market gyrated wildly, falling nearly 11 percent over a two-week period.[17]

In late July, a new controversy rocked the House when the news leaked that member Jim Jordan's (R-OH) staff had been conspiring with far-right outside groups to put pressure on Republican members to oppose any debt ceiling deal Boehner could negotiate with the Democrats.[18] This behavior was a stunning breach of House norms and Jordan was forced to apologize. Jordan was a founder of the Freedom Caucus in 2015 and ran for Speaker in 2023 but could not muster the necessary votes, in part because of incidents like this one. But the worst fallout was what the episode revealed about Boehner. As Nancy Pelosi, herself a former Speaker, told political reporter Alberta, "He could practically never deliver his votes."[19] When reporter Alberta repeated the quote to Boehner, his response was blunt and graphic: "It's hard to negotiate when you're standing there naked. It's hard to negotiate with no dick."[20]

As the debt ceiling expiration date grew close, Boehner took the exceptional step of relying on Democratic votes to get the ceiling raised. The Tea

Party rebels' willingness to walk the Republican leadership right up to the brink left fury and trepidation in its wake. The *New York Times* reported:

> In the seven months since the change of power in the House, the Washington discourse has shifted almost completely from the decades-long battle between both parties over how to allocate government resources to jousting over the moral high ground on imposing austerity, with seemingly none of the political or practical motivations that have historically driven legislation.[21]

Facing a grim future as House speaker, Boehner took an audacious chance: he engaged in highly secret negotiations with President Obama to develop a landmark budget deal. The two men negotiated the deal directly with each other, an unusual approach because members typically rely on staff even if they are monitoring the communications carefully. Their deal would have three components: curbing entitlements like Social Security, Medicare, and Medicaid, anathema to Democrats but catnip to deficit-conscious Republicans; imposing $1.2 trillion in cuts to discretionary spending, abhorred by Democrats but a victory for Republicans; and raising $800 billion in new revenue by eliminating tax deductions and loopholes, a victory for Democrats and a defeat for Republicans. Boehner told Alberta: "If I could have pulled this deal off, they could have thrown me out the next day. I would have been the happiest guy in the world."[22] As Boehner and Obama were on the brink of announcing their deal, a rump group of senators announced their own compromise, which had no chance of passing but threw the landmark Obama-Boehner negotiations off track. Each side blamed the other. When House Republicans found out about the negotiations, they were furious. Boehner's reputation as a speaker unable to control his members deepened.

In 2013, far-right members, including Senator Ted Cruz (R-TX), whom Boehner has described as "Lucifer in the flesh," sallied forth again. This time they refused to vote for legislation to appropriate enough money to keep the government operating.[23] The result was a government-wide shut down. A Washington Post–ABC poll conducted shortly after the government reopened found that 71 percent disapproved of the shutdown, 75 percent were dissatisfied with the "way this country's political system is working," and 63 percent had an unfavorable impression of the Republican party.[24]

Shutdowns demonstrate that Congress and the president cannot do their jobs. They also send a more potent message that government is expendable. Shutdowns did not happen until President Jimmy Carter asked Attorney General Benjamin Civiletti whether it was legal to continue government operations without funding approved by Congress. Civiletti reinterpreted an 1870 law known as the Anti-Deficiency Act and concluded that unfunded continuations were illegal.[25] Twenty-two shutdowns have occurred since, the vast majority for a handful of days. But three have been long enough to be widely publicized. The first was in 1995–1996 under President Clinton at the instigation of the Gingrich-led House. It lasted twenty-six days. The second, lasting two weeks, is the 2013 episode explained above. The third occurred under President Trump and lasted thirty-five days.

The next year, 2014, brought more upheaval caused by the Tea Party movement. Boehner's top deputy, House Majority Leader Eric Cantor (R-VA), was widely viewed as his successor. Cantor was part of an informal group of rising stars that also included Paul Ryan (R-WI) and Kevin McCarthy (R-CA), both of whom would become House Speakers. The three wrote a 2010 book entitled, with no apparent irony, *Young Guns: A New Generation of Conservative Leaders*.[26] On an upward trajectory in the House, Cantor appeared invincible in the 2014 open Republican primary to represent Virginia district 7, which is centered in Richmond. (In an open primary, a voter does not need to be registered as a member of a party to vote in its primary.) He faced a novice challenger named David Brat, a conservative economics professor at Randolph-Macon College, who was supported by local Tea Party activists. The unthinkable happened: Brat beat Cantor by more than ten percentage points. Brat was defeated in the

2018 midterm election by Democrat Abigail Spanberger, a former CIA operations officer and, like Brat, a political novice.

Cantor's loss had long-range implications for Republicans in both the House and Senate. It entrenched the perception, already suggested by previous Tea Party victories against prominent incumbents, that members of Congress who were not sufficiently supportive of far-right views could be "primaried," a fate as humiliating as it was career-ending. Political reporter Carl Hulse wrote that "Mr. Cantor's defeat will make incumbents much more reluctant to entertain any compromise with President Obama and the Democrats on issues like immigration, or to make votes that inflame the Republican base such as increasing the federal debt limit."[27]

Boehner had had enough. He announced his resignation from Congress on September 25, 2015, giving the newly created Freedom Caucus bragging rights for having taken down the most important Republican politician in Washington. Ways and Means Committee chair Paul Ryan (R-WI) reluctantly succeeded Boehner as speaker but retired in 2018, both because the Republican caucus remained near impossible to control and because he was rumored to be fed up with the stress of dealing with President Trump.[28] Ryan insisted that he left because he wanted to be a full-time parent while his children grew up.

After this upheaval in the House, ultraright conservatives and mainstream Republicans turned their attention to the battle over the future of the party. Overall, the mainstream lost. As just one example, former Florida governor Jeb Bush was an early favorite for his party's 2016 presidential nomination, but he failed to gain traction because he was perceived as too moderate. Brett Kavanaugh almost did not get nominated to the Supreme Court because he had worked for President George W. Bush, also perceived as insufficiently conservative. As Tea Party politicians and grassroots members and sympathizers fought their way to prominence, they pushed moderate Republicans to the railings and, by the 2016 national election, over the side of the ship.

In the wake of his defeat, Cantor said that he "had never heard of a football team that won by throwing only Hail Mary passes."[29] The remark indicates he did not fully appreciate what had happened to him. The Tea

Party takeover was done systematically, employing tactics that disrupted the routine order of congressional business with the melodrama of James Dean's "chickie run" performance in the 1955 movie *Rebel Without a Cause*.[30] Far from the desperation that motivates a Hail Mary pass, the Tea Partyers were disciplined, determined, and in the game for the long haul.

Pulling the Republican Party so far to the right is no small accomplishment. Indeed, it was a crucial factor—arguably, one of the two or three most important factors—in the election of President Trump. Some pundits spun these developments as the "death" of the Tea Party.[31] Others dismissed the Tea Party movement as an "astroturf" operation with no effective grassroots capacity.[32] Both characterizations are inaccurate. Instead, the Tea Party movement was absorbed into the Republican Party where, as commentator Paul Waldman predicted in 2013, it "has metastasized itself within its host."[33]

CONTRACTS WITH THE PEOPLE

Newt Gingrich's most fabled accomplishment—flipping the House to Republicans for the first time in four decades—is often credited to the centerpiece of his 1994 campaign strategy: proposing a "contract with America" based on national issues. Six weeks before the election, Gingrich released it at a press conference on the Capitol steps, with many of the three hundred members who signed it arrayed behind him. The contract could have provided the framework for a substantive policy agenda. But it did not succeed as anything more than a symbolic campaign promise. Only when grassroots activities were funded and steered by billionaires such as the Koch brothers did an agenda emerge, and the issues selected did more to advance the interests of the funders than the funded.

Gingrich and Republican Conference chair Dick Armey (R-TX) wrote the Contract with America at great expense and with much fanfare. They hired political consultants and pollsters to help them vet their drafts with Republicans, including candidates running for the first time. The pollsters gathered opinions on the sixty-seven items included in the original list of possibilities, and Gingrich and Armey circulated drafts to think tanks, trade associations, and business groups. Once they developed a near-final draft, they repeated the polling and focus groups.

The Contract with America pledged that within the first hundred days of taking back Congress, Republicans would introduce (but, cleverly, not necessarily pass) legislation to approve a balanced budget amendment to the Constitution. The bill would give the president line-item veto power over the budget and cut back welfare benefits, especially to single mothers who were minors. It would require longer prison sentences and strengthen the death penalty for federal crimes. (The prosecution of most crimes is handled at the state level.) United Nations officers would not be placed in command of American troops because far-right conservatives suspect the UN of nefarious intentions. The legislation would impose term limits on members of Congress. It would set limits on the money that could be recovered by consumers injured by defective products. Finally, it would eliminate congressional immunity from federal laws applying to conditions in private-sector workplaces. Two hot-button issues cherished by evangelicals—outlawing abortion and permitting prayer in schools—were left off the list.

In an interview with *Washington Post* political reporter Dan Balz, Gingrich explained, without apparent irony, that the Contract with America had two goals: to give the new Republican leadership and freshmen a "game plan" for the first one hundred days so that the freshmen would get "involved in changing the city, not learning how to be part of the city" and to offer "a positive set of things people actually want" as a "healthy antidote to the level of anger at Clinton and the level of negativism."[34] Armey said that the contract was "a seriously intended legislative agenda. We hope to pass every one of them, but we never made a guarantee we would do that."[35]

In the end, the only legislation Republicans passed was the application of federal workplace laws to Congress. Bits and pieces of other promises migrated into the statute books here and there. Welfare reform was negotiated with and announced by President Clinton. Overall, the entire resource-intensive and much publicized exercise had significant electoral benefits, but it was a flop as a practical matter, with one notable exception. Likely motivated by the Republican recapture of the House, Clinton announced that "the era of big government is over" in his 1996 State of the Union address.[36] The statement has had resounding political influence, taken to mean that Democrats had given up on the New Deal, the Great Society, and precautionary laws.

The Contract *from* America came out in 2010, soon after the Tea Party movement began to come together. It was the brainchild of Ryan Hecker, then a twenty-nine-year-old lawyer from Houston who worked on former New York City mayor Rudy Giuliani's presidential campaign. Hecker told *ABC News*, "We want to restructure our relationship with elected officials. This is a bottom-up, grassroots, transparent effort to call for real economic conservative reform."[37] The purpose, he explained, was to provide a document that politicians could sign to demonstrate their fealty to the Tea Party's grassroots.

To compile the list, Hecker established a website and solicited fellow activists to provide "planks" for the Contract from America. He whittled a thousand ideas down to fifty based on their popularity, as indicated by online votes. With Armey's advice, Hecker reduced the list to twenty items. He claimed that more than 450,000 people voted for their favorites. The top ten were released as the final Contract from America at a Tax Day rally near the Washington Monument convened by FreedomWorks, an organization headed by Armey.

The document was an amalgam of odd and ill-informed ideas. One proposal was to create a blue-ribbon task force that would audit every federal agency and program to identify whether it was duplicative, wasteful, and ineffective and its mission would be better left to the states. The contract also demanded that Congress repeal all tax laws on the books and replace them with a flat tax applicable to everyone, with the proviso that the legislation accomplishing this proposal must not be any longer than 4,543 words in length, the number of words in the original Constitution. Self-identified Tea Party members in Congress never pursued these ideas.

Party leaders warned Republicans to keep Tea Party voters in the fold.

For example, Haley Barbour, governor of Mississippi, chair of the Republican Governors Association, and former chair of the national Republican Party, warned in a speech to the Southern Republican Leadership Conference:

> How do we win in 2010? We stick together. The Democrats' fondest hope is to see the Tea Party or other conservatives split off and start a third party. Barack Obama is . . . praying for the conservative vote to be split in 2010. We can't let that happen. We've got to stay unified.[38]

THE DARK MONEY AGENDA

Based on a search of a huge inventory of documents obtained in lawsuits against the tobacco industry, Stanton Glantz, a medical doctor, and two colleagues, Amanda Fallin and Rachel Grana, published an article on the relations between the tobacco industry and the Tea Party.[39] They discovered several references to Citizens for a Sound Economy (CSE), a nonprofit think tank founded in 1984 by David Koch and Richard Fink, former professor of economics at George Mason University and executive at Koch Industries. The documents showed that CSE received substantial funding from Philip Morris, one of the largest tobacco companies in the nation. At the time, the industry was struggling against a growing body of health data documenting the diseases caused by its products. Proposals to curtail smoking included the imposition of excise taxes. CSE consulted on strategy and helped organize grassroots smokers' rights groups to oppose such taxes and other potential controls of tobacco products.

Seven years before the emergence of the Tea Party movement, CSE established a website dedicated to the "US Tea Party."[40] Internal strife over control split CSE into two new groups. The first, Americans for Prosperity, remained loyal to the Kochs. The second, FreedomWorks, hired former House majority leader Dick Armey (R-TX) as its most visible spokesman and was funded and overseen by the Scaife and Lande family foundations. Armey left FreedomWorks in 2012 following another internal battle, and the organization drifted. Today, Americans for Prosperity is substantially larger than FreedomWorks, with $64.5 million in revenue reported on its Internal Revenue Service Form 990 in fiscal year 2020, compared to $8.3 million for FreedomWorks.[41]

The Kochs are libertarians and oppose government interference in both personal and corporate affairs. They made their money through a dozen subsidiaries of Koch Industries, the second largest privately held company.[42] The Koch brothers' activities over the years are the well-publicized subject of two major books and numerous magazine and newspaper articles and online commentary.[43] David Koch died in 2019; Charles Koch is in his late eighties and continues to serve as the CEO of his company. They have invested hundreds of millions of dollars in politics, directly through campaign contributions and indirectly through the funding of groups like Americans for Prosperity.

As the organization's staff tracked political developments in the winter of 2009–2010, they noticed the emergence of local Tea Party groups and realized that such groups offered an exceptional opportunity to recruit ground troops to push their agenda. Financial support and training soon followed. On its website, Americans for Prosperity proclaimed:

> We believe every person has unique gifts that enable them to realize their American dream. This amazing potential of every individual to contribute to society is why we elevate the voices of grassroots activists in all 50 states who want to achieve policy reforms that open opportunities for all. . . .
>
> Our dedicated staff and passionate grassroots activists come from all different backgrounds and walks of life. What unites us is a steadfast belief in the power of the individual. We join together to tackle our country's biggest challenges, and we're committed to working with anyone to get good things done.[44]

Americans for Prosperity spent $20 million lobbying for the tax reform law enacted in 2017.[45] The new law distributed the largest cuts, as a percentage of after-tax income, to taxpayers like the Kochs, who are in the 95th to

99th percentiles of income distribution. The Congressional Budget Office predicted that the cuts would add $1.9 trillion to the federal deficit by 2028, a connection that got lost on people supporting the Tea Party who began their activism by abhorring deficits.[46]

In July 2022, the group, which claims three million members, listed "revealing the true cost of Washington" as its top issue and urged people to join the True Cost of Washington tour, a "grassroots movement to decrease the cost of living."[47] The target of the tour was inflation, then at the highest level in forty years and perceived as the most important political risk to Democratic candidates. The True Cost tour included rallies at multiple locations in seventeen states: Arkansas, Georgia, Illinois, Indiana, Iowa, Minnesota, New Hampshire, New Mexico, North Carolina, Ohio, Pennsylvania, South Carolina, South Dakota, Utah, Virginia, West Virginia, and Wisconsin. The website promised the announcement of more locations soon.[48]

Although they may be on the same side when business-friendly tax cuts are the issue, the relationship between Trump and the Koch brothers has been tense. In 2018, Trump tweeted that the brothers were "a total joke in real Republican circles" and "are against Strong Borders and Powerful Trade. I never sought their support because I don't need their money or bad ideas. . . . They love my Tax & Regulation Cuts, Judicial picks & more."[49] Charles Koch refused to support Trump's 2020 reelection campaign and confined contributions to other Republican candidates.

Americans for Prosperity also tackles state and local issues of interest to its benefactors. It is widely credited with turning Wisconsin into a right-to-work, anti-union state through its support of former governor Scott Walker. This campaign, which was duplicated in other states but was most successful in Wisconsin, was based on the theory that unions were the backbone of liberal Democratic politicians' success.

Researchers funded by the Ford Foundation reported that

> all told the Koch network has racked up important victories across many policy areas, like stymieing the implementation of the Affordable Care

> Act (and especially the expansion of Medicaid to poor uninsured adults) in states like Missouri and Tennessee, rolling back state efforts to address climate change (for instance, in Kansas and West Virginia), and passing massive tax cuts for wealthy individuals and companies (as in Kansas and Oklahoma).[50]

For example, Americans for Prosperity operatives organized a campaign in Nashville, Tennessee, against a $5.4 billion mass transit plan supported by the city's mayor and a coalition of local businesses.[51] The plan was subject to a voter referendum, and early polling suggested it would easily pass. The Kochs opposed it because they favor highways over mass transit (again, much of their money was generated by investments in oil and gas) and oppose the new taxes needed to fund the projects in the plan. The plan was defeated by some 42,000 phone calls and 6,000 door-knocks, all arranged by a sophisticated, computerized voter identification system called i360. Americans for Prosperity has coordinated door-to-door anti-transit canvassing campaigns for at least seven local or state-level ballots, winning the majority of them.[52]

INSURRECTION

The Freedom Caucus is fiercely loyal to Donald Trump. As mentioned earlier, Mark Meadows, a founder of the caucus, was Trump's chief of staff during and after the 2020 election. He kept in close touch with his former colleagues, setting the stage for their critical participation in the January 6, 2021, insurrection. In the days leading up to and including January 6, 2021, reporters from the *New York Times* wrote that

> a half-dozen right-wing members of Congress became key foot soldiers in Mr. Trump's effort to overturn the election, according to dozens of interviews and a review of hundreds of pages of congressional testimony about the attack on the Capitol. . . . The men were not alone in their efforts—most Republican lawmakers fell in line behind Mr. Trump's false

> claims of fraud, at least rhetorically—but this circle moved well beyond words and into action. They bombarded the Justice Department with dubious claims of voting irregularities. They pressured members of state legislatures to conduct audits that would cast doubt on the election results.[53]

The six Freedom Caucus members were Andy Biggs (R-AZ), Mo Brooks (R-AL), Matt Gaetz (R-FL), Louie Gohmert (R-TX), Scott Perry (R-PA), and Jim Jordan (R-OH). The first five asked the president for a blanket pardon from any criminal charges after the march to the Capitol turned violent. The sixth, Jim Jordan (R-OH) did not ask, perhaps because he thought Trump would not provide one. He was correct. Trump did not grant these requests. Out of 139 House members who voted to overturn the 2020 election results, 41 are members of House Freedom Caucus.

In the aftermath of the insurrection, former Speaker John Boehner published a book entitled *On the House: A Washington Memoir*.[54] He wrote, "I'll admit I wasn't prepared for what came after the election—Trump refusing to accept the results and stoking the flames of conspiracy that turned into violence in the seat of our democracy, the building over which I once presided," adding that "watching it was scary, and sad. It should have been a wake-up call for a return to Republican sanity."[55]

It was not a wake-up call, as no one could understand better than Boehner. The same group that drove him out of the House in 2015 were back with a vengeance. They must have spent time sheltering from the angry mob in an undisclosed location, but the chance to destabilize the same institutions the framers created in Article 1 of the Constitution was just too exciting to pass up.

Democrats controlled the House after Paul Ryan left, led by Speaker Nancy Pelosi (D-CA), during the 116th and the 117th Congresses. When the 118th Congress convened, Republicans had a narrow majority. Minority leader Kevin McCarthy (R-CA) soon announced he wanted to be Speaker. For the first time in American history and to the shock of everyone who works within and around Congress, it took fifteen ballots for McCarthy to eke out a victory because Freedom Caucus members refused to give him the handful of votes he needed to win. (Democrats consistently voted for their newly elected minority leader, Hakeem Jeffries [D-NY].) By the end of an embarrassing week, McCarthy had agreed to a series of unworkable demands, including the condition that a single member of the House could trigger a vote to remove him from the office. That motion was made within a few months of his election, again at the instigation of Freedom Caucus members. Three additional candidates tried to capture the office, but all failed. As this book goes to press, Representative Mike Johnson (R-LA), a close ally of Jim Jordan, has a tenuous hold on the office, and the government is once again threatened by a shutdown. At least as disconcerting as this profound dysfunction is the strong sense it conveys to the American people that one-third of the government is teetering on the edge of the precipice between governing and chaos.

FOUR

THE FEDERALIST SOCIETY

ORIGINALISM

The conservative conquest of the Supreme Court was the most important achievement of the Trump administration. The implications were brought home to millions of women of child-bearing age and the men who care about them when the six conservative justices issued *Dobbs v. Jackson Women's Health Organization*, overruling *Roe v. Wade* and ending the constitutional right to an abortion.[1] The decision reversed five decades of contrary law. It allowed the fifty states to decide whether, how, and when abortions would be available.

As just one example notable for its broad scope and punitive content, Texas, the nation's second most populous state, outlaws abortion except to save the mother's life or to prevent serious risk to her physical health. The law forces women to take to term pregnancies resulting from rape or incest unless they can afford to travel to a less restrictive state and find an opening at a clinic still providing abortions. The law also imposes criminal penalties up to life in prison on any person who performs an abortion. Two dozen abortion clinics in the state shut down almost immediately after the Dobbs decision.

The Federalist Society is the private sector organization responsible for the conservative capture of the Court. It worked for decades to achieve this and other victories by vetting conservative candidates seeking a judicial appointment and by advancing legal theories to reverse abortion rights, elevate religious rights, and undermine the federal government's authority to protect public health and the environment. All six conservative justices are Federalist Society members. As young lawyers, they enhanced their credentials as reliable candidates for the judiciary. Now they speak to enthusiastic audiences of conservative lawyers and law students.

A string of unexpected events beginning in 2016 created the opportunity for conservative capture of the high court. Democrat Hillary Clinton lost to Republican Donald Trump in the 2016 election; two justices died in office—Antonin Scalia in 2016 and Ruth Bader Ginsburg in 2020; and the Senate's Republican leadership refused to consider President Obama's nomination of District of Columbia Court of Appeals chief judge Merrick Garland to fill Scalia's seat.

The Garland nomination was sent to the Senate in March 2016, a full nine months before the end of President Obama's second term. Republicans claimed that considering a new nomination during an election year was undemocratic. But when Ruth Bader Ginsburg died in office just a few weeks before the 2020 election, Trump quickly forwarded the nomination of Amy Coney Barrett. She was confirmed with lightning speed by a party-line vote of 52 to 48, marking the first time in 151 years that a justice did not receive a single vote from the minority party. These events will endure in the history books as examples of ruthless political maneuvering for extraordinarily high stakes.

To fully understand the implications of the shift within the Supreme Court not just with respect to abortion but on many other issues, the first step is to examine "originalism," a core belief of conservative judges. This mode of analysis reads the Constitution and the Bill of Rights as dogma, the meaning of which is determined by finding out exactly what the authors of the language intended when they wrote it many years ago. The opposing view, embraced by more liberal judges and scholars, is that the ambiguous language in the two texts should be read as living documents in the context of evolving needs of the nation.

The 7–2 decision in *Roe v. Wade* depended on a right to privacy the Court thought was established by the Fourteenth Amendment. To discard *Roe*, Justice Samuel Alito, the author of the majority opinion in *Dobbs*, had to reinterpret the amendment. He wrote: "By 1868, the year when the Fourteenth Amendment was ratified, three-quarters of the States, 28 out of 37, had enacted statutes making abortion a crime even if it was performed before quickening."[2] He added that none of the supporters of the amendment thought it encompassed a right to abortion.

The Fourteenth Amendment was written in the immediate aftermath of the Civil War. Andrew Johnson was president, succeeding Abraham Lincoln. Johnson favored the quick restoration of seceding states to the Union and opposed any federal protections for freed slaves. But Congress was controlled by the fourteen-year-old Republican Party, which included a large contingent of abolitionists. The House approved articles of impeachment against Johnson, but he was acquitted by one vote in the Senate. These members drafted an amendment to protect Black Americans and sent it to the states, which ratified it in 1868.

Women in 1868—especially poor women—lived in sharply reduced circumstances from where we stand today, dependent on their husbands or fathers for sustenance, discipline, and permission. Women's suffrage would take another fifty-two years. As Justice Stephen Breyer wrote in a dissent to *Dobbs* on behalf of himself and Justices Kagan and Sotomayor:

> The majority's core legal postulate, then, is that we in the 21st century must read the Fourteenth Amendment just as its ratifiers did. . . . If those people did not understand reproductive rights as part of the guarantee of liberty conferred in the Fourteenth Amendment, then those rights do not exist.
>
> As an initial matter, note a mistake in the just preceding sentence. We referred there to the "people" who ratified the Fourteenth Amendment: What rights did those "people" have in their heads at the time? But of course, "people" did not ratify the Fourteenth Amendment. Men did.[3]

To drive his point home, Breyer cited an opinion issued by the Supreme Court in 1872. *Bradwell v. Illinois* involved the petition of Mrs. Myra Bradwell to the Illinois Supreme Court asking that the court grant her a license to practice law. The state court denied her petition and the United States Supreme Court upheld that decision, explaining:

> The civil law, as well as nature herself, has always recognized a wide difference in the respective spheres and destinies of man and woman. Man is, or should be, woman's protector and defender. . . . The harmony, not to say identity, of interest and views which belong, or should belong, to the family institution is repugnant to the idea of a woman adopting a distinct and independent career from that of her husband. . . . [A] woman ha[s] no legal existence separate from her husband . . . . [A] married woman is incapable, without her husband's consent, of making contracts which shall be binding on her or him.[4]

Without the ability to contract, a woman could not function as an attorney. Case closed.

The shock of the decision withdrawing the constitutional right to abortion drove large crowds into streets across the nation. But those protests were only the beginning. By allowing the states free rein to decide how to restrict abortion, the Court paved the way for a race to the bottom in red states.

In the years to come, states could follow the Texas example and criminalize the performance of an abortion. Such severe punishment could deter health care providers from offering the procedure even where abortions are legal. These dynamics played out when Indiana became the first state to adopt an abortion ban after *Dobbs*. The new Indiana law would allow abortion only in cases of rape, incest, or lethal fetal abnormality or when the procedure is necessary to prevent severe health effects or death. *Washington Post* columnist Ruth Marcus wrote that one exception was "if the pregnancy would result in 'substantial permanent impairment of the life of the mother.'" She asked, "Do you know what that means? Me neither—and neither will a doctor, facing the possibility of felony charges carrying a sentence of up to six years in prison."[5]

How the Federalist Society achieved its vision of a conservative Supreme Court is a remarkable story. A tight group of determined and savvy lawyers developed a radical agenda for legal reform while simultaneously pushing conservative judicial candidates, all the while claiming that the organization existed merely to debate exciting ideas. The new conservative majority turned the Supreme Court back into an activist court that is moving very fast.

TRUMP'S LISTS

During the 2016 Republican presidential primaries, Chris Christie, governor of New Jersey and a candidate, asked his friend Donald Trump, a real estate magnate and also a candidate, how he was planning to attract evangelical voters. Trump had been married three times and divorced twice. He had a reputation as an inveterate womanizer, characteristics sure to trouble evangelicals. Trump said he would ask the Federalist Society to produce a list of potential nominees for the Supreme Court and would reassure evangelical voters that he fully intended to use that list to deliver on their overriding goal: a conservative Court.

When Justice Scalia died two weeks before the South Carolina presidential primary, Donald McGahn, general counsel for the Trump campaign and Federalist Society member, primed the candidate to talk about his list. Trump pledged: "I'm gonna submit a list of justices, potential justices of the United States Supreme Court that I will appoint from the list. I won't go beyond that list. And I'm gonna let people know. Because some people say, maybe I'll appoint a liberal judge. I'm not appointing a liberal judge."[6] As explained will be explained in chapter 6, Trump was supported by 80 percent of white evangelical voters, and they are an indispensable part of the Republican base.

Many people helped prepare lists of potential candidates and steered Trump nominees toward confirmation, but none was more influential than Leonard Leo, then executive vice president of the Federalist Society and now co-chair of its board. Leo is one of the most talented lobbyists ever to work Capitol Hill. He played a crucial role in securing the Senate confirmations of Justices Samuel Alito, John Roberts, Neil Gorsuch, Brett Kavanaugh, and Amy Coney Barrett. No one deserves more credit for what the Court has become, except perhaps Senate majority leader Mitch McConnell (R-KY).

Leo is also a prodigious fundraiser. In August 2022, the *New York Times* broke the story that low-profile billionaire Barre Seid had given a nonprofit established and controlled by Leo an astounding $1.6 billion gift.[7] Seid, ninety and childless, gave all the stock in his company, Tripp Lite, an electrical device manufacturer, to Leo's nonprofit, the Marble Freedom Trust. Marble sold the stock to another company, pocketing the proceeds. Leo is using the money to expand his agenda to restricting abortion in the states, ending affirmative action, defending religious groups accused of discriminating against LGBTQ people, and fighting Democratic efforts to mitigate climate change. He explained:

> I had a couple of decades or more of experience rolling back liberal dominance in the legal culture, and . . . it was time to take the lessons learned . . . and see whether there was a way to roll back liberal dominance in other areas of American cultural, policy and political life.[8]

Among other projects, Leo has given millions of dollars to the Republican Attorneys General Association, a group that also received funds from the Chamber of Commerce and the Koch brothers. The money was used to fund Republican campaigns for attorney general and to bring litigation against agencies like the EPA. For example, the landmark Supreme Court case that curtailed the agency's authority to combat climate change was brought by a coalition of red states led by West Virginia. An affiliate of the organization, the Rule of Law Defense Fund, spent $150,000 to make robocalls encouraging recipients to attend the Trump rally that began the January 6, 2021, insurrection.

The Federalist Society was founded in 1982 by a small group of conservative law students at Yale University and the University of Chicago. Then professors Robert Bork and Scalia were their faculty advisers. The election of President Reagan renewed the determination of conservatives to retake the Court. The Federalist Society's maiden voyage was a symposium at Yale Law School in April 1982 to discuss federalism, or the balance of power between the national government and the states. Professor Scalia helped conservative law students raise money to support the event—about $25,000—from the private-sector Institute for Educational Affairs. "I sense," Ted Olson, then an assistant attorney general in the DOJ's Office of Legal Counsel, declared in his talk that weekend, "that we are at one of those points in history where the pendulum may be beginning to swing in another direction."[9] Olson went on to a long and successful career. Among other accomplishments, he was the top lawyer for presidential candidate George W. Bush when a divided Supreme Court voted 5–4 to stop the counting of votes in Florida and declare Bush the president.[10]

ROBERT BORK'S AMERICA

Already self-conscious about their minority status and aspiring to become influential, the founders of the Federalist Society were thrilled when, early in his first term, President Reagan nominated their most important mentors—Antonin Scalia and Robert Bork—to the prestigious D.C. Circuit Court of Appeals. At the beginning of his second term, Reagan decided to promote both men to the Supreme Court. Scalia went first, in 1986, and sailed through the process. Bork was nominated in 1987 and had a precedent-setting tough time. Members of the Federalist Society and, for that matter, conservatives throughout the legal community never got over the trauma of that fight. They became more determined than ever to dominate the federal courts.

Before Bork, the Senate norm was to defer to the president regarding judicial nominations because, having won election, he was entitled to choose candidates who reflected his own views on policy. Controversy over Supreme Court nominations broke out infrequently. The prequel to the contentious battle over Bork was the Senate's rejection, on a bipartisan basis, of President Nixon's nominations of Clement Haynsworth and G. Harrold Carswell.[11] Labor and civil rights organizations had strenuously opposed both men, who were southerners and embraced controversial positions on unions and race. But Nixon won confirmation of Justices Warren Burger, Harry Blackmun, Lewis Powell, and William Rehnquist, delighting conservatives and seemingly restoring stability to the process.

Reagan was determined to push the Supreme Court even further to the right. He elevated Justice William Rehnquist to chief justice and won confirmation for Justices Sandra Day O'Connor and Scalia. But a year later, when Reagan nominated Bork, liberals seemed to awaken, alarmed by the implications of another conservative appointment. The ensuing fight broke the fragile membrane insulating judicial candidates from harsh media attention and undermined the norm of deference to the president's choices.

Bork first gained national attention when he served as solicitor general during the Nixon administration. The president ordered Attorney General Elliot Richardson to fire Archibald Cox, the special prosecutor who was investigating Watergate. Richardson refused and resigned, as did Deputy Attorney General William Ruckelshaus. Bork, third in line, carried out the president's orders. No question, Bork was a self-righteous conservative. During his academic career at Yale, he wrote the nonfiction book *Slouching Toward Gomorrah: Modern Liberalism and American Decline*, which blamed liberals and the New Left for the decline of Western civilization.[12] He condemned affirmative action, the legalization of abortion, and cases guaranteeing one man, one vote. One of the first scholars to embrace originalism, he insisted that the framers did not intend to include a right to privacy in the Constitution.

When the White House announced the Bork nomination, liberal groups started to organize in opposition, lobbying every potentially sympathetic senator. The intensity of the battle is often characterized by the following quote from a nationally televised speech given by Senator Ted Kennedy (D-MA) on the floor of the Senate within hours after the nomination was made public:

> Robert Bork's America is a land in which women would be forced into back-alley abortions, blacks would sit at segregated lunch counters, rogue police could break down citizens' doors in midnight raids, schoolchildren could not be taught about evolution, writers and artists could be censored at the whim of the Government, and the doors of the Federal courts would be shut on the fingers of millions of citizens.[13]

In the end, the Bork nomination was rejected by a vote of 58–42, with three Republicans joining fifty-five Democrats.

Within a year, Bork stepped down from the court of appeals, explaining in his letter of resignation to President Reagan that he wished to escape "the constraints of propriety and seemliness" that prevent sitting judges from active participation in policy debates.[14] Bork remained an active member of the Federalist Society. When he died in 2012, Ethan Bronner of the *New York Times* wrote: "Judge Bork inspired a fervent generation of conservative legal thinkers. As America turned more conservative and President George W. Bush chose judges with views similar to his, many of Judge Bork's acolytes and admirers ended up on the federal bench."[15]

IT'S THE NETWORK—OR IS IT THE LISTS?

The battle over Bork intensified the Federalist Society founders' determination to build an institution that could provide an ideological counterweight to the mainstream legal community. In particular, they aspired to provide a conservative alternative to the American Bar Association (ABA). The ABA issues influential ratings for prospective judicial candidates and is responsible for accrediting law schools. With 194,000 members, it dominates the profession.

Overall, the Federalist Society succeeded in building its own network. Within a few years, conservative law students and young lawyers knew that if they were ambitious, anxious to network, and, especially, intent on becoming a judge, they should join Fed Soc, the group's website moniker and what law students call it. The organization's recruitment pitch is compelling. Membership affords extensive interaction with prominent public officials, judges, and legal scholars. The organization holds numerous national conventions, regional conferences, and local events. Members get a free subscription to the *Harvard Journal of Law and Public Policy*, where leading conservative scholars publish analytical pieces. Dues are modest in comparison to the ABA. Three decades after its first conference at Yale, the Federalist Society has 75,000 members, including 10,000 law students and 65,000 attorneys and legal scholars.[16]

The Federalist Society does not litigate and says it does not lobby, although executive vice president Leonard Leo's energetic activity shepherding Supreme Court nominees to confirmation sounds like lobbying by any reasonable standard. In an interview with *Washington Post* investigative reporters, Leo claimed he does this work on his "personal time," separating "my advocacy from the educational work of the Federalist Society. I put in a full day's work for the Society and spend a substantial amount of my personal time on the other public service work I also love."[17] He added:

> I have a very simple rule, which is, I'm engaged in the battle of ideas, and I care very deeply about our Constitution and the role of courts in our society. . . . And I don't waste my time on stories that involve money and politics because what I care about is ideas.[18]

But the *Washington Post* debunked his insistence that he was merely a volunteer doing good:

> The story of Leo's rise offers an inside look into the modern machinery of political persuasion. It shows how undisclosed interests outside of government are harnessing the nation's nonprofit system to influence judicial appointments that will shape the nation for decades. . . . Even as Leo counseled Trump on judicial picks, he and his allies were raising money for nonprofits that under IRS rules do not have to disclose their donors. Between 2014 and 2017 alone, they collected more than $250 million in such donations . . . according to a Post analysis of the most recent tax filings available.[19]

This story and others like it provided considerable information about potential violations of tax laws and lobbying rules committed by the network of organizations around Leo.[20] The IRS is responsible for taking enforcement actions against such violations but is woefully underfunded and politically cautious.

Apart from the lobbying it does in the judicial arena, the Federalist Society professes an agenda of stimulating debate, a disarming but insincere representation of what it intends to accomplish. The group conscientiously invites liberals to debate its most prominent members on conference panels. To emphasize its interest in opposing views, short biographies of speakers are included on its website with the disclaimer that the Federalist Society does not necessarily endorse what the speakers say. The postings are left on the website indefinitely. The impression of an ideologically balanced group of people discussing ideas should be fleeting. No one is convinced of a different position as a result of these sessions. Instead, their primary use is to help Federalist Society members develop the crucial skill of debunking arguments made by their ideological opponents.

The organization sponsors two distinct sets of activities to engage its most active members: practice groups and projects. Practice groups allow members to collaborate on their legal specialties. Most focus on traditional areas that are prominent at law firms across the country, such as corporations, financial services, international and national security law, labor and employment law, and intellectual property. But a practice group entitled Federalism and Separation of Powers is unique to the Federalist Society. As for projects, the website says its Regulatory Transparency Project is designed to promote "a national conversation about the benefits and costs of federal, state, and local regulatory policies and explores areas for possible improvement."[21] The ideological underpinnings of this work are deregulatory, and the goal of a national conversation is to convince others to embrace this view.

Two good books by political scientists characterize the core mission of the Federalist Society as networking. Both emphasize the importance of that activity. Amanda Hollis-Brusky writes that when she asked Gail

Heriot, a professor at the University of San Diego School of Law and a Federalist Society member, to explain the source of its influence, Heriot replied, "Like Verizon, it's the network."[22] Steven Teles writes that the organization has maintained a "clear, consistent, and limited mission over time" largely because of "its remarkably stable leadership cadre."[23] Four founders of the group—Steven Calabresi, David McIntosh, Gary Lawson, and Eugene Meyer—have served on its board of directors since its inception. Lawson told Teles:

> The reason we've succeeded . . . is that the same people who ran it twenty years ago, and the same people who will run it twenty years from now . . . all have a very clear vision of what this organization should do, which is promote ideas. Bring debates into law schools, bring debates into the legal community, and everything else that happens, we'll take it. If you ever view this as a device for organizing and galvanizing or anything else, it will blow up, and we all know that, and we're not going to let that happen.[24]

Lawson is certainly right that formulating specific positions for the purpose of lobbying or litigating is more strenuous and divisive than hosting a debating society. Yet his apparently guileless enthusiasm for debate should not distract from the Federalist Society's true mission: indoctrinating young lawyers regarding conservative legal ideology and grooming them to get influential jobs, especially judicial appointments under Republican presidents.

The Federalist Society's most consequential work has been the maintenance of the vaunted lists that made it possible to populate the federal courts with ultraconservative judges. *Washington Post* columnist Ruth Marcus devotes three dozen pages of her book *Supreme Ambition: Brett Kavanaugh and the Conservative Takeover* to the machinations of Kavanaugh's supporters to get him included on the highest order of such lists: candidates for the Supreme Court.[25] Kavanaugh's problem? He had a longtime association with former President George W. Bush, a politician considered too moderate by Federalist Society gatekeepers.

About a year after Trump became president, White House counsel Don McGahn spoke at the Federalist Society's annual meeting. He explained that President Trump ultimately ended up with two lists. One contained "mainstream folks, not a big paper trail, the kind of folks that will get through the Senate and will make us feel good that we put some pragmatic folks on the bench." But the administration also had a second group, made up of "some folks that are kind of too hot for prime time, the kind that would be really hot in the Senate, probably people who have written a lot, we really get a sense of their views—the kind of people that make some people nervous." According to McGahn, Trump threw the first list in the trash and went with the second. The president was "very committed to what we are committed to here, which is nominating and appointing judges that are committed originalists and textualists," he said. "The greatest threat to the rule of law in our modern society is the ever-expanding regulatory state. Regulatory reform and judicial selection are so deeply connected."[26]

By the end of his four-year term, Trump nominated and the Senate confirmed 234 federal judges, including the three Supreme Court justices. Trump succeeded in filling every vacancy on the federal appellate courts.[27] He could not have accomplished this feat without the help of Leonard Leo and Mitch McConnell. The latter's motto during Republican administrations has been to "leave no vacancy behind."[28] As points of reference, all four two-term presidents who preceded Trump did not do nearly as well: Reagan saw 402 judges confirmed (or an average of 201 per term); Clinton, 387 (193 per term); George W. Bush, 340 (170 per term); and Obama, 334 (167 per term).

THE ENERGIZER BUNNY OF CONSTITUTIONAL LAW

Three categories of cases decided after conservative justices Gorsuch, Kavanaugh, and Barrett joined justices Thomas, Alito, and Roberts are especially relevant to how the Court is curtailing government. The first and second dealt with the protection of public health during the pandemic, and the third involved the EPA's authority to mitigate climate change. The foundation of these decisions is the premise that Congress violates the constitutional principle of a separation of powers by delegating its legislative responsibilities to unelected bureaucrats who work in the executive, not the legislative branch. The flip side of this precept is that during Democratic administrations, agencies make decisions that are well beyond their statutory authority on so-called "major questions" of great economic and social significance that only Congress is authorized to solve.

Unlike the other federal courts at both the trial and appellate levels, which take appeals by the losing party as a matter of right, the Supreme Court has discretion to choose its cases. Aggrieved parties file somewhere in the vicinity of 7,000–8,000 requests for review annually. A minimum of four justices must vote in favor of taking a case, and the Court takes about eighty appeals annually. A single session of the Court lasts from the first Monday in October to the same date twelve months later. The justices do not conduct business together from the date of adjournment in late June or early July until their next session begins in October.

Since the conservative supermajority on the Court coalesced, it has prioritized cases involving overreach by agencies that protect public health, worker and consumer safety, and the environment, sending a clear message that it will overturn agency action that Congress has not explicitly authorized. The destructive implications for federal and state regulatory agencies are hard to overstate.

Law professor Lawson, Federalist Society board member and former clerk to Judge and then Justice Scalia, has specialized in promoting these ideas, which he characterizes under a broad theory called the "non-delegation doctrine." He describes it as "the Energizer Bunny of constitutional law: No matter how many times it gets broken, beaten, or buried, it just keeps going and going."[29]

Lawson argues that the framers of the Constitution never authorized the expansion of the administrative state and that large swaths of it are unconstitutional. True, the framers established an executive branch, and the president who heads it obviously needs people to help carry out his responsibilities. But the executive branch and the bureaucracy have expanded far beyond what the framers intended and must be cut back. Rather than step up to keep the executive branch under control, as the framers also intended, Congress is shirking its lawmaking function, writing laws that are so vague and expansive that in effect they authorize the bureaucracy to continue to legislate in violation of the separation of powers. Among Lawson's leading examples of offensive laws are the Securities Exchange Act, which created the Securities and Exchange Commission to ensure information relied on by investors in the stock market is accurate and available; the Communications Act, which created the Federal Communications Commission to administer access to public broadcast systems; and the Clean Air Act, which authorizes the EPA's most important work, including the reduction of greenhouse gases that cause climate change.

Lawson's description of the non-delegation doctrine as the Energizer Bunny is misleading. To be sure, the bunny has jumped up from time to time, exciting Federalist Society members. But until the conservative majority took over the Supreme Court, the first and last time the justices had overturned a law because it involved the constitutionally impermissible delegation of legislative power was eighty-seven years ago, during the first administration of Franklin Delano Roosevelt. The country was in the devastating grip of the Great Depression that began with the stock market crash of 1929 and did not end for a decade. Roosevelt was determined to create incentives for companies to put people back to work. Within his first one hundred days in office, Congress passed the 1933 National Industrial Recovery Act (NIRA), which, among other things, allowed private industry trade associations to develop codes prohibiting unfair competition. The president would approve the codes and they would be implemented not by federal agencies but by the associations themselves. Presidential approval meant violations of the codes were crimes that could be prosecuted in the federal courts.

Two Supreme Court cases decided within months of each other in the winter and spring of 1935 declared the NIRA unconstitutional, in effect wiping it off the books. The more important of the two, *A.L.A. Schech-*

ter Poultry Corporation v. United States, was decided by unanimous vote.[30] The case involved a Live Poultry Code drafted by industry leaders and approved by the president. The code was progressive, limiting the workweek to forty hours, setting a minimum hourly wage of fifty cents, prohibiting the employment of any person under sixteen years of age, and guaranteeing the right of collective bargaining to workers. It also regulated how wholesalers and retailers dealt with each other. Four brothers named Schechter ran a kosher slaughterhouse in New York City and sold their meat to retail stores. They were convicted of violating the code and appealed.

The Supreme Court rejected the framework of having the president approve a code written by private-sector business leaders as an unconstitutional delegation of lawmaking power. Roosevelt was furious, singling out the author of the opinion, chief justice Charles Evans Hughes, a staunch Republican, as the main target for subsequent attacks on the Court. But Justice Benjamin Cardozo, a progressive Democrat, joined the opinion, writing: "The delegated power of the legislation which has found expression in this code is not canalized within banks that keep it from overflowing. It is unconfined and vagrant."[31]

Roosevelt's disgust with the fall of the NIRA was a major reason that he pursued a court-packing plan that would have allowed him to increase the number of justices so that he could appoint a supportive majority. Despite his reelection by a wide margin in 1936, court-packing failed in Congress. In the meantime, a majority on the Supreme Court had come around and stopped trying to stymie the New Deal.

Roll the clock forward to 2001 and we reach the next significant effort by conservative federal judges to revive the non-delegation doctrine. Figuratively, large amounts of water had traveled under the bridge since the birth of the modern regulatory state during Roosevelt's New Deal. Thousands of pages were added to federal law authorizing a slew of agencies and departments to regulate a wide range of business conduct. Most of these laws contained provisions giving the agencies discretion in crafting rules that cost regulated industries billions of dollars but also delivered huge benefits to public health, worker and consumer safety, and environmental quality.

The 2001 case involved an effort by the Clinton administration's EPA to revise national air quality standards under the Clean Air Act. Among other provisions, the act requires the EPA administrator to set permissible levels—or national air quality standards—with respect to six common and harmful pollutants in the ambient air. These standards must protect public health with an "adequate margin of safety."[32] The pollutants at issue were particulate matter and ozone. Mounting scientific evidence showed that sixty thousand premature deaths were attributable to existing levels of particulate matter that are inhaled and lodge in the lungs, causing cardiovascular disease, among other serious health problems. High levels of ozone (smog) cause notable upticks in visits to the emergency room by asthmatic children. This evidence convinced the EPA that limits on acceptable levels of pollution should be made more stringent.

Soon after the EPA issued the new standards, a broad coalition of industry groups challenged the agency's decision before the D.C. Circuit Court of Appeals. A coalition of public health and environmental groups intervened on the EPA's side. The agency and its allies drew the short straw when the three-judge panel was appointed to hear the case. Two of the three—judges Douglas Ginsburg and Stephen Williams—were Reagan appointees. They zeroed in on the word *adequate* (referring to margin of safety), concluding that it was too imprecise to give the agency an intelligible principle for regulating. They concluded that the agency's interpretation of the statute was unconstitutional because it delegated too much discretion: "Here, EPA's freedom of movement between the poles is equally unconstrained, but the poles are even farther apart—the maximum stringency would send industry not just to the brink of ruin but hurtling over it, while the minimum stringency may be close to doing nothing at all."[33]

Understanding the implications of leaving the constitutionality of the entire Clean Air Act in question because of an adverse decision on one provision, the EPA appealed to the Supreme Court. A decision written by none other than conservative icon Justice Scalia briskly overturned the non-delegation portion of the D.C. Circuit's decision, concluding that the Clean Air Act's "scope of discretion" was "well within the outer limits of our non-delegation precedents."[34] Only Justice Clarence Thomas indicated willingness to revisit the non-delegation doctrine. But, in hindsight, Thomas was prescient. Lawson and other Federalist Society members' indefatigable advocacy of the non-delegation doctrine and its tenacious stepchild, the major questions doctrine, bore fruit. In rapid succession, the new conservative majority decided cases that undercut government in areas where it is needed the most.

COVID-19 AT WORK

American courts have long confirmed the "police power" of state governments to control what individuals may, must, and cannot do during public health emergencies to ensure the well-being of the community as a whole, often referred to as the "common good." As early as 1902, in *Jacobson v. Massachusetts*, the Supreme Court upheld a Massachusetts law compelling vaccination against smallpox, a disease that kills up to a third of the people it infects and for which no cure has ever been found.[35] Henning Jacobson argued that his Fourteenth Amendment rights had been violated because "a compulsory vaccination law is unreasonable, arbitrary, and oppressive, and, therefore, hostile to the inherent right of every freeman to care for his own body and health in such way as to him seems best."[36] Justice John Marshall Harlan wrote that the 1780 constitution of Massachusetts embraced

> a fundamental principle of the social compact that the whole people covenants with each citizen, and each citizen with the whole people, that all shall be governed by certain laws . . . "for the protection, safety, prosperity, and happiness of the people and not for the profit, honor, or private interests of any one man, family, or class of men."
>
> [I]n every well-ordered society charged with the duty of conserving the safety of its members the rights of the individual in respect of his liberty may at times, under the pressure of great dangers, be subjected to such restraint, to be enforced by reasonable regulations, as the safety of the general public may demand.[37]

Jacobson has long provided the grounds for judicial approval of emergency public health orders.

In mid-January 2022, the Supreme Court responded to a petition from the National Federation of Independent Business for an injunction against the implementation of an emergency standard issued by the Occupational Safety and Health Administration (OSHA) in response to the COVID-19 pandemic. The standard required some eighty-four million workers to *either* wear masks and obtain weekly tests *or* get vaccinated. (The standard was often misrepresented as a "vaccination mandate.") Petitioners seeking to enjoin government action must show that they are likely to prevail when the Court hears the case on the merits; they will suffer irreparable injury if the government proceeds; and if the Court grants an injunction, the decision will not harm the public interest.[38] The six conservative justices had no trouble granting the injunction in just a few pages of explanation, making it clear that they would overturn the emergency rule when they decided the dispute on its merits. OSHA abandoned the emergency rule and stopped working on a permanent standard.

The OSHA emergency standard was based on a provision of the Occupational Safety and Health Act stating that the secretary of labor "*shall*" issue an "emergency temporary standard" to take immediate effect if he determines that "employees are exposed to *grave danger* from exposure to substances or agents determined to be toxic or physically harmful or from new hazards" and action is "*necessary to protect* employees from such danger."[39]

To determine whether an agency correctly interprets what Congress has authorized it to do, federal courts apply a test based on another landmark Supreme Court opinion in *Chevron, U.S.A. v. Natural Resources Defense Council* and routinely referred to as the *Chevron* two step.[40] The case upheld a Reagan administration rule written at the request of industry and opposed by environmentalists. Or, in other words, deference to the Reagan EPA resulted in more regulatory flexibility that industry badly wanted. In the first step, judges inspect the statute's language to decide whether it has a plain meaning that authorizes—or conflicts with—what the agency did. If no plain meaning emerges, the judges move on to the second step, considering whether the agency's interpretation of the language seems reasonable. Ordinarily, at step two, judges do not substitute their own conclusions regarding the best outcome but instead defer to the agency's interpretation unless it is unreasonable.

In theory, the *Chevron* test applies to any regulation that is challenged during Republican and Democratic administrations. (Judges sometimes ignore it.) Environmentalists challenging Republican administration rules must satisfy both steps, just as industry groups must do when they challenge Democratic administration rules. But conservatives like Lawson find this approach unacceptable. They argue that deferring to agencies, even on technical matters within their expertise, is beyond the bounds of what the Constitution intended when it set up three distinct branches and gave Congress the power to make laws. The elimination of deference soon rose to the top of the Federalist Society agenda and it most ardent supporter on the Supreme Court, Justice Neil Gorsuch.

In the OSHA vax-or-test case, the new conservative majority spent very little time focusing on the language of the statute. Instead, during oral argument by solicitor general Elizabeth Prelogar, the chief of the Justice Department unit that represents agencies before the Supreme Court, Chief Justice John Roberts was preoccupied with the age of the statute that authorized OSHA to write protective rules, which was enacted in 1970. He told Prelogar, "You know, [1970] was 50 years ago that you're saying Congress acted. I don't think it had COVID in mind. That was almost closer to the Spanish flu than it is to today's problem."[41] The Spanish flu emerged in 1918, fifty-two years before enactment of the Occupational Safety and Health Act. The COVID-19 pandemic began in December 2020, fifty years after the act went on the books. The two pandemics have important similarities: they were both caused by infectious diseases that afflict the respiratory system and are highly contagious. They also have differences—different viruses, treatments, and categories of especially vulnerable people. But what Roberts seemed to be suggesting is that laws can get too old to be considered valid, and when they are, the Supreme Court can simply disregard them.

This formulation of the Constitution's procedures for making law was stunning. That document, so revered by the conservative justices, does not contain any provision resembling a sell-by date. Instead, the Constitution assumes that a law stays in effect until legislation changing its language is passed by both houses of Congress and signed by the president. If the Supreme Court really travels down this treacherous road, it will flout the understanding of every court up until now regarding what the Constitution requires. That outcome seems like a frighteningly long jump, even for the Energizer Bunny.

Prelogar argued that aspects of indoor work make the COVID pandemic more dangerous. People working in confined spaces have little autonomy over when and how they interact with other employees, outside customers, patients, suppliers, or members of the public. As a result, they face greater risk. The law requires the agency to make a scientifically supported finding that workers face grave danger, and it did so. Finally, the law does not require that a hazard be confined to the workplace. In fact, OSHA had routinely regulated other, more pervasive hazards, from fire threats to exposure to blood-borne pathogens, that arise in the home, the workplace, and public places.

The majority dismissed all of these arguments:

> The question, then, is whether the Act plainly authorizes the Secretary's mandate. It does not. The Act empowers the Secretary to set *workplace* safety standards, not broad public health measures. . . .
>
> Although COVID-19 is a risk that occurs in many workplaces, it is not an *occupational* hazard in most. COVID-19 can and does spread at home, in schools, during sporting events, and everywhere else that people gather. That kind of universal risk is no different from the day-to-day dangers that all face from crime, air pollution, or any number of communicable diseases. Permitting OSHA to regulate the hazards of daily life—simply because most Americans have jobs and face those

> same risks while on the clock—would significantly expand OSHA's regulatory authority without clear congressional authorization.[42]

The majority opinion did not address Prelogar's argument that COVID-19 was a greater risk to workers in confined spaces with little autonomy to avoid contact with members of the public. How that situation was analogous to crime, air pollution, or other communicable diseases was never explained.

The majority concluded that Congress must speak more clearly before it authorizes an agency to exercise powers of "vast economic and political significance."[43] Or, in other words, the Court announced a sharply different two-part test: (1) is the issue of "vast" economic and political significance, and (2) if so, has Congress spoken clearly enough to satisfy the non-delegation doctrine? This approach is now called the major questions doctrine. The new doctrine means that the Supreme Court has awarded itself the power to decide whether a law on the books is too old or too vague or just too ambitious to authorize agency action. Somehow, agencies must figure out whether Justices Roberts, Thomas, Alito, Gorsuch, Kavanaugh, and Barrett will approve of what they want to do unless Congress has given them very specific and recent instructions to go ahead.

From now on, every lawyer representing a client that objects to a regulation will make a major questions argument. Litigation over the doctrine will flourish in the lower federal courts. So far, the federal courts of appeal are split. Conservative judges have embraced it enthusiastically, but more moderate or liberal judges have resisted applying it too broadly. The D.C. Circuit Court of Appeals, which hears more regulatory cases than any other court and is often described as second only to the Supreme Court in influence, turned away a major-question-doctrine argument soon after the vax-or-test decision.[44] Instead, the Court returned to a traditional *Chevron* analysis on the grounds that the decision made by the Department of Commerce's National Marine Fisheries Service was not extraordinary or significant enough to qualify for the Supreme Court's new approach. The case involved a plan to manage and conserve overfishing of herring off the New England coast. The National Marine Fisheries Service had asked commercial fishing companies to contribute to the costs of monitoring to determine whether the plan was conserving enough fish.

Patrolling the perimeter of its decisions curbing the regulatory system to ensure that the lower courts complied, the conservative Supreme Court justices decided to review this decision and are likely to double down on their revival of the non-delegation doctrine.[45] If they find that a fishing industry cost-sharing requirement covering one section of the nation's coast is a question of vast economic and social importance, the major questions doctrine could become an all-encompassing threat to future health and safety regulation.

SUPERSPREADER WORSHIP

The terror that swept the country as COVID-19 took hold is as unforgettable as it is tempting to forget. Left on their own as the Trump administration fumbled and stepped aside, the states struggled to cope. The one obvious step the states could take was to set occupancy standards for indoor venues. California and New York wrote rules that restricted the number of people who could attend events like concerts and lectures, as well as religious services, based on the size of the facility and what people would do when they went there.

At first, Chief Justice Roberts created a majority supporting the state rules by voting with the liberals (Breyer, Ginsburg, Kagan, and Sotomayor). But when Justice Barrett was confirmed, the five conservatives (Thomas, Alito, Gorsuch, Kavanaugh, and Barrett) took over. The decisions froze state government efforts to control potential super-spreader events at the height of the pandemic.

The case decided by Roberts and the liberals involved a petition filed by the South Bay United Pentecostal Church for an injunction to block California's occupancy limits on church attendance.[46] Again, to get an injunction, the petitioner must show it is likely to win on the merits when the Supreme Court hears the case. The church argued that the California restrictions represented unconstitutional interference with religious freedom because "comparable secular businesses" were not subject to the same rules.[47]

California responded that religious services last for a considerable amount of time; congregants speak, sing, and sit close to each other; and, without capacity limits, such behavior heightens the risk of transmitting COVID-19 to unacceptable levels. The state explained that although it had looser restrictions on commercial venues such as stores, similar or more severe restrictions applied to "lectures, concerts, movie showings, spectator sports, and theatrical performances" where conduct similar to worship services could occur.[48]

Roberts's short opinion focused on the fact that because the state restricted large gatherings in a secular context, California had not discriminated on the basis of religion. Justice Kavanaugh dissented, ignoring these comparable restrictions and instead focusing on the state's leniency toward "pet grooming shops, bookstores, florists, hair salons, and cannabis dispensaries," dramatizing his point but opportunistically distorting the facts.[49]

Linda Greenhouse, the long-time Supreme Court reporter for the *New York Times*, wrote a column entitled "The Supreme Court, Too, Is on the Brink":

> The recognition that four Supreme Court justices—Clarence Thomas, Samuel Alito, Neil Gorsuch and Brett Kavanaugh—would have invoked the court's power to undermine fact-based public policy in the name of a misbegotten claim of religious discrimination was beyond depressing. It was terrifying. . . .
>
> Here's what's wrong with the Kavanaugh opinion: He throws words around imprecisely in a context where precision is everything. The state's rules "discriminate." We're all against discrimination. But what does this potent word mean? To discriminate, in the way law uses the word, means to treat differently things that are alike, without a good reason for doing so. That's why racial discrimination, for example, is almost always unconstitutional. . . .
>
> The concept of discrimination, properly understood, simply doesn't

> fit this case. California is not subjecting things that are alike to treatment that's different. Churches are not like the retail stores or "cannabis dispensaries" in Justice Kavanaugh's list of "comparable secular businesses." Sitting in communal worship for an hour or more is not like picking up a prescription, or a pizza, or an ounce of marijuana.[50]

The opinion upholding California's occupancy limit was overruled months later by a 5–4 vote in a case brought by the Roman Catholic Diocese of Brooklyn asking the Supreme Court to block implementation of a similar order by New York governor Andrew Cuomo. The New York restrictions were much like California's. The limits were more stringent for houses of worship than for stores, but less strict than restrictions on movie theaters and lecture halls. The stringency of restrictions in New York City was based on a sliding scale based on COVID-19 infection rates in the neighborhood where the house of worship was located.

The majority opinion gave no quarter: "Members of this Court are not public health experts, and we should respect the judgment of those with special expertise and responsibility in this area. But even in a pandemic, the Constitution[al right to freedom of religion] cannot be put away and forgotten."[51] In dissent, Justice Sotomayor wrote: "Justices of this Court play a deadly game in second guessing the expert judgment of health officials about the environments in which a contagious virus, now infecting a million Americans each week, spreads most easily."[52] A few months later, the Court considered a rematch between California and South Bay United Pentecostal Church, also on a petition for an injunction.[53] No important facts had changed. Vaccines were still six months away. California lost.

"For well over a hundred years—through polio, measles, HIV, and Ebola—*Jacobson* sailed the legal seas of public health as the accepted leading case, important both for its specific legal standards and its vision of the social contract in emergencies," wrote law professor Scott Burris in an essay questioning whether a new rash of "libertarian" cases puts *Jacobson*'s core premise at risk:[54] "The hypothetical risk of a governor using emergency power to become a tyrant becomes more urgent to forestall than the virus that is actually killing people."[55]

Whether these decisions will chill future government efforts to combat the next pandemic, when vaccines are unavailable and the death rate is high, is anyone's guess. But allowing indoor worship without occupancy limits means that many people who are not present at the service may be severely affected, starting with healthcare workers struggling to provide care in overrun emergency rooms. That trade-off, which harms one group for the sake of another when alternative forms of worship exist, seems like it should be unconstitutional.

COLLECTIVE ACTION OR COLLECTIVE SUICIDE

On June 30, 2022, the Supreme Court adjourned for the summer with a bang, not a whimper, issuing an extraordinarily important decision curbing the EPA's ability to mitigate climate change.[56] Mitigation requires polluting industries to lower greenhouse gas emissions that warm the planet. Scientists say that without aggressive mitigation, countries with high emissions, including the United States, will not succeed in meeting targets essential to avoid the worst consequences of climate change. Other tactics, such as trying to adapt to these consequences by building sea walls or subsidizing clean energy projects, will not be enough.

The Supreme Court climate case involved two defunct EPA regulatory actions dealing with power plants that burn fossil fuels, especially coal. Late in Obama's second term, the EPA issued a rule that required significant reductions in emissions but gave electric utilities flexibility on how to achieve them. They could (1) install carbon-capture equipment at individual plants, (2) switch from coal to less polluting fuel (natural gas, wind, or solar), or (3) trade credits with cleaner plants. This flexibility resulted in significantly lower compliance costs. But soon after the rule came out, the Supreme Court took the extraordinary step of issuing an order stopping implementation of the Obama rule. (Historically, such injunctions were rare.) Meanwhile, out in the real world, without any regulation in effect, power plants using fossil fuels had accomplished all the reductions required by the 2015 Obama rule.

Despite this remarkable achievement, when Trump took office, pledging to end the war on coal, his administration repealed the Obama rule and substituted a much weaker alternative. Environmentalists challenged the Trump rule in the D.C. Circuit Court of Appeals, and a three-judge panel invalidated it in 2021.[57] When the Biden administration took office in 2021, it announced that the EPA would not reinstate either the Obama or the Trump rule but instead would write a new one. That state of affairs—a regulatory agency contemplating what to do next with no regulation in effect—was the situation presented to the Supreme Court.

The state of West Virginia led a coalition of other red, coal-producing states and coal companies to petition the Supreme Court to review the D.C. Circuit's opinion. In another unprecedented development, the electric utilities came down on the EPA's side, supporting the Obama rule because it offered flexibility and lower compliance costs.

Solicitor General Prelogar asked the Supreme Court to dismiss the case as moot because no rule—or any other agency action—was on the table. By way of explanation, courts have the authority to hear only cases that arise between two opposing parties regarding an act or omission done by one party that aggrieves the other. Massachusetts officials were preparing to fine Henning Jacobson if he refused to have a smallpox vaccination. A New York judge convicted the Schechter brothers on the basis of codes issued under the National Industrial Recovery Act. California restricted occupancy in the South Bay Pentecostal church during the pandemic. In sum, a specific agency decision, identifiable parties, and an ample set of facts explaining events on the ground—all are indispensable. Or to describe the issue in a starker way, federal judges with lifetime appointments who conclude that they have the constitutional power to decide policy questions on the basis of how they think the world should work, without reference to a specific dispute between two opposing parties, are operating outside normal practice. The behavior deserves a label with darker connotations, such as autocratic or dictatorial.

The conservative majority ignored Prelogar's mootness argument. Its determination to take up the challenge in these circumstances did not bode well for the EPA. The gist of the majority's decision was that the Clean Air Act did not provide adequate authority for the Obama rule because it involved a major question of vast importance. Congress must pass a law to give the agency new authority to grant the flexibility the Obama rule had allowed. This flexibility, so valued by electric utilities, translated into an EPA effort to revamp the entire energy sector, a remit never contemplated by Congress.

The opinion, written by Chief Justice Roberts, also said that the trading aspect of the rule, which allowed cleaner utilities to sell credits to dirtier plants—called the "cap and trade" approach—was illicit because Congress had debated the concept but never passed legislation allowing it. The implications of this last observation are far-reaching: congressional *inaction* on any issue the Court thinks is a major question means the executive branch of government cannot act. Several thousand bills are introduced in the House and Senate annually. Almost all are shelved. Members introduce the bills to impress their constituents. The legislation's failure to be passed means nothing other than the sponsors did not have enough clout to get the leadership to bring it to the floor. The catch-22 represented by this approach could even invite sabotage by members of the House or Senate who could introduce legislation, push it along to some point in the process, and abandon it, knowing that if an agency embraces the approach included in the failed legislation, conservative judges could declare its actions illegal or unconstitutional.

The majority opinion spent very little time on the actual language of the Clean Air Act. But Justice Kagan, writing for the three dissenting justices (Breyer and Sotomayor joined her), took the traditional approach and read the law carefully. The provision at issue says that the EPA should formulate "the degree of emission limitation achievable through the *application of the best system* of emission reduction which (taking into account the cost of achieving such reduction and any non-air-quality health and environmental impact and energy requirements) the [EPA] Administrator determines has been adequately demonstrated."[58] Kagan wrote that congressional use of the broad word *system* was intentional:

> A "system" is "a complex unity formed of many often diverse parts subject to a common plan or serving a common purpose." . . . The majority complains that a similar definition . . . is just too darn broad. . . . Congress used an obviously broad word . . . to give EPA lots of latitude in deciding how to set emissions limits. And contra the majority, a broad term is not the same thing as a "vague" one. A broad term is comprehensive, extensive, wide-ranging; a "vague" term is unclear, ambiguous, hazy.[59]

May Congress put broad terms into the law and send an agency off to apply that law to a problem that Congress did not specifically debate at the time? Kagan said yes: "A key reason Congress makes broad delegations like Section 111 is so an agency can respond, appropriately and commensurately, to new and big problems."[60]

Congress and the agencies cannot know exactly what a major question is until the lower federal courts attempt to interpret the new doctrine. But the prospect that agencies will censor themselves is real. As law professor Lisa Heinzerling, a former EPA official responsible for overseeing rulemaking, wrote for *The Atlantic*, "One way to break the government is to make legislators and administrators look over their shoulder every time they think they might have a creative idea for addressing one of this country's many pressing problems."[61]

For decades, the world's scientists have issued increasingly dire warnings about the devastating consequences of further procrastination on reducing greenhouse gases. In 1988, up to then the hottest year on record, James Hansen, the director of the NASA Goddard Institute of Space Studies, delivered landmark testimony before the Senate Energy and Natural Resources Committee.[62] Hansen told the senators that he was 99 percent certain global warming was not a natural variation but instead was caused by anthropogenic pollutants in the atmosphere.

Twenty years later, nothing had been done. The scientific academies of thirteen countries begged leaders of the G8 nations to "act more forcefully to limit the threat posed by human-driven global warming."[63] The joint statement was signed by Brazil, Britain, Canada, China, France, Germany, India, Italy, Japan, Mexico, Russia, South Africa, and the United States.

Six years later, the world's scientists were finding it difficult to maintain their composure. The Intergovernmental Panel on Climate Change (IPCC), a sober, well-credentialed, and cautious group, warned that "without additional mitigation efforts beyond those in place today, and even with adaptation, warming by the end of the 21st century will lead to high to very high risk of severe, widespread and irreversible impacts globally (high confidence)."[64]

By 2018, a special IPCC report entitled *Global Warming of 1.5°C* warned that we are running out of time to avert catastrophic human health and ecological damage. If greenhouse-gas emissions continue at the same rate, the planet's atmosphere would warm up by as much as 1.5 degrees Celsius above pre-industrial levels, with disastrous effects for millions of people and ecological systems between 2030 and 2052.[65] These changes would produce a world of worsening drought, scarcity of potable water, food shortages, extreme weather events, and wildfires. The legally mandated fourth *National Climate Assessment* brought these findings home to the United States, confirming that the nation would also face such deadly consequences.[66]

In July 2022, UN Secretary General António Guterres said: "What troubles me most is that, in facing this global crisis, we are failing to work together as a multilateral community. . . . We cannot continue this way. We have a choice. Collective action or collective suicide. It is in our hands."[67]

A PERFECT CONGRESS

Most conversations about the potential expansion of the major questions doctrine include an eyeroll or headshake about how unlikely it is that the dysfunctional, intensely partisan, closely divided Congress will step up and take action, no matter how urgent the problem seems. Because the institution is such a mess, the reasoning goes, it will never respond to the Supreme Court's insistence that it get back to work. The cynicism is understandable.

But writing off Congress distracts attention from the questions raised by the dissenters: Has the Supreme Court really said that Congress may no longer write general grants of authority? If so, what kind of burden would this position impose? Could even the best-organized, exceptionally energetic, adequately funded, and most congenial Congress pass specific legislation fast enough? Does Congress have adequate bandwidth from members to address such an elaborate agenda, or a workforce large and specialized enough to deal with huge universe of problems agencies have managed for many years? When can an "old" law be ignored—after ten, twenty, fifty, or more years? If an old law is the basis of agency authority to address problems like climate change, how should Congress go about determining the level of specificity of language that is necessary?

The 116th Congress, which met between 2019 and 2021, had a total of 357 legislative days (when bills could be considered), or an average of 178 days annually. Congress includes 535 members—435 in the House and 100 in the Senate. Together, they employ approximately 12,500 employees in their individual offices, many of whom focus on constituent service and issues that arise in the member's district or state. Members sit on substantive committees with specified jurisdictions that employ an additional 6,000 staff. Updating all the old and overly general laws that the agencies have worked with for years would impose a staggering burden. Even in ideal circumstances, Congress would not be able to do it, and that outcome may very well be the point. As law professor Mark Lemley writes: "The Court has taken significant, simultaneous steps to restrict the power of Congress, the administrative state, the states, and the lower federal courts. . . . The common denominator across multiple opinions in the last two years is that they concentrate power in one place: the Supreme Court."[68]

Ironically, Attorney General William Barr, who was asked to deliver the nineteenth annual Barbara K. Olson Memorial Lecture at the Federalist Society's 2019 National Lawyers Convention, seemed to agree that the judicial branch is not the place to resolve power struggles between the legislative and executive branches:

> In recent years the Judiciary has been steadily encroaching on Executive responsibilities in a way that has substantially undercut the functioning of the Presidency. . . .
>
> The Framers did not envision that the Courts would play the role of arbiter of turf disputes between the political branches. . . .
>
> As Justice Scalia observed, the Constitution gives Congress and the President many "clubs with which to beat" each other. Conspicuously absent from the list is running to the courts to resolve their disputes.[69]

INSURRECTION

Lawyers enjoy a privileged position in America. The legal system depends on their willingness to represent clients otherwise reviled by the population at large. Television and movies have accustomed Americans to accepting a kind of immunity shield between lawyers and their clients—no matter how reprehensible the latter, the former continue to enjoy a decent reputation. The question of when a lawyer crosses from protected advocacy to join a client on the wrong side of these assumptions is a delicate one. But it does happen. If a lawyer is helping or encouraging a client to commit a crime, the ethics codes are clear. Both are in trouble.

High profile members of the Federalist Society supported President Trump before, during, and after the January 6, 2021, insurrection. Senators Ted Cruz (R-TX) and Josh Hawley (R-MO), graduates of Harvard and Yale law schools, respectively, where they presumably studied the Constitution in some depth, both voted against certifying the election. Cruz worked with Trump to develop a plan to delay congressional action in the wild hope of recruiting state legislators to declare that Trump won. Hawley pumped a fist in support of the rioters and was later filmed scurrying to safety as the Capitol was breached. But neither man was acting as a lawyer representing a specific client and covered by the ethics rules.

John Eastman and Jeffrey Clark, two unusually active members of the Federalist Society, also played key roles in Trump's campaign to overturn the election. Eastman gave Trump legal advice, and Clark importuned Trump to promote him to attorney general, the government's highest legal officer.

Eastman is a former law clerk to Justice Thomas. He served as the former dean of the law school at Chapman University and was a Chapman professor at the time of the insurrection. He has 283 entries on the Federalist Society's website for speeches and presentations he made to other members in Washington, D.C. and across the country. Jeffrey Clark joined the Federalist Society when he was still a law student in 1992. He, too, chaired a practice group. At the time of the insurrection, he was working at the Trump Justice Department.

Eastman created the discredited legal theory that Vice President Pence had the power to stop the certification of the election by the House and Senate and turn control of the final outcome over to state legislators. Eastman incited the crowd at the Trump rally held immediately before the march on the Capitol and spent his time blaming Vice President Pence for failing to stop the certification. The crowd screamed "Hang Mike Pence" on the march and inside the building. These threats to the vice president, who was sheltering with his Secret Service team, provoked them to fear for his and their lives.

> "We need to move now," an agent said, according to excerpts of radio traffic played by the [House January 6] committee. "If we lose any more time, we may lose the ability to do so." . . .
>
> A White House security official who was monitoring the traffic told the committee that agents were "starting to fear for their own lives."
>
> "There were calls to say goodbye to family members, so on and so forth," the security official said in audiotaped testimony. "For whatever the reason was on the ground, the VP detail thought that this was about to get very ugly."[70]

The House Select Committee to Investigate the January 6 Attack on the

United States Capitol subpoenaed emails Eastman exchanged with members of the White House on his Chapman University account. Eastman resisted turning the information over, and the dispute went to court. Federal district court judge David O. Carter ordered him to turn many of the documents over, writing that "Dr. Eastman and Mr. Trump launched a campaign to overturn a democratic election, an action unprecedented in American history. Their campaign was not confined to the ivory tower—it was a coup in search of a legal theory."[71] Eastman asked Rudy Giuliani to put his name on Trump's "pardon list" because, according to White House lawyer Eric Herschmann, he knew that he had incited violence at the rally.

Clark was still working at the Justice Department after the election and supported Trump's claim that it had been stolen. He drafted a threatening letter to Georgia election officials to be signed by acting attorney general Jeffrey Rosen. When Rosen refused to approve the letter, Clark went over his head, meeting with Trump twice. He offered to throw the department's considerable influence into the fight if Trump fired Rosen and made Eastman acting attorney general. At a third meeting with Trump that Rosen and his deputy attorney general Richard Donoghue attended, Donoghue told the president that DOJ lawyers would resign en masse were he to try such a maneuver, and Trump backed off.

As part of a criminal investigation of Eastman and Clark, the United States attorney in Virginia served warrants for their cell phones and a search of Clark's home. A letter signed by one hundred Chapman University faculty members condemning Eastman's behavior led to his resignation. Before he went into government, Clark had been a partner at Kirkland & Ellis, one of the largest (with 2,725 lawyers) and most lucrative ($4.8 billion in annual revenue) law firms in the country. The firm blocked Clark's return to its ranks, and he is now employed by the Center to Renew America, a small far-right group dedicated to attacking the teaching of critical race theory in the public schools.

The Federalist Society has maintained radio silence on both men and has never issued a public statement about the insurrection. As mentioned earlier, the Federalist Society was founded as an alternative to the American Bar Association (ABA), the mainstream group that most lawyers join. ABA president Patricia Lee Refo issued a statement on January 6, 2021, condemning "in the strongest terms" the assault on the Capitol as "criminal conduct."[72]

The Federalist Society's reaction to Trump's efforts to subvert the election give it the indelible characteristics of an ultraconservative political movement, as opposed to a professional society of smart conservative lawyers eager to debate ideas.

FIVE

FOX NEWS

MEET THE MURDOCHS

In the almost three decades since newspaper baron Rupert Murdoch hired Roger Ailes as the first CEO of Fox News, the network has disrupted the landscape of traditional media more than any other institution in the industry. It dominates cable television news and commentary, besting its competitors by large margins. Ambitious far-right politicians scramble for opportunities to appear on its prime-time shows. The network is the media core of the movement that has taken over the Republican Party and made the Trump presidency possible.

Fox News is also a newsmaker. Mainstream media outlets must cover the news made by Fox's influential guests, especially during Republican presidencies, and this attention has magnified its influence. Sean Hannity, a star of the prime-time lineup, was perceived as President Trump's shadow chief of staff; the two talked every night about Hannity's broadcast and other issues. Tucker Carlson, Fox News's leading prime-time host until April 2023, was a story unto himself, inspiring multiple profiles that examined the outrage that reliably attracted three million people each night.

One vivid example of the network making news was its promotion of Kyle Rittenhouse, the seventeen-year-old who drove to Kenosha, Wisconsin, during the fraught summer of 2020 to participate in a race riot triggered by the police shooting of Jacob Blake, a Black man. Armed with an AK-15-style automatic rifle, Rittenhouse killed two men and gravely wounded a third, claiming he acted in self-defense. His first television interview was on Tucker Carlson's prime-time show, now available as a YouTube video that has attracted 4.3 million views.[1] An invitation to Mar-a-Lago soon followed, with Trump pronouncing Rittenhouse a "nice young man."[2] Carlson made a documentary about him entitled *The Trial of Kyle*, which is streaming on Fox Nation, the subscription streaming service the network founded in 2018. Rittenhouse was acquitted of criminal charges and now hosts his own YouTube channel devoted to gun talk and the preservation of Second Amendment constitutional rights.

The Murdoch media empire operates newspapers and broadcast outlets around the world. It employed 10,600 employees in 2022. According to *Forbes*, the Murdoch family is worth over $17.4 billion.[3] In 2023, at the age of ninety-two, Rupert Murdoch relinquished his position as the chairman of the Fox Corporation's board of directors to his eldest son, Lachlan, who is also the corporation's CEO and has embraced his father's business model. Although the Murdochs live in Australia, Rupert was famous for keeping tight control over major editorial decisions made by his outlets around the world, and Lachlan seems to be following in these footsteps. With a few notable exceptions—the *Wall Street Journal* in America and *The Times* and *Sunday Times* in Britain are at the top of this short list—the Murdochs' print and broadcast outlets are styled as tabloids, with right-wing editorial leanings, an emphasis on sensational stories, and a steadfast impunity to criticism that their journalists have omitted, garbled, or misstated the facts.

In 2019, Rupert Murdoch decided to sell the film and television assets of 21st Century Fox, his multinational entertainment conglomerate, to Disney for a 25 percent stake in that company and $71.3 billion.[4] The sale followed a steady decline in revenues on the entertainment side of the Murdochs' business, the trauma of a sexual misconduct scandal at Fox News, and the Fox Corporation's failed attempt to buy Time-Warner. The Murdoch patriarch, who was in his late eighties but still in control of his empire, reportedly wanted to focus on the news side of the business. At the time, his two sons, Lachlan and James, were both perceived as possible successors, but Lachlan rose to CEO when the Disney sale closed and James receded into the background. Murdoch whisperers—and there are quite a few—speculate that the split resulted from Lachlan's embrace of his father's conservative politics and James's considerably more liberal stance. James was also discredited by his involvement in the phone hacking and police bribery scandal that engulfed Murdoch holdings in Britain, while Rupert walked away from the scandal, seemingly without a backward glance.

The Fox Corporation has a market value of $16.41 billion and carries $7.2 billion in debt. It is the seventh-largest media company in the world, but it is dwarfed by the first on the list—Comcast at $167.71 billion, and even the fourth, Warner Bros. Discovery at $33.72 billion. During its most successful programming, Fox News attracts an audience of between 2.5 and 3.5 million, who are widely perceived as the core of the Trump base. A smaller enterprise, Fox Business, is streaming on the web and operates from 9:30 a.m. to 5:00 p.m. EST. It attracts about 250,000–300,000 viewers.

As influential and lucrative as Fox News and its parent, the Fox Corporation, seem now, their future is unclear. Cable television is going the way of newspapers, steadily losing ground to more convenient streaming services. Between 2015 and 2021, cable and satellite TV viewership plunged from 76 percent to 56 percent.[5] Cable users constitute 39 percent of Americans ages 18–44; 43 percent of ages 45–64; and 50 percent of ages 65 and older.[6] In 2022, the Pew Research Center reported that Americans are transitioning away from all traditional news sources, including print, television, and radio, into "digital spaces."[7] Only 31 percent of Americans "often" got news from television of any sort in 2022, down from 40 percent in 2020, while 53 percent preferred digital devices.[8] Thirty-one is still a consequential number, given the Fox business model. But cable news's long-term future looks bleak.

This decline was on vivid display in May 2023, when CNN televised a live town hall with former President Trump. The one-hour show was heavily promoted but drew just 3.3 million viewers or, as media reporter Paul Farhi wrote, "about a third less than the number of people watching an episode of 'Celebrity Wheel of Fortune' on ABC the same night."[9] Aware of all these trends, mainstream broadcasters (NBC, CBS, and ABC) and their cable competitors (CNN, MSNBC, and Fox) are all pushing into streaming, investing many hundreds of millions of dollars.

The Murdochs' new streaming ventures are Tubi and Fox Nation. Tubi is a free streaming service offered with advertising. The platform provides access to 50,000 movies and TV shows and is developing a library of Tubi Originals. Its audience skews young, in the 18–34 demographic. Tubi is growing fast and claimed 64 million monthly "active" users in early 2023.[10] The Fox Corporation bought the site in 2020 for $440 million and has rejected recent offers to buy Tubi for as much as two billion dollars. Fox Nation is a subscription service dominated by Fox News spinoffs. For example, extensive programming developed by Tucker Carlson remains on the site, including his feverish three-part documentary *Patriot Purge*, which portrays the violence at the Capitol on January 6 as a "false flag" operation planned by elements within the FBI and the military.

Efforts to broaden Fox Nation's expansion into entertainment are proceeding slowly. Its two most prominent forays are *Duck Family Treasure*, a reality television series that features bearded men dressed in fatigues and carrying guns who hunt for treasures, rare artifacts, and hidden gems, and *Yellowstone One-Fifty*, a docu-series hosted by actor Kevin Costner that explores the history and wildlife of Yellowstone National Park. (Costner is the star of the first four seasons of *Yellowstone*, a popular drama created by Taylor Sheridan and broadcast on the Paramount network.) Lachlan Murdoch will not reveal the number of Fox Nation subscriptions, although he has claimed that it is doing very well.

For all Fox News's prominence and influence and beyond the challenges of shifting to streaming, troubling signs of corporate instability loom. Between my completion of the first and final drafts of this book, a matter of a few months, the news side of the Fox Corporation faced a mammoth, self-inflicted crisis for the third time in a little more than a decade. In 2011, a phone hacking and police bribery scandal forced Rupert Murdoch to shutter the 168-year-old British newspaper, the *News of the World*. After years of strategizing, he also lost the opportunity to buy the British Sky Broadcasting television channel. In 2017, a sex abuse scandal at Fox News resulted in the firing of CEO Roger Ailes, leading prime-time star Bill O'Reilly, and co-president of the news division Bill Shine. Then, in April 2023, the Fox Corporation paid $787.5 billion to settle a defamation case brought by Dominion Voting Systems regarding the network's coverage of the 2020 presidential election.[11] Dominion charged that Fox News had hosted guests who promoted blatantly false conspiracy theories that the company engineered its vote-counting machinery to switch votes from Trump to Biden. A second, similar lawsuit brought by Dominion's competitor, Smartmatic, seeks $2.7 billion in damages and is pending in a New York state court as this book goes to press. Lachlan Murdoch has insisted that Fox will fight Smartmatic's claims, although he said the same thing right up until the moment the Dominion settlement was announced.

THE FOX NEWS AUDIENCE

The loyal viewers of Fox News spend hours in front of the television. Shows feature attractive, well-groomed hosts, dazzling graphics, and disturbing videos. Fox commentators are far to the right ideologically and their audiences are enthusiastic and loyal. Of course, it is hard to tell which came first—Fox mantras or viewer beliefs. But the question likely does not matter.

Fifteen percent of Americans identify the network as the television news source they trust the most, an impressive figure when compared to the 16 percent who say they follow the combined total of NBC, ABC, and CBS news programs.[12] The Fox News audience is sharply partisan. Forty percent of Republicans, but just 8 percent of independents and 4 percent of Democrats favor the network as the most reliable source of news. The concentration of conservative Republicans on one source amplifies its influence not only among its viewers but among the politicians who hope to win their votes.

According to the Public Religion Research Institute (PRRI), the organization that emphasizes polling on religious preferences and attitudes, 36 percent of white evangelical Protestants trust Fox News, almost twice the percentage of any other religious group.[13] As will be discussed in chapter 6, white evangelicals are a critical part of the Republican base, further emphasizing the network's importance. PRRI reports that Fox News Republicans, who are 40 percent of the Republican base, are more likely to say they are conservative than the 60 percent of Republicans who do not identify Fox as their key source of news. Fox News Republicans are also whiter (81 percent versus 63 percent of all Americans); more male (57 percent versus 48 percent of all Americans); and older (32 percent of viewers are at least sixty-five years of age versus 21 percent of all Americans).

To define the nature and scope of the network's conservatism, PRRI staff surveyed the responses of Fox Republicans versus all Americans regarding the importance of critical issues, including the pandemic, climate change, the income gap, racial relations, gender differences, and immigration. Twice as many Americans as Fox Republicans thought the pandemic was a critical issue (60 percent of all Americans versus 32 percent of Fox Republican viewers). Forty-three percent of all Americans thought climate change is a critical issue, as opposed to 6 percent of Fox Republicans. Concern about the growing gap between the rich and the poor was considered a critical issue by 42 percent of all Americans versus 10 percent of Fox Republicans. Racial inequality was crucial for 43 percent of Americans but for 14 percent of Fox Republicans. Eighty-three percent of Fox Republicans thought discrimination against White Americans is as big a problem as discrimination against Black Americans and other minorities, as opposed to 42 percent of all Americans. Seventy percent of Fox Republicans thought society punishes men for acting like men, compared to 38 percent of all Americans. And 66 percent of Fox Republicans thought society has become too soft and feminine, compared to 39 percent of all Americans.

Unsurprisingly, immigration is a charged issue, with two-thirds of all Americans but only 41 percent of Fox Republicans favoring citizenship for children brought into the country illegally, commonly known as "Dreamers." On the heated issued of a border wall, 96 percent of Fox Republicans favored building it, compared to 42 percent of all Americans. Fifty-three percent of Fox News Republicans favored separating immigrant children from their parents at the border and charging the parents criminally, compared to 23 percent of all Americans.

The most important viewer during the Trump years was the president, who was so absorbed with the network that he talked openly about his reliance on Fox News at a press briefing shortly before the 2020 election. Trump was responding to a question about attorney general William Barr's decision to appoint John Durham as a special counsel to investigate potential improprieties involving Russia during the 2016 election:

> Now, what the Durham report is going to say, I can't tell you. But if they say half as much as I already know—just from seeing it. You know, you have people—I watch some of the shows. I watch [Fox Business reporter] Liz M[a]cDonald; she's fantastic. I watched Fox Business. I watched Lou Dobbs last night, Sean Hannity last night, Tucker last night, Laura. I watched "Fox and Friends" in the morning. You watch these shows; you don't have to go too far into the details. They cover things that are—it's really an amazing thing.[14]

Durham announced the end of his investigation in June 2023 without arriving at any definitive conclusion.

TUCKER CARLSON UNCHAINED

When Carlson took over from Bill O'Reilly in the wake of the network's sexual abuse scandal, he quickly absorbed strategies to make ratings climb. Carlson tracked his audience size in fifteen-minute increments. When his audience was most numerous, he looked at what he had been talking about at the time and doubled down on the topic. Through constant emphasis of these themes, Carlson grew his audience and his prominence in the Fox lineup. By 2020, he was the most popular prime-time cable host, beaten only on occasion by the cast that anchors *The Five*, a news commentary show that goes on air at 5:00 p.m. weekdays, three hours before Tucker Carlson's 8:00 p.m. prime-time slot. Over time, Carlson became a notorious prima donna, bucking the authority of executives working in the United States and viewing himself as accountable only to Lachlan Murdoch.

In one revealing incident, Carlson got in hot water for claiming that mass immigration made America "poor and dirtier."[15] Anxious about suffering reputational damage from the public backlash to the remark, prestige advertisers withdrew advertising from his show. Carlson walked into the annual Fox News holiday party deep in a cell phone conversation with Lachlan Murdoch and surrounded by an entourage of producers and assistants. At the end of the call, Carlson took the phone away from his ear and "grinning triumphantly," said, "We're good."[16]

More profiles were written about Carlson than any other cable personality over the last several years, and he reveled in the attention. But after protesters gathered at his home in Washington, D.C., and spray-painted his driveway, he decamped with his wife and four children to a family home in rural Maine, where Fox News built him a broadcast studio.

The *New York Times* conducted an exhaustive investigation of Tucker Carlson's background, career at Fox News, and programming content.[17] Reporters watched or read the transcripts of 1,150 episodes of *Tucker Carlson Tonight* between November 14, 2016, when the show first aired, through the end of 2021. They concluded that Carlson focused on five categories of assertions. First, the true enemy of the people is a ruling class that is intent on diminishing the influence of middle-class white Americans, a conspiracy theory called "white replacement." Second, these elites implement white replacement by welcoming into the country undesirable immigrants of color. Soon, these unfortunate additions will outnumber the white people who are the true Americans, electing Democrats rather than Republicans and ruining the country. Third, feminism and challenges to gender norms have undercut masculinity, resulting in falling birth rates and decimating the traditional family. Fourth, serious racism afflicts white people and they suffer when people of color are preferred by the law and the government. Fifth, crime-ridden cities, a dying middle class, and a weakened rural America are destroying civilization as we now know it.

Carlson worked with a staff of two dozen people. Every morning, he sent them a memo laying out that night's lead story and which guests he wanted to invite onto the show. Then he sat in his sauna thinking about what he wanted to say. A few hours before airtime, he drank coffee and wrote his monologue. *New York Times* reporter Nick Confessore summarized typical content:

> On "Tucker Carlson Tonight," events of the day are further evidence of truths already established; virtually any piece of news can be steered back to the themes of elite corruption, conspiracy and censorship, from gun control to marijuana legalization to paper drinking straws. . . . Accuracy isn't the point. . . . On the air, Mr. Carlson piles up narrative-confirming falsehoods and misleading statements so rapidly—about George Floyd's death, white supremacists who took part in the Jan. 6 riot, falling testosterone levels in men, COVID vaccines, the Texas power grid and more.[18]

Carlson's recorded commentary on climate change suggests that he may have been drinking more than coffee during his writing sessions. Here he is commenting on the issue in the context of the war in Ukraine (Carlson opposes America's efforts to support the Ukrainians, and the Putin government has aired his programs in Russia):

> Green energy cannot replace fossil fuels. Not now, not anytime soon. Fossil fuels remain what they have always been: the key to civilization. . . . So-called green energy is not close, is nowhere near replacing gas and oil and coal. . . .
>
> The Green New Deal . . . means poverty and the people pushing the Green New Deal must have known that all along. They don't actually

> believe climate change is an imminent threat. If they actually believe climate change was an imminent threat, an existential emergency, the first thing they would have done, the very first would be to ban private jets. Oh, but no. To this day, Al Gore still flies on private jets. Barack Obama owns tens of millions of dollars of beachfront property. He knows the oceans aren't rising. Come on. So, they're all in on it. It's a scam, but they don't care because they know they personally will escape the consequences of their own policies. . . .
>
> You can reach a place in your society where the people in charge and their lapdogs in the media become so completely disconnected from the concerns of actual people, become so totally uninterested in the lives of citizens, the society becomes very volatile, and we are fast approaching that point.[19]

Carlson's on-air persona was litigated in federal court in a defamation case brought by Karen McDougal, the former Playboy model who said she had a ten-month affair with Trump. Carlson had long defended Donald Trump from such charges. In one of his monologues, Carlson accused McDougal of extortion and she sued him for defamation. But federal Judge Mary Kay Vyskocil, a Trump appointee, dismissed the case because Carlson engaged in "rhetorical hyperbole and opinion commentary intended to frame a political debate" and should not be held to the standards that apply to conventional journalists.[20]

Defamation cases are difficult to prove against traditional journalists because freedom of the press was a core belief of the nation's founders and is incorporated into the Constitution by the First Amendment, which forbids Congress from making a law "abridging the freedom of speech, or of the press."[21] Defamation occurs when a journalist makes a statement that appears to be factual but it later turns out that the statement was false and was made with malice, defined as the journalist's knowledge that the statement was false. In effect, Judge Vyskocil stretched freedom of the press beyond those well-established boundaries when she concluded that Carlson had not defamed McDougal when he alleged that she extorted the money from Trump—a criminal offense—because his statements were opinions cloaked in rhetorical hyperbole. As explained below, three years later, a very different judge would apply the same law but conclude that hyperbole does not protect declarations that an audience would understand to be statements of fact.

Of all the volatile conspiracy theories Tucker Carlson promoted on Fox, the most dangerous was replacement theory. Embraced by white nationalists and other far-right groups, this construct fans the flames of racism, a perpetual problem in a nation with a history of slavery. For example, white nationalists at the Charlottesville, Virginia, Unite the Right rally in August 2017 chanted "Jews will not replace us," "Seig heil," and "Blood and soil" (another Nazi slogan) as they marched through the streets.[22]

In April 2021, Jonathan Greenblatt, CEO of the Anti-Defamation League, wrote a letter to Fox executives demanding that Carlson be fired. During the episode that had provoked Greenblatt, Carlson had said that the left and "all the little gatekeepers on Twitter" have a "hysterical" reaction if you suggest "that the Democratic Party is trying to replace the current electorate, the voters now casting ballots, with new people, more obedient voters from the Third World. . . . Let's just say it: That's true."[23]

Lachlan Murdoch replied:

> Fox Corporation shares your values and abhors anti-semitism, white supremacy and racism of any kind. . . .
>
> Concerning the segment of "Tucker Carlson Tonight" on April 8th, however, we respectfully disagree. . . . A full review of the guest interview indicates that Mr. Carlson decried and rejected replacement theory. As Mr. Carlson himself stated during the guest interview: "White replacement theory? No, no, this is a voting rights question."[24]

In May 2022, following a shooting spree in Buffalo by a self-described white nationalist that killed ten Black people, Senate majority leader Chuck Schumer (D-NY) wrote a letter to Rupert and Lachlan Murdoch, Fox News CEO Suzanne Scott, and the network's president and executive editor Jay Wallace exhorting them to "immediately cease the reckless amplification of the so-called 'Great Replacement' theory on your network's broadcasts."[25] Schumer's letter also highlighted the 2018 murder of eleven worshipers at a Pittsburgh synagogue by a white shooter who blamed Jews for allowing immigrant invaders into the country and the 2019 shooting of twenty-three people at an El Paso Walmart by a white man angry about "the Hispanic invasion of Texas." Schumer added that an investigation by the *New York Times* found that "Tucker Carlson alone amplified this dangerous and unfounded [replacement] theory in more than 400 episodes of his show." The letter said that "a recent AP poll found that nearly one-third of American adults believe that a group of people is trying to replace native-born Americans with immigrants for electoral gains."[26] The same poll found that Fox viewers "are nearly three times more likely to believe in Replacement Theory than other networks."

Lachlan Murdoch never responded to Schumer but in an interview with Axios scheduled to discuss Fox Nation's plans to expand its lifestyle programming, he attributed Schumer's distress to anxiety about the success of Fox News:

> I think when you're in the news business, and you're number one . . . you get a lot of heat and it just comes with the territory. You've got to realize what it is and how some of it is very organized kind of attacks—very coordinated—but it is what it is.[27]

As successful as Fox News has been in attracting an audience and advancing far-right ideology, the inner life of the company and its corporate owner, the Fox Corporation, have been in constant turmoil. Fox News and the Fox Corporation implicitly reject the journalistic norm requiring fact-based reporting. The Murdochs overlook unethical and illegal conduct of their reporters and commentators until other news outlets reveal the behavior and law enforcement is triggered. The result is that a global media empire ended up under catastrophic threat three times within little more than a decade.

THE GREAT HACK

The trilogy began in Britain in 1986 when Rupert Murdoch secretly built a modern printing plant in the East London district of Wapping. The plant used state-of-the-art technology that allowed editors to feed stories to the presses through computers, abandoning the hand-setting of type. The move to modernize resulted in the loss of thousands of printing jobs. Some six thousand workers went out on strike against News International, the version of Fox Corporation that operated in Britain and Ireland at the time. But the Wapping plant opened with the assistance of the members of another union, ensuring continued publication of the Murdoch newspapers. Aided by the labor policies of conservative prime minister Margaret Thatcher, including her pledge to deploy the police to defend plants against pickets, the strike failed, administering a body blow to the British labor movement.

During the strike, a close relationship was formed between the London Metropolitan Police and the reporting staff of the Murdoch newspapers, including the *News of the World*, the *Sunday Times*, and the *Sun*. "One thing everybody's missed is that in the battle of Wapping, when we were fighting the print unions, our lives became dependent on the police," Andrew Neil, former editor of Murdoch-owned *Sunday Times*, told Lowell Bergman, who reported on the controversy for PBS's *Frontline*.[28] A revolving door emerged: police inspectors would retire and become columnists at the newspapers, and reporters would leave their jobs to become public affairs employees with the police. Reporters began paying the police to give them stories, a criminal practice that remained undiscovered for many years. When cell phones went on the market, the police, reporters, and private investigators learned how to hack into the voicemails the phones recorded. This practice was also criminal.

Hacking by the *News of the World*, the most prominent of the Murdoch papers, was first revealed in 2005, when Prince William injured his knee playing soccer and called a couple of friends, leaving voicemails worrying about the severity of the injury. The knee got better, but the *News of the World* published a small story about it, exposing the source of the information as voicemail because the palace had not released any information about the incident. The paper's royal correspondent was arrested along with the private investigator who helped him discover the story. Both went to jail and the matter was dropped. Former *News of the World* editor Rebekah Brooks and then editor Andy Coulson claimed they knew nothing about the actions of one "rogue reporter."[29] Brooks was promoted to chief executive of News International UK, responsible for overseeing all the Murdoch operations in Britain, and Coulson resigned from the paper and went to work as the director of communications for prime minister David Cameron.

For a few years, the scandal was dormant because it appeared that the hacking involved only a small number of celebrities, politicians, and members of the royal family. But a chance encounter between *Guardian* investigative reporter Nick Davies and a senior police official at a social event tipped Davies to the fact that the practice was far more widespread. Building the story detail by detail over a period of years, Davies discovered a pattern of phone hacking and bribery involving thousands of people. The story was hard to report, in no small part because an English court had sealed the records of one of several lawsuits brought by prominent victims of hacking—in that case, Gordan Taylor, a soccer star.

Slowly but surely, the scope of the scandal emerged. Former *Sunday Times* editor Andrew Neil told the *Guardian* that the full scope of the hacking "suggests that rather than being a one-off journalist or rogue private investigator, it was systemic throughout the *News of the World*, and to a lesser extent the *Sun*. . . . Particularly in the *News of the World*, this was a newsroom out of control."[30] In July 2011 Davies broke the story that the *News of the World* had hacked the phone of a missing thirteen-year-old named Milly Dowler right after she had been abducted, when police were investigating her disappearance. Her dead body was discovered a few weeks later. Acting in real time, the journalists deleted messages to make room for additional calls, leaving the impression that Milly was accessing her voicemail and giving her parents false hope that she might still be alive. Although Davies's story appeared nine years after the murder, the Dowler disappearance had been front-page news and the revelations sparked a wave of public revulsion. Subsequent stories revealed the hacking of voicemail accounts of the relatives of British soldiers killed in Iraq and victims of a series of Islamic terrorist bombings in London on July 7, 2005, further exacerbating the public backlash.

Fox executive Rebekah Brooks and *News of the World* editor Coulson were tried criminally. She was acquitted but he was convicted, serving eighteen months in jail. Prime Minister Cameron said the jail sentence showed "no one is above the law."[31]

The Murdochs were forced to shut down the *News of the World*, their most profitable media investment in Britain. The scandal caused the resignation of Sir Paul Stevenson, commissioner of London's Metropolitan Police. Rupert Murdoch was forced to resign from the board of his own corporation, and James Murdoch, his son and apparent heir, withdrew as executive chairman of the company. Murdoch's bid to buy British Sky Broadcasting was scuttled by the scandal, frustrating his efforts to integrate similar channels he already owned in Germany and Italy.

Cameron, once a close ally of Rupert Murdoch, appointed Lord Justice Brian Leveson to lead an inquiry into the entire scandal. Leveson was a famous judge with an impeccable reputation and a long history of presiding over some of Britain's high-profile court cases. His report concluded that Rupert Murdoch had displayed "willful blindness to what was going on in his companies and publications," concluding that he was not a fit person to exercise the stewardship of a major international company."[32] Two years later, Murdoch was unrepentant, caught on tape claiming that investigators were "totally incompetent" and that the hacking and bribery were "part of the culture of Fleet Street."[33]

The Leveson report recommended that the government establish an independent regulator with power to control the most egregious practices of the tabloid press. One was established, but it did not have legal authority to enforce its findings. In 2015, Rupert Murdoch rehired Brooks as the CEO of his British businesses. The *Sun* widened its circulation by launching a new Sunday edition.

At a panel convened in 2021 by Hacked Off, an activist group advocating for a free but accountable press, the *Guardian's* Nick Davies evaluated the outcome of all his hard work:

> I thought we'd get a decent press regulator. So when people ask me what did we achieve [from breaking the phone hacking story]—nothing significant. . . . The basic problem, that the senior people in the power elite in this country are frightened of Rupert Murdoch, remains. To me the worst form of abuse of power isn't criminality or the privacy invasions or ethics. For me, the core abuse is that we haven't actually stopped them distorting the truth day after day.[34]

SEXUAL HARASSMENT

Having accumulated enough money in Britain to make his move in the United States, Rupert Murdoch hired Roger Ailes to establish and lead Fox News. The partnership was considered a coup for both men. Murdoch demonstrated business acumen and extended his far-flung media empire. Ailes was a fabled political operative who had established a largely favorable reputation in conservative Republican circles. He served as media consultant for presidents Nixon, Reagan, and George H. W. Bush. He had the temperament and the vision to jump-start the network and assemble stellar talent. Ailes occupied a lot of space at Fox News physically, intellectually, emotionally, and audibly.

Two decades after Ailes took over, the network was generating $1.48 billion in profit, roughly two and half times as much as CNN, its next-ranked competitor.[35] Interviewed by reporters writing a profile of Ailes in 2010, President Obama estimated that the "Fox effect" had cost him two or three points in the polls when he first ran for president. The profile concluded:

> This outsize success has placed Mr. Ailes, an aggressive former Republican political strategist, at the pinnacle of power in three corridors of

> American life: business, media and politics. In addition to being the best-paid person in the News Corporation last year, he is the most successful news executive of the last 10 years, and his network exerts a strong influence on the fractured conservative movement.[36]

From the beginning of his tenure, Ailes instilled ruthless competition among his on-air talent and a harsh strain of misogyny among his male executives. He hired extraordinarily attractive women for on-air jobs and insisted that they dress in outfits provided by a wardrobe room filled with snug, low-cut, short-skirted dresses worn with fashionably high heels. Ailes repeatedly propositioned the most attractive women for sex and, if they resisted, threatened retaliation that would stifle their careers.

In June 2016, Ailes fired Fox star Gretchen Carlson, one of the network's most popular on-air commentators, after steadily demoting her to less prominent programs and time slots and shutting her out of interviews with prominent newsmakers. Weeks later, her lawyers, Nancy Smith and Martin Hyman, filed a lawsuit in a New Jersey state court seeking damages from Ailes. The shrewd legal strategy of naming Ailes as the sole defendant circumvented a mandatory arbitration clause in Carlson's contract that barred employees from seeking relief in court. Publicity generated by the lawsuit would help her recover more money and encourage other women to come forward.

The complaint charged that Ailes had sabotaged Carlson's career because she refused his sexual advances. At one meeting, Ailes told her, "I think you and I should have had a sexual relationship a long time ago and then you'd be good and better and I'd be good and better," adding that "sometimes problems are easier to solve that way."[37] In meetings, Ailes would ask her to turn around so he could admire her posterior and her legs, comment on outfits that enhanced her figure, and tell her that if "he could choose one person to be stranded with on a desert island, [you] would be that person."[38]

When the lawsuit was filed, the scandal blew up, generating story after story in other media. The Murdochs hired a prominent law firm, Paul,

Weiss, Rifkind, Wharton & Garrison, to conduct a confidential investigation of the allegations. Reassured by promises that their identities would not be revealed to Fox management, more women began to come forward to talk with the investigators. But the crowning blow was testimony by Megyn Kelly, at the time one of a handful of prime-time stars that the network wanted to retain, who confirmed Carlson's account of Ailes's behavior.

Pressured by his sons, James and Lachlan, Rupert Murdoch fired Ailes two weeks after Carlson filed her complaint. Ailes left with a $40 million severance package. Fox settled with Gretchen Carlson for $20 million in September 2016, issuing a statement that apologized "for the fact that Gretchen was not treated with the respect and dignity that she and all of our colleagues deserve."[39] Ailes did not pay any portion of that settlement. Ten months later, he fell and hit his head at his home in Palm Beach, Florida. He was a hemophiliac and the condition worsened the consequences of those injuries. He died three days before his seventy-seventh birthday.

But Fox News was not yet out of the woods. Rupert Murdoch pledged a fresh start at the network reassuring employees, especially women, that the culture would change. In direct contradiction of this pledge, he appointed Bill Shine and Jack Abernethy, two veteran executives with close ties to Ailes, as co-presidents of Fox News. By the end of the scandal, Bill Shine would depart the network, accused of ignoring many complaints over the years from women who had experiences similar to Carlson's.

Other news outlets, including Fox News's most avid competitors, pursued the story energetically. A month after Ailes left, the *New York Times* published a story based on interviews with twelve women, some on the record and some anonymously, who described constant harassment by senior executives. The Murdochs stonewalled, issuing a statement claiming that the company did not tolerate such abusive behavior and that its business-standards manual contained instructions on how to report harassment.

A year later, the *New York Times* broke the story that Fox paid $32 million to settle sexual harassment allegations by Lis Wiehl, a long-time legal analyst, that Bill O'Reilly, the network's biggest prime-time star has harassed her sexually. The payment to Wiehl was but the latest in a string of similar cases involving O'Reilly, all of which had been settled secretly by the network. The women who brought the cases charged that O'Reilly's behavior included verbal abuse, lewd comments, unwanted advances, and late-night phone calls during which it sounded like he was masturbating. O'Reilly was fired two weeks later, after fifty advertisers abandoned his show and women's rights groups called for his departure. His payout when he left was estimated to be $25 million. In a letter to staff members, the Murdochs did not mention the allegations made by Wiehl, instead describing O'Reilly as "one of the most accomplished TV personalities in the history of cable news."[40]

The sexual harassment scandal rocked the network and caused the departure of important talent. Most major companies in that situation would get a firm grip on such illegal practices in the workplace for a slew of reasons, including public reputation and the need to attract top-flight talent. But in April 2023, seven years after Gretchen Carlson's lawyers filed her complaint, Abby Grossman, a veteran Fox producer, initiated a lawsuit alleging that employees working on Tucker Carlson's show, as well as Tucker Carlson himself, had fomented a hostile work environment that spanned the gamut from lewd comments about their female colleagues to anti-Semitic jokes. Grossman said that an office for the show had been decorated with a large picture of former House Speaker Nancy Pelosi wearing a bathing suit. Fox News settled the case for $12 million.

THE "BIG LIE"

The third scandal is ongoing. It began when, just before midnight on November 3, 2020, the news side of the Fox network called Arizona for Joe Biden. The reporters were in good company. The Associated Press made the same call, and its prediction was followed by many other news outlets. But some major networks held back, not just for a few hours, but for days as

Arizona struggled to come up with a definitive vote count. Biden did win the state, but by a much smaller margin than originally reported.

Within days after the election, Trump and his advisors were on the warpath, claiming that the election had been stolen by a conspiracy so broad and deep that it involved Democrat and Republican vote-counting officials in the contested states. The Trump organization brought sixty-two lawsuits challenging the vote, none of which succeeded in changing the win-loss column. Yet polls show that as many as 61–70 percent of Republicans think that Joe Biden stole the presidency.[41] Belief in what Democrats call the "Big Lie" is undermining American government to the point that four out of ten Americans think it possible the nation is heading toward civil war.[42]

Trump was so incensed by the Fox News call on Arizona that he blamed the network for shifting the election in Biden's favor, urging followers to watch conservative outlets Newsmax or One America News instead. In one tweet, he wrote: "@FoxNews daytime ratings have completely collapsed. . . . Very sad to watch . . . but they forgot what made them successful, what got them there. They forgot the Golden Goose."[43] For the first time in two decades, Fox News fell below CNN in the ratings. By nine days after the election, the Fox Corporation's stock price had fallen 6 percent and the Fox News audience for daytime and prime-time shows had fallen 34 percent and 37 percent, respectively.

To recoup, the network's executives fired Chris Stirewalt, its veteran politics editor and doubled down on coverage of Trump's claims. In an op-ed in *Politico* published after he was fired, Stirewalt wrote:

> Unable to sell large, diverse audiences to advertisers, news outlets increasingly focus on developing highly habituated users. To cultivate the kind of intense readers, viewers or listeners necessary to make the addiction model profitable, media companies need consumers to have strong feelings. Fear, resentment and anger work wonders. It helps news outlets create deep emotional connections to users not just as users of a product, but as members of the same tribe.[44]

As Fox executives thrashed about trying to regain their place in the Trump universe, the drift to the far right by Fox commentators became more and more troubling to hosts of the network's news shows, who operated independently from the opinion shows. Two of the network's most prominent news hosts—Shepard Smith and Chris Wallace—departed, further discrediting the network. As Smith said in his final broadcast: "Even in our currently polarized nation it's my hope that the facts will win the day. That the truth will always matter. That journalism and journalists will thrive."[45] After Smith landed at CNBC, he told CNN anchor Christiane Amanpour:

> Opine all you like, but if you're going to opine, begin with the truth and opine from there. When people begin with a false premise and lead people astray, that's injurious to society and it's the antithesis of what we should be doing: Those of us who are so honored and grateful to have a platform of public influence have to use it for the public good.[46]

In the same vein, Wallace said "I'm fine with opinion: conservative opinion, liberal opinion. But when people start to question the truth—Who won the 2020 election? Was Jan. 6 an insurrection? —I found that unsustainable."[47]

Fox executives decided to restore ratings by appearing to support Trump's claims about election fraud. But this time around, they were dealing with an isolated president. Figures willing to give him candid legal advice like Bill Barr, his attorney general, and Pat Cipollone, his White House counsel, had withdrawn into the background. Trump spent most of his time closeted with fanatic and unstable advisers, including Rudy Giuliani, the former mayor of New York, who described himself as Trump's personal lawyer, and Sidney Powell, a Texas lawyer who insinuated herself into Trump's inner circle by spinning the details of the stolen election conspiracy theory into a froth.

Giuliani and Powell realized that they needed a storyline to support their allegations. They settled on the narrative that Dominion Voting Systems, the company providing voting machines to twenty-eight states in 2020, was owned by Smartmatic, a company created in Venezuela to rig elections for socialist president Hugo Chavez. They added that Dominion machines had software allowing Democrats to steal huge numbers of votes from Trump and give them to Biden. In fact, Smartmatic is a competitor of Dominion and neither company had any connection to Hugo Chavez, who had died in 2013. Dominion was certified by U.S. Election Assistance, an independent bipartisan commission created by the Help America Vote Act of 2022 and chaired by a Trump appointee.

Anxious to curry favor with Trump after the ratings drop, Fox News commentators invited Giuliani and Powell on their shows and the two delivered increasingly elaborate versions of their conspiracy theories about Dominion and Smartmatic's role in the "steal." Dominion executives did not sit on their hands as the Fox attacks unfolded. They contacted Fox executives repeatedly, sending 3,600 emails debunking the claims made by Giuliani and Powell and echoed by the network's hosts. Dominion lawyers sent a lengthy letter explaining the problems with the broadcasts. Nothing worked. In some ways, this aspect of the unfolding fiasco is the most significant. Multiple, carefully documented warnings fell on deaf ears, whether for economic reasons such as assuaging Trump and restoring ratings or because of negligent mismanagement within the network, or both.

Dominion filed a lawsuit against Fox News in Delaware state court alleging that several of the network's commentators defamed its reputation when they broadcast and endorsed Powell and Giuliani's extravagant but baseless conspiracy theories. It asked for $1.6 billion in actual and punitive damages. The judge in the case, Eric M. Davis, was nominated by the state's governor, confirmed by the state senate, given a twelve-year term that lasts until December 2024, and is eligible for reappointment. Smartmatic filed its complaint in New York state court asking for $2.7 billion in damages. Its case is not likely to go to trial until 2024.

Attorneys for Fox News moved to dismiss Dominion's complaint for failure to state a legal claim that the court could resolve. Judge Davis rejected the motion, directing Fox News to answer the complaint and get ready for a trial. On April 19, 2023, after a jury was selected for the Dominion case and the trial was scheduled to begin, Fox agreed to pay Dominion $787.5 million to settle the case. Carlson was fired two days later.

The gist of Dominion's complaint was that Fox News provided a platform for Giuliani, Powell, and others to repeat defamatory comments about Dominion even though its producers and hosts knew these statements were false. Fox hosts endorsed these claims, repeating them on the air, the network's websites, and its social media accounts. The complaint alleged that 774 statements were made on the network challenging the election results and defaming Dominion in just the two weeks following the announcement that Biden was the president-elect. The hosts targeted by Dominion included Maria Bartiromo on *Morning with Maria*; Lou Dobbs on *Lou Dobbs Tonight*; Sean Hannity on *The Sean Hannity Show*; and Jeanine Pirro, host of *Justice w/Judge Jeanine.*

Bartiromo interviewed Trump shortly after the election. She endorsed the claim that Dominion rigged the election and called the company "disgusting and corrupt."[48] Powell appeared on Hannity's show claiming that Dominion machines "ran an algorithm that shaved off votes from Trump and awarded them to Biden. And they used the machines to trash large batches of votes that should have been awarded to President Trump."[49] Powell later pled guilty in a criminal case brought by Fulton County district attorney Fani Willis alleging that she and nineteen others, including Trump, interfered with vote counting in Georgia during the 2020 presidential election.

Even more damaging to the Fox News defense, in December 2020, the network tweeted a promotion for *Lou Dobbs Tonight*, a popular show on Fox Business. The text read: "The 2020 Election is a cyber Pearl Harbor: The leftwing establishment have aligned their forces to overthrow the United States government #MAGA #AmericaFirst #Dobbs."[50] It reached two million people.[51]

Dominion alleged that the facts in the case—primarily, transcripts of statements made on air, text messages and emails exchanged between network personnel, and statements made during depositions to prepare for the trial—proved that Fox News commentators knowingly or recklessly published conspiracy theories. It said that Rupert and Lachlan Murdoch and Fox News CEO Suzanne Scott knew that such claims were false and baseless but did not stop Fox News commentators from repeating such claims. Dominion argued that a reasonable viewer would have understood the claims to be assertions of fact. An expert-witness report submitted in the case by Mark Hosfield, a managing director of the investment bank Stout, estimated that Fox News's coverage had caused Dominion's equity and debt to drop $920.8 million.[52]

Fox News responded to Dominion's lawsuit by claiming that its employees were simply reporting an important news story and had no duty to verify the accuracy of the claims made by its guests.[53] It said that if Dominion were to win the case, any person who repeats a false allegation made by a public official would commit defamation. Fox said that Dominion bore the burden of proof and must show that the statements in question were made with actual malice.

At the end of March 2023, Judge Davis issued an opinion ruling on the parties' motions for summary judgment. Such motions ask the court to decide a case on the legal arguments and assume that the central facts of a case are not disputed. As a practical matter, when a judge grants summary judgment on key legal issues, the opinion should inspire the parties to settle. On the other hand, when the outcome of a case—or aspects of a case—depend on heavily disputed facts, judges should refuse to grant motions for summary judgment and cases should go to trial, where the credibility of witnesses can be tested by direct and cross examination when they take the stand. Judge Davis granted summary judgment, ruling against Fox News on several key points of law.

Most importantly, Judge Davis rejected the claim that Fox commentators were merely reporting newsworthy events. Instead, he wrote: "*The evidence developed in this civil proceeding demonstrates that it is* ***crystal clear*** *that none of the Statements relating to Dominion about the 2020 election are true.*"[54] (The italics and bold type are taken directly from the opinion.) Judge Davis left for trial the question of whether Fox hosts and guests were distorting the facts with actual malice, but the falsity finding significantly advanced Dominion's claims.

In a further blow to the defense, Judge Davis applied New York state law, which protects statements of opinion from liability but considers statements of fact made with malice to be defamatory. In an approach far different from Judge Vyskocil's opinion in the McDougal defamation case that applied blanket immunity to hyperbolic statements claimed to be mere opinion, he issued a forty-eight-page appendix that considered twenty separate excerpts from transcripts of Fox News shows. In each instance, Davis ruled that "the Statement uses precise and readily understood language to assert facts which are capable of being proven true or false, and the context in which the Statement is presented creates an inference to a reasonable viewer that it is factual."[55] So much for the idea that a person can use hyperbolic language and win immunity when stating a falsehood.

Beyond the judge's unfavorable rulings, the potential for embarrassment of the network's witnesses—including Rupert and Lachlan Murdoch—was undoubtedly an important factor in the decision to settle with Dominion. Rupert Murdoch's deposition was made public by the court and was generally viewed as undermining the company's case: "Rupert Murdoch said some Fox News hosts and commentators endorsed the false narrative that the 2020 election was stolen, according to testimony in an ongoing defamation lawsuit," reported the *Wall Street Journal*.[56] But

> Fox News itself didn't endorse that narrative. "I would have liked us to be stronger in denouncing it, in hindsight," Mr. Murdoch said, according to the [court] filing [of the deposition transcript]. Asked if he could have stopped the hosts from highlighting allegations on air, Mr. Murdoch responded, "I could have. But I didn't."[57]

TUCKER CARLSON'S DEMISE

The weekend before Fox News decided to settle with Dominion, its board of directors discovered the full extent and content of Tucker Carlson's tweets addressed to other Fox employees as the network struggled to manage Trump's stolen election claims.[58] During pretrial discovery in the Dominion case, Judge Davis ordered that the two parties exchange records from both company and personal cell phones. Fox lawyers had managed to get portions of these records redacted after months of battling with Dominion lawyers in court. But that protective wall could fall at any moment, especially if the case went to trial and Carlson was compelled to take the stand.

Consistent with his on-air personality, Carlson's text messages were blunt, hyperbolic, caustic, and profane. He called women "cunts," including Irena Briganti, head of the Fox News communications and public relations operation, and Trump spokesperson Sidney Powell.[59] He ridiculed the Fox hosts who were giving airtime to Giuliani and Powell but continued to identify with their claims on his broadcasts. In one particularly unfortunate tweet from the network's point of view, he announced that he hated Trump "passionately."[60]

In addition to Chair Rupert Murdoch and Executive Chair Lachlan Murdoch, the Fox Corporation's board of directors is composed of six people, most notably the former Speaker of the House of Representatives Paul Ryan (D-WI). Ryan resigned from the House in January 2019. He was a rising star in the Republican Party and he may fill this role again, although he has not been mentioned as a potential presidential candidate in 2024. Ryan said he was resigning because he did not want to miss participating fully in raising his children. But he accepted the speakership reluctantly after John Boehner (R-OH) was driven from the position. Ryan was worn down by the emotional dyspepsia of coping with the Trump White House and battling constantly with the House Freedom Caucus. Ryan is as conservative in demeanor and values as he is in intellect. It is tempting to imagine Ryan's role in this discussion. With a politician's appreciation of how such intemperance would play if made public and intuitive disgust at Carlson's lack of control, he may well have argued that Carlson's continued employment was a serious threat to the corporation, moving the Murdochs' imminent concerns about ratings to a longer-term perspective.

Shortly after it settled the Dominion case, Fox News announced that it was "parting ways" with Tucker Carlson. "We thank him for his service to the network as a host and prior to that as a contributor."[61] The delivery of the decision was harsh. Carlson did his regular show on Friday night, wishing viewers a good weekend. He was informed that he was fired the following Monday, ten minutes before the network released its statement.

When Rupert Murdoch fired Ailes, O'Reilly, and Shine, he reinforced the principle that the Fox brand came first and the talent a far distant second—a mantra preached by Ailes for years. But he had undoubtedly worried about what would happen to the network without the three men. Lachlan and Rupert Murdoch had reasons to be tired of Carlson despite his high ratings. In 2020, Carlson had carried out a failed attempt to depose Irena Briganti, the network's well-connected head of corporate communications.[62] He had become so recalcitrant in dealing with Fox executives in Washington and New York that Fox News had hired Raj Shah, a former Trump aide, to mediate between him and other top executives. Shah had been unsuccessful and the power struggle between Carlson and Briganti continued.

The relationship between Carlson and network executives remains tense. Fox News sent a team up to Carlson's property in Maine and removed the equipment in the studio it had built for him. When Carlson launched a "Tucker on Twitter" series, apparently with the approval of Twitter owner Elon Musk, Fox lawyers sent him a letter demanding that he stop posting videos on the streaming service because he was violating his employment contract. And the rumor mill is operating overtime. According to anonymous sources within the network, Briganti has assembled a dossier of harmful information about Carlson and stands ready to release it if he continues to defy network executives.[63]

WAXING OR WANING?

Many observers believe Fox News is on a steady upward trajectory for the foreseeable future, wielding considerable—at times definitive—influence over the Republican Party.[64] The most convincing evidence supporting this conclusion is the network's outsized influence on Republican politicians, who plead for appearances on such Fox programs as *The Five* and *Hannity*. While the steady decline of cable news remains a big problem for the network, Fox News is likely to continue as a potent force on the national scene for years to come.

A minority of commentators have argued that Fox News is not only waning but on an irreversible downward trajectory.[65] These critics focus on the facts that close to a third of Fox News loyal viewers are over sixty-five and disproportionately male and that their number seems to be capped at between three and three and a half million, depending on the time of day and the program. The critics also contest the Murdochs' reputation as influential "kingmakers," noting that they failed to support the winning Republican candidate in 2016 (Trump), 2012 (Romney), and 2008 (John McCain). The Murdochs were fervently opposed to Barack Obama but could not prevent his election and reelection. Of course, these observations must be tempered by the network's success in promoting Trump when he was president.

The obsessive pursuit of ratings at the expense of any meaningful effort to verify the truth of what comes out of its commentators' mouths has downsides that senior Fox executives seem incapable of managing. The Smartmatic case is likely to impose another punishing financial penalty. Coupled with the steady decline of cable television and the fact that the hard core of the Fox audience skews white and elderly, the network does not seem to be evolving rapidly enough to remain a powerhouse. The free-with-ads entertainment site Tubi may have a promising, long-term future. Fox cable news does not.

A further cautionary tale is provided by what has happened at CNN, Fox News's main competitor. Within a few months after Discovery Inc.

bought WarnerMedia, then the owner of CNN, and became Warner Bros. Discovery, the new company's executives cancelled CNN+, the network's long-planned, $300 million effort to break into streaming. They shut down CNN+ in part because they thought a streaming service devoted only to news and commentary could not survive in the highly competitive environment driven by the pandemic when many people increased their subscriptions to streaming programming. When most went back to work, so-called subscriber fatigue set in, and the overcrowded market for streaming services began to crash.[66] In those negative economic circumstances, the executives were convinced that only a full menu of news, commentary, and, crucially, entertainment could enter this marketplace and survive.

The decision to abandon CNN+ leaves up for grabs the question of what will happen to CNN, which is suffering from plunging ratings and loss of profits. In April 2022, Warner Bros. Discovery CEO David Zaslav hired Chris Licht, a veteran producer of single programs, to run CNN. A few months later, two stars of the network, John Harwood, its White House correspondent, and Brian Stelter, its chief media correspondent, left precipitously before their contracts expired. Both men were outspoken critics of Trump. Veteran media reporters began to speculate that CNN would move to the right and try to steal audience from Fox News. The rumors were prompted by public statements by John Malone, a Warner Bros. Discovery board member, multibillionaire, and well-known conservative funder. *Slate* reported that "Warner Bros. Discovery board member John Malone has gone on record as praising Fox News while noting that he'd like to see CNN "evolve back to the kind of journalism that it started with, and actually have journalists, which would be unique and refreshing."[67]

Licht tried hard to please, explaining that he saw a market for a middle-of-the-road CNN that would recapture Republican viewers who watched Fox News. But he was gone in a little over a year, after orchestrating a disastrous town hall with Trump that he consciously populated with an audience of enthusiastic Trump followers. Reporter Kaitlan Collins lost control and Trump got an hour of free airtime. A critical profile of Licht by veteran political reporter Tim Alberta for *The Atlantic* apparently sealed his fate.[68] Zaslav fired him a few days later.

As for the Murdochs, with the 2020 election in their rear view, Lachlan and Rupert seemed more ambivalent about the former president. Trump persisted with his stolen election claims, the FBI discovered classified documents at his Mar-a-Lago resort, and other potential Republican presidential candidates emerged. In July 2022, the Murdoch's two most prominent American newspapers—the *New York Post* and the *Wall Street Journal*—ran harsh editorials condemning Trump's behavior. The *New York Post* wrote: "It's up to the Justice Department to decide if this is a crime. But as a matter of principle, as a matter of *character*, Trump has proven himself unworthy to be this country's chief executive again."[69] The *Wall Street Journal* was similarly harsh:

> The brute facts remain: Mr. Trump took an oath to defend the Constitution, and he had a duty as Commander in Chief to protect the Capitol from a mob attacking in his name. He refused. He didn't call the military to send help. He didn't call Mr. Pence to check on the safety of his loyal VP. Instead he fed the mob's anger and let the riot play out.[70]

It is hard to imagine that the Murdochs were not consulted before such negative editorials appeared, on the same day no less, although the two newspapers are not nearly as vulnerable to MAGA loyalist backlash as Fox News. Four criminal indictments against Trump, two brought by federal prosecutors and two by their state counterparts, must exacerbate their wariness. Despite their newfound caution about Trump, how Fox News commentators will react if he becomes the Republican candidate for president in 2024 is anyone's guess. The Murdochs could easily return to promoting Trump's stolen election claims rather than risk another freefall in Fox News ratings.

INSURRECTION

In March 2023, a rare and gaping split emerged between Republican leaders in the House and Senate. To arouse the MAGA base, House Speaker Kevin McCarthy (R-CA) granted Tucker Carlson exclusive access to 41,000 hours of video footage of what happened at the Capitol on January 6, 2021, assembled by law enforcement. Carlson's team put together a short montage of the footage for his show a few days later. Carlson said the excerpts showed that most of the rioters were "orderly and meek" sightseers. In fact, they were entirely justified in traveling to the Capitol because "the 2020 election was a grave betrayal of American democracy given the facts that have since emerged about that election. No honest person can deny it."[71]

A portion of the montage showed Jacob Chansley, the "QAnon Shaman," walking through the halls followed by a handful of uniformed guards. Chansley was one of the most visible participants because he wore red, white, and blue face paint, was naked from the waist up, sported a Viking hat with horns protruding on either side, and carried an American flag and a bullhorn. Carlson claimed Chansley was acting peacefully because the uniformed guards made no effort to impede his progress. Chansley was also filmed in the Senate Chamber where he screamed from the balcony and later took a position on the podium to deliver a strange prayer at the top of his lungs.

The day after Carlson aired the montage, Senate minority leader Mitch McConnell (R-KY) stepped to the microphones on the Senate side of the Capitol. "With regard to the presentation on Fox News last night, I want to associate myself entirely with the opinion of the Capitol Police about what happened on Jan. 6."[72] He was referring to an internal memorandum authored by U.S. Capitol Police chief Tom Manger and addressed to serving officers that called out Carlson for "offensive and misleading conclusions" about the siege:

> One false allegation is that our officers helped the rioters and acted as "tour guides." This is outrageous and false. . . . I don't have to remind

> you how outnumbered our officers were on January 6. Those officers did their best to use de-escalation tactics to try to talk rioters into getting each other to leave the building. . . .
>
> The most disturbing accusation from last night was that our late friend and colleague Brian Sicknick's death had nothing to do with his heroic actions on January 6. The Department maintains, as anyone with common sense would, that had not Officer Sicknick not fought valiantly for hours on the day he was violently assaulted, Officer Sicknick would not have died the next day.[73]

Sicknick is a hero to the police who confronted the rioters. He died on January 7, 2021, after suffering two strokes. Law enforcement officials said he was struck with a fire extinguisher and died as a result, but this report was later disproven when medical examiners did an autopsy. The medical examiner said Sicknick had died from natural causes but agreed that Sicknick's engagement with the mob played some role in his fatal collapse.

Carlson repeated and expanded on his claims that forces in the government set up the rioters in *Patriot Purge*, a three-part "documentary" produced under a multiyear agreement to provide content for Fox Nation, the network's subscription streaming service. As this book goes to press, the film is still available on the site, but not on Fox News. *Patriot Purge*'s central narrative is that the January 6 insurrection was a "false flag" operation launched by Trump's deep-state foes who work inside the government, including the military and the FBI. The purpose of this conspiracy was to discredit Trump voters so that their constitutional rights could be taken away. Carlson explains: "Not, you should understand, a metaphorical war, but an actual war. Soldiers and paramilitary law enforcement, guided by the world's most powerful intelligence agencies, hunting down American citizens, purging them from society, and throwing some of them into solitary confinement."[74]

Carlson also claims that members of a loosely organized and violence-prone network known as "antifa" (short for *anti-fascist*) were also present and manipulated the crowd to commit more violence. Federal law enforcement has repeatedly debunked the idea that members of antifa were present, much less that they urged the protesters to commit more violence. As will be explained in chapter 8, the allegation makes no sense in the context of antifa's avowed purpose, which is to fight with people they perceive as fascists, including MAGA enthusiasts. But in text exchanges with NPR reporter David Folkenflik, Carlson insisted that "mainstream media" is lying, "in concert with Democrats," and that his own reporting "showed there was no insurrection."[75]

America has been working on its intricate constitutional system of checks and balances for less than 250 years, a short period by European standards. Whether the Murdochs have considered the implications of how they are disrupting this system is unknown. They are making a great deal of money and may sincerely believe that they are presenting a necessary counterweight to harmful liberal ideas. We cannot know the full price the country will pay for the cascading untruths, wildly irrational conspiracy theories, and systemic development of fury and paranoia Fox News and Fox Nation deliver to millions of viewers. But it seems like a risk far too serious for one family of billionaires to impose on the rest of us.

SIX

WHITE EVANGELICALS

GOD'S WILL

White evangelicals believe in the power of God's will and the End of Days, and they are fatalistic about urgent problems like climate change. To the extent that they see changes for the worse in the climate, they believe heat, drought, and floods are warning signs that the End of Days are nigh. The possibility provokes anxiety, wonder, and dread, but God controls the situation and will ensure the faithful are saved.

Despite their faith in God's will and the imperative of living a penitent life of observance and self-criticism, white evangelicals play a definitive role in the nation's politics because they are an indispensable component of the Republican Party's base. They deserve much of the credit for Donald Trump's election in 2016, did their best to support him in 2020, and will play a crucial role in choosing the candidate and determining the result of the 2024 presidential election. Their loyalty to the party led to the achievement of a crucial goal that eluded them for five decades: elimination of a constitutional right to abortion.

Political participation by white evangelicals began in the 1970s when ambitious pastors began to follow in the footsteps of Billy Graham, known as "America's pastor" and a towering figure worldwide. His charitable organization, Samaritan's Purse, reports that he "preached the Gospel of Jesus Christ to some 215 million people who attended one of his more than 400 crusades, simulcasts and evangelistic rallies in more than 185 countries and territories."[1]

Graham was especially proud that he had the opportunity to offer religious and other advice to presidents, starting with Harry Truman and ending with Barack Obama. His closest relationship was with Richard Nixon, who was not an overtly religious man. Graham treasured his easy access to the president and the opportunities it gave him to affect foreign and domestic affairs. Most of Graham's advice was conveyed in private meetings in the Oval Office or in written communications. When Nixon died in 1994, his papers and the tapes were released for public examination, revealing two embarrassing incidents when Graham gave advice that starkly departed from his religious beliefs.

Graham was adamantly opposed to Communism and supported the Vietnam War. As it raged on, he wrote a memorandum urging Nixon to bomb the dikes in North Vietnam, a battle plan that would have led to the death of an estimated one million people.[2] A tape recording of an Oval Office meeting in 1972 between Nixon and Graham contained a conversation revealing their mutual anti-Semitism, especially their conviction that Jews dominated American media.[3] Both men were preoccupied with the *New York Times*, owned by the Sulzbergers, a Jewish family. The paper endorsed Nixon's Democratic opponents (Hubert Humphrey and George McGovern) both times he ran for president. Graham told Nixon that if he won a second term, he could finally do something about the problem. At the end of his life, Graham said he had three regrets: neglecting his family, failing to march for civil rights with the Reverend Martin Luther King Jr., and succumbing to the "nearly insatiable pull of partisan politics."[4]

Unlike the Catholic Church, the institutional structure of white evangelicalism is not hierarchical with a single leader like the pope or a presiding institution like the Vatican. Instead, pastors are independent and preside with absolute authority over their congregation. The lack of hierarchy encourages cults of personality around the most charismatic and entrepreneurial pastors. Having a national presence through the achievement of political influence at the top tier of government is too tempting for most to resist.

The emergence of megachurches with congregations of several thousand has accelerated the prominence of ambitious white pastors and the political activism of their congregation. The scale of these institutions is unprecedented. The Hartford Institute for Religious Research defines *megachurch* as a Christian congregation with "sustained average weekly attendance of 2,000 persons or more in its worship services" and estimates that the United States hosted 1,650 Protestant megachurches in October 2019.[5]

The biggest is the nondenominational Lakewood Church in Houston, Texas, led by Pastor Joel Osteen. The church is a converted sports complex, where the average weekly attendance is 43,500.[6] Megachurches hold numerous worship services on Sunday and other days of the week to accommodate congregants, provide religious and psychological counseling, sponsor recreational centers for children and youth, and even furnish shopping venues for members' convenience. Apart from the occasional female author, professor, or televangelist, white evangelical leaders are male, but their wives are often active leaders in the social life of their congregations. No matter what their level of income, church members must tithe at the rate of 10 percent of their income to support church activities.

Osteen is a prominent leader of the "prosperity gospel" movement that is based on the belief that if congregants are devout and donate generously to the church, God will bless them with money. Osteen does not take a salary from the church and instead lives on the proceeds of his book sales, estimated to be in the tens of millions of dollars. Another high-profile prosperity gospel leader, Paula White, delivered the invocation at Trump's inauguration, chaired his evangelical advisory board, and gave a fiery speech at the rally organized for Trump followers on January 6, 2021, that culminated in the insurrection at the Capitol. Trump posed for photo ops with White and other evangelical leaders in the Oval Office.

Televangelism—the use of radio and television to reach followers nationwide—also provides a platform for leading pastors to accrue political power. Pioneered by evangelical leaders like Pat Robertson, Jim Bakker, Jerry Falwell, and Robert Jeffress, such programs attract millions of viewers and listeners. Robertson came to prominence as host of *The 700 Club*, a Christian variety show supported by donations from viewers and featuring prayers and religious musical performances. He was also the chairman of the Christian Broadcasting Network, which, along with his other media holdings, sold for $1.9 billion to the News Corporation in 1998. It is now owned by the Disney Corporation and has been renamed Freeform. *The 700 Club* remains on the air, attracting an audience estimated at one million each day. Robertson stepped down in 2021, handing the program over to his son Gordon.

Appointing a son to take over the father's ministry is common practice. Joel Osteen took over from his father, John Osteen; Franklin Graham stepped into Billy Graham's shoes; and Jerry Falwell Jr. became the president of Liberty University, the evangelical school his father, Jerry Falwell Sr., founded in Virginia, saving it from financial ruin by fundraising prodigiously. In 2020, Falwell Jr. was forced to resign in the wake of a sex scandal involving his wife's long-term affair with a much younger man.

White evangelicals have also become enmeshed in Christian nationalism, a widespread, well-funded, ultraconservative movement that played a prominent role in planning and executing the January 6, 2021, insurrection. Its core precept is that the United States is a Christian nation and must be ruled by Christian beliefs. The movement believes that God inspired the creation of the country and guided the drafting of both the Declaration of Independence and the Constitution. Members favor eliminating the Constitution's separation of church and state. Instead, interpretations of God's will and teachings should subsume judicial interpretations by non-believers. Overall, 81 percent of white evangelicals and 65 percent of Black Protestants endorse this vision compared to 45 percent of all Americans.[7] The numbers fall precipitously among non-Christians and younger people. In addition to declaring the United States a Christian nation, believers would stop federal officials from enforcing the separation of church and state and allow public school teachers to recite Christian prayers in the classroom.

Journalist Katherine Stewart, author of *The Power Worshippers: Inside the Dangerous Rise of Religious Nationalism*, a book on the origins, ideology, and activities of the Christian nationalist movement, writes that it

> is, first and foremost a political movement. Its principal goal, and the goal of its most active leaders, is power. Its leadership looks forward to the day when they can rely on government for three things: power and influence for themselves and their political allies; a steady stream of taxpayer funding for their initiatives; and policies that favor "approved" religious and political viewpoints.[8]

Christian nationalists should not be confused with white nationalists, the movement that organized the violent Unite the Right rally in Charlottesville, Virginia, in the summer of 2017.

However unified white evangelical support of Republican candidates, the national organization that convenes its largest denomination, the Southern Baptist Convention, is riven by severe internal problems. A sexual abuse scandal that extended over many years and involved pastors and other prominent male leaders is under investigation by the Justice Department for potential criminal offenses. At the Convention's annual meeting in June 2023, members voted by a large margin to exclude churches that allow women to preach in any capacity. A potential amendment to the group's constitution outlawing such behavior is pending and will become final in summer 2024. An attempted takeover of the Convention by ultraconservatives was thwarted, but provoked threats by Black pastors to leave the group. The attempted national takeover has been replicated by ultraconservative MAGA loyalists attacking "woke" pastors at individual churches across the country.

These debilitating conflicts are unlikely to be resolved in the short term, and trouble also looms over the longer-term horizon. Between 2006 and 2020, the number of Americans identifying as white evangelical Protestant declined from 23 percent to 14.5 percent.[9] Young evangelicals, beginning with Millennials (now 25–40) are falling away from the strict dogma embraced by their parents and grandparents. As veteran religion reporter Eliza Griswold writes:

> The separation of families at the border, climate change, and various progressive causes have galvanized young Christians. From a distance, evangelicalism can appear culturally monolithic . . . but many young evangelicals are more diverse, less nationalistic, and more heterodox in their views than older generations. Believing that being a Christian involves recognizing the sanctity of all human beings, they support Black Lives Matter and immigration reform, universal health care and reducing the number of abortions, rather than overturning *Roe v. Wade.*[10]

Robert P. Jones, CEO of the Public Religion Research Institute (PRRI), a social research firm that excels in reporting how religious groups perceive current events and controversy, agrees: "We are living in one of those interregnum moments between an old and new order."[11] The political influence of the white evangelical movement is likely to fade eventually, but during the Trump presidency more of his white Christian supporters identified as evangelicals than shed that identity.

For the time being, white evangelicals have one important political advantage that reflects their effective organization of congregants around the church and the discipline inherent to their faith. Overall voter turnout for national elections continues to hover between 54 and 62 percent. Yet white evangelicals turn out at higher levels than their numbers in the population. In 2020, they were 15 percent of the population but 28 percent of the electorate.[12] Anger over Trump's loss in 2020 has inspired ultraconservative pastors and their supporters to double down on political organizing. At least through the 2024 election and probably for several years beyond, polarization in the country and low voter turnout will amplify the electoral influence of this well-organized, ideologically homogenous, and highly motivated group.

This chapter focuses on white evangelicals and does not address the beliefs or political activities of Black and Latino evangelicals because the two groups are starkly different in their political attitudes and party affiliation. Eighty-six percent of evangelical churches are segregated by race.[13] A 2014 survey by PRRI found that 52 percent of white evangelicals believe whites and Blacks receive equal treatment in the criminal justice system, but 84 percent of Black Protestants disagreed.[14] Trump's strident attacks on immigrants and Black Lives Matter protests exacerbated the tension between the two groups.

Because the white evangelical community is distrustful of outsiders, reporting on its internal affairs can be difficult.[15] Internal battles between ultraconservative and moderate factions within the white evangelical movement are so charged that sources often insist on anonymity when talking to anyone who reports on these issues. The best insights are often contained in the writing of prominent evangelicals who have had careers in mainstream political jobs and are not in thrall to the MAGA movement. Two featured here are Michael Gerson, columnist for the *Washington Post* and former chief speechwriter for President George W. Bush, and Peter Wehner, contributing writer to the *New York Times* and *The Atlantic* and speechwriter for Presidents Reagan, George H. W. Bush, and George W. Bush. Gerson died in November 2022 after a long fight with kidney cancer, but Wehner is still reporting and analyzing.

RECRUIT AND REFORM

To qualify as an evangelical, a person must hold four beliefs, known as the "Bebbington quadrilateral" after their originator, historian David Bebbington:

> Biblicism: a high regard for and obedience to the Bible, especially the New Testament, which is to be taken literally as a historical record of the life and teachings of Jesus Christ and his followers and regarded as the ultimate authority regarding how believers should live their lives.

> Crucicentrism: a focus on Christ's crucifixion and its saving effects that make possible the redemption of humanity, to the point that all individual evangelicals must have a "born again" experience being touched by Christ and pursue a lifelong process of following Him as their Lord and Savior.
>
> Conversionism: the conviction that every person should be converted to evangelicalism and that those who follow other religions are heathen and will not be included in the End of Days when only evangelicals will be.
>
> Activism: the willingness to express and demonstrate the teachings of the Christian Gospel in missionary and social reform efforts.[16]

The movement's political activism is motivated by the last two beliefs. Constituents justify their favored public policy reforms as interpretations of God's will. For example, reforms to cut spending for social safety net programs are motivated by creating more opportunities for churches to step in, administer to the needy, and evangelize.

Evangelical leaders began to emphasize the top priority of overturning *Roe v. Wade* soon after the decision was issued in 1973. But their well-known focus on the issue obscured the true origin of Christian right activism. Historian Randall Balmer writes that, contrary to common belief, abortion was not the issue that first ignited white evangelical activism five decades ago.[17] Instead, its leaders were upset by efforts to withdraw nonprofit tax status from segregated evangelical schools like Bob Jones University. Conservative leader Paul Weyrich, a founder of the conservative think tank the Heritage Foundation, understood that segregation would not be a politically palatable issue to use in organizing evangelicals to support Republican Ronald Reagan over Democrat Jimmy Carter. Abortion was a far better cause than the tax problem and had the added advantage of uniting evangelicals with Catholics and mainstream Protestants. He was right. Five decades later, this coalition won, despite public opinion favoring retention of the right to abortion. (A Pew Research Center poll found that in June 2023, 61 percent of American adults thought abortion should be legal in all or most cases, as opposed to 37 percent who thought it should be illegal.[18])

The new conservative majority on the Supreme Court includes five Catholics (Justices John Roberts, Clarence Thomas, Samuel Alito, Brett Kavanaugh, and Amy Coney Barrett). Justice Neil Gorsuch was raised Catholic but now attends Episcopal services. The six are energetically delivering on goals that are the highest priorities of the Christian right. The conservative majority reversed *Roe v. Wade*, eliminating the constitutional right to abortion, overturned state restrictions on church occupancy during the pandemic intended to prevent exposure through close contact, invalidated restrictions on prayer in public school settings, and approved broader public funding of religious schools.[19] The next frontier is likely to be LGBTQ rights.

THE END OF DAYS AND THE POLITICS OF FEAR

All evangelicals believe in a central tenet known as the End of Days—also known as the End Times, the Apocalypse, Armageddon, or the Rapture. When the End of Days arrives, a catastrophic series of events will consume nonbelievers in horrific circumstances. Christ will elevate evangelicals who are sufficiently devout and have lived a good Christian life, saving them from torment. Many evangelicals watch for signs that the End of Days is imminent and discuss what the Apocalypse will be like. On Twitter, evangelicals have adopted the hashtag #RaptureAnxiety to gather and express emotional reactions to the perceived imminence of the End of Days. In a 2014 PRRI survey, 77 percent of white evangelicals said that recent natural disasters are attributable to the End of Days.[20]

A related belief is that God gave the Jewish people the Holy Land now encompassed by Israel and that Jews will safeguard it until the End of Days. In a 2017 poll conducted by LifeWay Research, 80 percent of respondents said that the creation of the state of Israel in 1948 was "fulfillment of Bible prophecy that shows we are getting closer to the return of Jesus Christ."[21] When President Trump announced he was moving the American embassy in Israel from Tel Aviv to Jerusalem, the hashtag saw a great deal of traffic because the decision was interpreted as bringing the End of Days closer.[22]

Evangelical culture reflects the pervasiveness, depth, and powerful impact of these beliefs, which are as awe-inspiring as they are terrifying. Robert Jones, CEO of PRRI, has written:

> As I came of age in Woodville Heights Baptist Church, . . . I internalized a cycle of sin, confession and repentance as a daily part of my life. Though I wasn't aware of it at the time, this was a double inheritance. Beneath this seemingly icy surface of guilt and culpability flowed a deeper current of innocence and entitlement. Individually, I was a sinner, but collectively, I was part of a special tribe. Whatever our humble social stations might be, we white Christians were God's chosen instruments of spreading salvation and civilization to the world.[23]

The paradoxical conviction that evangelicals must worship and repent strenuously until the End of Days arrive, and then they will be elevated to heaven, leaving behind all nonbelievers reenforces the insularity of the white evangelical community. If you believe the End of Days could occur in your lifetime, why bother entering into relationships with people who are nonbelievers unless you are confident you can convert them before the End of Days?

Sixteen best-selling novels written by evangelical authors Tim LaHaye and Jerry B. Jenkins and known as the "Left Behind" series dramatize the End of Days and Christ's return. Describing the books as "highly engaging reading for a mass market with elements drawn from sci-fi, romance, disaster porn, and political spy novels," *Christianity Today* critic-at-large Alissa Wilkinson wrote in the *Washington Post*:

> I was 12 when the first "Left Behind" book was published, and like many conservative evangelical kids growing up in church who could recite the timeline of the tribulation at the drop of a hat, I saw the books less like fiction and more like . . . Paul LaLonde's idea of them, as he described it to

> *Variety* in 2014: "It's also a historical account in a sense, because it's based on a true story, it just hasn't happened yet."[24]

LaLonde produced film adaptations of the novels.

Wilkinson explains that coauthors LaHaye and Jenkins are "dispensationalists," meaning they embrace the idea that the Jewish people were never replaced as God's chosen people and that the modern state of Israel is the biblical Israel that awaits the fulfillment of the Old Testament's warnings about the End of Days. The authors think that if Israel ever makes peace with its neighbors, that event will give rise to a disastrous one-world government, triggering the End of Days. Evangelicals will disappear from the earth en masse, and nonbelievers will begin seven years of tribulation. Christ and his followers will then return and, following a thousand-year period of peace, Satan will be defeated.

Historian John Fea is a white evangelical professor at Messiah University in Pennsylvania who has probed what he calls "the politics of fear." He writes that candidates appealing to white evangelicals during Republican primaries in 2015–2016 based their arguments on fear politics, which he defined as convincing "the faithful that the Christian fabric of the country was unraveling, the nation's evangelical moorings were loosening, and the barbarians were amassing at the borders, ready for a violent takeover."[25] Journalist Katherine Stewart agrees: "Christian nationalism today begins with the conviction that conservative Christians are the most oppressed group in American society. Among leaders of the movement, it is a matter of routine to hear talk that they are engaged in a 'battle against tyranny,' and that the Bible may soon be outlawed."[26]

Linked to these strong feelings of fear and persecution is the idea that Trump is a strongman who will defend white evangelicals against the forces of evil. Fea writes that during the 2016 Republican primary campaigns, Trump was at the head of the pack among white evangelicals until the fall of 2016, when Ben Carson briefly surged in popularity. Carson claimed superiority over Trump because he was a more devout practitioner of religion (he is a Seventh Day Adventist). Carson defended the right to fly Confederate flags on private property and compared the political correctness espoused by Democrats to the repression that occurred in Hitler's Germany. In response, Trump went on Fox News in the aftermath of the Islamic State's claim of responsibility for an attack in Paris that killed 130. He advocated the need to develop a strategy to kill the families of terrorists. Fea writes: "With terrorism filling the headlines, it was Trump, not Carson, who did a better job of playing the strongman."[27]

Robert Jeffress is the senior pastor at the First Baptist Church in Dallas, Texas, which has 13,000 members. He hosts television and radio programs called *Pathway to Victory* that are broadcast on hundreds of stations nationwide, and he appears regularly on Fox News. He has authored twenty-four books, including *Countdown to the Apocalypse* and *Not All Roads Lead to Heaven*, and he embraces Christian nationalism. In the run-up to the 2016 election, Jeffress explained his support for Trump in blunter terms:

> When I'm looking for a leader who's gonna sit across the negotiating table from a nuclear Iran, or who's gonna be intent on destroying ISIS, I couldn't care less about that leader's temperament or his tone or his vocabulary. Frankly, I want the meanest, toughest son of a gun I can fine. And I think that's the feeling of a lot of evangelicals. They don't want a Casper Milquetoast as the leader of the free world.[28]

THE POLITICAL AGENDA

White evangelicals have worked diligently for four decades to become politically powerful at the national, state, and local levels. Their grassroots are energetic and highly effective, in large measure because when they attend church, they become part of tight-knit, insular communities that exchange information, provide a place to organize with like-minded peers, and receive advice on political priorities. Their agenda on moral issues is the same as the Christian right: they oppose abortion and same-sex marriage and other civil rights for LGBTQ citizens. They advocate Christian displays in public places, the recital of Christian prayers in public schools, and federal funding for religious schools. Yet these religiously motivated beliefs are only one part of a significantly broader agenda.

The 2014 Pew Religious Landscape Study probed evangelical positions on broader public policy issues.[29] Sixty-four percent of evangelical Protestants said the country needs smaller government and fewer services. Sixty-eight percent of white evangelical Protestants said the nation had no responsibility to accept refugees.[30] Fifty-six percent of evangelical Protestants said that government aid to the poor did more harm than good, with every other religious group falling at least 10 percent lower than this number except Mormons, who weighed in at 64 percent. (Pew assumed that evangelical Protestants numbered 62 million and Mormons 6.5 million.) Forty-eight percent of evangelical Protestants said environmental laws cost too many jobs and hurt the environment, well above the number for any other religious group except Mormons, who endorsed the statement by 53 percent.

PRRI chief executive officer Melissa Deckman and three colleagues analyzed existing data to discover contemporary economic attitudes of evangelicals and other religious groups.[31] They concluded that the cross-fertilization between affiliation with the Tea Party and white evangelical communities has pushed the latter further to the right. Seventy-four percent of white evangelicals believe that the government should provide fewer services and reduce taxes compared to 58 percent of all Americans. Race makes a difference in this finding: white evangelicals "are about 1.3 times less likely than non-white evangelicals to favor a larger role for government" in domestic problems.[32] But class does not: "even among downscale white evangelical Protestants, there is a strong undercurrent of hostility toward government that is less pronounced among other downscale Americans."[33] These attitudes extend even to infrastructure and education: white evangelicals are "roughly 1.4 times less likely than other Americans to believe that public investment in infrastructure and education is the best way to spur economic growth."[34]

On the existential issue of climate change, much has been written about the emergence of evangelicals who believe it is their religious calling to be good stewards of God's creation.[35] But those progressives are greatly outnumbered. A Pew survey that came out in 2015 found that only 28 percent of white evangelicals believed the earth is getting warmer as a result of human activity, while 33 percent believed changes in climate were attributable to "natural patterns" and 37 percent thought "no solid evidence" existed that the earth was in fact getting warmer.[36]

In addition to the conviction that drought, storms, and other climate-related events are a sign that the End of Days is approaching, the religious basis for white evangelical rejection of climate change as a problem worthy of state intervention is dominionism, or the idea that all other creatures and inanimate natural sources are subservient to human needs. White evangelicals also believe that God is all-knowing and that He would save the planet from damage if that outcome was best for Christ's followers. Alternatively, if climate change is real, God may decide to allow these changes to run their course. If the dire predictions regarding climate change come true, the End of Days will be upon us. Christ will return, believers will be saved, and nonbelievers will perish.

TRUMP DELIVERS

President Trump did not disappoint white evangelicals in any major way and enjoyed strong and unwavering support throughout his presidency. His vice president and many members of his administration were white evangelicals. Trump delivered a solid conservative majority on the Supreme Court, and the six justices overturned the right to abortion.[37] On every other important case pitting religion against government requirements, the Christian right won. The court was more supportive of religious interests than at any time since the 1950s.[38]

Despite these huge victories, white evangelicals were disappointed with Trump appointee Justice Neil Gorsuch's opinion protecting LGBTQ rights against workplace discrimination.[39] Yet in June 2023, the Supreme Court ruled that a white evangelical web designer could refuse to work for a gay couple who wanted to commission a web design for their upcoming nuptials because forcing her to act against her beliefs would violate her First Amendment right to free speech.[40] A revised interpretation of the Constitution constricting such rights as privacy and due process might well form the basis for curtailing additional LGBTQ rights.

President Trump took multiple tough stands against immigration, assuaging evangelicals' and Christian nationalists' fears that nonbelievers would take over the country. He attacked social safety net programs by, for example, supporting state requirements to impose work requirements on recipients of Medicaid and Supplemental Nutrition Assistance Program (SNAP, formerly known as Food Stamps). He shut down any effort by the federal government to mitigate climate change and withdrew from the international Paris Agreement. About the only important promise Trump did not fulfill was the repeal of the Johnson amendment, a provision of tax law put in place by President Lyndon Johnson that bars pastors and other leaders of nonprofit institutions from endorsing political candidates from the pulpit.[41]

Much of the white evangelical community continued its passionate support for Trump after he lost the 2020 elections and beyond. Weeks after the 2020 election but before the attack on the Capitol on January 6, 2021, Franklin Graham, Billy Graham's son and as close to evangelical royalty as anyone can get, posted the following on Facebook:

> People have asked if I am disappointed about the election. When I think about my answer, I have to say honestly, that I am grateful—grateful to God that for the last four years He gave us a president who protected our religious liberties; grateful for a president who defended the lives of the unborn, standing publicly against abortion and the bloody smear it has made on our nation; grateful for a president who nominated conservative judges to the Supreme Court and to our federal courts; grateful for a president who built the strongest economy in 70 years with the lowest unemployment rate in 50 years before the pandemic; grateful for a president who strengthened and supported our military; grateful for a presi-

> dent who stood against "the swamp" and the corruption in Washington; grateful for a president who supported law and order and defended our police.[42]

After the riot at the Capitol, Graham urged Christians to pray for the Biden administration. But he also denounced the ten Republicans who voted to impeach the former president for the second time: "The House Democrats impeached him because they hate him and want to do as much damage as they can. And these ten, from [Trump's] own party, joined in the feeding frenzy. It makes you wonder what the thirty pieces of silver were that Speaker Pelosi promised for this betrayal."[43] (According to the Bible, Judas betrayed Christ right before the Crucifixion for thirty pieces of silver.)

PROSELYTIZING AT THE TOP OF GOVERNMENT

Capitol Ministries was founded in 1996 by Ralph Drollinger, a former professional basketball player, and his second wife, Danielle Drollinger, a former business lobbyist. The organization's motto is "Making disciples of Jesus Christ in the political arena throughout the world."[44] The organization works with counterparts in thirty-four state capitals. Drollinger operationalizes the goal of making politicians disciples of Christ by conducting prayer meetings where evangelical lawmakers read Scripture and he explains the policies that should follow from them.

During the Trump presidency, Drollinger ran Bible studies in three separate weekly sessions, one for members of the cabinet (location undisclosed and light refreshments served); one for the Senate (rotating offices of senators with hot breakfast served); and one for members of the House (Capitol Room H34 with dinner served). The Capitol Ministries website includes dozens of written Bible studies, versions of which were presented at such sessions.

Among Drollinger's "White House cabinet sponsors" during the Trump administration were Vice President Mike Pence, Agriculture secretary Sonny Perdue, EPA administrator Scott Pruitt, Education secretary Betsy DeVos, Energy secretary Rick Perry, Health and Human Services secretary Alex Azar, Housing and Urban Development secretary Ben Carson, Labor secretary Alex Acosta, NASA administrator Jim Bridenstine, and secretary of State Mike Pompeo. The Capitol Ministries website lists dozens of other politicians in Congress and the states who in some way support Drollinger's organization. Pruitt, who was forced out of office by ethical lapses, explained what Drollinger's Bible studies meant to him in an interview on Christian Broadcasting Network News:

> To be encouraged, to pray, to basically—each of us are dealing with large issues—and so to spend time with a friend, a colleague, a person who has a faith focus on how we do our job, whether it's through prayer or through God's Word, and to encourage one another in that regard is so, so important, and we have that in our Cabinet and it's such a wonderful thing.[45]

The first step in Drollinger's curriculum for federal officials is to convince them that applying Christian beliefs to decisions made in a secular context is essential. He preaches that Christians have a duty to affect the world in which they live and should not refrain from participating in political debates informed by their religious beliefs. That fundamental premise established, he considers public policy issues of the day. In September 2017, for example, he considered social welfare programs:

> Apart from those with genuine needs due to birth defects, war injuries, disease, developmental disabilities, etc., how many live in poverty because they are not *willing to work* or *willing to work* hard enough? In attempting to diminish the unmet needs of a society, this basic truth must not be overlooked by the Public Servant in his policy formation. . . . Proverbs 10:4 echoes this principle: *Poor is he who works with a negligent hand, But the hand of the diligent makes rich.*[46]

And in April 2018, he posted "Coming to Grips with the Religion of Environmentalism":

> *In our lifetime there has been a radical shift in aggregate, national religious belief. In essence and unfortunately, America has been in the process of changing horses: from the religion of Christianity to one of Radical Environmentalism. We are in the process of exchanging the worship of the Creator for the worship of His creation. This is a huge and dire error, with extreme consequences, and it presages disaster.*
>
> For years, global warming advocates have proffered that the California drought is a precursor of things to come.... What seems to go largely unnoticed is that the 180-degree turn around of the radical doomsday climate-change folks contradicts what God's Word states in this regard. ... God says *He causes His sun to rise on the evil and the good and sends rain on the righteous and the unrighteous.* Notice that God's common grace promises rain even to the unrighteous.[47]

Of course, leading white evangelical pastors make no apologies for their strenuous efforts to affect public policy in any venue they can find. They energetically develop political power of great importance. What is troubling about Drollinger's operation is the absence of any effort to distinguish between worship and lobbying. His "studies" involve elected and appointed officials, occupy federal government property, occur when attendees could be working, and push inappropriate religious justifications into policymaking.

THE BATTLES WITHIN

The Southern Baptist Convention is the leading national organization that convenes the people most active in Baptist churches at national conferences to make policy and exchange ideas. The Baptist denomination is the largest in the country, with an estimated fourteen million members. The Convention includes 47,000 churches nationwide. The 2014 Pew *Religious Landscape Study* reported that 85 percent of Convention members are white,

6 percent are Black, and 3 percent are Latino. The leadership is conservative, male, and white, although the membership includes an almost equal number of men and women.[48]

The National Association of Evangelicals (NAE) is a more moderate alternative to the Convention, although it is smaller and less visible. The NAE includes 45,000 churches from forty Protestant denominations. Its leadership has moved to the political center and is committed to diversity. In 2020, the group elected Walter Kim, a Korean American, as its president. He governs the group with the assistance of a ten-member board that includes three African Americans and two women. As commendable as this diversity is, the NAE is no match for the Convention.

Southern Baptists founded the Convention in 1845 because they supported slavery and their counterparts in Northern states did not. It did not repudiate that position until 1995 and waited until 2017 to pass a resolution condemning white slavery.

In June 2021, the Convention held a contentious vote on an effort by its ultraconservative members to take over its leadership. To prepare for the vote, the insurgents adopted a pirate flag as their symbol and talked about "taking the ship" back as a metaphor for their rebellion.[49] They complained about their fellow pastors' support for Black Lives Matter protests in the wake of the killing of George Floyd and claimed that too many pastors supported teaching critical race theory in the schools. The most prominent Black pastors within the Convention threatened to quit the organization if the ultraconservative faction won the vote. "I'm hanging on by a thread," Pastor Dwight McKissic told religion reporter Eliza Griswold. "Dozens of other pastors have already called me to ask what I'm going to do."[50] In the end, Ed Litton, a moderate candidate, won over his conservative competitors by 4 percent of the 14,000 votes cast. At a press conference after his election, Litton said "We are a family. At times it seems we're incredibly dysfunctional, but we love each other."[51] Litton was succeeded by Bart Barber, another mainstream conservative, who is serving his second term as this book goes to press.

Around the same time, the Convention was rocked by a sex scandal that involved abuse of women and children by pastors and other church personnel. Despite numerous reports and a campaign by the victims over several years, the Convention's leadership had managed to ignore the emerging scandal until May 2022, when internal dissenters pushed it to hire Guidepost Solutions, an independent consulting group, to write a four-hundred-page report about it.[52] The report documented how Convention leaders intimidated survivors of sexual assault and resisted proposals for change over two decades. It reported that an internal list of incidents identified 703 abusers, with 409 having a Convention affiliation at some point in time. The Convention appointed an "abuse reform implementation task force."[53] Among other major steps, the task force plans to hire another outside firm to establish a Ministry Check database that will contain the names of those "credibly accused of sexual abuse in order to ensure thorough information flow throughout the Convention" that will make it possible for member "churches to protect their congregations.[54]

Years earlier, D. August Boto, general counsel to the Convention's executive committee, was put in charge of managing these allegations before they evolved to a full-fledged scandal. For a decade, Boto maintained a long list of Baptist pastors and other male leaders who were accused of abuse. Boto sat on the list, taking no action to verify the accusations or hold accountable those found culpable. In an internal email about the problem, Boto wrote:

> This whole thing should be seen for what it is. It is a satanic scheme to completely distract us from evangelism. It is not the gospel. It is not even a part of the gospel. It is a misdirection play. Yes, Christa Brown [a survivor] and Rachael Denhollander [a survivor advocate] have succumbed to an availability heuristic because of their victimizations. They have gone to the SBC looking for sexual abuse, and of course, they found it. Their outcries have certainly caused an availability cascade. . . . But they are not to blame. This is the devil being temporarily successful.[55]

As the truth about the scandal began to emerge, Boto resigned, along with several other members of the Convention's executive committee.

Boto's use of the term *availability heuristic* is mistaken. The term connotes the psychological mistake of extrapolating from one rare, traumatic event to the generalization that such events are common. In essence, Boto was ridiculing the two women who had come forward to testify about their abuse by suggesting that their experience was rare and they were deluded enough to think it was common.

The Department of Justice is investigating the Convention and its members to determine whether crimes were committed by clergy and others. The Convention announced this development through its lawyers, acknowledging that the executive committee had received a subpoena. They pledged to cooperate fully.

The upheaval within the Convention was mirrored by upheaval within individual churches sparked by Trump's 2020 defeat. In an article for *The Atlantic* entitled "The Evangelical Church Is Breaking Apart," Peter Wehner reported that across the country, Trump loyalists were duplicating the racial controversy they provoked within the Southern Baptist Convention, attacking pastors who were either relatively uninvolved with politics or moderate in their approach to the aftermath of the 2020 presidential election.[56] If the pastors under fire did not renounce their moderate views, they faced the departure of dozens, and even hundreds, of congregants to other churches. Wehner's report was based on interviews, some with members of the evangelical community who wished to remain anonymous, and his reporting was largely anecdotal. Yet he is so prominent and well-respected as an evangelical leader that he is unlikely to either report falsely or be wrong about what is happening within a significant, albeit uncounted, number of churches across the country.

Wehner's leading example was the case of David Platt, a forty-three-year-old minister at the McLean Bible Church, a Baptist megachurch in an affluent Virginia suburb of Washington, D.C., that includes members of Congress as congregants. Platt authored the best-selling Christian book *Taking Back Your Faith from the American Dream* and was considered to have a bright future in the church in part because his personal style appeals to younger evangelicals. Trouble arrived when three elders of the church lost a routine election for internal leadership positions that should have been routine and should have had a positive result.

On July 4, 2021, Pastor Platt sermonized about disinformation that motivated the vote. A small, ultraconservative group within the congregation circulated the baseless rumor that if the three men ascended to power, they would sell the church to Muslims intent on converting it into mosque. The negative vote on the elders was reversed, but Platt's problems continued. The dissident group sued the church, claiming the election violated its constitution. Members alleged that Platt was left of center, was pushing a social justice agenda, and had promoted critical race theory. The messages said that the McLean Bible Church should be renamed the Melanin Bible Church. Melanin is a dark brown to black pigment (amino acid) that gives human skin and eyes a darker color.

According to Wehner's sources, the Platt incident was not an isolated example. A prominent evangelical pastor, speaking anonymously, told Wehner that "nearly everyone tells me there is at the very least a small group in nearly every evangelical church complaining and agitating against teaching or policies that aren't sufficiently conservative or anti-woke."[57] Historian George Marsden agreed with Wehner's source: "Tribal instincts have become overwhelming. . . . [Christian followers of Trump] have come to see a gospel of hatred, resentments, vilifications, put-downs, and insults as expressions of their Christianity, for which they too should be willing to fight."[58]

How prevalent are these problems? A survey conducted by the Barna Group, a polling outfit that specializes in tracking opinions on religious issues, found that as many as 42 percent of evangelical pastors are considering quitting their jobs, citing stress (34 percent), political divisions (32 percent), feelings of loneliness and isolation (18 percent), and the perception that their churches are in steady decline (10 percent). Whether these divisions within the church will become debilitating is unclear.

A small but prominent group of white evangelical dissidents has emerged in strong opposition to their community's direction. Three issues preoccupy them: unwavering support of Trump within the community, divisive racial and gender discord that is the byproduct of that support, and the alienation of young evangelicals. The dissidents with the highest public profile are Wehner and the now deceased Michael Gerson. Two others—Russell Moore and Robert Jones—are well-known within the evangelical community. Jones is the CEO at PRRI and the author of *White Too Long: The Legacy of White Supremacy in American Christianity*.[59] Moore is a theologian at *Christianity Today* and the former president of the Ethics and Religious Liberty Commission of the Convention.

Gerson wrote several anguished and eloquent pieces about evangelical support for Trump, but this is perhaps the best example:

> It is remarkable to hear religious leaders defend profanity, ridicule, and cruelty as hallmarks of authenticity and dismiss decency as a dead language. Whatever Trump's policy legacy ends up being, his presidency has been a disaster in the realm of norms. It has coarsened our culture, given permission for bullying, complicated the moral formation of children, undermined standards of public integrity, and encouraged cynicism about the political enterprise. . . .
>
> It is the strangest story: how so many evangelicals lost their interest in decency, and how a religious tradition called by grace became defined by resentment. This is bad for America, because religion, properly viewed and applied, is essential to the country's public life. The old "one-bloodism" of Christian anthropology—the belief in the intrinsic and equal value of all human lives—has driven centuries of compassionate service and social reform. Religion can be the carrier of conscience. It can motivate sacrifice for the common good. It can reinforce the nobility of the political enterprise. It can combat dehumanization and elevate the goals and ideals of public life.[60]

Jones warned that older white evangelicals' preoccupation with Trump could have drastic consequences for the future of the movement:

> White evangelicals' bargain with Trump is better understood as a desperate deal born of anxiety in the face of a changing nation than as a ful-

> fillment of their aspirations. . . . By tying themselves to the Trump brand, white evangelicals risk their movement's ability to grow. During the sea change in cultural attitudes over the last decade, white evangelical Protestants were also losing demographic ground. . . . Most of the declines in the overall evangelical population have come from young people, resulting in stark differences in generational representation. White evangelicals comprise 26 percent of seniors ages 65 and older, for example, but make up only 7 percent of Americans under the age of 30.[61]

In the wake of the Capitol insurrection, which represented a sharp turn away from the Christian values that are the foundation of evangelicalism, Moore wrote:

> You cannot stand for "law and order" while waving away lawlessness. You cannot champion the pro-life cause while waving away murder. You cannot support police by the murder of police officers. You cannot support religious liberty by trashing the United States.
>
> Beyond that, good policy cannot absolve bad character. Character matters. Integrity matters. That is not just about "manners" or "self-righteousness" or "elitism" or "aesthetics," but the ethics of Christ.[62]

INSURRECTION

In February 2022, the Baptist Joint Committee for Religious Liberty and the Freedom from Religion Foundation released *Christian Nationalism and the January 6, 2021 Insurrection*, a thorough, well-supported, and perceptive report explaining the leading role played by Christian nationalists before and during the Capitol insurrection.[63] Written by experts on the movement, it features color photographs of Christian nationalists demonstrating in Washington, D.C., during the weeks before January 6 and on the day itself. The most iconic shows a wooden cross towering above several men on the east side of the Capitol. One is pressing his forehead to the wood with his eyes closed.

The two groups that assembled the report were founded to consider the role of religion in the larger society. The Baptist Joint Committee for Religious Liberty (BJC) defines its mission as ensuring religious freedom for all, bringing what it describes as "our uniquely Baptist perspective of 'soul freedom' to 'defending the separation of church and state.'"[64] *Soul freedom* is a phrase connoting the Baptist belief that separation of church and state is the only arrangement that will allow voluntary faith to flourish. The organization lists its priorities as fighting the targeting of religious minorities, the rise of Christian nationalism, and the politicization of houses of worship. The Freedom from Religion Foundation "works as an umbrella for those who are free from religion and are committed to the cherished principle of separation of church and state."[65]

Both groups are preoccupied with Christian nationalism because they are dedicated to the polar opposites of these views and are opposed to the denial of religious freedom by forcing the conversion of the secular nation into a Christian one. As Amanda Tyler, executive director of the Baptist Joint Committee wrote in her introduction to the report:

> Christian nationalism demands a privileged place for Christianity in public life, buttressed by the active support of government at all levels. Christian nationalism is not Christianity, though it is not accurate to say that Christian nationalism has nothing to do with Christianity. . . . In other words, to oppose and work against Christian nationalism is not to oppose Christianity; in fact, many Christians see opposing Christian nationalism as key to preserving the faith.[66]

The report includes the results of opinion surveys showing that 73 percent of respondents most strongly attached to Christian nationalist beliefs said they believe in the conspiracy theories that compose QAnon.[67] Sociologists Andrew Whitehead and Samuel Perry explain that people who thought the Constitution was "divinely inspired" and that the federal government should declare America a "Christian nation" are far more likely to believe that "outside agitators like Antifa and Black Lives Matter were mixed into the crowd and started the violence."[68] Christian nationalists are more likely to resist state-imposed restrictions to curb the COVID-19 pandemic, to oppose vaccines, to fear immigrants, to endorse the practice of men leading and women following, and to deny the existence of voter suppression.[69]

Press accounts of what happened on January 6 typically omit any reference to demonstrations that happened during the weeks before, some of which ended in violence because they were attended by the far-right Proud Boys, a militia group known for street fighting. The omission makes the sudden eruption of thousands of angry rioters seem more anomalous than it would if the weeks of preparation were documented. Sections 5 and 6 of the report, written by attorney Andrew Seidel, fill that gap by explaining in detail the events he characterizes as practice runs for the insurrection. The first was the so-called Million MAGA March, held on November 14, 2020, and located at Freedom Plaza in Washington, D.C., a popular site for rallies and demonstrations. Christian nationalists, far-right cognoscenti, and members of the Proud Boys attended. Ed Martin, president of the Eagle Forum Education and Legal Defense Fund, delivered a prayer to the group as the Proud Boys among them took a knee:

> Lord, you said to us—"and you serve me in righteousness, I will give you prosperity and joy, and I will give you for the world, a light, a beacon on a hill." . . . We ask you Lord, strengthen us in the fight because the powers of darkness are descending. They're saying, "concession, not Constitution." . . . Finally, Lord, we ask you to expose the fraud.[70]

The event ended in violence as Proud Boys fought with counterdemonstrators after nightfall.

In the weeks leading up to January 6, pro-Trump Christian nationalists known as Jericho March organized demonstrations where groups of followers walked around notable buildings like state capitols to protest the 2020 election results, sometimes accompanied by the blowing of a shofar (a musical instrument usually made of a ram's horn). The marches were based on the Bible's description of a battle sparked by God's order to the Israelites that they should march around the walls of the Palestinian city of Jericho, located in the Jordan River Valley, carrying the Ark of the Covenant, a container used to store the law received by Moses on Mount Sinai. On the seventh day of marching, the Israelites blew their shofars and shouted, and the walls miraculously fell down. On December 12, 2020, members of the Jericho March organized a prayer rally on the National Mall. A three-minute trailer for the event, nicknamed "Let the Church Roar!" contained the following message:

> [The nation] is at a crossroads. One path leads to a return to our founding Judeo-Christian principles: love of God, life, liberty, justice, law, and order. The other path leads to socialism, globalism, destruction. . . . America is a gift entrusted to us by our Creator. . . . Now it is our moment to save our republic and protect our freedoms from the corrupt and destructive forces at work.[71]

After the December 12 rally, the Proud Boys again roamed the streets of Washington, D.C., starting fights and vandalizing African American churches.

The final dry run occurred on January 5, when Christian nationalists gathered near the Supreme Court to attend the One Nation Under God Prayer Rally. The most notable speaker was Roger Stone, Trump's former adviser, who was convicted on seven felony counts charging the crimes of perjury and interfering with a congressional investigation of Trump's 2016 election campaign. Trump pardoned Stone just before he started serving a forty-month prison sentence. Stone was escorted to the event by a squad of Oath Keeper militia members dressed in tactical gear. White evangelical Pastor Ken Peters, who runs the brick-and-mortar Patriot Church in Tennessee as well as a virtual "church" that organizes ad hoc demonstrations at Planned Parenthood facilities also spoke:

> If we don't hold up the shield of faith, Satan will take over this land. But I see a bunch of people here that will say, "No, no." We are not going to

> allow the enemy to destroy this beautiful and great land that our forefathers gave to us. We will rise up in this time and say like Paul Revere, "The leftists are coming!"[72]

Few figures were more visible during the insurrection than Jacob Chansley, the so-called QAnon Shaman, who was repeatedly photographed sitting in the presiding officer's chair on the floor of the Senate. Michael Luo broke the story of the most disturbing part of this astonishing scene for the *New Yorker*:

> As rioters milled about on the Senate floor, a long-haired man in a red ski cap bellowed, from the dais, "Jesus Christ, we invoke your name!" A man to his right—the so-called QAnon Shaman, wearing a fur hat and bull horns atop his head, and holding an American flag—raised a megaphone and began to pray. Others in the chamber bowed their heads. "Thank you, heavenly Father, for being the inspiration needed to these police officers to allow us into the building, to allow us to exercise our rights, to allow us to send a message to all the tyrants, the Communists, and the globalists, that this is our nation, not theirs, that we will not allow the America, the American way of the United States of America, to go down," he said. "Thank you, divine, omniscient, omnipotent, and omnipresent creator God for filling this chamber with your white light and love, your white light of harmony. Thank you for filling this chamber with patriots that love you and love Christ."[73]

The Justice Department charged Chansley with several felonies, including obstruction of an official proceeding (the certification of the election results by Congress). He pled guilty and was sentenced to forty-one months in prison. He was released early after he said in court: "Men of honor admit when they're wrong. Not just publicly but to themselves. I was wrong for entering the Capitol. I have no excuse. No excuse whatsoever. The behavior is indefensible."[74] As this book goes to press, Chansley has announced that he plans to run as a libertarian in the 2024 election for Arizona's eighth district seat in Congress.

Ample evidence indicates that the white evangelical movement is under great stress, celebrating the achievement of long-sought goals while simultaneously watching its premier national organization and individual churches convulsed by racial tension, a sexual abuse scandal, and furious debates over loyalty to Trump. Its membership overlaps with a Christian nationalist movement that is intolerant of all other religions and violent. But given white evangelicals' steadfast, decades-long commitment to the Republican Party in general and Donald Trump in particular, any hope that these tensions will change either their ideology or their determination to preserve its political influence is premature. The agenda of white evangelicals, as much as that of any other of the six groups profiled here, is gravely hostile to the government initiatives that a majority of Americans favor. That majority is diverse and unorganized. White evangelicals are not.

SEVEN

MILITIA

PAUL REVERE'S RIDE

Every American child learns about the midnight ride of Paul Revere, proud member of the Massachusetts militia, who alerted his compatriots that the British army was marching their way. Romanticizing the role of militia men in the American revolution is embedded in the nation's sense of itself. Members of today's "patriot militia" have done their best to co-opt that glory. They believe they walk in the steps of those 1776 forefathers, resisting enemies who are intent on destroying the constitutional rights won in the war for independence. Yet their ideology is libertarian and their beliefs are weighted down by elaborate conspiracy theories. They are as hostile toward American government as Paul Revere was hopeful about the new country.

Modern militia members and their allies perceive that they have many enemies, including the FBI; elected officials at all levels of government; the federal civil service, labeled by former President Trump as the "deep state"; African Americans and other people of color; Jews and other non-Christians; and Democrats. For reasons that are unclear, they refer to President Biden as ChiCom, short for Chinese Communist. Many believe they are fighting the New World Order, a conspiracy led by Jewish bankers and the United Nations to establish a totalitarian world government. From there, it is a short step to conclude, intellectually and emotionally, that arming yourself and joining like-minded comrades is as necessary as it was in 1776.

Three groups dominate this space: private militia groups, constitutional (or sovereign) sheriffs, and sovereign citizens. Militia men and a small number of women take advantage of lenient state laws to arm themselves with sophisticated weapons and organize at the national and, increasingly, the state and local levels. Members spend their spare time running firearms training, conducting military drills, attending gun shows, recruiting members, fundraising for their activities, and socializing. The most prominent militias with national reputations are the Oath Keepers, the Three Percenters, the Proud Boys, and the Boogaloo Bois. Before Donald Trump lost the 2020 election, instigated the Stop the Steal campaign, and provoked the January 6 insurrection, militia groups thought that protecting like-minded, unarmed fellow citizens was their most important role. Now they talk in grandiose terms about an imminent civil war.

In the aftermath of the January 6 insurrection, Justice Department prosecutors convened grand juries and obtained indictments of the leaders of the Oath Keepers and the Proud Boys. The charges were heavy and included seditious conspiracy. The first trials, in the spring of 2023, resulted in convictions and long prison terms.

Experts in right-wing extremism note a dramatic spike in militia activity after the election of Barack Obama. The most disturbing manifestation began in April 2014, when Bureau of Land Management agents began rounding up a small herd of cattle owned by Cliven Bundy, a rancher who refused to pay federal grazing fees. The agents arrested Cliven's son Dave for trying to obstruct them. Dozens of supporters and heavily armed militia men were mustered through social media to defend father Bundy. An armed standoff developed, with militia men photographed on a highway overpass aiming automatic weapons at police gathered in the road below. Men in Western dress rode horses around, waving American flags. The government ended the standoff by releasing the cattle.

Mark Potok, a senior domestic terrorism expert for the Southern Poverty Law Center, one of the groups tracking militia activities, emphasizes that the impact of what started as a small dispute was magnified by the spectacle of federal agents abandoning the scene:

> The bottom line about the Bundy standoff is that a large number of people in the militia movement pointed scoped, semi-automatic weapons at the heads of law enforcement officials and ultimately forced them to back down. It made people feel that you could win against the federal government and you needed to do it with a gun.[1]

Militia members made a second appearance two years later, when Cliven Bundy's son Ammon led a band of unarmed people in an occupation of Oregon's Malheur Wildlife Refuge headquarters to protest the imprisonment of two ranchers convicted of arson on federal land. Bundy and other sovereign citizens believe federal ownership of land is unconstitutional. The standoff lasted for fifty-one days, attracting hundreds of supporters. It ended when Bundy and his lieutenants left the refuge to attend a meeting in a nearby town. Federal and state law enforcement officers set up a roadblock and arrested all of them, except Bundy lieutenant LaVoy Finicum, who was fatally shot as he exited from his car reaching for a gun. Bundy and a few prominent lieutenants were indicted and tried, but they were acquitted by a jury.

In 2015, following the fatal police shooting of Michael Brown, a Black man, heavily armed white militia members showed up in Ferguson, Missouri. They claimed they were in the city to help the police guard small businesses against possible looting by demonstrators protesting Brown's death. The people in the streets were largely Black, and the police were out in force. Yet they did not interfere with the white militia men who took positions on the roofs of building, long guns pointing toward the street. When protesters confronted the militia men asking why they were allowed to openly carry weapons, one replied "I'm happy that we're able to defend ourselves. It's been our right for a long time."[2] Of course, had the protesters exerted their rights to open carry and marched with guns, the result might well have been considerably more violent.

Militia members mustered for the Unite the Right rally in Charlottesville, Virginia, in 2017, again walking the streets in camouflage and toting automatic weapons without interference from the police. They demonstrated at state capitols in Michigan and Idaho to protest pandemic restrictions, carrying their weapons into legislative sessions, in what some described as "dress rehearsals" for the January 6, 2021, insurrection.[3]

Watching heavily armed, untrained, and unauthorized white people haul automatic weapons through crowded public spaces is deeply troubling. But an even more disturbing development is the infiltration of far-right convictions within the ranks of state-supported law enforcement. So-called constitutional, sovereign, or sagebrush sheriffs believe that they are the highest government authority legitimized by the Constitution. Many belong to a group known as the Constitutional Sheriffs & Peace Officers Association, founded and led by former Arizona Sheriff Richard Mack, who is also a vocal supporter of the militia movement. The association claims to have four hundred members. Membership criteria, if any exist, are not public. The website proclaims that

> America needs to make a strong turn around to get back on the freedom track laid for us by our Founders. We believe it can't be done from the top down, due to many factors [including] corruption and entrenched bureaucracies in high places. We must, and we can, accomplish this turnaround starting locally at the county level, and lower. The office of county sheriff is the last hope of making this happen.[4]

Meanwhile, police departments in Montana, South Carolina, Texas, and Virginia have hired the sheriffs' group to provide proficiency training for their police officers.[5]

A splinter group of constitutional sheriffs has emerged named Protect America Now. Its website urges visitors to contribute $17.76 a month to support its member sheriffs' efforts to stand against those who "reject law and order"; "infringe on our 2nd Amendment rights"; "support massive illegal immigration"; and "want more government and want to raise taxes to the point where we become a socialist country."[6]

On the rationale that their authority supersedes those of any other government official, sovereign sheriffs have refused to enforce gun control regulations, federal land-use restrictions, and IRS demands for payment of back taxes. In the aftermath of the Sandy Hook elementary school shooting, Sheriff Mack spearheaded an aggressive letter-writing campaign joined by dozens of other sheriffs that threatened not to enforce "unconstitutional" new restrictions on gun ownership.[7] During the pandemic, sovereign sheriffs actively resisted efforts by local public health officials to implement restrictions, from mask mandates to stay-at-home orders.

Most militia members are drawn to Donald Trump, and he has embraced their support before, while, and after he was president. In the course of a debate with Joe Biden in September 2020, Trump told the Proud Boys to "stand back and stand by," presumably in the event their intervention would be necessary to fight in the streets in the event of a stolen election.[8] Most far-right militia members believe that the 2020 national election was stolen.

The protection of unarmed groups that promote their values is a priority for militia members and sovereign sheriffs. These protected groups include the Bundys and their allies in the West, anti-vaxxers, and supporters of Donald Trump. Many of the unarmed people that militia members protect are furious at government. They harbor conspiracy theories about what it might do. Libertarian is the label that comes closest to the common core of their beliefs. Experts on right-wing extremism classify those committed enough to exercise this belief as "sovereign citizens."[9]

Ammon Bundy, the leader of the Malheur occupation, is a sovereign citizen who does not carry weapons, but can summon militia protection to any place where he is engaged in a dispute. Bundy has moved on from rancher rights to found and lead People's Rights, a group of activists that is organized and deployed online. Its website articulates its agenda as protecting three "rights" that all "humans" possess:

> The right to life. "No other living thing (human, creature, plant or otherwise) has a higher claim upon your life than you do. It is yours, and yours alone, and it cannot be threatened or taken without serious legal and eternal consequences."
>
> The right to liberty. "Sometimes others, regardless of their supposed best intentions . . . try to make decisions for us—either by deciding what is 'right' for us, or by removing all possible 'wrong' choices from our selection. Any kind of act that prevents YOU from deciding what's best for YOU violates your right to be free."
>
> The right to exclusive ownership and control of property. "Just like every other human on Earth, you have the right to exclusively own and control *your* property. Property includes things like your home, your vehicles, your animals, your money, your time and talent. It especially includes your own *body*, and what you choose to put (or NOT to put) in it."[10]

The obvious contradiction here is whether women have the "freedom" to control their own bodies when they are pregnant or instead should be compelled by the state to carry pregnancies to term. Bundy is a Mormon and abortion overrides liberty for him. In 2022, he ran for governor in Idaho. His website for that failed endeavor characterizes abortion as "cruel and barbaric" but concedes that the "society and the culture" should "reflect an attitude of grace towards women" because both the mother and the baby are "victims" when an abortion takes place.[11]

Sovereign citizens are avid conspiracy theorists. Social scientist Sam Jackson writes that "political extremists of all types are motivated in part by the perception of a crisis that demands action, and they use this to whip up fear and recruit more members."[12] Jackson adds that the default assumption behind all these theories is that the people who run the federal government are constantly plotting to restrict liberty.

One prominent conspiracy theory is that the Federal Emergency Management Agency (FEMA) is building camps across the country where large numbers of Americans will be imprisoned. Another is that when the federal government responded to Hurricane Katrina, it was training for the future imposition of martial law. Closely related to this paranoia is the fear that the federal government is preparing to seize privately owned firearms. The enactment of the Brady Handgun Violence Prevention Act in 1993 exacerbated the spread and tenacity of these beliefs.[13] Patriot militia conspiracy theorists have also raised the possibility that the government has engineered publicity about "false flag" incidents that did not actually take place to justify further violations of individual rights. The Sandy Hook elementary school shooting in 2012 and the bombing of the Boston Marathon in 2013 are common examples.

A 2015 military training exercise nicknamed Jade Helm 15 caused near hysteria among far-right groups. The exercise was launched by the United States Special Operations Command, which is responsible for the most highly trained elite forces in the military, including SEAL Team 6 and Delta Force. Jade Helm 15 was planned to include sites in several states. Right-wing bloggers and conservative commentators alleged that the exercise was part of "a secret plan to impose martial law, take away peoples' guns, arrest political undesirables, launch an Obama-led hostile takeover of red-state Texas, or do some combination thereof."[14] Texas governor Greg Abbott went so far as to direct the Texas National Guard to keep a defensive watch over the federal military operation.

A final set of conspiracy theories involves the United Nations. The conspiracists believe that the UN is "an instrument of a malevolent cabal" that will be used to "erode American national sovereignty and crush Americans' individual liberties."[15] A related theory is that the UN will be used as a springboard for foreign troops to attack and take over the country.

Two tragic confrontations between small groups of armed extremists and federal law enforcement at Ruby Ridge, Idaho, and Waco, Texas, are often cited by patriot militia groups as a central inspiration. Both tragedies occurred in the early 1990s. Together, they motivated the most destructive domestic terrorist attack in the nation's history: the retaliatory bombing of a federal government office building in Oklahoma City two years to the day after the Waco siege ended in a crescendo of violence. The bombing killed 168 people, including 19 children at a daycare center in the building, and it remains the deadliest act of domestic terrorism in American history.

Militia and the far-right citizens groups have not forgotten Ruby Ridge, Waco, or Oklahoma City. Nor has Donald Trump. Thirty years after the Branch Davidian siege, Trump held the first big rally of his 2024 presidential campaign at the Waco regional airport. He pledged that "I am your warrior; I am your justice. . . . For those who have been wronged and betrayed . . . I am your retribution."[16]

BRINGING THE WAR HOME

In her excellent book *Bring the War Home: The White Power Movement and Paramilitary America*, historian Kathleen Belew traces the origin of today's militia movement back to the American military's withdrawal from Vietnam.[17] Tens of thousands of disaffected troops familiar with heavy-duty firearms returned to a country where they were regarded not as conquering heroes but as mentally unstable, possibly drug addicted, and often unemployable men who fought a bad war and lost. Their experience was a devastating contrast to the return of American troops from Europe a generation earlier. Belew writes, "As narrated by white power proponents, the Vietnam War was a story of constant danger, gore, and horror. It was also a story of soldiers' betrayal by military and political leaders and of the trivialization of their sacrifice."[18] For some, turning the rage outward was preferable to internalizing such acute distress.

Further endeavors in the Middle East, including the 1990 Gulf War, the Iraq war in 2003–2011, and the invasion and occupation of Afghanistan in 2001–2021, pushed out the trajectory of these unfortunate trends. Because discharged soldiers were at loose ends, resented government, and had ready access to weapons and because federal, state, and local law enforcement were armed far beyond their needs and competence, violent standoffs were inevitable.

Adding to the difficulty of absorbing these angry young men back into society was the military's grave error of redistributing leftover armament to police forces across the country.[19] The highest, best, and only appropriate use of such equipment is in an armed conflict against a foreign enemy. Instead, police fielded Special Weapons and Tactics (SWAT) teams clothed in black or camouflage using military grade weapons, tanks, and armored vehicles against Americans. Many years went by before police at all three levels of government were pressured into reducing such intimidation and, if you consider the worst that has happened at Black Lives Matter protests, they never did.

RUBY RIDGE

In 1992, federal marshals laid siege to the home of Randy and Vicki Weaver, who were living off the grid in a rustic cabin sited at the end of a dirt road in the Idaho forest.[20] The marshals were attempting to rearrest Randy Weaver because he had not appeared for a court date on a minor gun charge. The outcome was a federally engineered fiasco that cost three lives and instilled horrible memories in anyone paying attention to the events, then and for years after.

The Weavers had four young children, who ranged in age from sixteen to ten months old. The cabin did not have running water or electricity, and the Weavers were living a subsistence existence. Randy Weaver had enlisted in the military, serving in a support role to a Green Beret unit, but was not deployed outside the country. Vicki Weaver was a devout millennial Christian who was convinced that the End of Days would arrive, bringing with it a period of paradise on earth until the Last Judgment. Like evangelicalism, these beliefs are based on interpretations of the New Testament's Book of Revelations. She considered the family's retreat to the remote cabin the best way to live through the Bible's prophecies. Her husband shared these beliefs and was also a rabid white supremacist who often visited a nearby compound operated by the Aryan Nation. He maintained a small arsenal of weapons at his home, and members of the family, including the two oldest children—Sammy, 14, and Sara, 16—knew how to use them and were frequently armed as they walked around in the woods, often hunting game to supplement the family's subsistence diet.

The charges against Randy Weaver arose because a Bureau of Alcohol, Tobacco, and Firearms (BATF) informant named Ken Fadeley ran into him at an Aryan Nation retreat. Fadeley persuaded Weaver to sell him two sawed-off shotguns. When Weaver produced the illegal weapons, BATF agents arrested him and attempted to use the gun charges to force him into infiltrating a local militia group. Weaver refused and missed a court date to review his case. The presiding judge issued a bench warrant for his arrest. The charges were minor in comparison to the inexplicably lavish resources the BATF invested in rearresting him.

One unfortunate day, six BATF agents dressed in camouflage were prowling the woods near the Weaver cabin, surveilling the family's daily routine. They ran across the family's dog, Striker, and he began to bark. The Weavers' friend, Kevin Harris, who was visiting, and Sammy Weaver followed Striker, thinking he might have discovered some deer they could shoot. Striker was about to flush the agents out of their hiding place when one of them shot the dog. Sammy saw the shooting and started firing his own gun at the agents. They fired back and when Sammy turned to run away, they shot him fatally in the back. By now Randy Weaver and Harris were both alerted and started firing at the intruders. Deputy U.S. Marshal Francis Degan was killed in the melee. From the federal agents' point of view, the death of one of their own escalated the situation and made the Weavers even higher-value targets. The FBI deployed its hostage rescue team to the site.

The FBI team had two components: assaulters and sniper/observers. As journalist Jess Walter describes their tactics in his best-selling book on Ruby Ridge:

> The snipers would crawl into place on the perimeter of a crisis site, keeping their eyes and guns on the situation, and then the assault team would move into place on the ground, bust down all the doors that needed to be busted down, wrestle the bad guys to the ground and—in the sanitized vernacular of federal law enforcement—"stabilize the situation."[21]

The snipers were operating under rules of engagement that were heavily criticized in the bitter aftermath of the siege. As a team leader explained to his men, the rules were that "if Randall Weaver, Vicki Weaver, Kevin Harris are observed with a weapon and fail to respond to a command to surrender, deadly force can be used to neutralize them."[22] From the law enforcement perspective, the siege had morphed into a confrontation with armed criminal targets. They had lost the reality of an anguished family with a dead child, plagued by paranoia, and holed up in an isolated cabin in the forest. Or, as Walter describes it, "the brutality of bureaucracy" had taken over.[23]

On the second day of the siege, Randy Weaver, Kevin Harris, and Sara Weaver were all armed as they explored what they considered the perimeter of the cabin's grounds. On their way back to the cabin, Randy Weaver stopped at an outbuilding where Sammy Weaver's body lay. FBI sniper Lou Horiuchi fired, wounding Randy Weaver in the arm. Everyone ran to the house, and Vicki Weaver, carrying her ten-month-old baby Elisheba, opened the door for them. As Harris entered the house, Horiuchi fired again, missing Harris but hitting Vicki Weaver in the head, killing her instantly. Her dead body lay in the living room for days as the siege dragged on.

Unaware that Horiuchi had killed Vicki Weaver, FBI agents appealed to her repeatedly over bullhorns, convinced that she was the most rational and decisive of the three adults. Their amplified messages urging her to come out of the cabin to talk compounded the misery inside the cabin. At one point, the agents even invited her to join them for a pancake breakfast.

Randy Weaver and Kevin Harris were both wounded, Harris especially badly, and without medical supplies, their conditions grew worse. The remaining children were terrified. In adulthood, Sara Weaver told interviewers for a PBS documentary that everyone in the cabin was convinced they would never get out of the situation alive.

Ruby Ridge became a national news story. Over the eleven days of the siege, four hundred law enforcement personnel were deployed to the bottom of the road that led to the cabin. They were heavily armed, driving large trucks and Humvees, and staying in huge tents. FBI negotiators were unable to motivate Randy Weaver to speak with them, and in desperation, they decided to take up the offer of Bo Gritz, a decorated Special Forces officer during the Vietnam War and hero to the far-right white supremacist movement. Ten days after the siege began, Gritz talked Randy Weaver into allowing federal agents to carry Harris out of the cabin so that he could receive medical treatment. Weaver and his children surrendered the next day.

The federal government tried Weaver and Harris for murder in the death of Deputy Marshal Decan before a jury in Boise, Idaho. The government's witnesses were so incoherent and inconsistent and the circumstances of Vicki Weaver's death so poignant that the two men were acquitted of murder. Weaver was sentenced to eighteen months in prison for failing to appear in court regarding his 1991 weapons charge. The Weavers sued the government for damages, ultimately settling for $3.1 million in 1995. The surviving Weaver children received $1 million each, and Randy Weaver received $100,000.

The Justice Department formed a task force to investigate its own mistakes and concluded that the FBI's conduct at Ruby Ridge was plagued by numerous problems both during the siege and when the case was prepared for court.[24] Specifically, it criticized inadequate investigation of the circumstances when the FBI first arrived on the scene, the overly aggressive rules of engagement, and the U.S. Attorney's choice to seek the death penalty for Weaver and Harris.

In a 2017 appearance on an NPR program commemorating the twenty-fifth anniversary of Ruby Ridge, Jess Walter traced the confrontation to diametrically opposed versions of the facts advanced by Weaver supporters and the government. He said that people on the right believed Weaver was an innocent farmer when the government "tricked him into sawing the barrels off shotguns, and then gave him the wrong court date and threatened to throw him off his land, and then provoked a gunfight with him and shot his son and his dog, and then the next day murdered his wife."[25] The government saw Weaver as a "white separatist who went to Aryan Nation meetings and was hanging out with the worst of the worst, and because of that became the target of federal investigation."[26] Walter added that the Right continues to use Ruby Ridge as a rallying cry "because this is their very worst nightmare. This is the thing that they warn can happen to Americans."[27]

WACO

Despite all the internal recriminations and negative publicity, six months after Randy Weaver's surrender, the same institutional players repeated many of the same errors at the Branch Davidian compound in Waco, Texas, with even more horrendous consequences. The seventy-seven acre compound housed a religious sect that was an offshoot of the Seventh Day Adventists, a Christian denomination closely associated with millennial or End of Days theology. Like the Weavers, the Davidians believed the Second Coming of Christ was imminent. They spent much of their time studying the Bible, especially the Book of Revelation, to discover when this event would occur and what it would mean to those who would be saved.

The sect was led by David Koresh, a charismatic leader whose given name was Vernon Howell. The Book of Revelation includes several obscure passages regarding the "seven seals," or messages inscribed by God that prophesize about the End of Days. An interpreter known as the Lamb is identified as the person who could unlock the seven seals and reveal their secrets, triggering the End of Days. Koresh persuaded the Davidians that he was the Lamb and therefore qualified to lead them in hours of daily Bible study.

As his authority within the community grew, Koresh initiated the divisive practice of taking numerous "spiritual wives" from among all the women and girls of the congregation. Some were as young as twelve. Koresh fathered several children. During the siege, the Davidians made home videos of Koresh and several of his children to prove that the children were safe. Those tapes are still available online.[28] The practice roiled the small community, but Koresh was so charismatic and persuasive that even after federal police placed the Davidians under siege and they were offered an opportunity to surrender peacefully, very few left.

The Davidians provoked the attention of the BATF because they ran a small business selling guns. BATF agents obtained warrants to search the compound for illegal weapons and arrest Koresh. For reasons that again are unclear, eighty armed BATF agents descended on the compound on February 28, 1993. At the time, the Davidian community consisted of about 150 people, including men, women, and children. The Davidians, taken by surprise, resisted. In the gun battle that followed, four agents and six Davidians were killed. Again, the shootout prompted the arrival of the FBI hostage rescue team. Why the BATF agents did not take the far lower-key approach of arresting Koresh on the street during his frequent trips into town for supplies remains a disturbing question.

Over the course of the siege, about eight hundred law enforcement officers assembled around the compound and the military brought in heavy tactical weapons, including ten Bradley tanks, two Abrams tanks, and four combat-engineering vehicles. To break the Davidians down and supposedly motivate a peaceful surrender, the FBI cut off electricity and supplies, trained spotlights on the property, and set up giant speakers that blasted noise day and night, including the sounds of rabbits being slaughtered and loud music.

In an article for the *New Yorker* entitled "Sacred and Profane: How Not to Negotiate with Believers," journalist Malcom Gladwell identified the costly mistakes made by the FBI negotiators in assessing the Davidians and what it would have taken to end the siege peacefully. Negotiators expected the Davidians to be intimidated and to turn "paranoid and defensive."[29] They did not grasp that they were dealing with "a very different kind of group—the sort whose idea of a good evening's fun was a six-hour Bible study wrestling with a tricky passage of Revelation."[30] Because the negotiators did not grasp the depth of religious fanaticism that animated the Davidians, they had nothing but disdain for Koresh, calling his theology "Bible-babble" and dismissing him a "'self-centered liar,' 'coward,' 'phony messiah,' 'child molester,' 'con-man,' [and] 'cheap thug who interprets the Bible through the barrel of a gun.'"[31] Federal agents also speculated that child abuse was ongoing and a mass suicide was possible.

The FBI negotiators thought they could negotiate with the Davidians as they would with common criminals. Gladwell wrote:

> There was no pragmatism hidden below a layer of posturing, lies, and grandiosity. They were "value-rational"—that is to say, their rationality was organized around values, not goals. A value-rational person would accept his fourteen-year-old daughter's polygamous marriage, if he was convinced that it was in fulfillment of Biblical prophecy. Because the F.B.I. could not take the faith of the Branch Davidians seriously, it had no meaningful way to communicate with them.[32]

Rumors of child abuse and the potential for mass suicide were prominent in the briefings presented to Attorney General Janet Reno, who would make the call about ending the siege. She had just arrived in Washington, D.C., from Florida and did not understand the internal machinations of President Clinton's newly elected administration or the public acceptability of using a potentially violent assault to persuade the Davidians to surrender.[33] Worried especially by the reports of child abuse, Reno decided to break the gridlock by introducing supposedly nonlethal tear gas to force them out of the compound. But this tear gas was military grade and capable of igniting fires. Masks did not exist to protect small children from its potentially lethal effects. Whether Reno was informed of these dire possibilities is unclear.

The tear gas was delivered by tanks that broke through the walls of compound buildings. Fires started and shooting began. The bodies of seventy-five people—fifty adults and twenty-five children under age 15—were discovered in the wreckage, Koresh among them. The government estimated that seventeen had died from gunshot wounds, including several children. Twelve survivors were indicted. Eight were convicted on various weapons and involuntary manslaughter charges, and four were acquitted.

For right-wing people who were already deeply suspicious of the national government, Ruby Ridge and Waco were apocalyptic. In the immediate aftermath of Waco, the commitment to protect innocents from government violence spread and strengthened among militia groups. Michael Vanderboegh, founder of the Three Percenters militia, told the *New York Times*:

> My reaction to Waco was horror. It was the defining moment, I think, of the late 20th century in terms of the relationship between the citizen and government. Waco proved to us that citizen disarmament was coming. It scared the crap out of us and it mobilized us. Do we serve the government or does the government serve us? These kinds of fundamental questions hardly ever get settled without violence. Waco can happen at any given time but the outcome will be different this time, of that I can assure you.[34]

OKLAHOMA CITY

Two years to the day after the final Waco conflagration, Timothy McVeigh, a veteran of the Gulf War and recipient of the Bronze Star, one of the military's highest honors, and his friend, Terry Nichols, also a veteran, loaded a Ryder truck with motor oil and fertilizer and parked it in front of the Alfred P. Murrah Building in Oklahoma City. McVeigh ignited two fuses and a huge blast killed 168 people, including 19 children, and injured 680 more. McVeigh was tried, convicted, and received the death penalty in 2001. Nichols was tried, convicted, and sentenced to 161 consecutive life terms without the possibility of parole. He is still in prison.

The various stories in the press about McVeigh's life described him as a loner, obsessed with guns, and alienated from family and friends. Investigators discovered pictures of McVeigh watching the Waco siege unfold from a bluff above the compound. McVeigh was inspired by far-right movements, including militias, and hung out on the fringes of them. In one strange twist, McVeigh met with members of the Wolverine militia in Michigan before he carried out the bombing. Three decades later, Wolverine members were indicted for plotting to kidnap Michigan Governor Gretchen Whitmer in response to the stringent restrictions she imposed during the pandemic.[35] Two leaders of the plot, Adam Fox and Barry Croft, were found guilty and sentenced to sixteen and nineteen years respectively.[36]

McVeigh studied *The Turner Diaries*, a 1978 novel written by William Luther Pierce under the pseudonym Andrew MacDonald, described by the FBI as the bible of the extremist right. The book depicts the violent overthrow of the United States government, a nuclear war, and a race war that leads to the extermination of non-whites and Jews. In addition to its virulent racism and brutal fantasies, it includes crude plans for carrying out acts of terror against the government. Today, copies of the book are almost impossible to find. It is not available from book sellers, online, or in public libraries.

After Oklahoma City, militias across the country lowered their profile, and some are likely to have disappeared forever. Two decades later, as it did with other groups profiled in earlier pages, most notably the Tea Party, the election of the nation's first African American president revived militia groups.[37] The Southern Poverty Law Center, one of the handful of national public interest groups that specializes in tracking white nationalist terror groups, estimates that between 2000 and 2008, some 150 militia groups existed. By 2009, that number increased to 500. In 2012, the number had more than doubled to 1,300.

Militias and far-right groups have not forgotten Ruby Ridge, Waco, or Oklahoma City, as indicated by the thousands of people who traveled to the Waco regional airport to attend the Trump rally in March 2023. In the aftermath of January 6 and the Justice Department's exhaustive criminal investigation, many have turned away from the nation's capital toward state and local activism. The emphasis on interventions close to home, especially during the pandemic, is at least as threatening to government stability and the public interest as their passionate claims that they are ready to fight a civil war.

Jared Holt, a domestic extremism researcher with the Atlantic Council's Digital Forensic Research Lab, confirmed that the shift to state and local action is happening in an interview with *The Guardian*: "A lot of this push to decentralize these organizations and push them into local venues is explicitly spelled out by leadership figures . . . hoping to evade scrutiny from law enforcement and the public."[38] The *Guardian* story quoted a message posted on the website of Ammon Bundy's People's Rights network: "No more protesting at the Capitol. It's not going to work. You hit them in their district offices, local neighborhoods. . . . Think local government."[39]

"DR. BERRY SHOULD BE ATTACKED 'ON SIGHT'"[40]

A mere five months after the pandemic began, the *Journal of the American Medical Association* published an article by three nationally known public health experts who wrote that "harassment of health officials for proposing or taking steps to protect communities from COVID-19 is extraordinary in its scope and nature, use of social media, and danger to the ongoing pandemic response. It reflects misunderstanding of the pandemic, biases in human risk perception, and a general decline in public civility."[41]

The *New York Times* published an extensive follow-up story on the state of public health departments across the country in October 2021.[42] Reporters Mike Baker and Danielle Ivory interviewed more than 140 local health officials, public health experts, and lawmakers, examined state laws and local government documents, and analyzed three hundred responses to a survey they sent to county health departments across the country. They concluded that public health agencies have seen a "staggering exodus of personnel, many exhausted and demoralized, in part because of abuse and threats."[43] Dozens of departments reported that they had not hired, but instead lost employees during the pandemic. More than five hundred top health officials left their jobs. State legislatures approved some one hundred new laws that constrain public health agencies' ability to combat the next pandemic. On top of the inevitable pandemic miseries of long hours, stressful work, inadequate staffing, low pay, and a scourge of pandemic deaths, public health officials confronted threats to their own and their families' safety.

Despite this substantial evidence, the crisis was heavily underreported in media across the country, although individual episodes did get some attention. When Dr. Allison Berry, a popular family physician and local health officer in Port Angeles, Washington, announced a mask mandate in response to an alarming increase in COVID-19 Delta variant cases, she became a target for outraged constituents. They confronted her during a pandemic briefing and demonstrated in front of her house. A county sheriff escorted her to the parking lot when she left the office, and she watched to see if vehicles were trailing her as she drove home. "The places where it is most needed to put in more stringent measures, it's the least possible to do it," Berry said. "Either because you're afraid you're going to get fired, or you're afraid you're going to get killed. Or both."[44]

In Wilson County, Kansas, Dr. Jennifer Bacani McKenney attracted such vehement verbal attacks when she moved a bit more slowly than other health departments to lift lockdown orders that she told her children to do their homework away from windows. Dr. Nichole Quick, the chief health officer of Orange County, California, was confronted at one public meeting by an unidentified woman who read her home address out loud and threatened to organize a group of protesters to demonstrate on Quick's lawn. Dr. Quick resigned. Dr. Amy Acton, director of the Ohio Department of Health, quit after armed protesters wearing MAGA hats and carrying Trump flags showed up at her house.

Other, equally serious threats emerged. A movement of far-right county sheriffs claiming preposterously broad legal authority under the Constitution jumped into the public spotlight. Sheriff Mark Lamb of Pinal County, Arizona, appeared at an anti-vaccine protest in Phoenix patrolled by heavily armed men in camouflage. Lamb said, "We're going to find out what kind of patriots you are. We're going to find out who is willing to die for freedom."[45] Lamb supports the Stop the Steal movement and has spoken out in support of forming private militias that he insists are "well within the Constitution."[46] He has built an online network of like-minded colleagues.

Bob Songer, sheriff of Klickitat County, Washington, announced that he was going to arrest any public official who enforced "unconstitutional" mandates, including those issued by the state.[47] These threats may seem outlandish from a distance, but people living in the county took them quite seriously. County health department director Erinn Quinn wrote to the elected county commissioners asking if she could be arrested because she was following state pandemic mandates. The county's prosecuting attorney said he had installed additional security at his home and retained his own attorney in case the sheriff came after him. School district superintendent Brian Freeman sent the sheriff an email acknowledging that he was enforcing a state-mandated mask mandate for all students, staff, and visitors while they were on campuses. Freeman offered to turn himself into the sheriff to avoid an arrest in front of the students.

A couple of days later, Freeman and another district superintendent issued a statement demanding that the sheriff withdraw his statement and warning that it violated a state law prohibiting the intimidation of school officials and staff. At an open meeting where the sheriff's statement was discussed, David Sauter, the chair of the board of county commissioners, said:

> The more I read it, it actually upsets me more . . . because it is not limited to health care and the response to COVID. It is a general statement about any bureaucrat or government official, mayor, commissioner, whoever, that is perceived by a single individual, namely the sheriff, to be violating somebody's constitutional rights being subject to arrest. That is a chilling thing to say. That is the path to authoritarian regimes.[48]

Well on his way to becoming another far-right hero, Songer spoke at a We the People rally organized by the county's Republican Party. He said that the Black Lives Matter movement is a

> Marxist, Socialist, Communist organization. . . . There's a master plan to overthrow our government and change it from a constitutional government to a socialist government. . . . It'll be a cold day in Hell before I allow that to happen and I know you patriots will not allow that to happen. If they come to our county and start that crap, I'll guarantee you

> they're not going to like the results. They will be thrown in jail and I will use high-pressure firehoses from the fire department, and we'll use every means we've got to put them down and put them down hard.[49]

The emergence of heavily armed militia members protesting pandemic restrictions introduced the possibility of lethal violence on a larger scale. In what some have called a dress rehearsal for the January 6 insurrection, heavily armed men dressed in camouflage, most with face coverings, swarmed the Michigan state capital in Lansing to protest pandemic restrictions ordered by the state's Democratic governor Gretchen Whitmer.[50] They were photographed outside and inside the building, including within the Senate chamber while the legislators were in session. Senator Dayna Polehanki tweeted: "Directly above me, men with rifles yelling at us. Some of my colleagues who own bullet-proof vests are wearing them."[51] Within months, the Michigan State Capitol Commission banned the open carry of guns in and around the statehouse.

In Idaho, a crowd of two hundred, many armed, stormed the state legislature to protest mask mandates and other restrictions.[52] They threatened to overwhelm state troopers trying to keep them out of the balcony where members of the public may sit to watch proceedings. Attempting to avoid violence, Speaker of the House Scott Bedke said they could enter if they would behave. "Bad day to forget my gun," said one masked Republican representative.[53]

Ammon Bundy, the leader of the Malheur siege, organized the Idaho action. These days, Bundy runs a network of militants and militia members called People's Rights, organized through Facebook with an unknown number of members spread across the West. Bundy leads teams that rush to sites of confrontations between government officials and individuals perceived to be exercising their constitutional rights to take the challenged action. The teams include armed militia men who might intimidate the officials into backing down. Just a rumor of his imminent arrival elevates the tension. As Travis McAdam, leader of the Montana Human Rights Network, explained to the *High Country News*, "We all know what the

Bundy family playbook is, and we know how that ends. It ends in armed standoffs with the government."[54]

Bundy appears addicted to the attention he receives when he arrives on the scene of a dispute, especially when he is supported by armed militia. Simply by showing up, Bundy, Stewart Rhodes of the Oath Keepers, and their successors—for they will inevitably have apprentices, copycats, and rivals—wreak havoc in communities when they attack a broad public interest, such as remaining safe during a pandemic or protecting children from parental neglect.

In May 2022, Bundy pulled his strangest stunt yet when he led demonstrations to protest the hospitalization without parental consent of the grandson of his close friend, Diego Rodriguez.[55] The ten-month-old baby was suffering from severe malnutrition, could not sit up on his own, and was so underweight that doctors thought his condition life-threatening. He was hospitalized at St. Luke's Meridian Medical Center in Idaho.

Bundy's position was that the state had overreached and violated the parents' absolute right to care (or not care) for the child free from interference by the state. Bundy and supporters continued demonstrating not just at the hospital but at the homes of people involved in the child's case. The hospital, one of the largest in Idaho, was forced to divert ambulances to other hospitals and lock its doors to members of the public. The hospital sued Bundy and the baby's grandfather, Diego Rodriguez, for damages. A statement issued by Chris Roth, president and CEO of the St. Luke Health System, reads: "It is important for us to stand up to the bullying, intimidation and disruption and the self-serving and menacing actions of these individuals, for the protection of our employees and patients."[56] The jury ordered the two men to pay $26.5 million in compensatory damages and $26 million in punitive damages but is unlikely to collect because Bundy has boycotted court proceedings and does not seem to have the money.

All of this mayhem is enabled by the open carry of guns.[57] Twenty-five states do not require a permit to carry a gun in public, despite the eruption of mass shootings in recent years. Four states (California, Florida, Illinois, and New York) and the District of Columbia prohibit the open carry of handguns. Nine states require a permit or license for open carry. The remainder allow open carry of handguns with some restrictions on location (for example, not at schools). Three states (California, Florida, and Illinois) and the District of Columbia prohibit open carry of long guns. In forty-one states, open carry of long guns is legal, although in one state the gun must be unloaded and two states limit open carry in certain cities.

The targets of right-wing animus are getting the message. In an article for *Harper's Magazine* in November 2021, reporter Rachel Monroe described the experience of gun shop owner Michael Cargill right after COVID-19 was declared a pandemic. "Cargill realized that people were not only caching toilet paper in response; they were arming themselves," she wrote.[58] Cargill sold out his inventory and then scoured pawnshops to buy as many Glocks and Berettas as he could find. Cargill is Black. A study published in the *Journal of the American Medical Association* showed that an "estimated 2.9 percent of U.S. adults (7.5 million) became new gun owners from 1 January, 2019, to 26 April, 2021. Most (5.4 million) had lived in homes without guns."[59] Half of all new gun owners were female and 40 percent were Black (20 percent) or Hispanic (20 percent).

In the same epic term when the Supreme Court overruled precedent establishing a legal right to abortion and curtailed the EPA's authority to mitigate climate change, the conservative majority also limited states' authority to regulate concealed guns in public places.[60] The case involved two adult men who wanted to carry concealed guns for self-protection. New York denied their application for a license on the grounds that they had not proven they had a "proper cause" for the license. The court concluded that the state had violated their Fourteenth Amendment right to keep and bear arms in public for self-defense. The case is expected to produce extensive litigation in the states that have tried to impose limits on concealed or open carry of handguns or long guns.[61]

The pandemic caused 1.05 million deaths in America, or 16 percent of global deaths, in a country with just 4 percent of the world population. The nation was ranked first among nations in pandemic preparedness but could not deliver on that potential. Americans should have learned some profound lessons from the experience. Yet experts warn that another lethal pandemic is inevitable and the country is far from ready for it. *Atlantic* reporter Ed Yong, who won a Pulitzer Prize for his coverage of the pandemic after predicting with frightening accuracy that it would happen, writes:

> As the global population grows, as the climate changes, and as humans push into spaces occupied by wild animals, future pandemics become more likely. We are not guaranteed the luxury of facing just one a century, or even one at a time. . . .
>
> But domestically, many public-health experts, historians, and legal scholars worry that the U.S. is lapsing into neglect, that the temporary wave of investments isn't being channeled into the right areas, and that COVID-19 might actually leave the U.S. *weaker* against whatever emerges next.[62]

The serious challenges Yong and others have identified are well known among national policymakers, although the prospects for meaningful reform of the public health system are dim.

As far-right groups move away from national protests and decentralize their activities, armed militia, sovereign citizens, and constitutional sheriffs could make rudimentary public health protections impossible in wide swaths of the country. If they do, the next pandemic will be even worse.

THE OATH KEEPERS

Soon after January 6, the Justice Department launched the most ambitious, resource-intensive investigation in its—and probably any other law enforcement agency in the world's—history. Attorney General Merrick Garland was determined to deliver justice to the police who were killed and injured during the insurrection and to deter any similar future attack on the basic functions of American democracy. Low-hanging fruit in the massive accumulation of evidence were defendants affiliated with three prominent national militia groups—the Oath Keepers, the Proud Boys, and the Three Percenters, who spoke, chatted, and texted for weeks on what they thought were encrypted lines. Several members of the groups were indicted for serious felonies, including seditious conspiracy, and some chose to go to trial. The Oath Keepers went first and are the focus here because the group has the most coherent ideology and history.

Elmer Stewart Rhodes announced the founding of the Oath Keepers in 2009 on the Lexington Green in Massachusetts, where 234 years earlier, the first shots were fired in the American Revolution. (He has dropped the Elmer.) On that March day in Lexington Square, Rhodes was joined by two well-known far-right colleagues—Richard Mack, founder of the Constitutional Sheriffs and Peace Officers Association, and Mike Vanderboegh, founder of the Three Percenters. The Oath Keepers' most important characteristic is a determination to center recruitment efforts on active and retired members of the military, law enforcement officers, and first responders. They are convinced that when the wrong people run government, it becomes tyrannical and must be opposed, if necessary by violence.

> Oath Keeper bylaws describe the organization as a non-partisan association of currently serving military, reserves, National Guard, veterans, Peace Officers, and Fire Fighters who will fulfill the Oath we swore, with the support of like-minded citizens who take the Oath to stand with us, to support and defend the Constitution against all enemies, foreign and domestic, so help us God. Our Oath is to the Constitution.[63]

Members must take the following pledge:

> I do solemnly swear (or affirm) that I will support and defend the Constitution [of the U.S.] against all enemies, foreign and domestic, that I will bear true faith and allegiance to the same, and that I take this obligation freely, without any mental reservation or purpose of evasion, pledging my life, my fortune, and my sacred honor. So help me, God.[64]

The pledge is borrowed from the version administered to military recruits, but the Oath Keepers omit one crucial sentence, which reads: "I will obey the orders of the President of the United States and the orders of the officers appointed over me, according to regulations and the Uniform Code of Military Justice."[65] Or, in other words, the pledge omits any mention of a command hierarchy based on training, vetting by experience, and meritorious promotion.

Further defining Oath Keeper values is the expectation that members will "refuse" to follow ten "unconstitutional" orders.[66] The authority that would issue such orders is left unclear. Several reflect far-right conspiracy theories:

> We will NOT obey orders to disarm the American people.
>
> We will NOT obey orders to conduct warrantless searches of the American people.
>
> We will NOT obey orders to detain American citizens as "unlawful enemy combatants" or to subject them to military tribunal.
>
> We will NOT obey orders to impose martial law or a "state of emergency" on a state.
>
> We will NOT obey orders to invade and subjugate any state that asserts its sovereignty.
>
> We will NOT obey any order to blockade American cities, thus turning them into giant concentration camps.
>
> We will NOT obey any order to force American citizens into any form of detention camps under any pretext.
>
> We will NOT obey orders to assist or support the use of any foreign troops on U.S. soil against the American people to "keep the peace" or to "maintain control."
>
> We will NOT obey any orders to confiscate the property of the American people, including food and other essential supplies.
>
> We will NOT obey any orders which infringe on the right of the people to free speech, to peaceably assemble, and to petition their government for a redress of grievances.

As several of the above statements indicate, Oath Keepers are preoccupied with threats, real and imagined. Social scientist Samuel Jackson characterizes the central message of the group as warnings "that the federal government is preparing to attack its own citizens and it urges Americans to prepare for that conflict by gathering supplies and engaging in paramilitary training."[67]

The Oath Keepers recruit members online and through social media. People hear about the organization from right-wing media outlets and celebrities, including Alex Jones of Infowars and Fox News commentators. The organization claims that it has 30,000 members; the Anti-Defamation League estimates that it has 1,000-3,000; and the Center for Strategic and International Studies says that "most research settles on about 5,000 members."[68] Jackson estimates that the number of pre-January 6 active members was in the range of 5,000. That number would make it one of the largest militia groups in the country.

Oath Keepers founder and chief organizer Rhodes is indefatigable, articulate, and vivid. He is skilled in dealing with the media, promoting himself and the organization. Media stories about Rhodes and the Oath Keepers most often mention that he is a former paratrooper and a graduate of the Yale Law School without qualifying those attributes. Rhodes did enlist in the Army and was trained as a paratrooper, but an accident during a training jump resulted in an honorable discharge. Rhodes was unlucky again when he dropped a loaded handgun in 1993 and it fired, blinding him in his left eye. He wears an eye patch, which adds to his swashbuckling appearance. Rhodes did attend Yale Law School, a prestigious and elite institution that carries with it a patina of intellectual superiority and credibility but does not ensure good behavior by its graduates. In fact, Rhodes was earning a living as a lawyer in Montana, but abruptly decided to abandon his practice and his clients. When they complained about his neglect of their cases, he was disbarred. His former wife divorced him because he was violent and abusive to her and their three children. Most articles about Rhodes—and dozens, if not hundreds, have been written—mention his Yale degree but omit these confounding details, entirely missing how difficult Rhodes has made his own life and what that conclusion means about his stability.

In 2021, a crude database of supposed Oath Keeper members compiled by assistants to Rhodes was made public. Mike Giglio, a reporter for *The Atlantic*, analyzed the database, estimating that two-thirds of its entries had a background in military or law enforcement. He interviewed dozens of those listed:

> As I pored through the entries, I began to see them as a window into something much larger than the Oath Keepers. Membership in the group was often fleeting—some people had signed up on a whim and forgotten about it. The Oath Keepers did not have 25,000 soldiers at the ready. But the files showed that Rhodes had tapped into a deep current of anxiety, one that could cause a surprisingly large contingent of people with real police and military experience to consider armed political violence. He was like a fisherman who sinks a beacon into the sea at night, drawing his catch toward the light. . . .
>
> The dominant mood was foreboding. I found people far along in deliberations about the prospect of civil conflict, bracing for it and afflicted by the sense that they were being pushed toward it by forces outside their control. Many said they didn't want to fight but feared they'd have no choice.[69]

Giglio stresses the importance of gun rights as an organizing tool and principle for militias like the Oath Keepers. Each year, Virginia holds a "lobby day" when people concerned about pending legislative proposals can rally and meet elected officials. In 2020, with the legislature just transferred into Democratic hands, some 22,000 people descended on the state capitol in Richmond, many of them "carrying AR-15s and political signs: OPPOSE TYRANNY. GUNS SAVE LIVES. TRUMP 2020."[70] Oath Keepers, Three Percenters, and Proud Boys were prominent in the group.

The Oath Keepers have a national office with a small staff that included Rhodes, who received a salary for full-time work. State and local affiliates pay dues to support the national operation. Local groups are typically organized into two divisions—a "quick reaction force," composed of the "fittest and most mobile patriots," and a "Home Guard or Family Safe Unit, which aims to protect homes, families, and communities of the expeditionary force."[71]

The Oath Keepers existed in relative obscurity until 2014, when, mustered by social media, several heavily armed members traveled to Cliven Bundy's cattle dispute. The experience was heady, especially for Rhodes, who received a great deal of attention from national media during the standoff, likely because he was the most articulate person speaking on Bundy's behalf.

To their edification, the experience established the Oath Keepers as a dependable private police force available to protect far-right activists. Summoned by social media, they would appear, heavily armed, in fraught circumstances that threatened or ended in violence. They went to Ferguson, Missouri, and the Malheur Wildlife Refuge. Oath Keepers were present at polling places in 2016 and 2020, supposedly to discourage election fraud. They offered security to business owners who defied COVID-19 public health safety measures.[72]

The Oath Keepers' appearance in Ferguson was especially controversial because members of the group came to a city roiled by racial conflict, with the stated purpose of helping the police ensure that Black protesters did not loot small businesses. Rhodes denies that Oath Keepers are racist, telling an *Al Jazeera* reporter reporting on the group's presence in Ferguson that "I'm a quarter Mexican, so it's kind of hard for me to be a white supremacist. And we have Black members, and we're guarding a Black lady's bakery. . . . So why would we do that if we're some kind of racist organization?"[73]

When Oath Keepers showed up at Black Lives Matters protests following the fatal police shooting of George Floyd, Rhodes posted the following message on the organization's Facebook page:

> I see some of you conflicted about how to handle what's going on in the streets of this country, I too was conflicted but let me say this. Maybe you better read that Oath again it said protect the constitution from all enemies foreign and or here's the part you better read slowly. . . . Domestic.

> . . . Once these thugs turned to burning, killing and looting, they became domestic enemies.[74]

The statement is as hyperbolic as it is typical of Rhodes. Thousands of Black Lives Matter demonstrations happened that summer, and they were overwhelmingly peaceful.[75]

INSURRECTION

The Justice Department has charged more than one thousand defendants for their role in the January 6 insurrection, who have been arrested in nearly all fifty states and the District of Columbia.[76] As of November 2023, 683 rioters had entered guilty pleas, including 201 who pled to felonies and 482 who pled to misdemeanors. A total of 86 have pled guilty to felonies that involve assaulting the police and 41 more pled to feloniously obstructing the police during a civil disorder.

On the first anniversary of the insurrection, Attorney General Merrick Garland gave a speech reaffirming the Justice Department's commitment to holding all "January 6th perpetrators, at any level, accountable under the law—whether they were present that day or were otherwise criminally responsible for the assault on our democracy."[77] He reviewed the consequences: eighty Capitol police and sixty D.C. Metropolitan police were assaulted, including being knocked unconscious, dragged down stairs facedown, crushed in a door, attacked with chemical agents, and battered with pipes and poles. Five died, along with four people voluntarily participating in the events of the day.

The depth and scope of the Justice Department's investigation of the January 6 insurrection is unprecedented. Prosecutors issued five thousand subpoenas and search warrants, seized two thousand or more devices, watched over twenty thousand hours of video footage, and examined about fifteen terabytes of computer data. They received and evaluated three hundred thousand tips from members of the public. In determining how to charge potential defendants, Garland explained that the Justice Department was following "well-worn prosecutorial practices."[78] People "who assaulted officers or damaged the Capitol" and "those who conspired with others to obstruct the vote" faced "greater charges."[79]

The long list of felony charges brought against militia members included assaulting, resisting, or impeding police officers; using a deadly or dangerous weapon; causing serious bodily injury to an officer; destruction of government property; corruptly obstructing, influencing, or impeding an official proceeding (in this context, a joint session of Congress to count Electoral College ballots); and, most serious of all, seditious conspiracy. Indictments including this crime alleged that the defendant conspired to commit offenses, including sedition, defined in the statute as "conspir[ing] to overthrow, put down, or to destroy by force the Government of the United States [including] to prevent, hinder, or delay the execution of any law."[80] Other charges carry similar prison terms—up to twenty years—but this one goes to the heart of the matter.

The Oath Keeper contingent put on trial first included Rhodes; Kelly Meggs, a car dealer and leader of the Florida Oath Keepers; Kenneth Harrelsen, a welder and Army veteran, also from Florida; Jessica Watkins, a trans woman, bar owner, and Army veteran who founded an Ohio affiliate; and Thomas Caldwell, a former naval officer from Virginia who once held a top-secret clearance.[81] The grand jury indictment in the case tells a story as chilling as it is bizarre.

Two days after the 2020 election, Rhodes sent a message to an encrypted group chat including several of his alleged co-conspirators, urging them to refuse to accept the election result and declaring, "We aren't getting through this without a civil war. Too late for that. Prepare your mind, body, spirit."[82] He followed up on December 11, 2020, with a message to another group chat stating that if President-elect Biden were to assume the presidency, "It will be a bloody and desperate fight. We are going to have a fight. That can't be avoided."[83]

On December 14, 2020, Rhodes published a letter on the Oath Keepers' website urging the use of force to stop the transfer of presidential power. On December 22, 2020, in a conversation with a regional leader of the Oath Keepers, Rhodes said, "We will have to do a bloody, massively bloody revolution against them. That's what's going to have to happen."[84] On December 23, he posted another open letter claiming that "tens of thousands of patriot Americans, both veterans and non-veterans, will already be in Washington D.C., and many of us will have our mission-critical gear stowed nearby just outside D.C."[85]

In his open letters, Rhodes urged Trump to invoke the Insurrection Act to bolster their chances of overturning the election. The act authorizes the president to deploy armed units—specifically, "state militia" and the military—against Americans if necessary to suppress rebellion or domestic violence.[86] Rhodes thought the Oath Keepers qualified as state militia under the act and that if Trump invoked it, they could enter the District of Columbia with their guns and fight alongside other insurgents and—hopefully—the military, which would follow the commander in chief's orders. The Oath Keepers would have the same authority as deployed troops but without rules of engagement, commanding officers, or any similar constraints.

In July 2020, Trump had threatened to invoke the Insurrection Act to quell peaceful demonstrations across the country protesting the police killing of George Floyd unless the nation's governors called up National Guard troops "to dominate the streets."[87] General Mark Milley, chairman of the Joint Chiefs of Staff, opposed the idea of using the military for this purpose, and Trump eventually dropped the idea.[88]

In Oath Keeper lexicon, "mission critical equipment" refers to a stockpile of weapons, ammunition, and other gear that they hauled to Washington, D.C., and stored in hotel rooms in nearby suburban Virginia. If necessary, they would muster what they called "quick reaction force" teams to take the weapons into the District of Columbia or elsewhere to fight. Their reasoning for stockpiling the weapons in Virginia may have been based on the District of Columbia's stringent laws that require guns to be registered, prohibit concealed carry unless the gun is registered in the District, and ban open carry altogether. In one especially strange communication, defendant Thomas Caldwell asked members of the Three Percenters militia if they knew of a boat on a trailer that the owner would be willing to lend to the Oath Keepers "in support of our efforts to save the Republic" so that the quick response team could travel across the Potomac River from Virginia to Washington, D.C., with "heavy weapons."[89]

The indictment reveals which hotels the Oath Keepers selected and the kind of armament they stockpiled. It lists the equipment they carried to the Capitol: hard-knuckle tactical gloves, tactical vests, chemical sprays, goggles, scissors, and sticks. Once at the Capitol, all the defendants except Rhodes organized themselves into two "stacks," a military term for troops walking in a tight single file line with one hand on the shoulder of the person marching ahead of them, and entered the Capitol.

At the trial, Rhodes took the stand, a highly unusual move for a defendant who was facing up to sixty years in prison and had left such a lavish record leading up to and including January 6. Rhodes, always reluctant to relinquish an opportunity to inform an audience, made matters worse. He testified, "I think it was stupid to go into the Capitol. . . . One, because it wasn't our mission. And, two, it opened the door for our political enemies to persecute us. And that's what happened and here we are."[90] The jury was unimpressed. Rhodes and Meggs were convicted of seditious conspiracy, as well as other charges. Three co-defendants—Kenneth Harrelson, Jessica Watkins, and Thomas Caldwell—were acquitted of the sedition charge but convicted of other felonies.

Sentencing in major cases like this one typically follows weeks after the decision by judge or jury to convict. Prosecutors prepare sentencing memoranda that justify the sentences they ask the judge to propose, explaining why the charges they filed and proved at trial justify the imposition of that punishment. In their sentencing memorandum asking that Rhodes serve a twenty-five-year sentence, prosecutors said he led and organized

> a conspiracy to forcibly oppose the authority of the government of the United States and an attack on the Capitol and Congress during the certification of a presidential election, and for his unabashed lack of remorse for these crimes, Rhodes presents a current and unique danger to the community and to our democracy.[91]

Judge Amit Mehta sentenced Rhodes to eighteen years in prison, telling him: "You, sir, present an ongoing threat and a peril to this country, to the republic and to the very fabric of our democracy. . . . You are smart, you are compelling, and you are charismatic. Frankly, that is what makes you dangerous."[92]

The Oath Keepers' focus on recruiting former and current members working in law enforcement and the military presents an important conundrum. They participated in a violent attack where serving police were injured and several lost their lives. Yet they saw themselves as allied with the police in confronting Black Lives Matter demonstrators. During the Cliven Bundy cattle dispute, Oath Keepers pointed automatic weapons at the police in broad daylight and avoided a violent confrontation only because the police stood down. During the insurrection at the Capitol, Rhodes hoped his followers would be fighting alongside the military after Trump invoked the Insurrection Act. It would be easy to dismiss all of the above as the product of gun-loving, disturbed people who had unrealistic ideas about what would happen if they persisted. But the relationship between the far-right militia and the police is far more complicated.

New Yorker staff writer Luke Mogelson has done exceptional reporting on far-right extremism, including the book *The Storm Is Here: An American Crucible*. In an article entitled "How Trump Supporters Came to Hate the Police," he described the contradictions in militia members' attitudes toward the police and police attitudes toward them.[93] He describes this scene on the Senate floor:

> My impression was that a simple contract—sometimes tacit, sometimes explicit—governed most interactions between Trump supporters and law enforcement on January 6th: the insurrectionists would attack only those officers who stood in their way, while bestowing the usual respect and deference on those who stood down. Still, the vicious brutality encountered by officers who fought back makes the passivity of some of their peers all the more confounding. I'd been in the Senate chamber for about twenty minutes when a large phalanx of Metropolitan Police

> entered. The Trump supporters were suddenly corralled, with no avenue of escape. Assuming that everyone in the chamber would be detained and that our phones would be confiscated, I withdrew my wallet and prepared to show my press card. But no arrests were made. No one was searched. Nobody questioned. The red-bearded officer approached a rioter and spoke to him privately, after which the rioter announced, "We gotta go, guys, otherwise we're goin' in handcuffs." As we filed out through the main door, the sergeant with the shaved head told us, "Be safe. We appreciate you being peaceful." . . .
>
> Strategic forbearance is one thing. But can we really attribute such outright solicitude, in the midst of what one officer called a "medieval battle," to some tactical shrewdness intended to beguile a volatile adversary? I don't think so. I think that the complex, often contradictory actions of officers on January 6th flowed from their complex, often contradictory relationship with that adversary.

Police deciding to stand down is not a new phenomenon in America, especially in the biggest cities wracked by violent crime. But if this reaction extends to marauding mobs motivated by political conflict, the consequences for the country could be catastrophic. On their own, militia members have no chance to achieve the revolutionary overthrow of the federal government, and their leaders' threats are nothing more than insane delusions of grandeur. Were a critical mass of police—or, more dire, members of the military—to join them, the upheaval could destabilize the government to an extent that is hard to imagine.

In that vein, it is worth remembering a statement by former defense secretary James Mattis condemning Trump's actions in ordering the military (among others) to clear the square outside the White House of protesters, using clubs and tear gas:

> I have watched this week's unfolding events, angry and appalled. The words 'Equal Justice Under Law' are carved in the pediment of the United States Supreme Court. This is precisely what protesters are rightly

demanding. It is a wholesome and unifying demand—one that all of us should be able to get behind. . . .

Donald Trump is the first president in my lifetime who does not try to unite the American people—does not even pretend to try. Instead, he tries to divide us. We are witnessing the consequences of three years of this deliberate effort. . . . We can unite without him, drawing on the strengths inherent in our civil society. This will not be easy, as the past few days have shown, but we owe it to our fellow citizens; to past generations that bled to defend our promise; and to our children.[94]

EIGHT

THE LEFT

UNFORCED ERRORS

The preceding chapters tell depressing stories. Powerful groups with lots of money and a candidate for president who uses government as a whipping boy are gearing up for the 2024 election and have a decent chance of reinstalling Donald Trump in the White House. Once there, he could pardon the January 6 defendants and pick up where he left off in crippling health, safety, and environmental agencies with budget cuts and constant ridicule. If far-right Republicans control both houses of Congress, the outcome would be worse. Even if Trump is defeated or does not run, the Freedom Caucus will continue to sabotage Congress, corporations will lobby or litigate climate change rules to a standstill, Fox News will sell conspiracy theories, and so on.

It is tempting to leave these possibilities out in the ether without considering the other side of the equation: why have left-leaning interest groups not been more effective in counteracting the six? Fully answering that question could take several more volumes. Yet one possibility at the heart of this book is worth considering. Have left-leaning groups failed because they are unable to understand the threats posed by the six and where their own vulnerabilities lie? Is it possible that because they underestimated and misunderstood their opponents, left-leaning activists strode off in the wrong direction and made costly mistakes? Two cautionary tales provide useful answers to these questions.

In offering these examples, I do not intend to paint with a broad negative brush the large, diverse, and extraordinarily capable public interest community that operates out of Washington, D.C., and focuses on the decisions made by the national government. Rather, the two examples focus on strategies and tactics that simply did not work and have important ramifications for the future.

The first was the effort to pass comprehensive climate mitigation legislation as soon as Barack Obama became president. That effort was the first and last time liberal legislators and environmentalists had the opportunity to take the action that is so desperately needed to avert the worst consequences of a warming planet. The climate story begins in 2009, shortly after Obama became president, when Washington-centered environmental groups decided to negotiate an inside deal with thirty big companies affected by climate change. Their theory was that a group of "strange bedfellows" would so impress members of Congress that the deal they negotiated would provide the blueprint for successful legislation. The exclusivity, secrecy, and high-handedness of the negotiations caused a backlash that contributed to the demise of the legislation in the Senate.

During the fraught years when Trump was president, radical left antifa cells disrupted peaceful demonstrations by fighting in the streets. People who identify as antifa are generally white, middle class, and relatively young. Their core belief is that they must prevent fascists from speaking in public, violently if necessary. Their definition of fascism is murky and their commitment to ad hoc street fighting causes significant collateral damage.

In one high-profile episode, they attacked the police with firecrackers and Molotov cocktails and went on a rampage of window-breaking and setting fires in Berkeley, California, to disrupt a speech by a far-right provocateur named Milo Yiannopoulos. In addition to providing Yiannopoulos with a golden opportunity to raise his profile on social media and make more money, antifa created the impression that left-leaning activists oppose free speech.

Then, in the summer of 2020, when thousands of demonstrations were held to protest the murder of George Floyd, a Black man, by Derek Chauvin, a white police officer, antifa went into the streets again. Antifa men and women were especially active in Portland, Oregon, where protests extended over an astonishing one hundred straight days. At the end of the summer, a cavalcade of trucks and cars waving Trump flags drove into downtown Portland. Antifa people and the far-right fought each other with pipes, bear spray, and paintball guns. Michael Reinoehl, a self-appointed antifa security guard, killed Aaron Danielson, a member of the far right militia group called Patriot Prayer. Federal police assassinated Reinoehl the following week. These events illustrated the deep pitfalls of violence as tactic, much less a strategy, when the other side is better armed, better resourced, and spoiling for a fight.

Climate change mitigation falls squarely within the focus of this book: attacks on government efforts to protect public health, consumer and worker safety, and the environment. Antifa's activities are admittedly farther afield. Those events are included because antifa gave Donald Trump the opportunity to portray its loose network as a major threat, camouflaging the far more serious domestic terrorism threat posed by far-right groups and patriot militia.

DOOMSDAY SCENARIOS

In 1979, researchers told the Carter administration that "man is setting in motion a series of events that seem certain to cause a significant warming of world climate unless mitigating steps are taken immediately."[1] The implications of this warning were not lost on investors in fossil fuels (coal, oil, and natural gas). Their response had dual components—first, to discredit the scientific research that was revealing the nature and scope of climate change and, second, to emphasize the feasibility of adapting to climate change rather than attempting the significantly more expensive alternative of imposing pollution controls.

The National Academies of Science (NAS) represent the gold standard in American science. The institution's modus operandi is to convene panels of the best experts available and ask them to investigate and evaluate a set of hypotheses known as a "charge." The NAS established its first panel to evaluate what scientists knew about climate change in 1983. Among its members was a politically conservative physicist named William Nierenberg. Rather than considering what the research showed regarding the urgency of reducing industrial emissions of the greenhouse gases that cause climate change, Nierenberg persuaded his colleagues to focus on whether humans could adapt to climate change if and when it got serious. The panel concluded that our ability to adapt was sufficient.

Science historians Naomi Oreskes, Erik Conway, and Matthew Shindell characterize Nierenberg's efforts as the "social *deconstruction* of scientific knowledge."[2] This strategy had been perfected in industry campaigns to debunk scientific findings on the health consequences of smoking, the irreversible neurological damage children under six suffer when exposed to lead in gasoline and paint, and the fatal childhood leukemia resulting from illegal dumping of trichloroethylene that migrated into the drinking water of Woburn, Massachusetts, to name just a few. Polluting industries fund scientists to pick apart such research. During deconstruction, each individual piece of research is subjected to minute examination, made possible by the reality that scientific studies are rarely perfect or comprehensive in design. As each study is cast into doubt, the body of research justifying action is reduced and weakened.

Deconstruction is the opposite of the traditional weight-of-the-evidence approach followed by all reputable scientists. Weight of the evidence aggregates all the available research and develops a consensus view on what the collection reveals about a problem. The tension between deconstruction and weight-of-the-evidence methodologies has played out in every consequential regulatory dispute starting with tobacco control, proceeding to the elimination of lead in gasoline and control of other toxins, and culminating with climate change.[3]

Nierenberg's interference threw off track policymakers' recognition of emerging science documenting the danger of failing to mitigate emissions. Eventually, scientists arrived at the conviction that anthropogenic greenhouse gas (GHG) emissions were pushing the climate irrevocably toward intolerable warming. In 1988, up to then the hottest year on record, James Hansen, the director of the NASA Goddard Institute of Space Studies, delivered landmark testimony before the Senate Energy and Natural Resources Committee. Hansen told the senators that he was 99 percent certain global warming was not a natural variation but instead was caused by pollutants in the atmosphere. "Global warming is now large enough that we can ascribe with a high degree of confidence a cause and effect relationship to the greenhouse effect. . . . Our computer climate simulations indicate that the greenhouse effect is already large enough to begin to affect the probability of extreme events such as summer heat waves."[4] When Hansen testified, modeling showed that if the buildup of GHGs continued, temperatures were likely to increase by three to nine degrees Fahrenheit between 2025 and 2050, melting ice to the point that the sea level would rise between one and four feet.[5]

On the eve of a meeting of the G8 nations in June 2008, the scientific academies of thirteen countries, including the American NAS, signed a document begging the nations' leaders to "act more forcefully to limit the threat posed by human-driven global warming."[6] The G8 included Canada, England, France, Germany, Italy, Japan, Russia, and the United States. The countries represented by the scientific academies included Brazil, Britain, Canada, China, France, Germany, India, Italy, Japan, Mexico, Russia, South Africa, and the United States.

Six years later, the world's scientists were finding it difficult to maintain their composure. The Intergovernmental Panel on Climate Change (IPCC) was founded in 1988 by the World Meteorological Organization and the United Nations Environmental Programme. It has attracted the participation of most qualified scientists engaged in research regarding the nature, scope, and future of the climate. The IPCC reported that anthropogenic (manmade) greenhouse gas emissions mean that "many aspects of climate change and associated impacts will continue for centuries, even if anthropogenic emissions of GHGs are stopped. The risks of abrupt or irreversible changes increase as the magnitude of the warming increases."[7]

By 2018, a special IPCC report entitled *Global Warming of 1.5°C* warned that we are running out of time to avert catastrophic human health and ecological damage. If GHG emissions continued at the rate they were then, the planet's atmosphere would warm by as much as 1.5° Celsius above pre-industrial levels, with disastrous effects for millions of people and ecological systems between 2030 and 2052.[8] (One degree Celsius is about 1.8 degrees Fahrenheit.) Warming would produce a world of worsening drought, scarcity of potable water, food shortages, extreme weather events, and wildfires as soon as 2040.

The same year, the legally mandated fourth National Climate Assessment brought these findings home to the United States.[9] Written by the top experts at thirteen departments and agencies from Commerce, State, Defense, and Agriculture to the EPA, its *Report-in-Brief* warned of deadly consequences unless the nation undertook mitigation of GHG emissions, as opposed to mere adaptation to a changing climate. When the fifth assessment came out in November 2023, scientists warned that the nation is warming 60 percent more quickly than the world as a whole and predicted sea level rise of eleven inches by 2050.[10]

In 2021, the IPCC issued its sixth assessment, warning (again) that without rapid and drastic reductions in the emissions of GHGs, the human race could not dodge the catastrophic results of rising temperatures. Elizabeth Kolbert, author of the Pulitzer Prize–winning book *The Sixth Extinction: An Unnatural History,* explained that the IPCC had sketched out several possible futures. The most optimistic was that "carbon emissions will fall to zero during the next few decades, and new technologies will be developed to suck tens of billions on tons of CO_2 from the air."[11] Even in that unrealistic scenario, temperatures would rise by 1.6° Celsius by the middle of the century. A far more likely scenario would be warming by 2° Celsius by 2050 and 3° Celsius by the end of twenty-first century, an outcome that would be bad enough. But

> in a not-at-all-implausible scenario temperatures will rise by 3.6 degrees Celsius—or 6.5 degrees Fahrenheit—by around 2090. What will summer be like as temperatures continue to rise? In the carefully vetted formulation of the IPCC, "many changes in the climate system become larger in direct relation to increasing global warming." In other words, we really don't want to find out. But unfortunately, we are going to.[12]

Throughout this period, from 1995 to the present, the United Nations convened dozens of conferences involving many nations to craft agreements that would reduce emissions. The United States bears a great deal of responsibility for undermining these efforts, participating in and pulling out of the negotiations depending on whether a Democrat or Republican was president. All the agreements depended on voluntary reductions and were not enforced.

Midway between Hansen's warning and Kolbert's prediction, it seemed possible that Congress might take a first step to mitigate climate change.

A CROWDED WINDOW OF OPPORTUNITY

When Barack Obama was elected, virtually every one of the public interest groups that are part of the Democratic base went on point like a hunting dog. As the first African American to achieve the nation's highest office was inaugurated before a record-setting crowd of 1.1 million exuberant supporters, national environmental groups began lobbying to elevate action on climate change to the new administration's top legislative priority. They joined a long line of other groups beseeching the new president to choose their issues instead.

Obama was up to his knees in alligators and everyone knew it. The 2008 market crash was crushing middle- and low-income Americans, throwing them out of their homes, sucking away their jobs, and shredding national safety net programs. A stimulus bill was the first priority and any proposal on that or any other reform had to run a gauntlet of increasingly hostile congressional Republicans. Progressive groups knew that the window for any legislative agenda beyond the stimulus bill was closing fast and might slam shut as soon as the 2010 midterm elections. They turned out to be right. Republicans retook control of the House by a large margin, ending any possibility of passing climate change legislation. The window was exactly two years wide, with the 2008 crash occupying a large part of that short period. There was no time to waste.

One reason environmental groups gave for putting climate change first was a political miracle in the House. As the 111th Congress organized itself in 2009, Henry Waxman (D-CA), who chaired one of several subcommittees within the powerful Energy and Commerce Committee, accomplished a political coup of great significance by wresting the chairmanship of the full committee from the apparently invincible John Dingell (D-MI). The Committee was the best launching pad in the House for climate change legislation. Waxman was a liberal with an outstanding record of legislative accomplishments and a long-standing commitment to environmental issues. Dingell was far less liberal especially when it came to air pollution controls on cars and trucks made in Detroit. Waxman's elevation meant that he controlled the Committee's agenda and could exert considerable pressure on members to vote his way. He joined with Congressman Ed Markey (D-MA), another long-time member of the Energy and Commerce Committee, to introduce comprehensive legislation incorporating a cap-and-trade approach to drive down GHG emissions.

Cap-and-trade programs put a cap, or aggregate limit, on the amount of covered pollution that regulated sources can emit on an annual basis. The Waxman-Markey bill awarded annual permits, or allowances, to sources of GHGs with the assumption that when the allocations of covered sources were tallied, the total would fall at or below the quantity authorized by the cap. No source—for example, a coal-fired power plant—could emit more than the amount covered by its annual allowances. Holders of allowances could trade (buy or sell) them with other companies. This approach meant that owners of dirty plants (for example, power plants burning dirty coal) could avoid installing expensive pollution equipment by buying allowances to cover their excess emissions from owners of cleaner plants (for example, power plants running on natural gas). The cap was what environmental groups wanted, and trading was what industry wanted.

With the crucial support of House Speaker Nancy Pelosi (D-CA), Waxman and Markey began the arduous fight to get H.R. 2454, the Clean Energy and Security Act of 2009, to the House floor. As often happens in such battles, the sponsors won crucial votes by granting financial benefits to regulated sources. In the first few years of the program's operation, more than a third of allowances would be given to electric utilities at no charge. By the time the bill reached the House floor, it incorporated caps that would reduce GHGs by 17 percent below 2005 levels by 2020 and by 83 percent below 2005 levels by 2050, a good start with much more work to be done.

Sharp divisions afflicted both the left and the right. On the left, Greenpeace opposed the Waxman-Markey bill, as did James Hansen, the scientist who first sounded the alarm about climate change. Hansen wrote that the legislation was "a monstrous absurdity hatched in Washington after energetic insemination by special interests [that] locks in fossil fuel business-as-usual and garlands it with a Ponzi-like 'cap and trade' scheme."[13] On the right, the National Association of Manufacturers announced that it had launched a "multistate, multimillion-dollar comprehensive advertising campaign opposing the . . . Waxman-Markey climate change bill."[14]

In the end, the House passed the legislation by an uncomfortably close margin, 219–212, with forty-four Democrats voting against it and eight Republicans voting for it. The bill was sent to the Senate, where it eventually died without ever reaching the floor. The national environmental groups that staked their prestige and credibility on the effort were bitterly disappointed. To be sure, they had strong forces arrayed against them. But they had had a strategy they were sure would work. What went wrong?

STRANGE BEDFELLOWS

The "Big Green" groups that launched the effort to push Waxman-Markey through Congress included the Environmental Defense Fund, the Natural Resources Defense Council, the Pew Center on Global Climate Change, the World Resources Institute, and the Nature Conservancy. All were old hands at getting controversial legislation passed in better times, and they had faith that, although outnumbered, they were far superior to industry experts in the science, technology, and public policy needed to solve the climate change problem. This superior expertise would allow them to outwit their industry opponents.

The group was led by Fred Krupp, the long-time head of the Environmental Defense Fund, who had a reputation for working with industry and saw himself as a consummate dealmaker.[15] Krupp argued that if the environmental groups could assemble a coalition with major industry players and come up with a negotiated compromise, they could sell it to key players on Capitol Hill and finally get something done. This plan was overconfident, even in a town where lobbyists drive much of the action. In effect, the group would negotiate behind closed doors, hand their detailed compromise to legislators, circumvent the hundreds of parties excluded from the negotiations, and stand smiling behind the president when he signed the legislation into law. Krupp ultimately recruited about two and a half dozen large corporations, including electric utilities, oil refiners, automakers, chemical companies, and other manufacturers, to join the Big Green groups in a coalition named the U.S. Climate Action Partnership (USCAP). Months later, USCAP emerged with a compromise to be used as the blueprint for the House legislation. Participants were proud of their efforts, but far more daunting challenges were still ahead.

Politics in the country were changing faster than Krupp or the other environmental members of USCAP realized. As explained in chapter 3, the emergence of the Tea Party meant that mainstream Republicans were sharply challenged from the right. The Tea Party seemed to have activists in every Republican district and they were unalterably opposed to big government, as typified by Democratic proposals to widen access to health care and combat climate change. Equally challenging, the country was still suffering from the recession caused by the 2008 crash. The unemployment rate was 8.2 percent by the time Obama gave his 2009 State of the Union address. For better or worse, a bad economy can doom environmental legislation, which is widely portrayed by industry as too costly regardless of the benefits it provides.

The companies that joined USCAP were powerful, but they were outnumbered and outspent by the hundreds of other industry players excluded from the group, including powerful trade associations like the American Petroleum Institute, the Chamber of Commerce, and the National Association of Manufacturers. The rationale of the elite corporate members of USCAP was that by sitting down with the environmentalists, they could steer the legislation in industry's favor. The perception of all the other companies was that the corporate members of USCAP were capitulating to a small group of environmental organizations that were negotiating from a position of weakness. They thought Republicans had a good chance of flipping one or both chambers of Congress in the midterms and that Obama was weakened by the 2008 crash. Why rush and why concede?

The self-selected USCAP environmental groups had problems with their left flank. Exclusion of other national organizations—most notably Friends of the Earth, Greenpeace, and especially the Sierra Club, the best grassroots environmental organization in the nation—made it difficult to muster local support as the legislative process lurched along. The other groups had not played any role in formulating the deal and resented the Big Green groups' arrogance. USCAP had some money for organizing at the local level, but much of it was spent on media and political advertising rather than direct personal contacts between voters and members of Congress.

As problematic, the cap-and-trade concept was hard to explain, not least because it was a closed circuit, helping companies but not people. The most important environmental laws were based on the premise that polluters should pay to reduce their pollution, making the environment cleaner for people and nature. Cap and trade turned this logic on its head: rather than reduce pollution, the government was giving companies permission to pollute and allowing them to buy and sell pieces of that permission to each other. Pollution would decrease over time if the limits assumed by the cap were enforced, but giving away permissions to pollute confused people.

The trade-offs became even more perplexing when the White House and USCAP insisted on leaving out of their routine talking points any discussion of the legislation's advantages in averting the dire perils of climate change. Instead, they presented the legislation as a way to create green jobs. Somehow, they must have reasoned, talking jobs without mentioning looming environmental problems would slip by industry opponents and raise enthusiasm from people battered by the 2008 crash.

Convinced by Krupp and the other leaders of the Big Green groups that they had a winning strategy, environmental funders spent unprecedented amounts on the battle, estimated as almost $394 million in 2008, $602 million in 2009, and $630 million in 2010.[16] But although the foundations were remarkably generous, these sums had one critical drawback. Most environmental foundations are tax-exempt nonprofits, so they are prohibited from making campaign contributions. Industry groups not only were free of this constraint but outspent their opponents by large margins.

When the campaign collapsed in the Senate, the funders were surprised, frustrated, and wary of the explanations offered by the five environmental groups that led the effort. The Rockefeller Family Fund decided to commission two outside reports that would critically analyze the debacle and suggest better ways forward. The first report was a granular explanation of who did what to whom written by journalists Petra Bartosiewicz and Marissa Miley.[17] The second was a normative analysis written by widely respected Harvard political scientist Theda Skocpol.[18]

Skocpol wrote that the central, indispensable missing ingredient in the environmentalists' strategy was the organization of a widespread network of grassroots organizations in key states that could have put pressure on wavering lawmakers:

> The USCAP campaign was designed and conducted in an insider-grand-bargaining political style that, unbeknownst to its sponsors, was unlikely to succeed given fast-changing realities in U.S. partisan politics and governing institutions. . . .
>
> Climate change warriors will have to look beyond elite maneuvers and find ways to address the values and interests of tens of millions of U.S. citizens. To counter fierce political opposition, reformers will have to build organizational networks across the country, and they will need to orchestrate sustained political efforts that stretch far beyond friendly Congressional offices, comfy board rooms, and posh retreats.[19]

To prove her point, Skocpol analyzed the success of the Affordable Care Act, more commonly known as Obamacare, which the president signed into law in March 2010.[20] She wrote that the "health care arena" included "physicians' and nurses' associations, associations of hospitals, insurance companies, and pharmaceutical manufacturers . . . labor unions [and] consumer groups, nonprofits, and charities."[21] Not only was this assembly more diverse than USCAP, but public interest funders established a "slightly left-of-center effort called 'Health Care for America Now' (HCAN) that managed networks of supporters in dozens of states conducting local events and pressuring members of Congress from beyond the Beltway."[22] She concluded that the addition of this grassroots lobbying made all the difference.

A second example of a broad coalition that accomplished major public interest law reform during the 111th Congress was the coalition that lobbied for the creation of the Consumer Financial Protection Bureau as part of the Dodd-Frank Wall Street Reform and Consumer Protection Act.[23] Public interest groups representing consumers, current members of the military, veterans, low-income consumers, and students at for-profit colleges fought successfully to protect the provisions establishing the agency despite intense opposition from the financial services industry.

Skocpol was also critical of the structure of the cap-and-trade program USCAP had negotiated. In 2001, environmentalist and businessman Peter Barnes proposed that the cap-and-trade system be changed to a "cap-and-dividend" formula that would take the money raised by auctioning off the permits to emit pollution and return it to American consumers. During the 111th Congress, Senators Maria Cantwell (D-WA) and Susan Collins (R-ME) introduced legislation based on Barnes's idea.[24] Neither senator was much of a player on environmental issues, and the bill went nowhere. It probably would have provoked even more intense industry opposition. But had it been the vehicle supported by environmentalists, a major problem of communication would have been solved:

> Instead of building political support by bargaining with industrial interests about how many permits they may get cheaply or for free, the cap and dividend approach makes it possible to speak with average citizens about what they might gain as well as pay during the transitional period of increasing prices for energy from carbon sources. . . . No opaque, messy, corrupt insider deals. The dividend payments also deliver a relatively greater economic pay-off to the least-well off individuals and families, precisely the people who, as energy prices rise, would have to spend more of their incomes as home heating, electricity, and gasoline.[25]

These arguments are pragmatic and well-placed as a matter of populist politics. But Skocpol extended them one vital step further: "Environmentalism has a reputation for appealing mostly to white, upper-middle-class educated citizens, even as stagnating wages for less privileged Americans have made it easy for right-wing forces to demonize carbon-capping as a new tax that will burden already hard-pressed families."[26] She added: "The most powerful kind of reformist policymaking uses an initial law to create material benefits and normative claims that, in turn, reinforce and enlarge the supportive political coalition behind the new measure. A classic example is Social Security."[27]

Some of the environmentalists most invested in passage of the legislation attacked Skocpol's motives, intellect, reasoning, and conclusions. The most vehement was Joseph Romm, a blogger on climate issues. He described the Skocpol report as a "lengthy new opinion piece" and an "incredibly long but oddly incomplete essay" that "aims to pin the blame for the failure of the climate bill on the environmental community."[28] Instead,

> opponents of action—the fossil fuel companies, the disinformers, the right-wing media, and anti-science, pro-pollution ideologues in the Senate—deserve 60 percent of the blame.... The lame-stream media gets 30 percent for its generally enabling coverage.... Then the "think small" centrists and lukewarmers get 5 percent for helping to shrink the political space in the debate.[29]

The upshot, according to Romm? Five percent of the blame should be allocated between "team Obama and environmental groups (along with Senate Democrats, scientists, progressives, and everyone else, including me)."[30] For that last 5 percent, he declares, "the lion's share has to go to Obama.... He is the agenda-shaper. He has the biggest megaphone by far. He made most of the decisive blunders."[31]

Romm was especially irritated by Obama's chief of staff, Rahm Emanuel, who kept telling USCAP members to find some Republican senators to support their proposal. The legislation needed sixty votes to impose cloture on the inevitable filibuster, after all, and that total could be reached only by getting some Republican supporters. For months, Senator Lindsey Graham (R-SC) negotiated with Senators Joe Lieberman (I-CT) and John Kerry (D-MA) to produce a compromise, but Graham ended up pulling out of the deal. Romm said that had Obama taken on this task of recruiting Republicans, he would have been far more persuasive than USCAP. Given Republicans' determination to deprive the president of reelection in 2012, this argument seems both unrealistic and opportunistic.

As time ran out and midterm electoral prospects looked bad for Democrats, Obama and his advisers made another choice that infuriated the USCAP environmentalists. Obama chose the health care bill as a priority over climate change. Romm argued that this choice was an egregious failure because the climate bill "was far more important for the future of the nation and the world."[32] In other blogs, he identified it as the reason why the Obama presidency failed.[33]

Not all leaders of the environmental movement condemned Obama and Skocpol. Bill McKibben, author and activist, had just founded 350.org, the first planetwide, grassroots climate change movement. He wrote:

> If the inside-the-Beltway groups had been able to turn to a real grassroots activist movement, the outcome might have been different. But that movement didn't really exist, and many of the big players had only disdain for its embryonic form—they liked talking with corporate honchos more than treehuggers. And so the lobbyists from the green groups were walking naked into the offices of senators, who recognized that they lacked the ability to inflict pain or offer reward. The result was the rout we saw.[34]

Defeat in a legislative battle to which you have devoted years of your life is heartbreaking and infuriating, especially when you know that the stakes are huge and urgent. But Skocpol was not working as a toady for the oil and gas industry. Nor is she stupid, shallow, or self-serving. Her bottom line deserves consideration: if you cannot explain what the legislation would do at Thanksgiving dinner with the family, you have a real problem.

ILLIBERAL POLITICS

The anti-fascist movement began with resistance to the Nazis across Europe in the 1920s and 1930s. Antifa groups rioted to keep Oswald Mosley's fascist followers off the streets in October 1936 in a confrontation known as the Battle of Cable Street. The antifa movement in the United States—generally pronounced an-tee-fah and short for *anti-fascism*—has existed for decades but became prominent when Trump used it as one of his favorite foils. Antifa protesters participated in outbreaks of violence in Charlottesville, Virginia; Portland, Oregon; and Berkeley, California. In Portland, a man associated with antifa shot dead a right-wing demonstrator and then was assassinated by federal police. Along with his allies at Fox News and other right-wing media outlets, Trump distracted attention from right-wing militia activities by insisting that left-wing violence wrought by antifa was much worse.

Antifa does not have a centralized, hierarchical management structure. Instead, the movement operates as a loosely organized collection of small groups of like-minded people who do not coordinate activities. As FBI director Christopher Wray testified before the House Homeland Security Committee, "It's not a group or an organization. It's a movement or an ideology."[35] A Congressional Research Service background paper for members of Congress agreed: "[The] movement appears to be decentralized, consisting of independent, radical, like-minded groups and individuals. . . . Its tenets can echo the principles of anarchism, socialism, and communism . . . . Among many other things, [its members] may also support environmentalism, the rights of indigenous populations, and gay rights."[36]

Antifa's most prominent American interpreter is Mark Bray, the author of *Antifa: The Anti-Fascist Handbook*.[37] Bray describes himself as a communist and states unequivocally that he supports the antifa movement: "I hope *Antifa* will aid and inspire those who will take up the fight against fascism in the years to come so that someday there will be no need for this book."[38] Or, in other words, the book actually is a handbook and not an independent analysis of the movement.

When the antifa handbook first came out, activities on the Berkeley campus were in the news and Bray was a lecturer at Dartmouth College. He emerged as the leading academic able to explain the movement and was soon invited to participate in a series of high-profile interviews on television, radio, and in print. On *Meet the Press*, he said that "when pushed, self-defense is a legitimate response to white supremacist and neo-Nazi violence. We've tried ignoring neo-Nazis in the past. We've seen how that turned out in the '20s and '30s. . . . It's a privileged position to say you never have to defend yourself from these kinds of monsters."[39]

The day after the show aired, Dartmouth president Philip Hanlon posted a statement declaring that Bray's support for violent protest does not "represent the views of Dartmouth [because the institution] embraces free speech and open inquiry in all matters."[40] The paradox that Hanlon was advocating an absolute right to free speech but chastising Bray for exercising it did not go unnoticed. One hundred faculty members wrote a letter asking Hanlon to withdraw the statement.[41] He did not. Bray left Dartmouth and now teaches at Rutgers University.

Bray dedicates his book to the Jews of Knyszyn, Poland, the site of Nazi atrocities that resulted in the death of the Jewish population in the area. Bray is also Jewish. He exhibits a "never again" mindset common among Jews who have immersed themselves in the Holocaust. He writes, "After Auschwitz and Treblinka, anti-fascists committed themselves to fighting to the death the ability of organized Nazis to say anything."[42]

Bray makes dutiful efforts to define fascism and anti-fascism but ends up with ambiguous and confusing results. He acknowledges that fascism is "notoriously difficult to pin down," but ends up relying on historian Robert Paxton's explanation that fascists "reject any universal value other than the success of chosen peoples in the Darwinian struggle for primacy."[43] Bray adds: "Postwar (after World War II) fascists have experimented with an even more dizzying array of positions by freely pilfering from Maoism, anarchism, Trotskyism, and other left-wing ideologies and cloaking themselves in 'respectable' electoral guises on the model of France's Front National and other parties."[44]

His explanation of anti-fascism is not much clearer:

> Anti-fascism is an illiberal politics of social revolutionism applied to fighting the Far Right, not only literal fascists. As we will see, anti-fascists have accomplished this goal in a wide variety of ways, from singing over fascist speeches, to occupying the sites of fascist meetings before they could set up, to sowing discord in their groups via infiltration, to breaking any veil of anonymity, to physically disrupting their newspaper sales, demonstrations, and other activities. Militant anti-fascists disagree with the pursuit of state bans against "extremist" politics because of their revolutionary, anti-state politics and because such bans are more

> often used against the Left than the Right.
>
> Some antifa groups are more Marxist while others are more anarchist or antiauthoritarian. In the United States, most have been anarchist or antiauthoritarian since the emergence of modern antifa under the name Anti-Racist Action (ARA) in the late eighties.[45]

In addition to its strategy of preventing speech by anyone it considers to be fascists, the movement's credibility is undermined by murky definitions of who is and who is not a fascist and its lack of a coherent explanation of how it chooses its targets. When up against a leader of the opposition who is not only the president of the United States but a master of arousing his followers with colorful and paranoid attacks, the ambiguity of antifa's mission became a high-profile problem.

BLACK BLOC AT BERKELEY

Milo Yiannopoulos (born Milo Hanrahan) is a handsome British man in his late thirties who dresses flamboyantly and is an expert at attracting attention. Sometimes he describes himself as Jewish and sometimes he says he is Catholic. For many years, as he rose to prominence on the right, he said he was gay. In 2017, he announced on Instagram that he had married an unidentified man. In 2021, he said he was "ex-gay" and "sodomy free," saved by conversion therapy, adding: "The guy I live with has been demoted to housemate, which hasn't been easy for either of us. It helps that I can still just about afford to keep him in Givenchy and a new Porsche every year. Could be worse for him, I guess."[46] In 2023, he announced that he had signed on as the director of political operations for rapper Kanye West, who says he is running for president.

Yiannopoulos began his career in 2014 as an editor at Breitbart and a prodigy of Steve Bannon, who briefly served as Donald Trump's first chief of staff. In 2016, Yiannopoulos and fellow Breitbart reporter Allum Bokhari coauthored a widely read article entitled "An Establishment Conservative's Guide to the Alt-Right."[47] They described the alt-right as consisting of people who are "young, creative and eager to commit secular heresies, [who] have become public enemy number one to beltway conservatives—more hated, even, than Democrats or loopy progressives."[48] The article insisted that the key difference between "old-school racist skinheads" and the alt-right is the latter's stunning intelligence: "Skinheads, by and large, are low-information, low-IQ thugs driven by the thrill of violence and tribal hatred. The alternative right are a much smarter group of people—which perhaps suggests why the Left hates them so much. They're dangerously bright."[49] Or, in other words, these explanations leave the unmistakable impression that the coauthors are describing themselves.

The Anti-Defamation League (ADL), a nonprofit group committed to tracking extremists, has established a category called the "alt lite," which it defines as "a loosely connected movement of right-wing activists who reject the overtly white supremacist ideology of the alt right, but whose hateful impact is more significant than their 'lite' name suggests. The alt lite embraces misogyny and xenophobia and abhors 'political correctness' and the left."[50] The ADL places Yiannopoulos among this group.

In 2015, Yiannopoulos began what he called the Dangerous Faggot Tour with the goal of visiting college campuses in England and the United States at the invitation of conservative student groups. His goal was to provoke controversy and generate content for the social media outlets he uses to earn a living. His behavior at these events was not just provocative but nasty. For example, while speaking at the University of Wisconsin, he mocked a transgender student, displaying her name and photo on a screen before an audience of about 325 people and ridiculing her for insisting that she should be able to use the women's locker room at the campus recreation center. The student dropped out of school.

At the beginning of February 2017, Berkeley College Republicans invited Yiannopoulos to speak on campus. A nonviolent protest was organized, bringing out a crowd of about 1,500 in Sproul Plaza, which is adjacent to the student union, the site of his talk. (The plaza is also the site where the Berkeley Free Speech Movement was founded in 1964.) Unbeknownst to the organizers of that rally, a group of about 150 black bloc demonstrators was marching to the plaza. The term *black bloc* refers to antifa members' practice of dressing all in black, with face coverings to mask their identities. When they reached the plaza, the black bloc members dived into the crowd, hitting people with crude weapons, and using pepper spray. Why they attacked people who were also demonstrating against Yiannopoulos is unclear. Antifa members threw Molotov cocktails at buildings and smashed windows. They hurled fireworks at the police and pulled down a light tower, setting it on fire. The speech was canceled and Yiannopoulos was hustled out of the building. Intent on demonstrating its support of free speech, the University of California Berkeley administration allowed a campus group to invite Yiannopoulos to speak a second time in September 2022. After addressing a small crowd, he departed, flanked by police.

The Dangerous Faggot Tour became part of a concerted effort by right-wing figures, including neo-Nazi Richard Spencer. They would show up on campuses and provoke demonstrations, providing fodder for media allies like Fox News commentator Tucker Carlson. Two implications were drawn: the people demonstrating were afraid to tolerate free and open debate, a cornerstone of American democracy, and left-wing demonstrators were violent and out of control. In a *Politico* story headlined "Universities Fear a Violent 2018," Mark Bray, as usual, was preoccupied with explaining antifa: "[Antifa] refuses to grant white supremacist or fascist politics the status of being worthy of debate or conversation and argues these kinds of groups and politics ought to be shut down from the very beginning before they have the smallest opportunity to grow."[51]

Yiannopoulos continued to enjoy financially fruitful, semi-mainstream career as a provocateur and pundit until his appearance in 2016 on the podcast "Drunken Peasants." During the broadcast he said that teenage boys as young as thirteen could profit from friendly sexual relationships with older men. The *Daily News* reported that when a host of the podcast fired back that his comment "sounds like Catholic priest molestation to me," Yiannopoulos said "I'm grateful for Father Michael. I would not give nearly such good head if it wasn't for him."[52]

This time, he had gone too far. He was forced to resign from Breitbart; the Conservative Political Action Coalition withdrew an invitation to speak at an upcoming meeting; and Simon & Schuster canceled his $250,000 book contract. Yiannopoulos self-published the book, sold an unknown number of copies, and served as a voluntary summer intern for Representative Marjorie Taylor Greene (R-GA). He continues to give speeches and generally agitate opponents, but without a reliable platform.

In a short post entitled "Milo Yiannopoulos: Five Things to Know," the ADL described him as a "misogynistic, racist, xenophobic, transphobic troll who is extremely good at getting people to pay attention to him."[53] If this harsh description is reasonably accurate, the question then becomes whether paying attention to him in the way antifa members did at Berkeley is a good idea, especially given the fallout that his appearances and their attacks cause. In other words, people like Yiannopoulos thrive on exactly what antifa does to shut perceived fascists down.

Jelani Cobb, dean of the Columbia University Journalism School and staff writer for the *New Yorker*, argues that demonstrating against Yiannopoulos turns provocateur into victim and obscures the damage to the people who are the targets of his attacks:

> Last year, Yiannopoulos was permanently banned from Twitter for his role in a campaign of racist, sexist harassment directed at Leslie Jones, a "Saturday Night Live" cast member. When Twitter suspended his account, Yiannopoulos denounced it as "cowardly" and declared himself a martyr for the cause of free speech. . . .
>
> The further fact of Yiannopoulos's fervent support for President Trump is not, then, surprising. Few figures in American history have better weaponized the imaginary grievances of entitled people who consider themselves oppressed than Trump has. This is precisely the reason the black-clad rioters among the protesters at Berkeley . . . served his ultimate interests. It was a tactical error that ignored everything 2016 should have taught us. . . .
>
> We are witnessing the rebirth of alchemy as a serious endeavor, an undertaking in which we transform abuse into victimhood, billionaires

into besieged outsiders, and the vulnerable into vectors of mass danger. It is no more empirically sound than the old mutations of lead into gold—but it is far more marketable. And it is far more dangerous than the inept rogues who showed up on Berkeley's campus that evening.[54]

RAGE AND GRIEF IN PORTLAND

Antifa made headlines again during the summer of 2020 when Derek Chauvin, a white police officer, murdered George Floyd, a Black man, prompting thousands of protests across the country, the vast majority of which were peaceful.[55] Portland, Oregon—the hip home of co-ops and bike lanes—became the poster child for Donald Trump's perverse effort to sell his followers on the idea that it was antifa and other left-wing groups that were causing an epidemic of violence in America. Portland protests of George Floyd's murder lasted an astonishing one hundred straight nights. Several times, the protests deteriorated into violence involving demonstrators versus the police or members of far-right groups, or both.

The Portland, Oregon, metropolitan area has a population of 2.2 million. About 641,000 people live within the city limits. Portland is the whitest large city in America, a surprising legacy with a grim background.[56] Oregon entered the Union in 1859 as a "whites-only" state because its laws banned African Americans (slaves and former slaves) from living within its boundaries even though the state constitution banned slavery. The economic motivation for the law was to protect white settlers who were granted free land by the federal government. In 1922, Portland's chief of police posed with hooded Ku Klux Klan members. During World War II, the city was the site of camps that imprisoned Japanese Americans.

More recently, far-right groups have proliferated in and around Portland. In the 1970s, Posse Comitatus—a Christian identity movement that was notoriously racist and anti-Semitic—launched from the city. The movement no longer exists, not because the people who shared those beliefs changed their mind but because Posse Comitatus was replaced by far-right groups with similar attitudes. In 2016, Joey Gibson, a man of Irish and Japanese descent who served time for felony theft, founded Patriot Prayer in Vancouver, Washington, a small city a short distance north of Portland. The group is avidly pro-Trump and has focused on fighting antifa. The Proud Boys militia, one of the leading groups in the January 6 insurrection, is also active in the area. Both groups have sponsored demonstrations in cities they consider too liberal throughout the Pacific Northwest and northern California.

Portland elects progressive Democrats and has a variety of nonviolent, left-leaning activists and organizations. The city is also home to Rose City Antifa, one of the oldest antifa groups in the nation. Like other liberal cities located in swing and red states (Madison, Wisconsin, and Austin, Texas, come to mind), Portland's progressive activists must navigate the considerable strain caused by periodic incursions of right-wing groups during times of trouble.

The relationship between the Portland police and left-wing activists has been troubled for years. In 2014, the Justice Department's Civil Rights Division reached a settlement with the Portland Police Bureau based on allegations that the police had used excessive force, especially against people with mental illness or suffering a mental health crisis.[57] Those claims were revived during the Floyd protests. About sixty officers were trained to respond to violence during demonstrations and they were spread thin. Compounding the situation, a few weeks after the protests started, the city council voted to cut $15 million out of the police budget in response to community groups that had lobbied for a cut of $50 million. During the Floyd protests, Portland police wove between intervening and standing down. When they intervened, they sometimes used excessive force. When they refused to intervene, they left protesters and provocateurs to fight each other with fists, clubs, pepper spray, and makeshift shields.

Trump soon realized that the sheer longevity of nightly protests and Portland's blue politics provided an opportunity to turn the city into a case study of bad government under liberal Democrats. In July, with the full cooperation of Attorney General William Barr, he deployed federal police from the Department of Homeland Security and the U.S. Marshals

Special Operations Group to Portland on the disingenuous excuse that protesters had congregated, night after night, near the federal courthouse in downtown Portland and his administration was determined to protect the building. People out on downtown streets late at night reported being seized by men wearing camouflage and thrown into unmarked vans.[58] Federal police arrested ninety protesters, charging them with a mix of felony and misdemeanor offenses. Once Trump was out of office, one-third of these cases were dismissed "with prejudice" (never to be reinstated).

On one particularly inauspicious evening, Portland resident Donavan LaBella was participating in a peaceful demonstration outside the federal courthouse. He was standing on the street across from the building holding a boombox over his head. Federal police fired a supposedly nonlethal munition, hitting him in the head, fracturing his skull, and causing serious brain injury. LaBella has sued the government for damages in federal court. The government is fighting to keep secret the names of federal officers on duty in Portland during the protests.

Investigative reporting published in 2021 revealed that in addition to the federal police, dozens of FBI employees were sent on temporary assignments to Portland.[59] The Trump administration was plagued by internal debate, with FBI intelligence agents insisting that white nationalists are the leading domestic terrorism threat versus Department of Homeland Security officials arguing that antifa and radical leftists should be the priority. Each week at national security briefings with the FBI, Barr demanded updates on antifa.

The low point of the Portland protests came in late August when a cavalcade of hundreds of trucks waving American and pro-Trump flags entered the city. Leaders of the truck brigade had planned to drive on highways around Portland, but some number veered off and drove downtown. They were received by black bloc demonstrators wearing helmets and brandishing makeshift pipes and other weapons. Scuffles broke out between the two groups, including the shooting of paintballs, spraying of toxic chemicals, assaults with makeshift clubs, and fistfights.

During the mayhem, antifa member Michael Reinoehl shot Aaron

Danielson, a Trump supporter and member of right-wing Patriot Prayer. Reinoehl was a constant presence at the protests who viewed his role as providing security for his fellow demonstrators, much like the Oath Keepers. After the shooting, he went into hiding. He gave an interview to Vice News to tell his side of the story, claiming that Danielson approached him holding a knife and that he fired in self-defense. Several days later, the federal Marshals Service discovered Reinoehl's location. As he got into his car, unmarked sport utility vehicles screeched to a halt in front of his bumper. The marshals jumped out, started to fire, and Reinoehl died on the pavement.

Several witnesses at the scene told reporters that they did not hear the marshals either identify themselves or give any warning before they fired thirty-seven rounds from two rifles and two handguns almost immediately after stopping their vehicles. Some of the bullets hit neighboring homes. Reinoehl had a handgun in his pocket but the only bullet fired from that gun was found inside his car.

Attorney General Barr called the operation a "significant accomplishment" that eliminated a "violent agitator."[60] Trump said "This guy was a violent criminal and the U.S. Marshals Service killed him. And I will tell you something, that's the way it has to be. There has to be retribution when you have crime like this."[61]

In a deeply troubling juxtaposition, four days before the Portland shooting, seventeen-year-old Kyle Rittenhouse appeared in Kenosha, Wisconsin, to serve as a self-appointed peacekeeper during protests over the nonfatal shooting of Jacob Blake, a Black man, by Rusten Sheskey, a white policeman. Rittenhouse was armed with an AK-15-style automatic rifle. In an interview with the far-right, twenty-four-hour news site the Daily Caller, which had been founded by Fox News commentator Tucker Carlson, Rittenhouse said, "People are getting injured and our job is to protect this business."[62]

Rittenhouse attracted a great deal of attention as he circulated through the streets with his gun and eventually attracted a group of men who tried to disarm him. He shot two dead and badly wounded a third. He was arrested peacefully at his home in Antioch, Illinois, the following day and went on trial for first-degree intentional homicide, among other felony charges. The jury acquitted him after four days of deliberations.

ANARCHIST JURISDICTIONS

The Trump effort to scapegoat antifa and distract attention from right-wing militia violence accelerated as the 2020 election heated up. Five days after George Floyd was murdered in May 2020, Trump said: "The memory of George Floyd is being dishonored by rioters, looters and anarchists. The violence and vandalism are being led by antifa and other radical left-wing groups who are terrorizing the innocent, destroying jobs, hurting businesses and burning down buildings."[63] He repeated the claim twenty times in the next three weeks, and his attack was amplified by allies online. He also threatened to designate antifa a "terrorist organization."[64]

In June 2020, as Black Lives Matter protests spread across the country, Trump tweeted: "I don't see any indication that there were any white supremacist groups mixing in. This is an ANTIFA Organization. It seems that the first time we saw it in a major way was Occupy Wall Street. It's the same mindset. @kilmeade @foxandfriends TRUE!"[65] Trump spoke about the protests the same day in the Rose Garden, identifying antifa as the leading instigator of intolerable violence:

> In recent days, our nation has been gripped by professional anarchists, violent mobs, arsonists, looters, criminals, rioters, Antifa, and others. A number of State and local governments have failed to take necessary action to safeguard their residents. Innocent people have been savagely beaten. . . .
>
> These are not acts of peaceful protest. These are acts of domestic terror. The destruction of innocent life and the spilling of innocent blood is an offense to humanity and a crime against God. . . .
>
> If a city or state refuses to take the actions that are necessary to defend the life and property of their residents, then I will deploy the United States military and quickly solve the problem for them.[66]

Sociologists Kerby Goff and John McCarthy set out to discover whether any factual basis existed for the claim that antifa had infiltrated Black Lives Matter.[67] They studied two databases that collect information on protest events in the U.S. and discovered 14,000 racial justice protests in 2020. Antifa was mentioned as present in thirty-seven. The researchers also discovered that when antifa did appear, the incidence of violence increased, whether or not a right-wing group was present. Further research by political scientists Erica Chenoweth and Jeremy Pressman showed that, dating back to 2017, Black Lives Matter protests were overwhelmingly peaceful.[68] Police made arrests in only 5 percent of the 7,305 events they studied, and protesters or bystanders were reportedly injured in 1.6 percent.

During a debate with Democratic candidate Joe Biden at the end of September 2020, moderator Chris Wallace at Fox News, asked Trump if he was willing to "condemn white supremacists and militia groups and to say that they need to stand down and not add to the violence in a number of these cities as we saw in Kenosha and we've seen in Portland."[69] Trump responded, "I would say almost everything I see is from the left wing not from the right wing."[70]

Conspiracy theories were also prominent in Trump's repertoire. During one of his frequent interviews with Fox News, Trump talked about an airplane "almost completely loaded with thugs, wearing these dark uniforms, black uniforms, with gear and this and that [linked to] people that are in the dark shadows [controlling] Joe Biden."[71] When severe wildfires broke out in Oregon, forcing forty thousand people to evacuate and killing nine, QAnon members picked up this narrative, promoting the false allegation that antifascists had started the fires. Frantic calls to 911 about antifa arsonists slowed evacuation efforts.

The nadir of this campaign was an incident in Buffalo, when two police officers, one holding a baton, pushed seventy-five-year-old Martin Gugino, a white man, to the ground during a peaceful protest of the Floyd killing. Gugino fell over backward, cracking his head open on the ground. As blood trickled from Gugino's right ear, the officers strode on without breaking stride. Trump tweeted: "Buffalo protester shoved by Police could be an ANTIFA provocateur. 75-year-old Martin Gugino was pushed away after appearing to scan police communications in order to black out the equipment. @OANN [One America News Network] I watched, he fell harder than was pushed. Was aiming scanner. Could be a set up?"[72] In fact, Gugino had a cell phone in his hand.

In August, Attorney General William Barr joined the chorus, accusing Black Lives Matter protestors of employing "fascistic" tactics. "They are a revolutionary group that is interested in some form of socialism, communism. . . . They're essentially Bolsheviks."[73] Barr alleged that Black Lives Matter had been corrupted by violent antifa members who were trying to push Trump out of office. He announced that the Justice Department had compiled a list of "anarchist jurisdictions" pursuant to a memorandum from the president. The list included New York City, Portland, and Seattle. Barr said,

> We cannot allow federal tax dollars to be wasted when the safety of the citizenry hangs in the balance. It is my hope that the cities identified by the Department of Justice today will reverse course and become serious about performing the basic function of government and start protecting their own citizens.[74]

A study conducted by the Center for International and Strategic Studies examined an original dataset of 893 terrorist plots and attacks in the United States between January 1994 and May 2020.[75] The data set was compiled by the START Global Terrorism Database (GTD), a project of the University of Maryland College Park, considered one of the best compendia of information about global terrorism in the world.[76] The researchers concluded that far-right terrorism has "significantly outpaced" terrorism from other categories of perpetrators.[77]

INSURRECTION

In the aftermath of the January 6 insurrection, Trump allies revived allegations that participants were actually affiliated with antifa. Within two days of the riot, Zignal Labs, a private company that has software capable of monitoring the content of social media communications across the internet, counted 411,099 mentions of antifa as causing or participating in the violence.[78] In testimony before the Senate Judiciary Committee, FBI director Christopher Wray said his agency had not developed any information that antifa, anarchists, or provocateurs opposed to Trump were present at the Capitol on January 6, 2021. Among the Trump base, the conspiracy theory persisted.

Severe problems between the police and the communities they serve have convinced both the far right and the far left that they must provide their own armed security at public events. Exacerbated by the nation's permissive gun laws, such circumstances are disasters waiting to happen. But antifa's calculus that if they brawl in the streets, they have a chance to defeat right-wing forces is deluded. It does not take much to become the target of a demagogue like Trump. If anything, recent history suggests fighting in the streets with an ill-defined enemy accelerates autocracy's spread.

NINE

SOLUTIONS

CITIZENS UNITED

None of the six interest groups profiled here has any incentive to moderate their war on government. Top-tier corporations, the Freedom Caucus in the House, the Federalist Society, Fox News and the Murdochs, white evangelicals, and far-right militia groups will continue as they have for the foreseeable future, waxing, waning, and waxing again.

A widespread, durable outbreak of grassroots violence could destabilize the economy to the point that the stock market and long-term business profitability are threatened. Or the Freedom Caucus could crash the economy by blocking extension of the debt ceiling and be pushed out of office. Donald Trump could win again and move the country into an autocracy. Any of those developments should motivate a critical mass of the largest and most influential corporations—by far the most powerful one of the six—to intervene in a constructive way. Yet their political infrastructure is so fragmented that they lack a reliable mechanism for organizing their response other than press statements that are here today and gone tomorrow.

One constituency of the six is likely to evolve in a more positive direction. Young, white evangelicals differ in attitudes and goals from their parents. They display more tolerance of racial differences, more concern about climate change, and less acceptance of rigid political loyalty to far-right Republicans. They are in the process of either trying to change the church from within or stepping away from worship. The numerous self-inflicted wounds that are weakening the Southern Baptist Convention should motivate those who want to stay in the church to push for strong reforms. But this trajectory could take years to develop.

The progressive response to the country's crises has failed miserably in some key areas. Chapter 8 chronicled the efforts of one of the most politically successful public interest lobbies, large national environmental groups, responding to their most important issue, climate change, by cutting an insider deal with a small group of CEOs. That strategy failed miserably. No grassroots movement has yet emerged that is capable of blunting the power of fossil fuel producers' resistance to mitigating climate change despite the increasingly rapid manifestation of symptoms from excessive heat to drought, floods, storms, and melting ice caps.

Deeply embedded in American culture is the idea that people should not complain about a problem without offering solutions. Finding solutions these days requires recognition of a conceptual fork in the road. You can go big and risk looking naïve, even foolish, because any significant proposal will not be feasible until, as Barack Obama once said, "we can break this fever."[1] Or you can go small and end up with a long list of very specific fixes that take more time to explain than they are worth discussing in a book intended for a general audience. As I reached the end of this book and it was time to develop a solution, I decided to go big by endorsing the elusive goal of reforming campaign finance rules. This book opens with a chapter on the huge amounts of money that large corporations spend on Capitol Hill, within the executive branch, and in the courts, and it seems fitting to end there as well. The tidal wave of money from the very rich has undermined the two most important prerequisites of a functioning democracy: voting and making laws. More than most other major reforms, this one has the potential to displace the clog of fury that paralyzes Congress.

This solution is out of reach at the moment for a few converging reasons. The highest hurdle is *Citizens United v. Federal Election Commission*, the most destructive Supreme Court decision ever written from the perspective of destabilizing American democracy.[2] By a vote of five to four, conservative justices granted corporations "personhood" under the First Amendment, making them equivalent to an individual person. Instead of talking about public policy and voting with their pocketbooks, which business leaders were doing already, corporations and people who made fortunes from business released a tidal wave of money into the electoral system, sabotaging the principle of one person, one vote. Of course, Congress could lessen the corrupting impact of the money, but it is gridlocked for the foreseeable future because Democratic politicians believe they cannot afford to disarm without a guarantee that Republicans would be compelled to follow suit and vice versa.

If it became possible to restore constraints on donations from dark money sources and megadonors and increase federal matching shares for candidates on a bipartisan basis, the internet provides the technology to make small donations possible. All we would need then is the will to restore the principles that in the United States, individual people choose their leaders, voting has consequences, campaign funding is in equipoise, and only human beings are people for the purposes of the Constitution's Bill of Rights.

THE GRIM LEGACY OF CITIZENS UNITED

Citizens United was decided by a five-to-four vote in 2010, two years into Obama's first term and the year of his first midterm election, which went quite badly. The conservative justices in the majority—Kennedy, Roberts, Scalia, Thomas, and Alito—faced off against four liberal dissenters—Stevens, Breyer, Ginsburg, and Sotomayor. Justice Anthony Kennedy was the swing vote and authored the opinion. The upshot of the decision was that so long as donors neither contributed directly to a candidate nor coordinated with the candidate's campaign, they could spend unlimited amounts of money to steer election outcomes. *Citizens United* inflicted savage damage on members of Congress, who were already struggling to raise the mounting expenses of campaigns. The flood of money caused those costs to reach unprecedented levels, with the result that candidates spent more and more time raising money.

The case arose out of a 2008 film styled as a feature-length documentary and titled *Hillary: The Movie*. It was produced by Citizens United, a right-wing, nonprofit corporation led by David Bossie, a conservative activist who became Donald Trump's deputy campaign manager in 2016. Clinton was a candidate for president and the movie consisted of intensely negative propaganda regarding her fitness for the office. *Hillary: The Movie* was distributed in theaters and on DVDs, but Citizens United also wanted to show it through video-on-demand in the weeks right before the election. This last aspiration was illegal under existing campaign finance laws. Bossie decided to go to court to challenge those requirements. His case took a long time to reach the Supreme Court, as these matters typically do, and the decision was not issued until Obama beat Clinton in the primaries and became president.

The law at stake was the Bipartisan Campaign Reform Act of 2002, nicknamed McCain-Feingold after its two principal authors, senators John McCain (R-AZ) and Russ Feingold (D-WI). Citizens United challenged provisions of the law that regulated campaign contributions made by for-profit corporations. The law prohibited campaign ads and other forms of communications during the thirty days before a primary if the ads advocated election of specific candidates and might reach at least fifty thousand people.[3] Citizens United was a nonprofit corporation but a small portion of the money used to make the movie was donated by for-profit corporations. If the movie was shown through video-on-demand, it might reach audiences totaling more than fifty thousand people.

Before *Citizens United*, for-profit corporations had many legal routes to influence elections. They could create political action committees, or PACs, that donated directly to candidates and coordinated with their campaigns. The Congress of Industrial Organizations, an organization representing labor unions, created the first PAC in 1943 to support Franklin Roosevelt's reelection campaign. As discussed in chapter 2, after the Powell memo circulated in the early 1970s, for-profit corporate PACs grew quickly. For-profit corporations are also allowed to spend unlimited amounts on "issue advertising." Paying for ads that feature hot-button problems like a weak economy, crime, the operation of public schools, or social issues like abortion gives corporations significant influence over elections. Given all these avenues for spending their money, the thirty-day restriction was a relatively small restraint until the five-justice majority turned it into a crossroads for constitutional law.

The Supreme Court could have handed a victory to Citizens United on narrower grounds, sidestepping the Constitution entirely. For example, the five justices in the majority could have explored the option of exempting the movie because for-profit corporations contributed only a very small amount of its funding. True, Citizens United had lost its case before the Federal Election Commission, the agency that implemented and enforced McCain-Feingold. But the Supreme Court issues opinions correcting agencies on their interpretations of the law all the time.

Two additional legal norms supported a narrow ruling. A mere seven years before Bossie petitioned to have his case heard by the Supreme Court, the Court had reaffirmed cases holding that corporations did not have First Amendment rights.[4] Under the judge-crafted doctrine of stare decisis, meaning the practice of leaving precedents settled if at all possible, a narrow interpretation confined to the specific facts of Citizen United's situation would preserve that conclusion, doing far less damage. Second, the well-established avoidance doctrine, meaning the principle of refraining from deciding cases on constitutional grounds if at all possible, supported a decision handing Citizens United a victory without confronting the First Amendment's application to all corporations. Instead, the majority made the case into a blockbuster, concluding that the thirty-day restriction undercut vital, irreplaceable free speech interests:

> The Court cannot resolve this case on a narrower ground without chilling

> political speech, speech that is central to the meaning and purpose of the First Amendment. . . . Speech is an essential mechanism of democracy, for it is the means to hold officials accountable to the people. . . . Premised on mistrust of governmental power, the First Amendment stands against attempts to disfavor certain subjects or viewpoints.[5]

Once it had turned the case into a constitutional challenge, another extraordinarily important barrier remained for the majority to traverse. The judicial litmus test for assessing the constitutionality of campaign finance law was whether the restrictions imposed by the law served the permissible purpose of preventing corruption or the appearance of corruption that might arise between the donor and the candidate if the candidate won and took office. The cause and effect seem intuitive. Donors contribute not only to affect an election's results. They hope to gain access to and influence over victorious candidates once they become officeholders and have power. When candidates become officeholders, they can do favors for large donors, increasing the likelihood that they continue to receive similar donations for future campaigns. So, common sense would suggest, if donations buy such access or influence, the government should step in and level the playing field by limiting those contributions.

The most disturbing aspect of Justice Kennedy's majority opinion was its reality-defying definition of corruption. He described his test for contributions that could be prohibited consistent with the First Amendment as "quid pro quo corruption." The familiar Latin phrase in his view meant literally exchanging X for Y immediately:

> The fact that [donors] may have influence over or access to elected officials does not mean that these officials are corrupt. . . . The appearance of influence or access, furthermore, will not cause the electorate to lose faith in our democracy. By definition, an independent expenditure is political speech presented to the electorate that is not coordinated with a candidate. . . . Independent expenditures do not lead to, or create the appearance of, quid pro quo corruption. In fact, there is only scant evidence that

> independent expenditures even ingratiate. Ingratiation and access, in any event, are not corruption.[6]

Or, in other words, if a donor contributes a large sum to a candidate without coordinating with the candidate's campaign and the candidate is elected to office—say, to a congressional office in the district where the donor's company is headquartered—the newly elected candidate will not try to keep the donor happy by doing favors. Instead, the opinion assumed that candidates do not know or do not care about the sources of large donations made during a campaign and that donors do not have the opportunity to visit with candidates at a variety of events during the campaign and afterwards, making requests for help. The new standard seemed to require evidence of communications between a candidate and a donor where they literally exchange money for specific votes. This read of human nature is as unrealistic as any ever proposed by the Supreme Court. As important, it does not reflect what the average American thinks is going on as verified by opinion polls explained shortly.

The only sliver of light in the opinion was its unabashed embrace of disclosure as a preferable remedy to constraints on donations:

> A campaign finance system that pairs corporate independent expenditures with effective disclosure has not existed before today. . . . With the advent of the Internet, prompt disclosure of expenditures can provide shareholders and citizens with the information needed to hold corporations and elected officials accountable for their positions and supporters. . . . The First Amendment protects political speech; and disclosure permits citizens and shareholders to react to the speech of corporate entities in a proper way. This transparency enables the electorate to make informed decisions and give proper weight to different speakers and messages.[7]

Unfortunately, as the decision was implemented on the ground, disclosure bit the dust.

Kennedy concluded with the astounding statement that the Supreme

Court was compelled to enter the campaign spending debate because existing laws could be used to ban the famous 1939 film *Mr. Smith Goes to Washington*, starring Jimmy Stewart. He wrote:

> When word concerning the plot of the movie *Mr. Smith Goes to Washington* reached the circles of Government, some officials sought, by persuasion, to discourage its distribution. Under [the precedent set in] *Austin*, though, officials could have done more than discourage its distribution—they could have banned the film. After all, [*Mr. Smith Goes to Washington*], like *Hillary*, was speech funded by a corporation that was critical of Members of Congress. *Mr. Smith Goes to Washington* may be fiction and caricature; but fiction and caricature can be a powerful force.[8]

Or, in other words, because a handful of members of Congress disliked being caricatured in a Hollywood movie, for-profit corporations needed First Amendment rights that would allow them to make unrestricted contributions under broad circumstances.

The case Justice Kennedy cited to illustrate the stupidity of existing law was *Austin v. Michigan Chamber of Commerce*, decided by the Court two decades earlier by a vote of six to three.[9] The majority opinion in that case was written by Justice Thurgood Marshall, who was joined by Chief Justice William Rehnquist and Justices William Brennan, Byron White, Harry Blackmun, and John Paul Stevens, with Justices Kennedy, O'Connor, and Scalia in dissent. The opinion upheld a Michigan law that barred for-profit corporations from using their "treasury money"—generally any money they earned from their business activities—for "independent contributions" to support or oppose candidates.

Justice Marshall's majority opinion upheld the Michigan law because the majority was worried about "the corrosive and distorting effects of immense aggregations of wealth that are accumulated with the help of the corporate form and that have little or no correlation to the public's support for the corporation's political ideas."[10] He said the circumstances of the case led the Court to identify

> as a serious danger the significant possibility that corporate political expenditures will undermine the integrity of the political process, and it has implemented a narrowly tailored solution to that problem. By requiring corporations to make all independent political expenditures through a separate fund made up of money solicited expressly for political purposes, the Michigan Campaign Finance Act reduces the threat that huge corporate treasuries amassed with the aid of favorable state laws will be used to influence unfairly the outcome of elections.[11]

Justice Kennedy is not the only member of the Supreme Court to make extreme, borderline irrational statements in an opinion. But his prediction was a whopper as these things go. Using a well-reasoned, strong majority opinion signed by a diverse group of justices to predict the appearance of an all-powerful censor in Hollywood the next time members of Congress got upset about being caricatured in a movie surely must be a-bridge-too-far reasoning at the highest level of judicial law.

It is not an exaggeration to say that the four judges voting in the minority were horrified by the majority opinion. Justice Stevens, writing for the dissenting four, accused the majority of operating "with a sledgehammer rather than a scalpel" in striking down one of Congress's "most significant efforts to regulate the role that corporations and unions play in electoral politics" and "compounds the offense by . . . striking down a great many state laws as well."[12] The dissenters said that the majority was relying on a flawed interpretation of the law when it insisted that the First Amendment prohibits regulatory distinctions based on a speaker's identity:

> The basic premise underlying the Court's ruling is . . . the proposition that the First Amendment bars regulatory distinctions based on a speaker's identity, including its "identity" as a corporation. While that glittering generality has rhetorical appeal, it is not a correct statement of the law. . . . The conceit that corporations must be treated identically to natural persons in the political sphere is not only inaccurate but also inadequate to justify the Court's disposition of this case. . . .

> Although they make enormous contributions to our society, corporations are not actually members of it. They cannot vote or run for office. Because they may be managed and controlled by nonresidents, their interests may conflict in fundamental respects with the interests of eligible voters.[13]

To bolster this point, the dissent offered a list of examples where speech is restricted on the basis of identity.[14] Members of the military enjoy the right to free speech, but not in certain circumstances, such as when they are preparing for battle. Civil servants employed by the federal government are prohibited from engaging in federal election campaigns. Foreign nationals may not, directly or indirectly, make contributions to specific candidates or provide independent expenditures in any American election. Students are not entitled to the same freedom of speech in school as adults enjoy in other settings. Prisoners are constrained in how they may speak while serving their time.

As for the majority's crabbed definition of corruption:

> The difference between selling a vote and selling access is a matter of degree, not kind. And selling access is not qualitatively different from giving special preference to those who spend money on one's behalf. Corruption operates along a spectrum, and the majority's apparent belief that quid pro quo arrangements can be neatly demarcated from other improper influences does not accord with the theory or reality of politics.[15]

The upshot was that the majority's "blinkered and aphoristic approach to the First Amendment" will "undoubtedly cripple the ability of ordinary citizens, Congress, and the States to adopt even limited measures to protect against corporate domination of the electoral process. Americans may be forgiven if they do not feel the Court has advanced the cause of good government today."[16]

The reach of the *Citizens United* decision grew as the lower federal courts applied the decision to other aspects of campaign funding. *Speech-*

Now.org v. Federal Election Commission, decided by the Court of Appeals for the District of Columbia Circuit months after *Citizens United*, gave birth to super PACs when it concluded that individuals, corporations, and labor unions could make unlimited contributions to those organizations so long as they did not coordinate their activities with candidates.[17] *McCutcheon v. Federal Election Commission*, decided in 2014 by another five-to-four vote, invalidated aggregate limits on dollars donated over a two-year period.[18]

As for the impact of *Citizens United* and its progeny on public confidence in government, the dissenters were right. In 2019, an ambitious Gallup poll measured public satisfaction with respect to twenty-two aspects of the "state of the nation."[19] The highest ranked attribute was military strength and preparedness, with 78 percent of respondents satisfied. The lowest was the nation's campaign finance laws, with 80 percent dissatisfied. A second poll by Scott Rasmussen for RealClear Politics found that 53 percent of voters believe political corruption is a "crisis in the United States, while 36 percent believe it is a significant problem but not a crisis. . . . This is truly an issue that cuts across partisan and demographic lines."[20]

WE THE PEOPLE VERSUS OR "WE THE CORPORATIONS"?[21]

As devastating as it proved to electoral politics, *Citizens United* did not spring forth instantly. The history of this deeply destructive precedent is long, surprising, and important to know. In 2018, law professor Adam Winkler published a history of how American corporations fought a long and successful campaign to win their constitutional rights.[22] He opens his account in 1882, when former senator Roscoe Conkling (R-NY) argued before the Supreme Court on behalf of his client, the Southern Pacific Railroad. Conkling was challenging a decision by the California state legislature to deny railroads the opportunity to deduct their debts from the taxable value of their property. The deduction was available to individual Californians. Conkling argued that the ratifiers of the Fourteenth Amendment intended its grant of equal protection to "persons" to apply to corporations and not just individual people. If corporations were entitled to the same protection, California's financial penalty could not stand.

Conkling had special influence on the point because he had participated in the drafting of the Fourteenth Amendment. He produced a personal journal containing what he claimed were his contemporaneous notes made while the text of the amendment was drafted. The Supreme Court's decision in *Santa Clara County v. Southern Pacific Railroad Company* did not squarely address the application of the Fourteenth Amendment to corporations.[23] But a headnote written by the reporter who recorded the judges' decisions confirmed that Conkling had prevailed on the point. No final ruling was ever entered in Southern Pacific's case, but the Court assumed that it meant corporations were entitled to Fourteenth Amendment rights, and subsequent cases were decided on that basis.

"In the years that followed," Winkler writes, "the Supreme Court would invoke those corporate rights to invalidate numerous laws governing how businesses were to be run, supervised, and taxed."[24] Conkling's case was one among many lawsuits of similar import, even though the Fourteenth Amendment was inspired by the need to guarantee equal protection to freed slaves. Between 1868, when the amendment was ratified, and 1912, the Supreme Court decided twenty-eight cases dealing with the rights of African Americans and "an astonishing 312 cases dealing with the rights of corporations."[25]

Winkler concludes that *Citizens United* was the culmination of the corporate rights movement and cautions that "it would be a mistake to view *Citizens United* as a novelty, as an ungrounded intervention of the Roberts Court with little basis in law or history. . . . While corporate rights reached new heights with *Citizens United*, the scaffolding had been built up over two centuries of Supreme Court decisions."[26]

President Obama, who taught constitutional law at the University of Chicago for twelve years, understood the implications of the opinion as soon as he read it. A few days later, he took the opportunity of his State of the Union Address to openly rebuke the Supreme Court justices in attendance:

> With all due deference to separation of powers, last week the Supreme Court reversed a century of law that I believe will open the floodgates for special interests—including foreign corporations—to spend without limit in our elections. I don't think American elections should be bankrolled by America's most powerful interests, or worse, by foreign entities. They should be decided by the American people.[27]

The remarks triggered enthusiastic applause from Democratic members of Congress sitting in the House chamber to hear the speech, and a visible frown from Justice Alito, who mouthed the words "not true."[28]

A few weeks later, Chief Justice John Roberts announced that he was "'very troubled' by the 'setting, circumstance and decorum' of the State of the Union speech because the justices were forced to sit expressionless while Congress 'literally surrounds them,' at times cheering and hollering."[29] He added, "To the extent the State of the Union has degenerated into a political pep rally, I'm not sure why we are there."[30] As it turned out, decorum aside and politics front and center, Obama's criticism was understated.

Representative Jim Leach (D-IA) was one of the last moderate Republicans to serve in Congress. In an article entitled "*Citizens United*: Robbing America of Its Democratic Idealism," he wrote in 2013:

> Brazenly, in *Citizens United*, the Court employed parallel logic to the syllogism embedded in the most repugnant ruling it ever made, the 1857 Dred Scott decision. To justify slavery, the Court in Dred Scott defined a class of human beings as private property. To magnify corporate power a century-and-a-half later, it defined a class of private property (corporations) as people. Ironies abound. Despite overwhelming evidence to the contrary, the mid-nineteenth-century Court could see no oppression in an institution that allowed individuals to be bought and sold. In the Citizens United ruling, despite overwhelming evidence to the contrary, the Court implied that corporations were somehow oppressed—in this case considered to be censored—and therefore should be freed to buy political influence and sell opposing candidates down a river of nega-

tivity. . . .

To advance the sophistic argument that more money in campaigns equates to more democracy, the Court had to employ a linguistic gyration. It presumed that *money* is *speech* and that a *corporation* is an *individual*. But where in any dictionary or in any found documents are these equivalencies made?[31]

"THE WILD WEST WORLD OF POLITICAL MONEY"[32]

After *Citizens United*, *SpeechNow*, and *McCutcheon*, three entirely predictable things happened.

The incoming tide of campaign contributions rose and rose and has yet to crest. Elections have become so expensive that fundraising is an inescapable priority for candidates, especially new ones. The following figures come from the website OpenSecrets, run by the Center for Responsive Politics, the preeminent nonprofit group that tracks political contributions.[33] In 2008, two years before the *Citizens United* decision, the aggregate cost of congressional races was $3.4 billion but by 2012, when the Tea Party stormed Congress, those costs had risen to $4.7 billion. A decade after the decision, costs had taken another, massive jump. Congressional races cost $9.9 billion in 2020. The total cost of the presidential election jumped from $3.4 billion in 2012 to $6.5 billion in 2020.

Super PACs became ubiquitous, used by both parties in wars of attrition. They are required to identify the groups and individuals that donate money; they file tax returns; and they must remain independent from the campaigns of specific candidates. But federal enforcement in this area is rare and noncompliance blatant. Convincing evidence has emerged that super PACs coordinate behind the scenes. Often, former campaign staff or political operatives who worked with the candidates in Congress take the top jobs at super PACs and communicate informally on strategies, tactics, and timing. For example, in the 2022 election cycle, moderate incumbent representative Kurt Schrader (D-OR) was facing a threat from his left in his upcoming primary. He wanted to send a message to the outside groups supporting him that it was time to go on the attack. On an obscure corner of his website, he inserted an inconspicuous red box that proposed a strategy for discrediting his challenger and sported a link to an opposition-research document about her qualifications. A super PAC funded by the pharmaceutical industry began running television ads that tracked the Schrader materials. Shane Goldmacher, the *New York Times* reporter who broke the story, wrote:

> The practice is both brazen and breathtakingly simple. To work around the prohibition on directly coordinating with super PACs, candidates are posting their instructions to them inside the red boxes on public pages that super PACs continuously monitor.
>
> The boxes highlight the aspects of candidates' biographies that they want amplified and the skeletons in their opponents' closets that they want exposed.[34]

Goldmacher added that Republicans "work hand in glove with their super PACs, too, but in different ways."[35] When Republican J. D. Vance, author of the best-selling book *Hillbilly Elegy: A Memoir of a Family and Culture in Crisis*, ran successfully for an Ohio Senate seat in 2022, he outsourced polling.[36] The super PAC supporting him, which was funded by a $15 million contribution from conservative Silicon Valley investor Peter Thiel, posted the polling data it gathered on an unpublicized Medium page that Vance campaign staff accessed constantly.

Often, donors who wish to remain anonymous give their money to what are known as 501(c)(4)s after the section of the tax code that authorizes them.[37] These nonprofit corporations must file tax returns but are not obligated to reveal the identities of their donors. In effect, donor identities become secret when the money is first given to the 501(c)(4) and remain secret when the money lands in a super PAC bank account. This practice of donating while keeping the name of the donor secret is commonly referred to as "dark money."

Dark money donors have a variety of reasons for remaining anonymous. People with a high profile in public-facing corporations may not want to attract attention for donations that could seem controversial. As grateful as recipients of the money may be, they often prefer not to reveal the association. Election-related spending by dark money groups ballooned to $4.5 billion in the decade following *Citizens United*, more than six times what had been spent in this category in the two decades before the decision.

Super PACs come and go, reorganizing and renaming, emerging and receding. As of October 24, 2023, 2,476 groups organized as super PACs operated in American elections, reporting total receipts of $2.7 billion and total expenditures of $1.36 billion in the 2021–2022 election cycle.[38] Conservative groups provided 60 percent of that money, while liberal groups contributed 34 percent.[39] But these discrepancies between conservative and liberal percentages must be qualified by the fact that the 2020 national election cycle drew $1 billion in dark money.[40] The dark money raised by liberal groups was 257 percent more than the offsetting funds raised by conservative groups, $514 million to $200 million. This development was likely an outlier brought on by widespread fear among Democrats and independents that Trump would win reelection.

Although corporations were perceived as the focus of *Citizens United* at the time, a different phenomenon soon began to emerge—very wealthy individuals, dubbed "megadonors," contributed far more than corporations. During the 2022 midterm election cycle, the top ten wealthy individual donors contributed $642 million. At the top of the list were conservatives Sheldon and Miriam Adelson, who donated $215 million, and liberal Michael Bloomberg, who gave $152.5 million.

When asked to explain the significance of these developments, Sheila Krumholz, the executive director of the Center for Responsive Politics said that "this is a crucial sector of the contribution base because they are able to nimbly put in whatever amounts are needed at any moment."[41] Although both parties have billionaire supporters, Republicans have more. Of the top twenty-five donors in the most recent midterm cycle, eighteen are Republicans. Billionaires contribute 20 percent of total Republican donations and 14.5 percent of Democratic money.

DIALING FOR DOLLARS

All this money-bundling through super PACs, megadonors, and reliance on dark money has exacerbated congressional dysfunction to the breaking point. According to Issue One, a bipartisan organization of two hundred former governors, ambassadors, and members of Congress that works on election and voting issues, the average senator up for reelection in 2020 raised an average of $19,100 a day, and the typical House member raised $2,400.[42] In a toss-up race, the typical House member was compelled to raise $7,200 a day.

In addition to funding their own races, members must contribute large sums to party war chests if they want to receive coveted committee assignments or rise in the leadership.[43] Committee chairmanships and ranking member status (the leading member from the minority party on a committee) are scored A, B, or C by party leaders.[44] Top positions—for example, the chairmanship of appropriations or financial services—can mean a levy of as much as $2 million–$3 million.

Raising money on property owned by the federal government is illegal, so both parties have set up call centers where members spend many hours each week "dialing for dollars." *Sixty Minutes* reporter Norah O'Donnell interviewed Congressman Rick Nolan (D-MN), who served three terms in 2013–2019. Nolan said that "both parties have told newly elected members of the Congress that they should spend 30 hours a week in the Republican and Democratic call centers across the street from the Congress, dialing for dollars."[45] *Sixty Minutes* disclosed a leaked script for such a call prepared by the National Republican Congressional Committee (NRCC).[46] David Jolly, a former Republican from Florida, had the following exchange with O'Donnell:

> Jolly: We sat behind closed doors at one of the party headquarter back rooms in front of a white board where the equation was drawn out. You have six months until the election. Break that down to having to raise $2 million in the next six months. And your job, new member of

> Congress, is to raise $18,000 a day. Your first responsibility is to make sure you hit $18,000 a day.
>
> O'Donnell: How were you supposed to raise $18,000 a day?
>
> Jolly: Simply by calling people, cold-calling a list that fundraisers put in front of you, you're presented with their biography. So please call John. He's married to Sally. His daughter, Emma, just graduated from high school. They gave $18,000 last year to different candidates. They can give you $1,000 too if you ask them to. And they put you on the phone. And it's a script.

Jolly added that the work schedule for Congress was arranged around hours that were convenient for such calls. During the 117th Congress, which ran from January 3, 2021, to January 3, 2023, the House met for 160 days in 2021 and 112 days in 2022, and the Senate met for 158 days in 2021 and 171 days in 2022. These meager schedules set both institutions up to fail even if their many other problems were resolved.

The dominance of super PACs does not always lead to sensible political decisions that win votes or, for that matter, improve the diversity of Congress. About two thousand people have served in the Senate since it was created in 1787. A vanishingly small number have been people of color—fourteen Hispanic and eleven African American over the entire period, despite the fact that Hispanic people make up 18.9 percent of the population, and Black Americans 13.6 percent, for a total of 32.5 percent. Even discounting the number of people of all races who are living in the nation illegally, the inconsistencies are troubling and have a great deal to do with how campaigns are funded. A 2022 paper by political scientists Jacob Grumbach, Alexander Sahn, and Sarah Staszak concluded that Black and Hispanic shares of donors are far smaller than their shares of the population, and that these disparities are reflected in candidates selected.[47]

Democracy in Color, a nonprofit focused on political strategy and analysis at the intersection of race and politics, asked Democratic super PACs active in the 2020 national elections how they were deploying their money and submitted the answers to a team of data scientists and political experts for analysis.[48] The report focused on four criteria: whether the super PAC provided adequate information to contributors regarding its strategic plans, geographic information about where it was targeting spending, the demographics of the people it targeted, and the rigor of the data supporting spending decisions.

The report explained that 46 percent of Democratic voters were people of color in the 2016 national election, and that seven million teenagers of color have reached eighteen years of age since that election. But the Democrats' Senate Majority PAC, which raised $166.7 million for the 2020 election cycle, had not spent any money in Georgia, where a Black candidate, Raphael Warnock, ended up winning. Instead, it wasted money on races in Iowa, which was considered hopeless, and Michigan, where the Democratic candidate was eight points ahead.

THE NUCLEAR OPTION

Amending the Constitution would be the most effective way to reverse *Citizens United*, but the risks of making other crucial problems worse are too high to undertake such arduous and uncertain effort. The Constitution establishes two paths to add amendments, both devised to make any but the most innocuous, consensus changes difficult. The first requires two-thirds of House members and two-third of senators to propose an amendment.[49] If approved by the legislatures of three-fourths of the states, the amendment is ratified and added to the Constitution. This process produced all the twenty-seven amendments added so far.

Alternatively, the legislatures of two-thirds of the states may call a convention for proposing amendments.[50] Whatever amendments are developed during the convention become part of the Constitution if approved by three-fourths of state legislatures. This approach produced the Constitution in 1789 but has never been implemented from start to finish again.

Over the last two decades, a small group of academics, pundits, and activists have debated the merits of convening a constitutional convention.[51] Because the Constitution does not address the qualifications or the number of participants allowed to attend or the procedures for reaching a final decision, the possibility of a "runaway convention" is a significant risk, especially because the two political parties have such different ideas about the content of amendments that would be offered.[52]

Conservatives have argued for an amendment to require that federal budgets be balanced, jeopardizing social welfare programs. Far-right participants could advance proposals to eliminate the separation of church and state or increase protection of gun rights. Liberals would urge amendments to protect a woman's right to abortion and the rights of women and LGBTQ people in general. Because the two sides of our polarized political system have too much to lose and no way to control the outcome, a constitutional convention is unlikely to happen in the foreseeable future.

THE FOR THE PEOPLE ACT

At the beginning of the 117th Congress, convened just as Trump was leaving office, Democrats introduced the For the People Act as S. 1 in the Senate and H.R. 1 in the House.[53] The designation "1" means that the leadership of both houses orchestrated the introduction of the bill as the first of the session intending to emphasize the legislation's importance. The House passed the legislation on a party line vote of 220–210 on March 3, 2021. But when Majority Leader Chuck Schumer (D-NY) brought it up on the Senate floor, Republicans blocked it with a filibuster threat. Because this scenario could happen again until and unless the filibuster is abolished and Democrats hold the House, the Senate, and the White House, the effort seems fruitless. Nevertheless, the legislation was constructed by the best advocates for deep set campaign finance reform and if it survived mostly intact, it would go long way to solving the problems explained above.

Both parties take full advantage of dark money, super PACs, loopholes, and lack of IRS enforcement. But Democratic candidates are most often on the losing end of campaign financing. Biden's experience of raising significantly more dark money than Trump in 2020 was an outlier. An OpenSecrets chart compared the top ten 501(c)(4) groups and the total amounts they raised during 2008–2014, a period covering two national and two midterm elections. In ninth place was the only "liberal" (likely to support Democrats) group—the League of Conservation Voters, which contributed $28 million.[54] The nine conservative groups contributed $548.8 million.

Republican opposition to H.R. 1 was likely motivated by one of the party's most important donors, Charles Koch and Koch Industries, the corporate powerhouse he built with his now-deceased brother David. Soon after the For the People Act was introduced in the Senate, *New Yorker* reporter Jane Mayer wrote an article about a leaked recording of a private conference call to discuss the legislation.[55] Participants included Steve Donaldson, a policy adviser to minority leader Mitch McConnell, and Kyle McKenzie, the research director for the Koch-run group Stand Together.

McKenzie told the group he had a "spoiler" to discuss—namely, the popularity of the legislation when it was described in neutral terms, adding that a "very large chunk of conservatives [are] supportive of these types of efforts."[56] He added that focus groups found a message "condemning billionaires buying elections" to be "most convincing, and it riled them up the most."[57] To stop the legislation, the group of allies would have to rely on "under-the-dome-type strategies"—namely, the filibuster—because turning public opinion could be "incredibly difficult."[58] Donaldson told the group, "When it comes to donor privacy, I can't stress how quickly things could get out of hand. . . . We have to hold our people together."[59] He predicted that the fight over the legislation is going to be a long and messy one, but he did not expect McConnell to back down.[60]

The For the People Act contains reforms in five areas: voting rights, election security, congressional redistricting or gerrymandering, campaign finance, and ethical reforms applicable to lobbying the White House, the courts, and Congress. The campaign finance provisions include federal matching shares for elections, disclosure of dark money donors, ending coordination between super PACs, and restructuring the Federal Election Commission (FEC). (The following references to H.R. 1 also apply to S. 1.) The legislation opens with blunt findings regarding *Citizens United* that explain why Congress is writing the law: "The Supreme Court's misinterpretation of the Constitution to empower monied interests at the expense of the American people in elections has seriously eroded over 100 years of congressional action to promote fairness and protect elections from the toxic influence of money."[61]

MATCHING SHARES FOR SMALL DONATIONS

Between 1976 and 2008, almost every major presidential candidate took advantage of the federal matching share program.[62] The law limited a candidate's overall spending to $45 million, a reasonable sum in what now look like the good old days. *Citizens United* was decided in 2010. In 2016, Martin O'Malley, the former Democratic governor of Maryland, made headlines when he tried to resuscitate his flagging presidential campaign by taking federal funds. An analyst with the Sunlight Foundation, a group that focuses on transparency in politics, summed it up bluntly: "So while taking public financing was once a sign that a candidate was a serious player, or at least had a broad base of support in a number of states, it's now an indication that a candidate can't hope to compete financially."[63]

New candidates face serious barriers to entry. An analysis by the Brennan Center for Justice released in August 2022 found that in the House, Republicans had 178 safe seats and Democrats 177.[64] Such analyses do not account for the need to assemble a war chest to discourage primary challenges from people who are members of one's own party, and this method of threat is used to keep conservative but not quite conservative enough Republican members in line.

H.R. 1 offered congressional and presidential candidates the opportunity to apply for matching shares based on small—up to $200—donations they receive from individual voters. Candidates in primaries and elections were invited to opt into the system. Matching shares were offered at a six-to-one ratio. For example, a single $200 donation would receive a matching share of $1,200, or a $1,400 total return. The proposal would encourage campaigns to concentrate on what Michael Waldman, president of the Brennan Center for Justice, called "the most encouraging trend in campaign fundraising, the rise of small donors."[65] Almost half the money donated to President Obama's 2012 reelection campaign came from people who gave $200 or less.

The Congressional Budget Office, which develops cost estimates for provisions in federal legislation, estimated that the H.R. 1 matching share program would cost about $475 million annually. To avoid spending general taxpayer money on the program, the bill imposed a 4.75 percent surcharge on criminal fines and civil and administrative penalties assessed against corporate defendants and their executive officers and collected by the federal government. In the absence of this requirement, the money would be transferred into general funds supervised by the Treasury Department. The Justice Department has assessed billions of dollars in settlements with large companies in several recent cases, including $5 billion against Facebook for mishandling users' personal information, $4.9 billion against the Royal Bank of Scotland for misleading investors prior to the 2008 market crash, $4.3 billion against Volkswagen for cheating on diesel emission tests, and $5.5 billion against BP for damages caused by the Deepwater Horizon oil spill.

DARK MONEY DISCLOSURE

Existing law allows funding entities to keep donor names secret unless the funds are used to expressly advocate for or oppose the election of specific candidates *and* are coordinated with the candidates they support. This constraint is easily circumvented by airing negative ads that do not urge viewers to vote for the subject of the ad. In 2020, according to the Campaign Legal Center, "Major dark-money groups spent tens of millions of dollars on TV ads that promoted or attacked candidates without expressly telling viewers to 'vote for' or 'vote against' the candidate."[66] For example, the Republican dark money group American Action Network ran TV ads prior to the sixty-day window that praised three House incumbents running for reelection and attacked House Speaker Nancy Pelosi's "extreme agenda."[67] A Democratic dark money group Majority Forward also ran TV ads, including one in North Carolina attacking Republican senator Thom Tillis and urging voters to "tell Thom Tillis: Stop cutting healthcare and put our families first."[68]

H.R. 1 would close these loopholes by requiring disclosure of contributors' identity to the FEC whenever dark money groups spend over $10,000 on paid advertising at any time that "promotes or supports . . . or attacks or opposes the election of a named candidate."[69] The disclosures must include each "disbursement" of campaign funds, the names of the people who control the group, and the names of all other donors. Most ads cost considerably more and would exceed the $10,000 limit.

A second justification for disclosure is to prevent dark money contributions by foreign governments. The most notorious example is Russian operatives who paid for internet ads "focused on stoking and amplifying social discord in the U.S. electorate; lowering turnout (especially among Black voters); and, once Donald Trump became the Republican nominee, helping him defeat Hillary Clinton."[70]

The FEC has opined that dark money groups need only disclose donors who explicitly say their contributions are made to further specific independent expenditures the group intends to make (independent in the sense that they are not coordinated with a candidate) or electioneering communications (again, those made to oppose or support the election of a specific candidate). Donors who make open-ended contributions without mentioning these end points remain anonymous. Courts have struck down the FEC interpretation, but the agency has not bothered to issue a new rule mandating disclosure. The legislation corrects this problem by mandating disclosure if a group spends more than $10,000 on political ads and it has donors that each contribute more than $10,000. Donors can sidestep this requirement if they specify that their money should not be used for any campaign-related ads.[71]

As mentioned earlier, during the 2020 election cycle, dark money groups gave $660 million to super PACs, and the donors to the dark money group remained anonymous. The conservative group One Nation gave more than $85 million to Senator McConnell's Senate Leadership Fund used to support Republican Senate campaigns. The wealthy individuals or corporations that provided the money are secret. A Democratic super PAC named Future Forward collected $70 million from dark money groups and took advantage of the same legal gap. H.R. 1 addresses this "dark money daisy chain problem" by requiring that all large political contributions over $10,000 be traced back to their original source and disclosed.[72]

NO SHERIFFS IN TOWN

Existing campaign financing requirements, as mangled by *Citizens United*, are weak, doing little to control the huge amounts of money required to run a campaign, the barriers to entry the system erects against new candidates, the frenetic and inordinately time-consuming fundraising, the fundraising crises that afflict members of Congress, and the opacity of who gives money to whom for what. Compounding these problems is the reality that even these meager requirements are rarely enforced.

The Internal Revenue Service (IRS) is responsible for verifying the credentials of the nonprofit "social welfare" corporations authorized by section 501(c)(4) of the Internal Revenue Code and its implementing regulations.[73] The FEC is responsible for ensuring the public disclosure of donations to candidates, candidate committees, PACs, and super PACs. Both agencies are in bad shape, even by today's low standards, underfunded for years, lobbied to distraction by special interests, repeatedly dragged into hostile courts, and attacked at every turn by former President Trump and his far-right allies in Congress.

The provision in the tax code that authorizes dark money groups requires that they be "civic leagues or organizations not organized for profit but operated exclusively for the promotion of social welfare."[74] *Social welfare* is an expansive term and has been stretched to include both lobbying and elections. The imprecision of these requirements and the vast amounts of money channeled into campaigns through this category mean that rigorous government oversight and enforcement are crucial to prevent abuses.

As just one admittedly unusual example, a group claiming 501(c)(4) status, Women for America First, was implicated in organizing the March to Save America that became the January 6, 2021, insurrection.[75]

The IRS has long served as a whipping boy for anti-government conservatives. In 2012, its staff launched an effective attack. Conservative groups reported that the IRS was sending detailed questionnaires to groups that had applied for 501(c)(4) status, identifying some of them by searching for "tea party" or "patriot" in their names.[76] Tea Party conservatives newly arrived in Congress seized the moment and dragged the IRS and responsible employees through the mud in the press. By the end, the IRS unit responsible for overseeing 501(c)(4) compliance was gun-shy and shirked enforcement in the area.

An audit by the Government Accountability Office (GAO), the investigative agency that staffs oversight activities for Congress, discovered that between 2010 and 2017, the IRS conducted and closed 226 examinations regarding whether tax-exempt nonprofits were complying with political campaign rules.[77] Most of these exams focused on 501(c)(3) organizations that are prohibited from participating in political campaigns under any circumstances.[78] Only fourteen examinations, or 6 percent, focused on 501(c)(4) organizations. IRS officials admitted that the regulations they had written on the standards for determining a violation of 501(c)(4) were unclear and confusing, making it harder to pursue violations. Before the agency could rewrite the rules, Congress attached riders to IRS appropriations bills that prohibit the IRS from writing any new rules to solve this problem. In 2015, the Obama administration gave up on challenging such riders, in effect abandoning the fight to force disclosures of dark money donors.

In 2022, congressional Democrats passed the Inflation Reduction Act and President Biden signed it into law. The new law allocated $80 billion to the IRS to improve its technology, process returns faster, and expand enforcement. Congressional Republicans are fiercely opposed to this new funding, portraying the IRS as bullies who will use the extra resources to plague the average American. Senator Chuck Grassley (R-IA) told Fox

News that the new money could be used to deploy an IRS "strike force that goes in with AK-15s already loaded, ready to shoot some small businessperson in Iowa."[79] Democrats have responded that they intend to focus expanded auditing on people who make more than $400,000 a year and large corporations. As this book goes to press, Republicans got Democrats to agree to reduce this funding by $21 billion as a condition of extending the debt ceiling. They have threatened to demand more as a condition of voting in favor of legislation to keep the government open at the beginning of the new fiscal year in October 2023.

If anything, the FEC is in even worse shape. Structured as an independent agency, it is governed by commissioners appointed for set terms and removable only for cause, rather than a single political appointee chosen by the president and removable for any reason. In theory, this structure allows an independent agency to be less beholden to the party occupying the White House. In practice, because most independent agencies are chaired by a person who is appointed by the president and the chair controls the staff, they must heed what the administration in power wants them to do.

Independent agencies typically have odd numbers of commissioners from both parties so they do not deadlock. But the FEC has six commissioners, with the proviso that no more than three can be from the same party, meaning the lineup is always three to three unless seats are left open. The agency has a staff in the vicinity of three hundred, a very small number given the volume of money at stake and the difficulty of monitoring the complex web of organizations that take advantage of vague rules. Small staff, huge mission creep, and a potential for endless deadlock are not an auspicious setup for the agency that must oversee a contentious, fiercely competitive field.

Enter Senate majority (or minority) leader Mitch McConnell (R-KY), who has led Senate Republicans since 2007. Conservative judicial appointments are typically identified as the centerpiece of McConnell's legacy, especially his successful effort to get three new justices onto the Supreme Court. But throughout his long career he has opposed campaign finance controls with unsurpassed ardor. McConnell became a senator in 1985.

Anxious to make a name for himself within the Senate, he spent his first decade as the "spear catcher" on legislation to reform campaign reform, meaning he opposed it noisily, becoming the target of the figurative spears thrown by liberals and the media. In a lengthy profile published in 2019, McConnell said that most senators "were more interested in being seen as supporting campaign finance reform than actually enacting it."[80] He added that although such proposals were popular with the public, he did not think he would lose elections because of his high profile on the issue.

McConnell believes that Republicans are most successful when campaign finance remains unregulated and that *Citizens United* was a vindication of his preoccupation with installing conservative judges on the federal bench. Over time, McConnell has become one of the most prodigious fundraisers in Congress, building strong loyalty among his fellow Republicans whether they controlled the Senate or not.

When McCain-Feingold passed in 2002, McConnell had already assembled a team to challenge it before the Supreme Court. The Court ruled against him at first and it took eight more years for a conservative majority to engineer *Citizens United*.[81] But McConnell never lost focus, deciding that if he did not like the law, his next best bet was to sabotage the agency. As Heather McGehee, who lobbied for years on the other side, told the *New York Times*, "McConnell understood pretty quickly, faster than other folks, that you can have the best laws on the books, but if there's no law enforcement, it doesn't matter."[82]

McConnell has the power as Senate Republican leader to select and vet potential appointees, and he actually took the time to interview every candidate for the FEC personally. This level of attention is highly unusual, especially in the Senate and for a leader with such broad responsibility. It was possible because McConnell was already powerful, not given to conversing with the media, and fervently devoted to the campaign finance issue. After the George W. Bush administration nominated conservative election law specialist Don McGahn, an avowed fan of the First Amendment rights of corporations, super PACs, and dark money who had worked with McConnell during fight against McCain-Feingold legislation, the two saw an opportunity to disrupt the FEC that was not to be missed. McConnell quietly steered the appointment to conclusion and McGahn took his seat.

The FEC requires four votes to authorize any consequential action, including giving the green light to enforcement actions. When the FEC deadlocks, parties seeking enforcement action against their rivals can challenge its inaction in court, but judges typically side with the agency. McGahn hit the ground running and smartly engineered an agreement among the three Republican commissioners to vote together no matter what the issue. Their agreement was ironclad. In the five years leading up to 2008, when McGahn arrived, the FEC held 3,364 votes on enforcement actions and deadlocked only 39 times. Between 2008 and 2013, it considered only 866 enforcement proposals and deadlocked on 123. When he left in 2013, McGahn said, "I didn't need this job. I came here to work, to change the way the place thinks. I was proven right time and time again by court cases."[83]

The voting deadlock created a rapidly expanding universe of unofficial enforcement policies. Republican commissioners have loosened restrictions on candidates and outside groups simply by signaling what standards they are willing to enforce.[84] Election lawyers began advising their clients that a stalemate was good news because it meant that half the commissioners supported their position. One enterprising lawyer at Covington & Burling tried to market the situation, posting an article on the powerful firm's website with the title: "The F.E.C.: Where a 'Tie' Can Be (Almost) a 'Win.'"[85] The situation was a classic case of what political scientists call capture—without a majority, conservative Republicans who did not believe in the agency's mission had made its enforcement program close to moribund.

In 2013, President Obama nominated Ann Ravel to the FEC, where she served until 2017 before leaving in frustration. Ravel had extensive experience as a government lawyer and had just served a two-year term on California's Fair Political Practices Commission. She was so disgusted when she decided to resign that she took the unusual step of issuing a report entitled "Dysfunction and Deadlock: The Enforcement Crisis at the Federal Election Commission Reveals the Unlikelihood of Draining the Swamp."[86] In an op-ed published at around the same time, she wrote: "When citizens feel that their voice doesn't matter, that their vote cannot make a difference, and that they are powerless, our democracy is in danger."[87]

The FEC is also underfunded. In the five years after *Citizens United*, its budget was flat and staffing levels fell to a fifteen-year low. During this period, it did not write any rules to interpret the many issues raised by *Citizens United* or *SpeechNow*, including such critical problems as how to determine whether a super PAC is insulating itself from coordination with candidates or their campaigns.

In 2019, the FEC responded to questions posed by Zoe Lofgren (D-CA), the chair of the House Committee on Administration, which has oversight authority over the FEC. Little had changed.[88] The FEC had 289 unresolved enforcement cases on its docket, some of which dated back to the 2013 election cycle. The agency admitted that it had not penalized a single entity for illegally coordinating with candidates or their campaigns since *Citizens United* was decided in 2010. Two of six commissioner slots were open. Because commissioners can sit until their replacements arrive, the four remaining commissioners have collectively served for thirty-six years on "holdover status."

The For the People Act would reduce the number of commissioners at the FEC to five (from six). The legislation retains six-year terms and the requirement that commissioners be appointed by the president and confirmed by the Senate.[89] A person who has served a six-year term would not be eligible for reappointment. Unrestricted holdover terms would be eliminated. Members could continue to serve for only one year if a successor is not available. The president would select a chair from among the serving commissioners. The chair would serve as the chief administrative officer with power to prepare its budget, hire and fire its staff director and general counsel, and issue subpoenas for witnesses and production of documents.

The legislation would reform the enforcement process by giving the general counsel the power to review and report on every complaint filed with the FEC.[90] The general counsel would determine whether the complaint indicates a violation has or is about to occur, as well as whether to open an investigation or dismiss the complaint. The FEC commissioners would have thirty days to make a decision before the general counsel's recommendation goes into effect, creating a strong incentive for avoiding the endless delays that have plagued the institution for the last several years.

If H.R. 1–like legislation is ever considered by Congress, it will undergo revisions, likely significant ones. Conceivably Democrats could pass it on their own, avoiding Republican effort to derail reforms. Or the fever could break and bipartisan support would be possible. Even then, the House vote that approved it during the 117th Congress was accomplished under the assumption that the legislation would never come up in the Senate. Once it looks like legislation could pass, members focus and changes are made. Yet even revised versions of the reforms explained above would improve the dismal situation we live with now. When people across the political spectrum think the government is corrupt, government shakes to its foundation.

ACKNOWLEDGMENTS

I have worked on this book on and off for a few years, intending to explain how the six far-right interest groups disabled government public health, worker and consumer safety, and environmental programs by stealth: cutting budgets to the bone, never updating the law, harassing civil servants, opening the doors of White House and congressional staff to lobbyists with any manner of complaint, and using the courts to jam the system. Then the January 6, 2021, insurrection happened, and the goals of the book expanded into an examination of how much American democracy is threatened by the sabotage the six have accomplished.

Thousands of people, including militia members dressed for combat, marauded through the halls of Congress as members and staff sheltered in place, some just feet away, crouching under tables and praying the door locks held. Seven people died, most of them police, and for a few hours, the president of the United States watched the revolt unfold on television without doing anything about it. I can only hope that my foray into the individual and cumulative effect of the six before, then, since, and in the future helps readers come to grips with these twisted roots of the country's problems.

Many people helped me take this painful journey through the inaccurate, opportunistic, self-serving, and hysterical campaigns against government. My editor at Stanford University Press, Marcela Cristina Maxfield, was unfailingly supportive and astute—I could not have done this project without her. Lisa Heinzerling and Shana Jones, my brilliant friends, gave invaluable advice. Thanks also to Susan McCarty, the managing research fellow in the Thurgood Marshall Law Library at the University of Maryland Carey Law School, who reviewed countless drafts, improving the vital sourcing of information over and over again. My colleague Tom McGarity and I were going to write a book together, but decided we had different ideas about it; our initial discussions helped me conceive of this volume, and his book *Demolition Agenda: How Trump Tried to Dismantle American Government, and What Biden Needs to Do to Save It* came out in 2022. I talked often to my savvy former colleagues from the Center for Progressive Reform, including Matt Freeman, James Goodwin, and Matt Shudtz. My friend Ernie Isenstadt was ready to combat my ideas with kindness. John Richard helped me gain perspective on the left. And I learned a great deal from the dozens of students who have taken my government law courses over the years—truly, this volume is for you. Special thanks to Kennedi Fichtel, Kaitlyn Johnson, Saul Slowik, , and Matt Williams. My son Daniel Espo deserves the final acknowledgment not only because I love him dearly but because his energy, intelligence, and determination to change the country offsets the darkness of what could happen to America and the planet if we keep going as we have .

Research by other scholars and journalists was invaluable, including books by Frank Ackerman and Lisa Heinzerling (*Priceless: On Knowing the Price of Everything and the Value of Nothing*); Michael Avery and Danielle McLaughlin (*The Federalist Society: How Conservatives Took the Law Back from Liberals*); Kathleen Belew (*Bringing the War Home*); John Boehner (*On the House: A Washington Memoir*); Jefferson Cowie (*Stayin' Alive: The 1970s and the Last Days of the Working Class* and *Freedom's Dominion: A Saga of White Resistance to Federal Power*); E. J. Dionne (*Why the Right Went Wrong, Conservatism—From Goldwater to Trump and Beyond*); Frances Fitzgerald (*The Evangelicals: The Struggle to Shape America*); Jacob Hacker and Paul Pierson (*American Amnesia: How the War on Government Led Us to Forget What Made America Prosper*); Sam Jackson

(*Oath Keepers: Patriotism and the Edge of Violence in a Right-Wing Anti-government Group*); Kathleen Hall Jamieson and Joseph Cappella (*Echo Chamber: Rush Limbaugh and the Conservative Media Establishment*); Robert Jones (*White Too Long: The Legacy of White Supremacy in American Christianity*); Thomas Mann and Norman Ornstein (*It's Even Worse Than It Was: How the American Constitutional System Collided with the New Politics of Extremism*); Ruth Marcus (*Supreme Ambition: Brett Kavanaugh and the Conservative Takeover*); Jane Mayer (*Dark Money: The Hidden History of the Billionaires behind the Rise of the Radical Right*); Jon Meacham (*The Soul of America*); Naomi Oreskes and Erik Conway (*Merchants of Doubt: How a Handful of Scientists Obscured the Truth on Issues from Tobacco Smoke to Global Warming*); Christopher Parker and Matt Barreto (*Change They Can't Believe In: The Tea Party and Reactionary Politics in America*); Kim Phillips-Fein (*Invisible Hands: The Businessmen's Crusade against the New Deal*); Ruth Marcus, *Supreme Ambition Brett Kavanaugh and the Conservative Takeover*); Gabriel Sherman (*The Loudest Voice in the Room: How the Brilliant, Bombastic Roger Ailes Built Fox News—And Divided a Country*); Theda Skocpol and Vanessa Williamson (*The Tea Party and the Remaking of Republican Conservatism*); Ganesh Sitaraman (*The Crisis of the Middle Class Constitution: Why Economic Inequality Threatens Our Republic*); Steven Teles (*The Rise of the Conservative Legal Movement*); David Vogel (*Fluctuating Fortunes, The Political Power of Business in America*); Jess Walter (*Ruby Ridge: The Truth and Tragedy of the Randy Weaver Family*); Andrew Whitehead and Samuel Perry (*Taking America Back for God: Christian Nationalism in the United States*); Adam Winkler (*We the Corporations: How American Businesses Won Their Civil Rights*); and Julian Zelizer (*Burning Down the House: Newt Gingrich, the Fall of a Speaker, and the Rise of the New Republican Party*).

The journalism of Tim Alberta, Michael Gerson, Mike Giglio, Luke Mogelson, and Peter Wehner is outstanding and I am a fan. Alberta and Mogelson have also written relevant books: *American Carnage* and *The Storm Is Here*, respectively. The anguish of Gerson and Wehner over what the white evangelical movement has become is both moving and incisive.

NOTES

CHAPTER 1

1. Charles M. Blow, "Trump's Army of Angry White Men," *New York Times*, October 25, 2020, https://www.nytimes.com/2020/10/25/opinion/trump-white-men-election.html.

2. David Brooks, "Our Pathetic Herd Immunity Failure," *New York Times*, May 6, 2021, https://www.nytimes.com/2021/05/06/opinion/herd-immunity-us.html.

3. David Frum, "How to Build an Autocracy," *The Atlantic*, March 2017, https://www.theatlantic.com/magazine/archive/2017/03/how-to-build-an-autocracy/513872/.

4. Paul Krugman, "Notes on Excessive Wealth Disorder," *New York Times*, June 22, 2019, https://www.nytimes.com/2019/06/22/opinion/notes-on-excessive-wealth-disorder.html.

5. Ronald Reagan, "Inaugural Address," *Public Papers of the Presidents of the United States*, 1981, no. 1, 1, January 20, 1981, https://www.govinfo.gov/app/details/PPP-1981-book1.

6. Pew Research Ctr., "American's View of Government: Decades of Distrust, Enduring Support for Its Role," June 6, 2022, https://www.pewresearch.org/politics/2022/06/06/americans-views-of-government-decades-of-distrust-enduring-support-for-its-role/.

7. Jeffrey M. Jones, "Congress' Job Approval Drops to 13%, Lowest Since 2017," Gallup, October 27, 2023, https://news.gallup.com/poll/513410/congress-job-approval-drops-lowest-2017.aspx.

8. "In Depth: Topics A to Z, Supreme Court," Gallup, https://news.gallup.com/poll/4732/supreme-court.aspx, accessed November 20, 2023.

9. Karl Evers-Hillstrom, "Most Expensive Ever: 2020 Election Cost $14.4 Billion," OpenSecrets, February 11, 2021, https://www.opensecrets.org/news/2021/02/2020-cycle-cost-14p4-billion-doubling-16/.

10. Amisa Ratliff, "Seven Numbers to Know about the Campaign Money that Flowed to House and Senate Members in 2020," Issue One, December 17, 2020, https://issueone.org/articles/seven-numbers-to-know-about-the-campaign-money-that-flowed-to-house-and-senate-members-in-2020/.

11. Taylor Giorno, "Federal Lobbying Spending Reaches $4.4 Billion in 2022—The Highest since 2010," OpenSecrets, January 26, 2023, https://www.opensecrets.org/news/2023/01/federal-lobbying-spending-reaches-4-1-billion-in-2022-the-highest-since-2010/.

12. Ibid.

13. John L. Dorman, "Former GOP House Speaker John Boehner Calls Fellow Republican Jim Jordan a 'Political Terrorist,'" *Insider*, April 10, 2021, https://www.businessinsider.com/boehner-lambasts-republican-jim-jordan-political-terrorist-2021-4.

14. Caleb Ecarma, "Tucker Carlson, Promoter of Racist 'Replacement' Theory, Insists He's Not a Racist," *Vanity Fair*, July 7, 2022, https://www.vanityfair.com/news/2022/07/tucker-carlson-racist-replacement-theory.

15. Yair Rosenberg, "'Jews Will Not Replace Us': Why White Supremacists Go after Jews," *Washington Post*, August 14, 2017, https://www.washingtonpost.com/news/acts-of-faith/wp/2017/08/14/jews-will-not-replace-us-why-white-supremacists-go-after-jews/.

16. Oliver Darcy, "Fox Has No Problem with Tucker Carlson's 'Replacement Theory' Remarks, Says Lachlan Murdoch," CNN, April 12, 2021, https://www.cnn.com/2021/04/12/media/murdoch-response-adl-tucker-carlson/index.html.

17. 10 U.S.C. § 252, which reads: "Whenever the President considers that unlawful obstructions, combinations, or assemblages, or rebellion against the authority of the United States, make it impracticable to enforce the laws of the United States in any State by the ordinary course of judicial proceedings, he may call into Federal service such of the militia of any State, and use such of the armed forces, as he considers necessary to enforce those laws or to suppress the rebellion."

18. 18 U.S.C. § 2384.

19. Josh Levin, "The Judge Who Coined 'Indict a Ham Sandwich' Was Himself Indicted," *Slate*, November 25, 2014, https://slate.com/human-interest/2014/11/sol-wachtler-the-judge-who-coined-indict-a-ham-sandwich-was-himself-indicted.html.

20. Ryan Fuhrmann, "How Large Corporations Avoid Paying Taxes," *Investopedia*, February 7, 2023, https://www.investopedia.com/financial-edge/0512/how-

large-corporations-get-around-paying-less-in-taxes.aspx; Dave Davies, "How the Ultrawealthy Devise Ways Not to Pay Their Share of Taxes," *NPR*, August 25, 2022, https://www.npr.org/2022/08/25/1119412217/how-the-ultrawealthy-devise-ways-to-not-pay-their-share-of-taxes.

21. Brown v. Board of Education, 347 U.S. 483 (1954). Government Accountability Office, *K-12 Education: Student Population Has Significantly Diversified, but Many Schools Remain Divided along Racial, Ethnic, and Economic Lines*, No. GAO-22-104737, July 14, 2022, https://www.gao.gov/products/gao-22-104737. The report found that during 2020–2021, more than a third of students (about 18.5 million) attended schools where 75 percent or more of the students were of a single race. The worst problems were in the Midwest and the Northeast.

22. Citizens United v. FEC, 588 U.S. 310 (2010).

23. Thomas Mann and Norman Ornstein, *The Broken Branch: How Congress Is Failing America and How to Get It Back on Track* (New York: Oxford University Press, 2006). Mann and Ornstein wrote their book before the Tea Party emerged in 2010. They have followed up with two additional volumes: *It's Even Worse Than It Looks: How the American Constitutional System Collided with the New Politics of Extremism* (New York: Basic Books, 2012); and *It's Even Worse Than It Was* (New York: Basic Books, new and expanded edition, 2016). The authors are careful to explain that while Democrats broke Congress to some degree by rigging procedural rules in their favor, Republicans are to blame for the damage that has paralyzed Congress.

24. As just one example, Jill Lepore, the Harvard historian who wrote the well-received and extensive book *These Truths: A History of the United States*, does not identify this period as remarkable and barely touches on what occurred during it. Lepore, *These Truths* (New York: W.W. Norton, 2018), 681. The blind spot must be deliberate; the index of the book contains only two references to climate change.

25. The phrase "bureaucracy bashing" was coined by political scientists. See, e.g., R. Sam Garrett, James A. Thurber, A. Lee Fritschler, and David H. Rosenbloom, "Assessing the Impact of Bureaucracy Bashing by Electoral Campaigns," *Public Administration Review* 66 (2006): 228–240.

CHAPTER 2

1. Adam Winkler, *We the Corporations: How American Businesses Won Their Civil Rights* (New York: Liveright Publishing, 2018).

2. Thomas Jefferson to George Logan, November 12, 1816, Founders Online, National Archives, https://founders.archives.gov/documents/Jefferson/03-10-02-0390.

3. Detached memoranda by James Madison, ca. January 31, 1820, Found-

ers Online, National Archives, https://founders.archives.gov/documents/Madison/04-01-02-0549.

4. Winkler, *We the Corporations*, 5.

5. Ibid.

6. Ibid.

7. Ibid.

8. Citizens United v. FEC, 588 U.S. 310 (2010).

9. Jeffrey M. Jones, "Confidence in U.S. Institutions Down; Average at New Low," Gallup, July 5, 2022, https://news.gallup.com/poll/394283/confidence-institutions-down-average-new-low.aspx.

10. Amina Dunn and Andy Cerda, "Anti-Corporate Sentiment in U.S. Now Widespread in Both Parties," Pew Research Center, November 1, 2022, https://www.pewresearch.org/short-reads/2022/11/17/anti-corporate-sentiment-in-u-s-is-now-widespread-in-both-parties/.

11. See, e.g., Jacob S. Hacker and Paul Pierson, *Winner-Take-All Politics: How Washington Made the Rich Richer—and Turned Its Back on the Middle Class* (New York: Simon & Schuster, 2010), 117–18; Kim Phillips-Fein, *Invisible Hands: The Businessmen's Crusade against the New Deal* (New York: W.W. Norton, 2009), 162.

12. Lewis Powell, memorandum to Eugene B. Sydnor, chairman, Education Committee, U.S. Chamber of Commerce, "Attack on the American Free Enterprise System," August 23, 1971, Lewis F. Powell Jr. Papers, Washington and Lee University School of Law Scholarly Commons, https://scholarlycommons.law.wlu.edu/cgi/viewcontent.cgi?article=1000&context=powellmemo.

13. Jack Anderson, "Powell's Lesson to Business Aired," *Washington Post*, September 28, 1972, F7.

14. Powell memorandum, 1–3, 7-10.

15. Ibid., 34.

16. Powell memorandum, 5. Powell footnoted the Alsop quote as deriving from an article by the columnist, "Yale and the Deadly Danger," *Newsweek*, May 18, 1970.

17. Ibid.

18. Ibid., 6.

19. Ibid. Powell cites the May 1971 issue of *Fortune*, at page 145, as the source of this quotation.

20. Ralph Nader, *Unsafe at Any Speed, The Designed-In Dangers of the American Automobile* (New York: Grossman Publishers, 1965).

21. 23 U.S.C. § 401 et seq.

22. Powell memorandum, 24.

23. Ibid., 18–19.

24. Linda Greenhouse, "Lewis Powell, Crucial Centrist Justice, Dies at 90," *New York Times*, August 26, 1998, A1 (emphasis in original).

25. Phillips-Fein, *Invisible Hands*, 162.

26. Ibid., 188.

27. David Vogel, *Fluctuating Fortunes: The Political Power of Business in America* (New York: Basic Books, 1989), 59.

28. Ibid., 197-98.

29. OpenSecrets, "Top Spenders," https://www.opensecrets.org/federal-lobbying/top-spenders?cycle=2021, accessed November 14, 2022.

30. OpenSecrets explains: "The lobbying data that form the basis of this site are compiled using the lobbying disclosure reports filed with the Secretary of the Senate's Office of Public Records (SOPR) and posted on its website. . . . Quarterly reports are due on the 20th day of January, April, July, and October and are incorporated into OpenSecrets.org after they appear on the SOPR website. Previously posted data are subject to change as new amendments are filed. Additional details about lobbyists and their activities since 2011 are collected from data provided by the Clerk of the House. . . . Lobbying firms are required to provide a good-faith estimate rounded to the nearest $10,000 of all lobbying-related income from their clients in each quarter. (Lobbying firms sometimes double as law, accounting, or public relations firms—income for non-lobbying activity is supposed to be excluded from the lobbying reports.) A lobbying firm does not have to file for clients that do not spend at least $3,000 during a quarter. Likewise, organizations that hire in-house lobbyists must provide good-faith estimates rounded to the nearest $10,000 of all lobbying-related expenditures in a quarter." OpenSecrets, "Methodology," https://www.opensecrets.org/federal-lobbying/methodology#reports, accessed November 14, 2022.

31. U.S. Chamber of Commerce, "About the U.S. Chamber of Commerce," https://www.uschamber.com/about-us-chamber-commerce, accessed November 14, 2022. In 1967, the Chamber had 36,000 members; by 1974, 80,000 companies belonged. Vogel, *Fluctuating Fortunes*, 199.

32. OpenSecrets, "Top Lobbying Firms," https://www.opensecrets.org/federal-lobbying/top-lobbying-firms?cycle=2021, accessed November 14, 2022.

33. "Heritage Foundation Releases 'Mandate for Leadership' and 'Solutions 2020,'" July 30, 2020, https://www.heritage.org/press/heritage-foundation-releases-mandate-leadership-and-solutions-2020.

34. The Heritage Foundation, *A Season of Growth, A Year of Achievement, 2017 Annual Report* (Washington, D.C.: Heritage Foundation, May 2018), 3, https://www.heritage.org/sites/default/files/2018-05/2017_AnnualReport_WEB.pdf.

35. Jason Webb Yackee and Susan Webb Yackee, "A Bias toward Business? Assessing Interest Group Influence on the U.S. Bureaucracy," *Journal of Politics* 64 (2006): 128–139.

36. Wendy Wagner, Katherine Barnes, and Lisa Peters, "Rulemaking in the

Shade: An Empirical Study of EPA's Air Toxic Emission Standards," *Administrative Law Review* 63 (2011), 119.

37. 42 U.S. C. § 7409(b)(1).

38. Whitman v. American Trucking Associations, 531 U.S. 457 (2001).

39. William D. Ruckelshaus, "Stopping the Pendulum," *Environmental Forum*, 12, no. 6 (November–December 1995), 25. Ruckelshaus led the agency from January 1970 to April 1973, during the Nixon administration, and served again during the Reagan administration.

40. Summary Minutes, National Industrial Pollution Control Council Meeting, February 10, 1971, at 3, cited in William H. Rodgers Jr., "The National Industrial Pollution Control Council: Advise or Collude?," *Boston College Law Review* 13 (1972): 719–747.

41. Pub. L. No. 96-511, 94 Stat. 2812, codified at 44 U.S.C. §§ 3501-3521.

42. Executive Order no. 12291, 46 Fed. Reg. 13,193 (February 17, 1981).

43. Executive Order no. 12866, 58 Fed. Reg. 51,735 (October 4, 1993).

44. The best, most readable critique of cost-benefit analysis is Lisa Heinzerling and Frank Ackerman, *Priceless: On Knowing the Price of Everything and the Value of Nothing* (New York: New Press, 2004).

45. For an excellent explanation of how and why the costs are inflated, see Thomas O. McGarity and Ruth Ruttenberg, "Counting the Cost of Health, Safety, and Environmental Regulation," *Texas Law Review* 80 (2002): 1,997–2,058.

46. Jerry Ellig, "What Are the Indirect Costs of Regulation?" Regulation: Expert Commentary, Mercatus Center, George Mason University, December 1, 2011, https://www.mercatus.org/expert_commentary/what-are-indirect-costs-regulation.

47. Newt Gingrich, "Healthcare Rationing: Real Scary," *Los Angeles Times*, August 16, 2009, https://www.latimes.com/archives/la-xpm-2009-aug-16-oe-gingrich16-story.html.

48. Ibid.

49. Nicole V. Crain and W. Mark Crain, *The Impact of Regulatory Costs on Small Firms* (Small Business Administration Office of Advocacy, September 2010), 6. The Small Business Administration Office of Advocacy, which commissioned the study using government funds, is unabashedly pro-business. The Government Accountability Office criticized its lax review of the Crain reports, and they have been removed from the agency's internet site. GAO, *Small Business Administration, Office of Advocacy Needs to Improve Controls over Research, Regulatory, and Workforce Planning Activities*, No. GAO-14-525, July 2014, 13–14, https://www.gao.gov/assets/gao-14-525.pdf.

50. Crain and Crain, *The Impact of Regulatory Costs on Small Firms*, iv..

51. Ibid., 4. Emphasis added.

52. Daniel Kaufman, Aart Kraay and Massimo Mastruzzi, *The Worldwide Governance Indicators: Methodology and Analytical Issues*, World Bank Policy Research Working Paper No. 5430 (2010), http://papers.ssrn.com/sol3/papers.cfm?abstract_id=1682130.

53. Lisa Heinzerling and Frank Ackerman, "The $1.75 Trillion Lie," *Michigan Journal of Environmental & Administrative Law* 1 (2012): 127, 134.

54. Ibid., 134. Emphasis added.

55. Ibid., 131. Emphasis in original.

56. Curtis Copeland, "Analysis of an Estimate of the Total Costs of Federal Regulations," Congressional Research Service, No. R41763, April 6, 2011, 2.

57. Ibid.

58. W. Mark Crain and Nicole V. Crain, *The Cost of Federal Regulation to the U.S. Economy, Manufacturing and Small Business, a Report for the National Association of Manufacturers* (National Association of Manufacturers, September 10, 2014), 1, https://www.nam.org/wp-content/uploads/2019/05/Federal-Regulation-Full-Study.pdf.

59. Ibid.

60. Richard W. Parker, "The Faux Scholarship Foundation of the Regulatory Rollback Movement," *Ecology Law Quarterly* 45 (2019): 845, 863–865.

61. Ibid., 863.

62. W. Mark Crain and Nicole V. Crain, *The Cost of Federal Regulation to the U.S. Economy, Manufacturing and Small Business, a Study Conducted for the National Association of Manufacturers* (National Association of Manufacturers, October 2023), https://nam.org/wp-content/uploads/2023/11/NAM-3731-Crains-Study-R3-V2-FIN.pdf.

63. Competitive Enterprise Institute, "Clyde Wayne Crews," https://cei.org/experts/clyde-wayne-crews/, accessed November 14, 2022.

64. Clyde Wayne Crews Jr., *The Ten Thousand Commandments: An Annual Snapshot of the Federal Regulatory State, 2021 Edition* (Competitive Enterprise Institute, 2021), 5, https://cei.org/wp-content/uploads/2021/06/Ten_Thousand_Commandments_2021.pdf.

65. Ibid.

66. Ibid.

67. Ibid., 43.

68. Ibid., 46.

69. Ibid., 5.

70. Ibid., 42.

71. Romney for President, "Believe in America: Mitt Romney's Plan for Jobs and Economic Growth" (2011) at 57, https://grist.org/wp-content/uploads/2012/01/believeinamerica-planforjobsandeconomicgrowth-full.pdf.

72. C-Span, "Donald J. Trump Rally in Toledo, Ohio," September 21, 2016, https://www.c-span.org/video/?415667-1/donald-trump-campaigns-toledo-ohio.

73. See, e.g., James Rosen, "Regulation Nation: As Firms Grow, Regs Follow," Fox News, December 23, 2015, https://www.foxnews.com/politics/regulation-nation-as-firms-grow-regs-follow; Richard Rahn, "How to Create Jobs Now," Newsmax, June 7, 2011, https://www.newsmax.com/rahn/jobcreation-governmentspending-stimulusprogram-keynes/2011/06/07/id/399088/; Alex Swoyer, "Report: 3,853 New Federal Rules Issued in 2016, 211 New Laws Passed," Breitbart, January 2, 2017, https://www.breitbart.com/politics/2017/01/02/5847167/; Clyde Wayne Crews Jr., "Joe Biden's Year in Federal Regulation, 2021," *Forbes*, December 31, 2021, https://www.forbes.com/sites/waynecrews/2021/12/31/joe-bidens-year-in-federal-regulation-2021/?sh=55fc22c66240; Nicole V. Crain and W. Mark Crain, "The Regulation Tax Keeps Growing," *Wall Street Journal*, September 27, 2010, https://www.wsj.com/articles/SB10001424052748703860104575508122499819564; Editorial, "So Many Rules, So Few Opportunities," *Wall Street Journal*, May 6, 2016, https://www.wsj.com/articles/so-many-rules-so-few-opportunities-1462575067; David W. Kreutzer, "Taxes, Regulations Hurt Economy," *USA Today*, August 15, 2017, https://www.usatoday.com/story/opinion/2017/08/15/regulations-taxes-hurt-growth-editorials-debates/104627838/.

74. Pew Research Center, "In a Politically Polarized Era, Sharp Divides in Both Partisan Coalitions," December 17, 2019, https://www.pewresearch.org/politics/2019/12/17/in-a-politically-polarized-era-sharp-divides-in-both-partisan-coalitions/.

75. Pew Research Center, "Public Trust in Government: 1958–2022," June 6, 2022, https://www.pewresearch.org/politics/2022/06/06/public-trust-in-government-1958-2022/.

76. Pew Research Center, "In a Politically Polarized Era," 24.

77. Ibid., 11.

78. See, e.g., Nicholas Reimann, "Top Business Leaders Plea for Debt Ceiling Raise Ahead of 'Complete Catastrophe,'" *Forbes*, October 6, 2021, https://www.forbes.com/sites/nicholasreimann/2021/10/06/top-business-leaders-plea-for-debt-ceiling-raise-ahead-of-complete-catastrophe/?sh=26e47ccf6684.

79. See, e.g., Ellen Gilmer, "Trump Record Marked by Big Losses, Undecided Cases," *Bloomberg Law*, January 11, 2021, https://news.bloomberglaw.com/us-law-week/trump-environmental-record-marked-by-big-losses-undecided-cases.

80. See, e.g., Charles Piller, "Exclusive: FDA Enforcement Actions Plummet under Trump," *Science*, July 2, 2019, https://www.science.org/content/article/exclusive-fda-enforcement-actions-plummet-under-trump; Naveena Sadisivam, "Inside Biden's Uphill Battle to Restore EPA after Trump," *Grist*, March 1, 2021, https://grist.org/politics/epa-joe-biden-environmental-law-enforcement-trump/.

81. The two most notorious examples are Scott Pruitt as EPA administra-

tor and Ryan Zinke as secretary of the Department of the Interior. Both men were driven from office by ethical lapses. See, e.g., Rebecca Hersher and Brett Neely, "Scott Pruitt Out at EPA," National Public Radio, July 5, 2018, https://www.npr.org/2018/07/05/594078923/scott-pruitt-out-at-epa; Nathan Rott and Shannon Van Sant, "Ryan Zinke Is Leaving the Interior Department, Trump Tweets," National Public Radio, December 15, 2018, https://www.npr.org/2018/12/15/663597698/ryan-zinke-is-leaving-the-interior-department. With respect to the science brain drain, see Joe Davidson, "Federal 'Brain Drain' Threatens American Scientific Leadership, New Report Says," *Washington Post*, March 17, 2021, https://www.washingtonpost.com/politics/science-federal-trump-epa/2021/03/17/8663d58a-86b5-11eb-8a67-f314e5fcf88d_story.html.

82. Kathryn Dunn Tenpas, "Tracking Turnover in the Trump Administration," Brookings, January 2021, https://www.brookings.edu/research/tracking-turnover-in-the-trump-administration/.

83. Remarks by President Trump at American Center for Mobility, Ypsilanti, MI, *Daily Compilation of Presidential Documents*, March 15, 2017, Office of the Federal Register, National Archives, 1, https://www.govinfo.gov/content/pkg/DCPD-201700168/html/DCPD-201700168.htm.

84. 42 U.S.C. § 7543(b).

85. They are Colorado, Connecticut, Delaware, Maine, Maryland, Massachusetts, New Jersey, New Mexico, New York, Nevada, Oregon, Pennsylvania, Rhode Island, Virginia, Vermont, and Washington, plus the District of Columbia.

86. Joe Garofoli, "Five Ways Trump Changed California—Including One that Helped Democrats," *San Francisco Chronicle*, January 17, 2021, https://www.sfchronicle.com/politics/article/Five-ways-Trump-changed-California-including-15878137.php.

87. Chris Cameron, "These Are the People Who Died in Connection with the Capitol Riot," *New York Times*, January 5, 2022, updated October 13, 2022, https://www.nytimes.com/2022/01/05/us/politics/jan-6-capitol-deaths.html.

88. National Association of Manufacturers, "Manufacturers Call on Armed Thugs to Cease Violence at Capitol," press release, January 6, 2021, https://www.nam.org/manufacturers-call-on-armed-thugs-to-cease-violence-at-capitol-11628/.

89. Todd C. Frankel, Jeff Stein, Jena McGregor, and Jonathan O'Connell, "Companies Backed Trump for Years. Now They're Facing a Reckoning after the Attack on the Capitol," *Washington Post*, January 8, 2021, https://www.washingtonpost.com/business/2021/01/08/trump-policies-corporate-america/.

90. Gerald F. Seib, "How Corporate America Became a Political Orphan," *Wall Street Journal*, July 23, 2021, https://www.wsj.com/articles/how-corporate-america-became-a-political-orphan-11627052148.

91. Pub. L. No. 111-203, Title X, 124 Stat. 1376, 1955 (2010).

92. Ari Berman and Nick Surgey, "Leaked Video: Dark Money Group Brags

about Writing GOP Voter Suppression Bills across the Country," *Mother Jones*, May 13, 2021, https://www.motherjones.com/politics/2021/05/heritage-foundation-dark-money-voter-suppression-laws/.

93. "Statement Signed by Major Corporations Opposing Laws That Restrict Voting Rights," *Washington Post*, April 14, 2021, https://www.washingtonpost.com/context/statement-signed-by-major-corporations-opposing-laws-that-restrict-voting-rights/dd5c9bdf-b441-47ea-98c5-07d6a2b8a223/.

94. David Gelles and Andrew Ross Sorkin, "Hundreds of Companies Unite to Oppose Voting Limits, but Others Abstain," *New York Times*, April 14, 2021, https://www.nytimes.com/2021/04/14/business/ceos-corporate-america-voting-rights.html.

CHAPTER 3

1. Smoking Argus, "Rick Santelli Calls for Tea Party on Floor of Chicago Board of Trade," *YouTube*, February 19, 2009, https://www.youtube.com/watch?v=wcvSjKCU_Zo.

2. Ibid.

3. Tim Dickinson, "Meet the Right-Wing Rebels Who Overthrew John Boehner," *Rolling Stone*, October 6, 2015, 3, 4, https://www.rollingstone.com/politics/politics-news/meet-the-right-wing-rebels-who-overthrew-john-boehner-73320/.

4. President Harry Truman coined the phrase "do-nothing Congress" when he ran for reelection in 1947–1948; he was referring to the 80th Congress, which was Republican led. Alfred Steinberg, "Harry S Truman," *Britannica*, updated July 4, 2023, https://www.britannica.com/biography/Harry-S-Truman/Succession-to-the-presidency. A modern example of this charge centers on the 114th Congress (2015–2017), which passed 329 laws. Aaron Blake, "The 'Do-Nothing Congress' Graduates to the 'Do-Nothing-Much Congress,'" *Washington Post*, December 20, 2016, https://www.washingtonpost.com/news/the-fix/wp/2016/12/20/the-do-nothing-congress-graduates-to-the-do-nothing-much-congress/.

5. U.S. Constitution, art. I, § 8.

6. Tim Lau, "The Filibuster Explained," Brennan Center for Justice, April 26, 2021, https://www.brennancenter.org/our-work/research-reports/filibuster-explained.

7. Andy Barr, "The GOP's No-Compromise Pledge," *Politico*, October 28, 2010, https://www.politico.com/story/2010/10/the-gops-no-compromise-pledge-044311.

8. Ibid.

9. *The Federalist Papers*, Federalist No. 22 (1787) (Alexander Hamilton), https://guides.loc.gov/federalist-papers/text-21-30#s-lg-box-wrapper-25493335.

10. Molly E. Reynolds, "What Is the Senate Filibuster, and What Would It Take to Eliminate It?," Brookings, September 9, 2020, https://www.brookings.

edu/policy2020/votervital/what-is-the-senate-filibuster-and-what-would-it-take-to-eliminate-it/.

11. Max Cohen, "Obama Calls for End of 'Jim Crow Relic' Filibuster If It Blocks Voting Rights Reforms," *Politico,* July 30, 2020, https://www.politico.com/news/2020/07/30/barack-obama-john-lewis-filibuster-388600.

12. Thomas Mann and Norman Ornstein, *The Broken Branch: How Congress Is Failing America and How to Get It Back on Track* (New York: Oxford University Press, 2006). Mann and Ornstein wrote their book before the Tea Party emerged in 2010. They have followed up with two additional volumes: *It's Even Worse Than It Looks: How the American Constitutional System Collided with the New Politics of Extremism* (New York: Basic Books, 2012) and *It's Even Worse Than It Was* (New York: Basic Books, new and expanded edition, 2016). The authors are careful to explain that while Democrats broke Congress to some degree by rigging procedural rules in their favor, Republicans are to blame for the damage that has paralyzed Congress.

13. McKay Coppins, "The Man Who Broke Politics," *The Atlantic,* November 2018, https://www.theatlantic.com/magazine/archive/2018/11/newt-gingrich-says-youre-welcome/570832/.

14. Julian Zelizer, *Burning Down the House: Newt Gingrich, the Fall of a Speaker, and the Rise of the New Republican Party* (New York: Penguin Press, 2020), 292–293.

15. Tim Alberta, "John Boehner Unchained," *Politico Magazine,* November–December 2017, https://www.politico.com/magazine/story/2017/10/29/john-boehner-trump-house-republican-party-retirement-profile-feature-215741/. Alberta's article is among the finest pieces of political reporting and profile reporting I have ever read.

16. See Cut, Cap, and Balance Act of 2011, H.R. 2560, 112th Cong. (2011); Alberta, "John Boehner Unchained."

17. Graham Bowley, "Stocks Plunge on Fears of Global Turmoil," *New York Times,* August 5, 2011, https://www.nytimes.com/2011/08/05/business/markets.html.

18. Alberta, "John Boehner Unchained."

19. Ibid.

20. Ibid.

21. Jennifer Steinhauer, "Debt Bill Is Signed, Ending a Fractious Battle," *New York Times,* August 2, 2011, https://www.nytimes.com/2011/08/03/us/politics/03fiscal.html.

22. Alberta, "John Boehner Unchained."

23. Cruz was closely aligned with the Tea Party class and played a central role in the shutdown. Libby Nelson, "Boehner on Ted Cruz: 'I Have Never Worked

with a More Miserable Son of a Bitch in My Life,'" *Vox*, April 28, 2018, https://www.vox.com/2016/4/28/11526234/boehner-cruz.

24. Dan Balz and Scott Clement, "Poll: Major Damage to GOP after Shutdown, and Broad Dissatisfaction with Government," *Washington Post*, October 22, 2014, https://www.washingtonpost.com/politics/poll-major-damage-to-gop-after-shutdown-and-broad-dissatisfaction-with-government/2013/10/21/dae5c062-3a84-11e3-b7ba-503fb5822c3e_story.html.

25. 31 U.S.C. §§ 101 et seq.

26. The title was probably borrowed from a 1988 movie of the same name that starred Kiefer Sutherland, Emilio Estevez, Lou Diamond Phillips, and Charlie Sheen as a group of downtrodden but hard-riding and charismatic young cowboys who seek vengeance for the death of their mentor, a distinguished British gentleman played by Terence Stamp.

27. Carl Hulse, "Incumbents Fear Cantor's Loss Will Fill Tea Party's Sails," *New York Times*, June 12, 2014, https://www.nytimes.com/2014/06/13/us/politics/incumbents-fear-cantors-loss-will-fill-tea-partys-sails.html.

28. Mark Leibovich, "This Is the Way Paul Ryan's Leadership Ends," *New York Times Magazine*, August 7, 2018, https://www.nytimes.com/2018/08/07/magazine/paul-ryan-speakership-end-trump.html; Tina Nguyen, "Paul Ryan Claims He Secretly Saved America from 'Tragedy' under Trump," *Vanity Fair*, August 7, 2018, https://www.vanityfair.com/news/2018/08/paul-ryan-claims-he-secretly-saved-america-from-tragedy-under-trump.

29. Hannah Hess, "What Happened to the Young Guns?," *Roll Call*, October 13, 2015, https://rollcall.com/2015/10/13/what-happened-to-the-young-guns/.

30. In the 1955 movie *Rebel Without a Cause*, the male stars—Sal Mineo, James Dean, and Corey Allen—have a car race called the "chickie run" that will result in the death of anyone who does not jump out of his car before it hurtles off a bluff. The characters played by Mineo and Dean exit in time, but Allen's character crashes to his death. The movie came out one month after Dean's death in a car crash. Lee Pfeiffer, "Rebel Without a Cause," *Britannica*, December 15, 2009, updated May 23, 2023, https://www.britannica.com/topic/Rebel-Without-a-Cause.

31. See, e.g., Paul H. Jossey, "How We Killed the Tea Party," *Politico Magazine*, August 14, 2016, https://www.politico.com/magazine/story/2016/08/tea-party-pacs-ideas-death-214164.

32. See, e.g., George Monbiot, "The Tea Party Movement: Deluded and Inspired by Billionaires," *Guardian*, October 25, 2010, https://www.theguardian.com/commentisfree/cifamerica/2010/oct/25/tea-party-koch-brothers.

33. Paul Waldman, "The Tea Party, Now and Forever," *American Prospect*, October 18, 2013, https://prospect.org/article/tea-party-now-and-forever.

34. Dan Balz, "GOP 'Contract' Pledges 10 Tough Acts to Follow," *Washington Post*, November 20, 1994, https://www.washingtonpost.com/archive/poli-

tics/1994/11/20/gop-contract-pledges-10-tough-acts-to-follow/50fdd611-035e-41d9-8827-e0231de5c105/.

35. Ibid.

36. William J. Clinton, "Address Before a Joint Session of the Congress on the State of the Union," *Public Papers of the Presidents of the United States*, 1996, no.1, 79–86, https://www.govinfo.gov/app/collection/ppp/president-42_Clinton,%20William%20J./1996/01%21A%21January%201%20to%20June%2030%2C%201996.

37. Teddy Davis, "Tea Party Activists Unveil 'Contract from America,'" *ABC News*, April 15, 2010, https://abcnews.go.com/Politics/tea-party-activists-unveil-contract-america/story?id=10376437.

38. Ibid.

39. Amanda Fallin, Rachel Grana, and Stanton Glantz, "'To Quarterback behind the Scenes, Third-Party Efforts': The Tobacco Industry and the Tea Party," *Tobacco Control* 23 (2014): 322–331.

40. Ibid., 324.

41. Americans for Prosperity, data from 2020 IRS Form 990 (2021), https://projects.propublica.org/nonprofits/organizations/753148958; FreedomWorks, 2020 IRS Form 990 (2021), https://projects.propublica.org/nonprofits/organizations/521526916.

42. "America's Largest Private Companies," *Forbes*, 2021, https://www.forbes.com/largest-private-companies/list/#tab:rank_search:koch%20industrie.

43. See, e.g., Jane Mayer, *Dark Money: The Hidden History of the Billionaires behind the Rise of the Radical Right* (New York: Doubleday, 2016); Christopher Leonard, *Kochland: The Secret History of Koch Industries and Corporate Power in America* (New York: Simon & Schuster, 2019).

44. Americans for Prosperity, https://careers.americansforprosperity.org/.

45. Tax Cuts and Jobs Act, Pub. L. No. 115-97, 131 Stat. 2054 (2017); Philip Elliott, "The Koch Brothers Have a Plan to Make the Tax Bill Popular," *Time*, December 21, 2017, https://time.com/5075076/koch-brothers-tax-bill-campaign/.

46. Congressional Budget Office, "Cost Estimate of H.R. 1," November 13, 2017, https://www.cbo.gov/publication/53312.

47. Americans for Prosperity, "Join the True Cost of Washington Tour," https://americansforprosperity.org/true-cost-overview/, accessed July 25, 2023.

48. Americans for Prosperity, "Join Us at a Location Near You," https://americansforprosperity.org/true-cost-tour-dates/, accessed July 25, 2023.

49. Veronica Stracqualursi, "Trump Says Koch Brothers Are 'Total Joke,'" *CNN Politics*, July 31, 2018, https://www.cnn.com/2018/07/31/politics/trump-koch-brothers/index.html.

50. Alexander Hertel-Fernandez, Caroline Tervo, and Theda Skocpol, "How the Koch Brothers Built the Most Powerful Rightwing Group You've Never Heard of," *Guardian*, September 26, 2018, https://www.theguardian.com/us-

news/2018/sep/26/koch-brothers-americans-for-prosperity-rightwing-political-group.

51. Hiroko Tabuchi, "How the Koch Brothers Are Killing Public Transit Projects around the Country," *New York Times*, June 19, 2018, https://www.nytimes.com/2018/06/19/climate/koch-brothers-public-transit.html.

52. Ibid.

53. Katie Benner, Catie Edmondson, Luke Broadwater and Alan Feuer, "Meadows and the Band of Loyalists: How They Fought to Keep Trump in Power," *New York Times*, December 15, 2021, https://www.nytimes.com/2021/12/15/us/politics/trump-meadows-republicans-congress-jan-6.html.

54. John Boehner, *On the House: A Washington Memoir* (New York: St. Martin's Press, 2021).

55. Ibid., 246.

CHAPTER 4

1. Dobbs v. Jackson Women's Health Organization, 142 S. Ct. 2228, 2242 (2022); Roe v. Wade, 410 U.S. 113 (1973). *Roe* held that once the fetus became viable, a state could ban abortion.

2. *Dobbs*, 2252–53.

3. *Dobbs*, 142 S. Ct. 2228, 2324 (2022) (Breyer, J., dissenting).

4. Bradwell v. Illinois, 83 U.S. 130, 141 (1872).

5. Ruth Marcus, "Indiana's Cruel Abortion Bill Is a Warning of Post-Roe Reality," *Washington Post*, July 31, 2022, https://www.washingtonpost.com/opinions/2022/07/31/indiana-abortion-bill-cruel-new-reality/.

6. Ruth Marcus, *Supreme Ambition: Brett Kavanaugh and the Conservative Takeover* (New York: Simon & Schuster, 2019), 19.

7. See, e.g., Kenneth Vogel and Shane Goldmacher, "An Unusual $1.6 Billion Donation Bolsters Conservatives," *New York Times*, August 22, 2022, https://www.nytimes.com/2022/08/22/us/politics/republican-dark-money.html; Robert O'Harrow Jr. and Shawn Boburg, "A Conservative Activist's Behind-the-Scenes Campaign to Remake the Nation's Courts," *Washington Post*, May 21, 2019, https://www.washingtonpost.com/graphics/2019/investigations/leonard-leo-federalists-society-courts/.

8. Kenneth P. Vogel, "Leonard Leo Pushed the Courts Right. Now He's Aiming at American Society," *New York Times*, October 12, 2022, https://www.nytimes.com/2022/10/12/us/politics/leonard-leo-courts-dark-money.html.

9. Olson quoted in Michael Kruse, "The Weekend at Yale That Changed American Politics," *Politico Magazine*, September/October 2018, https://www.politico.com/magazine/story/2018/08/27/federalist-society-yale-history-conservative-law-court-219608/.

10. Bush v. Gore, 531 U.S. 98 (2000).

11. Alfonso A. Narvaez, "Clement Haynsworth Dies at 77: Lost Struggle for High Court Seat," *New York Times,* November 23, 1989, D21.

12. Robert Bork, *Slouching Toward Gomorrah: Modern Liberalism and American Decline* (New York: Regan Books, 1996).

13. Kennedy quoted in James Reston, "Washington: Kennedy and Bork," *New York Times* July 5, 1987, https://www.nytimes.com/1987/07/05/opinion/washington-kennedy-and-bork.html.

14. Linda Greenhouse, "Judge Bork Is Stepping Down to Answer Critics and Reflect," *New York Times,* January 15, 1988, https://www.nytimes.com/1988/01/15/us/judge-bork-is-stepping-down-to-answer-critics-and-reflect.html.

15. Ethan Bronner, "A Conservative Whose Supreme Court Bid Set the Senate Afire," *New York Times,* December 19, 2012, https://www.nytimes.com/2012/12/20/us/robert-h-bork-conservative-jurist-dies-at-85.html.

16. For a relatively recent discussion of the Federalist Society's origin and influence on judicial appointments, see Jason Zengerle, "How the Trump Administration Is Remaking the Courts," *New York Times Magazine,* August 22, 2018, https://www.nytimes.com/2018/08/22/magazine/trump-remaking-courts-judiciary.html.

17. O'Harrow and Boburg, "A Conservative Activist's Behind-the-Scenes Campaign."

18. Ibid.

19. Ibid.

20. See, e.g., Robert Maguire, "Group behind Trump SCOTUS Picks Brought in Nearly $50 Million in Secret Money," *Citizens for Responsibility and Ethics in Washington,* June 15, 2022, https://www.citizensforethics.org/reports-investigations/crew-investigations/group-behind-trump-scotus-picks-brought-in-nearly-50-million-in-secret-money/; Anna Massoglia and Andrew Perez, "New 'Dark Money' Group Led by Trump Judicial Adviser Ties to Network Promoting His Court Picks," OpenSecrets, February 27, 2019, https://www.opensecrets.org/news/2019/02/dark-money-group-led-by-trump-judicial-adviser-scotus-picks/.

21. "What Is the Regulatory Transparency Project?," video, Federalist Society, July 17, 2019, https://fedsoc.org/commentary/videos/what-is-the-regulatory-transparency-project; Regulatory Transparency Project, Federalist Society, https://rtp.fedsoc.org/.

22. Amanda Hollis-Brusky, *Ideas with Consequence: The Federalist Society and the Conservative Counterrevolution* (New York: Oxford University Press, 2015), 16.

23. Steven Teles, *The Rise of the Conservative Legal Movement: The Battle for Control of the Law* (Princeton, NJ: Princeton University Press, 2008), 161.

24. Ibid., 162.

25. Marcus, *Supreme Ambition,* 10–45.

26. McGahn quoted in Zengerle, "How the Trump Administration."

27. Molly Riley, "Obama's Legacy on Judicial Appointments, by the Numbers," Reuters, January 19, 2017, https://www.nbcnews.com/storyline/president-obama-the-legacy/obama-s-legacy-judicial-appointments-numbers-n709306. The article explains that Obama's appointments were admirably diverse, but that he started too slowly in his first year and had many appointments delayed when Republicans controlled the Senate.

28. Carl Hulse, "With Wilson Confirmation, Trump and Senate Republicans Achieve a Milestone," *New York Times*, June 24, 2020, https://www.nytimes.com/2020/06/24/us/trump-senate-judges-wilson.html.

29. Gary Lawson, "Delegation and Original Meaning," *Virginia Law Review* 88 (2002): 327, 330.

30. A.L.A. Schechter Poultry Corp. v. United States, 295 U.S. 519 (1935).

31. Ibid., 551.

32. 42 U.S.C. § 7409(b)(1).

33. American Trucking Associations v. EPA, 175 F.3d 1027, 1037 (D.C. Cir. 1999).

34. Whitman v. American Trucking Associations, Inc., 531 U.S. 457, 475 (2001).

35. Jacobson v. Massachusetts, 197 U.S. 11, 13 (1905).

36. Ibid.

37. Ibid., 29.

38. National Federation of Independent Business v. Department of Labor, 142 S. Ct. 661, 671 (2022).

39. 29 U.S.C. § 655(c)(1). Emphasis added.

40. Chevron U.S.A., Inc. v. NRDC, 467 U.S. 837 (1984).

41. Ruth Marcus, "Chief Justice Roberts's Jarring Vaccine Jurisprudence," *Washington Post*, January 9, 2022, https://www.washingtonpost.com/opinions/2022/01/09/conservative-supreme-court-justices-could-harm-covid-fight/.

42. National Federation of Independent Business v. Department of Labor, 142 S. Ct. 661, 665 (2022). Emphasis in original.

43. Ibid., 665 (citation omitted).

44. Loper Bright Enters. v. Raimondo, 45 F.4th 359 (D.C. Cir. 2022), *cert. granted*, No. 22-451 (May 1, 2023) (granting certiorari on question 2 of the petition for certiorari, "Whether the Court should overrule *Chevron* or at least clarify that statutory silence concerning controversial powers expressly but narrowly granted elsewhere in the statute does not constitute an ambiguity requiring deference to the agency").

45. Loper Bright Enters. v. Raimondo, 143 S. Ct. 2429 (2023) (order granting certiorari).

46. South Bay United Pentecostal Church v. Newsom, 140 S. Ct. 1613 (2020).

47. Ibid., 1614 (Kavanaugh, Thomas, and Gorsuch, J.J., dissenting). Securities Exchange Act.

48. Ibid., 1613 (Roberts, C.J., concurring).

49. Ibid., 1614.

50. Linda Greenhouse, "The Supreme Court, Too, Is on the Brink," *New York Times*, June 4, 2020, https://www.nytimes.com/2020/06/04/opinion/sunday/supreme-court-religion-coronavirus.html.

51. Roman Catholic Diocese of Brooklyn v. Cuomo, 141 S. Ct. 63, 68 (2020).

52. Ibid., 79.

53. South Bay Pentecostal Church v. Newsom, 141 S. Ct. 1294 (2021).

54. Scott Burris, "Individual Liberty, Public Health, and the Battle for the Nation's Soul," *The Regulatory Review*, June 7, 2021, https://www.theregreview.org/2021/06/07/burris-individual-liberty-public-health-battle-for-nations-soul/.

55. Ibid.

56. West Virginia v. Environmental Protection Agency, 142 S. Ct. 2587 (2022).

57. American Lung Association v. EPA, 985 F.3d 914 (D.C. Cir. 2021).

58. 42 U.S.C. § 7411(a)(1). Emphasis added.

59. 142 S. Ct. at 2630 (Kagan, J., dissenting) (citations omitted).

60. Ibid., 2628.

61. Lisa Heinzerling, "The Supreme Court Is Making America Ungovernable," *The Atlantic*, July 26, 2022, https://www.theatlantic.com/ideas/archive/2022/07/supreme-court-major-questions-doctrine-congress/670618/.

62. *Greenhouse Effect and Global Climate Change: Hearing before the S. Comm. on Energy and Natural Resources*, 100th Cong., 1st Sess. (1988), statement of Dr. James Hansen, Director, NASA Goddard Institute for Space Studies.

63. Joint Science Academies, "Climate Change Adaptation and the Transition to a Low Carbon Society," June 2008, http://insaindia.res.in/pdf/Climate_05.08_W.pdf.

64. IPCC, *Climate Change 2014 Synthesis Report, Summary for Policymakers* (2014), 4, 16, 17, https://www.ipcc.ch/site/assets/uploads/2018/02/AR5_SYR_FINAL_SPM.pdf. "High confidence" is IPCC-speak for conclusions that are so strongly supported by available research that the group regards them as dispositive. The IPCC was founded in 1988 by the World Meteorological Organization and the United Nations Environmental Programme. It has attracted the participation of thousands of the most qualified scientists engaged in research regarding the nature, scope, and future of climate changes.

65. IPCC, *Global Warming of 1.5°C* (2018), 4, https://www.ipcc.ch/sr15/. See also Coral Davenport "Major Climate Report Describes a Strong Risk of Crisis as Early as 2040," *New York Times*, October 7, 2018, https://www.nytimes.com/2018/10/07/climate/ipcc-climate-report-2040.html.

66. U.S. Global Change Research Program, *2018: Impacts, Risks, and Adap-*

tation in the United States: Fourth National Climate Assessment, Volume II: Report-in-Brief, ed. D. R. Reidmiller et al. (Washington, D.C.: U.S. Global Climate Change Research Program, 2018), https://nca2018.globalchange.gov/.

67. Catherine Clifford, "UN Leader Warns against Climate 'Collective Suicide' as Heat Wave Grips Europe," CNBC, July 18, 2022, https://www.cnbc.com/2022/07/18/guterres-warns-against-climate-suicide-as-heat-wave-grips-europe.html.

68. Mark A. Lemley, "The Imperial Supreme Court," *Harvard Law Review Forum* 136 (2022): 97.

69. William P. Barr, "19th Annual Barbara K. Olson Memorial Lecture at the Federalist Society's 2019 National Lawyers Convention," Washington, D.C., November 15, 2019, https://www.justice.gov/opa/speech/attorney-general-william-p-barr-delivers-19th-annual-barbara-k-olson-memorial-lecture. Olson was the wife of Ted Olson, quoted earlier in this chapter. She died on September 11, 2001, when she was a passenger on the plane the terrorists forced to crash into the Pentagon.

70. Ashley Parker, Isaac Stanley-Becker, and Carol Leonnig, "Frantic Secret Service Radio Traffic Show How Close Pence Was to Danger," *Washington Post*, July 22, 2022.

71. Order re Privilege of Documents Dated January 4–7, 2021, at 44, John C. Eastman v. Bennie Thompson et al., No. 8:22-cv-00099-DOC-DFM (D.C. Cal., March 22, 2022), https://www.courthousenews.com/wp-content/uploads/2022/03/eastman-select-committee-order.pdf.

72. American Bar Association, "Statement of ABA President Patricia Lee Refo Re: Violence at the U.S. Capitol," January 6, 2021, https://www.americanbar.org/news/abanews/aba-news-archives/2021/01/statement-of-aba-president-patricia-lee-refo-re--violence-at-the/.

CHAPTER 5

1. "Kyle Rittenhouse Speaks to Tucker Carlson in First TV Interview," YouTube, November 22, 2021, https://www.youtube.com/watch?v=do7sbWaZstQ.

2. Teaganne Finn, "Trump Says He Met with Kyle Rittenhouse after Verdict, Calls Him a 'Nice Young Man,'" *NBC News*, November 24, 2021, https://www.nbcnews.com/politics/donald-trump/trump-says-he-met-kyle-rittenhouse-after-verdict-calls-him-n1284513.

3. "Billionaires: #99, Rupert Murdoch," *Forbes*, April 4, 2023, https://www.forbes.com/profile/rupert-murdoch/?list=billionaires&sh=38058882b1af.

4. Brooks Barnes, "Disney Moves from Behemoth to Colossus with Closing of Fox Deal," *New York Times*, March 20, 2019, https://www.nytimes.com/2019/03/20/business/media/walt-disney-21st-century-fox-deal.html.

5. Lee Rainie, "Cable and Satellite TV Use Has Dropped Dramatically in the

U.S. Since 2015," Pew Research Center, March 17, 2021, https://www.pewresearch.org/fact-tank/2021/03/17/cable-and-satellite-tv-use-has-dropped-dramatically-in-the-u-s-since-2015/.

6. Statista, "Share of Adults Who Subscribe to a Cable TV Service in the United States as of February 2022, by Age Group," https://www.statista.com/statistics/322958/pay-tv-penetration-rate-usa/.

7. Naomi Forman-Katz and Katerina Eva Matsa, "News Platform Fact Sheet," Pew Research Center, September 20, 2022, https://www.pewresearch.org/journalism/fact-sheet/news-platform-fact-sheet/.

8. Ibid.

9. Paul Farhi, "The Looming Existential Crisis for Cable News," *Washington Post*, May 23, 2023, https://www.washingtonpost.com/media/2023/05/23/cable-news-demise-trump-cnn-ratings-streaming/.

10. "Tubi Releases New Findings on Streaming TV Trends in Its Annual Report, The Stream 2023: Actionable Audience Insights for Brands," press release, February 14, 2023, https://corporate.tubitv.com/press/tubi-releases-new-findings-on-streaming-tv-trends-in-its-annual-report-the-stream-2023-actionable-audience-insights-for-brands/.

11. I will not discuss the legal distinctions between the parent and subsidiary corporations here.

12. PRRI Staff, "Trumpism after Trump? How Fox News Structures Republican Attitudes," Public Religion Research Institute, November 18, 2020, https://www.prri.org/wp-content/uploads/2020/11/PRRI-Nov-2020-Fox-News-1.pdf.

13. PRRI Staff, "Trumpism After Trump? How Fox News Structures Republican Attitudes," November 18, 2020, https://www.prri.org/research/trumpism-after-trump-how-fox-news-structures-republican-attitudes/.

14. Remarks by President Trump in press briefing, September 10, 2020, https://trumpwhitehouse.archives.gov/briefings-statements/remarks-president-trump-press-briefing-091020/.

15. Nicholas Confessore, "American Nationalist, Part 1, How Tucker Carlson Stoked White Fear to Conquer Cable," *New York Times*, April 30, 2022, https://www.nytimes.com/2022/04/30/us/tucker-carlson-gop-republican-party.html.

16. Ibid.

17. Karen Yourish, Weiyi Cai, Larry Buchanan, Aaron Byrd, Barbara Harvey, Blacki Migliozzi, Rumsey Taylor, Josh Williams, and Michael Zandlo, "Inside the Apocalyptic Worldview of 'Tucker Carlson Tonight,'" *New York Times*, May 1, 2022, https://www.nytimes.com/interactive/2022/04/30/us/tucker-carlson-tonight.html. See also Nicholas Confessore, "What to Know About Tucker Carlson's Rise," *New York Times*, April 30, 2022, https://www.nytimes.com/2022/04/30/business/media/tucker-carlson-fox-news-takeaways.html; Confessore, "How Tucker Carlson Stoked White Fear."

18. Confessore, "How Tucker Carlson Stoked White Fear."

19. Tucker Carlson, "Tucker Carlson: The Green New Deal Means Poverty," *Fox News Live*, August 29, 2022, https://www.foxnews.com/opinion/tucker-carlson-green-new-deal-means-poverty.

20. Opinion and Order Granting Motion to Dismiss, Karen McDougal v. Fox News Network, LLC, Case 1:19-vc-11161 (MKV), (S.D.N.Y. Sept. 23, 2020), https://law.justia.com/cases/federal/district-courts/new-york/nysdce/1:2019cv11161/527808/39/. See also Elliot Hannon, "Judge Rules Tucker Carlson Is Not a Credible Source of News," *Slate*, September 25, 2020, https://slate.com/news-and-politics/2020/09/judge-rules-fox-news-tucker-carlson-not-source-of-news-defamation-suit-mcdougal-trump.html.

21. U.S. Const. amend. I.

22. Yair Rosenberg, "'Jews Will Not Replace Us': Why White Supremacists Go after Jews," *Washington Post*, August 14, 2017, https://www.washingtonpost.com/news/acts-of-faith/wp/2017/08/14/jews-will-not-replace-us-why-white-supremacists-go-after-jews/.

23. Ibid.

24. Oliver Darcy, "Fox Has No Problem with Tucker Carlson's 'Replacement Theory' Remarks, Says Lachlan Murdoch," CNN, April 12, 2021, https://www.cnn.com/2021/04/12/media/murdoch-response-adl-tucker-carlson/index.html.

25. "Read Senator Chuck Schumer's Letter to Fox News about Tucker Carlson and Replacement Theory," *New York Times*, May 17, 2022, https://www.nytimes.com/interactive/2022/05/17/nyregion/senator-chuck-schumer-s-letter-to-fox-news-executives.html.

26. The poll was part of a study issued on the tenth anniversary of the Associated Press–NORC Center for Public Affairs Research several days before Schumer's letter. Polling showed that "roughly one in three (32%) adults agree that a group of people is trying to replace native-born Americans with immigrants for electoral gains. A similar share (29%) also express concern that an increase in immigration is leading to native-born Americans losing economic, political, and cultural influence." AP-NORC Center for Public Affairs Research, "Immigration Attitudes and Conspiratorial Thinkers," May 2022, 1, https://apnorc.org/wp-content/uploads/2022/05/Immigration-Report_V15.pdf.

27. Sara Fischer, "Lachlan Murdoch Responds to Criticism That Fox News Is Polarizing," Axios, May 24, 2022, https://www.axios.com/2022/05/24/lachlan-murdoch-criticism-fox-news-polarizing.

28. "Murdoch's Scandal," transcript, PBS *Frontline*, March 27, 2012, https://www.pbs.org/wgbh/frontline/documentary/murdochs-scandal/transcript/.

29. Ibid.

30. Vikram Dodd, "Ex-Murdoch Editor Andrew Neil: News of the World Revelations One of the Significant Media Stories of Our Time," *The Guard-*

ian, July 8, 2009, https://www.theguardian.com/media/2009/jul/09/andrew-neil-murdoch-andy-coulson.

31. Lisa O'Carroll, "Andy Coulson Jailed for 18 Months for Conspiracy to Hack Phones," *The Guardian*, July 4, 2014, https://www.theguardian.com/uk-news/2014/jul/04/andy-coulson-jailed-phone-hacking.

32. John Burns and Ravi Somaiya, "Panel in Hacking Case Finds Murdoch Unfit as News Titan," *New York Times*, May 1, 2012, https://www.nytimes.com/2012/05/02/world/europe/murdoch-hacking-scandal-to-be-examined-by-british-parliamentary-panel.html.

33. Andy Davies, "Revealed: the Rupert Murdoch Tape," *4News*, July 3, 2013, https://www.channel4.com/news/murdoch-rupert-tape-police-the-sun-journalists.

34. Hacked Off, "8th Annual Leveson Lecture Event," YouTube, December 10, 2021, https://www.youtube.com/watch?v=9SLgb0478Ps.

35. Pew Research Center, "Total Profit for Cable TV (Fox News, CNN and MSNBC)," July 13, 2021, https://www.pewresearch.org/journalism/chart/sotnm-cable-total-profit-for-cable-tv/.

36. David Carr and Tim Arango, "A Fox Chief at the Pinnacle of Media and Politics," *New York Times*, January 9, 2010, https://www.nytimes.com/2010/01/10/business/media/10ailes.html.

37. Complaint and Jury Demand at 5–6, Gretchen Carlson v. Roger Ailes, No. L-005016-16 (N.J. Super. Ct. Law Div. July 6, 2016).

38. Ibid., 5.

39. Michael Grynbaum and John Koblin, "Fox Settles With Gretchen Carlson over Roger Ailes Sex Harassment Claims," *New York Times*, September 7, 2016, https://www.nytimes.com/2016/09/07/business/media/fox-news-roger-ailes-gretchen-carlson-sexual-harassment-lawsuit-settlement.html.

40. Emily Steel and Michael Schmidt, "Bill O'Reilly Is Forced Out at Fox News," *New York Times*, April 19, 2017, https://www.nytimes.com/2017/04/19/business/media/bill-oreilly-fox-news-allegations.html.

41. Those polls are cited and summarized in Jon Greenberg, "Most Republicans Still Falsely Believe Trump's Stolen Election Claims. Here Are Some Reasons Why," *Poynter*, June 16, 2022, https://www.poynter.org/fact-checking/2022/70-percent-republicans-falsely-believe-stolen-election-trump/. The Poynter Institute is a nonprofit that specializes in media ethics and runs the Pulitzer Prize–winning website PolitiFact, which fact-checks statements in the mainstream media.

42. Taylor Orth, "Two in Five Americans Say a Civil War Is at Least Somewhat Likely in the Next Decade," *YouGov America*, August 26, 2022, https://today.yougov.com/topics/politics/articles-reports/2022/08/26/two-in-five-americans-civil-war-somewhat-likely.

43. Ken Meyer, "Trump Goes on Warpath against Fox News amid Reports He's Set to Launch Competitor: 'They Forgot the Golden Goose,'" *Mediaite*, November 12, 2020, https://www.mediaite.com/trump/trump-goes-on-the-warpath-against-fox-news-amid-reports-hes-set-to-launch-competitor-they-forgot-the-golden-goose/.

44. Chris Stirewalt, "What I Learned about Media Rage after Getting Fired from Fox," *Politico*, August 8, 2022, https://www.politico.com/news/magazine/2022/08/28/fox-news-trump-journalism-00053991.

45. Mamta Badkar, "Veteran Fox Anchor and Trump Critic Shepard Smith Steps Down," *Financial Times*, October 11, 2019, https://www.ft.com/content/76f99406-ec63-11e9-85f4-d00e5018f061.

46. Alexis Benveniste, "Shep Smith Breaks His Silence about Why He Left Fox News," CNN, January 20, 2021, https://www.cnn.com/2021/01/20/media/shep-smith-fox-amanpour/index.html.

47. Michael M. Grynbaum, "Chris Wallace Says Life at Fox News Became 'Unsustainable,'" *New York Times*, March 27, 2022, https://www.nytimes.com/2022/03/27/business/media/chris-wallace-cnn-fox-news.html.

48. Complaint at 56, US Dominion v. Fox Corp. and Fox Broadcasting Co., No. N21C-11-082 EMD (Del. Super. Ct. Nov. 8, 2021).

49. Ibid., 57.

50. Ibid., 60–61.

51. Ibid.

52. Tiffany Hsu, "What to Know about Dominion, the Voting Machine Company Suing Fox," *New York Times*, April 17, 2023, https://www.nytimes.com/2023/04/17/business/media/dominion-fox-lawsuit.html.

53. US Dominion v. Fox News Network, LLC, Nos. 21C-02-257 EMD, N21C-11-082 EMD, at 31–32 (Del. Super. Ct. Mar. 31, 2023), 2023 WL 2730567.

54. Ibid., 43.

55. Ibid., 87, 89, 92, 96, 102, 105, 111, 112, 114, 117, 118, 121, 124, 125, 127, and 129.

56. Erin Mulvaney and Keach Hagey, "In Deposition, Rupert Murdoch Says Fox News Hosts Endorsed False 2020 Election Claims," *Wall Street Journal*, March 3, 2923, https://www.wsj.com/articles/in-deposition-rupert-murdoch-says-fox-news-hosts-endorsed-false-2020-election-claims-c9348fc0.

57. Ibid.

58. Jim Rutenberg, Jeremy Peters and Michael Schmidt, "On Eve of Trial, Discovery of Carlson Texts Set Off Crisis atop Fox," *New York Times*, April 26, 2023, https://www.nytimes.com/2023/04/26/business/media/tucker-carlson-dominion-fox-news.html.

59. Keach Hagey, Joe Flint, and Isabella Simonetti, "Tucker Carlson's Vulgar, Offensive Messages about Colleagues Helped Seal His Fate at Fox News," *Wall*

Street Journal, April 26, 2023, https://www.wsj.com/articles/tucker-carlsons-vulgar-offensive-messages-about-colleagues-helped-seal-his-fate-at-fox-news-e52b3cc5.

60. Ibid.

61. Brian Flood, "Fox News Media, Tucker Carlson Part Ways," *Fox News*, April 24, 2023, https://www.foxnews.com/media/fox-news-media-tucker-carlson-part-ways.

62. Asawin Suebsaeng and Diana Falzone, "Inside the 'Death Match' That Helped Doom Tucker Carlson at Fox," *Rolling Stone*, May 7, 2023, https://www.rollingstone.com/politics/politics-features/tucker-carlson-fox-news-power-struggle-text-messages-1234731076/.

63. Diana Falzon and Asawin Suebsaeng, "Fox Has a Secret 'Oppo File' to Keep Tucker Carlson in Check, Sources Say," *Rolling Stone*, April 25, 2023, https://www.rollingstone.com/politics/politics-features/fox-news-tucker-carlson-secret-dossier-oppo-file-1234723855/.

64. Kevin Drum, "The Real Source of America's Rising Rage," *Mother Jones*, September–October 2021, https://www.motherjones.com/politics/2021/07/american-anger-polarization-fox-news/; Eric Wemple, "Yes, Fox News Matters. A Lot," *Washington Post*, April 11, 2019, https://www.washingtonpost.com/opinions/2019/04/11/yes-fox-news-matters-lot/; Jane Mayer, "The Making of the Fox News White House," *New Yorker*, March 4, 2019, https://www.newyorker.com/magazine/2019/03/11/the-making-of-the-fox-news-white-house.

65. Jack Shafer, "The Incredible Shrinking Fox News," *Politico*, April 9, 2019, https://www.politico.com/magazine/story/2019/04/09/fox-news-rupert-murdoch-226612/; Michael Socolow, "Fox News Isn't the Problem, It's the Media's Obsession with Fox News," *The Conversation*, April 9, 2019, https://theconversation.com/fox-news-isnt-the-problem-its-the-medias-obsession-with-fox-news-114954; Frank Rich, "Stop Beating a Dead Fox," *New York Magazine*, January 24, 2014, https://nymag.com/news/frank-rich/fox-news-2014-2/.

66. See, e.g., Toni Fitzgerald, "5 Valuable Lessons from the Abrupt Failure of CNN+," *Forbes*, April 30, 2022, https://www.forbes.com/sites/tonifitzgerald/2022/04/30/5-valuable-lessons-from-the-abrupt-failure-of-cnn/; John Koblin, Michael Grynbaum, and Benjamin Mullin, "Inside the Implosion of CNN+," *New York Times*, April 24, 2022, https://www.nytimes.com/2022/04/24/business/media/cnn-plus-discovery-warner.html.

67. Justin Peters, "Why CNN Is Booting All the Trump Critics Who Work There," *Slate*, September 10, 2022, https://slate.com/business/2022/09/cnn-trump-harwood-stelter-licht.html.

68. Tim Alberta, "Inside the Meltdown at CNN," *The Atlantic*, June 2, 2023, https://www.theatlantic.com/politics/archive/2023/06/cnn-ratings-chris-licht-trump/674255/.

69. Editorial Board, "Trump's Silence on Jan. 6 Is Damning," *New York Post*,

July 22, 2022, https://nypost.com/2022/07/22/trumps-jan-6-silence-renders-him-unworthy-for-2024-reelection/. Emphasis in original.

70. Editorial Board, "The President Who Stood Still on Jan. 6," *Wall Street Journal*, July 22, 2022, https://www.wsj.com/articles/the-president-who-stood-still-donald-trump-jan-6-committee-mike-pence-capitol-riot-11658528548.

71. Nikki McCann Ramirez, "Tucker Carlson's Jan. 6 Footage Dump Delivers the Sloppy Propaganda Kevin McCarthy Wanted," *Rolling Stone*, March 6, 2023, https://www.rollingstone.com/politics/politics-news/tucker-carlson-jan-6-footage-kevin-mccarthy-1234691769/.

72. Katherine Faulders, Rachel Scott, and Luke Barr, "Capitol Police Chief Slams Carlson's Comments about Jan. 6 Video as 'Offensive and Misleading' in Internal Video," *ABC News*, March 7, 2023, https://abcnews.go.com/Politics/capitol-police-chief-slams-carlsons-comments-jan-6/story?id=97686463.

73. The full text of the memo is available here: https://s3.documentcloud.org/documents/23697943/from-the-desk-of-the-chief-235-truth-justice.pdf.

74. Bill McCarthy, "Tucker Carlson's 'Patriot Purge' Film on Jan. 6 Is Full of Falsehoods, Conspiracy Theories," *Politifact*, November 5, 2021, https://www.politifact.com/article/2021/nov/05/tucker-carlsons-patriot-purge-film-jan-6-full-fals/.

75. David Folkenflik and Tom Dreisbach, "'Off the Rails': New Tucker Carlson Project for Fox Embraces Conspiracy Theories," NPR, November 3, 2021, https://www.npr.org/2021/11/03/1051607945/tucker-carlson-fox-news-insurrection-conspiracy-new-show.

CHAPTER 6

1. "Billy Graham," Samaritan's Purse, https://www.samaritanspurse.org/media/bio-billy-graham/#:~:text=Preaching,than%20185%20countries%20and%20territories, accessed July 28, 2023.

2. Jeff Greenfield, "When Richard Nixon Used Billy Graham," *Politico*, February 21, 2018, https://www.politico.com/magazine/story/2018/02/21/billy-graham-death-richard-nixon-217039/.

3. Associated Press, "Billy Graham Apologizes to Jews for His Remarks on Nixon Tapes," *New York Times*, March 3, 2002, https://www.nytimes.com/2002/03/03/us/billy-graham-apologizes-to-jews-for-his-remarks-on-nixon-tapes.html.

4. Paul Batura, "Billy Graham's Regrets," Fox News, February 28, 2018, https://www.foxnews.com/opinion/billy-grahams-regrets.

5. Hartford Institute for Religion Research, "Megachurch Definition," http://hirr.hartsem.edu/megachurch/definition.html, accessed July 28, 2023.

6. Elisha Fieldstadt, "America's Biggest Megachurches, Ranked," CBS News,

November 28, 2018, https://www.cbsnews.com/pictures/30-biggest-american-megachurches-ranked/.

7. Gregory Smith, Michael Rotolo, and Patricia Tevington, "Views of the U.S. as a 'Christian Nation' and Opinions about 'Christian Nationalism,'" Pew Research Center, October 27, 2022, https://www.pewresearch.org/religion/2022/10/27/views-of-the-u-s-as-a-christian-nation-and-opinions-about-christian-nationalism/.

8. Katherine Stewart, "Network of Christian Nationalism Leading Up to January 6," in *Christian Nationalism and the January 6, 2021, Insurrection* (Freedom from Religion Foundation, 2022), 10, https://ffrf.org/uploads/legal/Christian_Nationalism_and_the_Jan6_Insurrection-2-9-22.pdf.

9. PRRI Staff, "The 2020 Census of American Religion," July 8, 2021, https://www.prri.org/research/2020-census-of-american-religion/.

10. Eliza Griswold, "Millennial Evangelicals Diverge from Their Parents' Beliefs," *New Yorker*, August 27, 2018, https://www.newyorker.com/news/on-religion/millennial-evangelicals-diverge-from-their-parents-beliefs.

11. Robert P. Jones, *White Too Long: The Legacy of White Supremacy in American Christianity* (New York: Simon & Schuster, 2020), 11.

12. Dana Milbank, "Trump's Racist Appeals Powered a White Evangelical Tsunami," *Washington Post*, November 13, 2020, https://www.washingtonpost.com/opinions/2020/11/13/trumps-racist-appeals-powered-white-evangelical-tsunami/.

13. Jennifer Cotto, "Racial Segregation Still Prevalent in Church Communities," WTTW News, August 29, 2022, https://news.wttw.com/2022/08/29/racial-segregation-still-prevalent-church-communities.

14. Daniel Cox, Juhgem Navarro-Rivera, and Robert P. Jones, "Economic Insecurity, Rising Inequality, and Doubts about the Future, Findings from the 2014 American Values Survey," PRRI, 2014, https://www.prri.org/research/survey-economic-insecurity-rising-inequality-and-doubts-about-the-future-findings-from-the-2014-american-values-survey/.

15. See, e.g., Religion News Service, "Russell Moore to ERLC Trustees: 'They Want Me to Live in Psychological Terror,'" June 2, 2021, https://religionnews.com/2021/06/02/russell-moore-to-erlc-trustees-they-want-me-to-live-in-psychological-terror/. Russell Moore is a highly regarded theologian who quit the Southern Baptist Convention in 2020 over what he says were deeply personal attacks against him when he tried to facilitate reconciliation and reform in the face of a widespread sex abuse scandal within Baptist churches and the Convention itself. At the time of his resignation, he was the president of the Convention's Ethics and Religious Liberty Commission.

16. See D. W. Bebbington, *Evangelicalism in Modern Britain: A History from the 1730s to the 1980s* (London: Routledge, 1989), 2–3.

17. Randall Balmer, "The Real Origins of the Religious Right," *Politico*, May 27, 2014, https://www.politico.com/magazine/story/2014/05/religious-right-real-origins-107133/.

18. Hannah Hartig, "About Six-in-Ten Americans Say Abortion Should Be Legal in All or Most Cases," Pew Research Center, June 13, 2022, https://www.pewresearch.org/short-reads/2022/06/13/about-six-in-ten-americans-say-abortion-should-be-legal-in-all-or-most-cases-2/.

19. Dobbs v. Jackson Women's Health Organization, 142 S. Ct. 2228 (2022) (abortion); Roman Catholic Diocese of Brooklyn v. Cuomo, 141 S. Ct. 63 (2020) (pandemic restrictions on church attendance); Kennedy v. Bremerton School Dist., 142 S. Ct. 2407 (2022) (prayer during public school sporting events); Carson v. Makin, 142 S. Ct. 1987 (2022) (public assistance to religious schools).

20. Robert P. Jones, Daniel Cox, and Juhem Navarro-Rivera, *Believers, Sympathizers, and Skeptics: Why Americans Are Conflicted about Climate Change, Environmental Policy, and Science* (Public Religion Research Institute and American Academy of Religion, 2014), 4, https://www.prri.org/wp-content/uploads/2014/11/2014-Climate-Change-FINAL1-1.pdf.

21. Joel C. Rosenberg, Chosen People Ministries, *Evangelical Attitudes toward Israel Research Study*, Lifeway Research, 2017, http://lifewayresearch.com/wp-content/uploads/2017/12/Evangelical-Attitudes-Toward-Israel-Research-Study-Report.pdf.

22. What will happen to the Jewish "remnant" during the End of Days is a complex topic beyond my scope here. Much depends on their acceptance of Jesus Christ as their savior, an unacceptable belief in the Jewish faith.

23. Robert P. Jones, "The Unmaking of the White Christian Worldview," *Time*, September 29, 2021, https://time.com/6102117/white-christian-americans-sins/.

24. Alissa Wilkinson, "The 'Left Behind' Series Was Just the Latest Way America Prepared for the Rapture," *Washington Post*, July 13, 2016, https://www.washingtonpost.com/news/act-four/wp/2016/07/13/the-left-behind-series-was-just-the-latest-way-america-prepared-for-the-rapture/.

25. John Fea, "The Fear Sweepstakes: How Trump Captured the White Evangelical Vote," *Christian Century* 35, no. 14 (2018): 22–25.

26. Katherine Stewart, "Christian Nationalism Is One of Trump's Most Powerful Weapons," *New York Times*, January 6, 2022, https://www.nytimes.com/2022/01/06/opinion/jan-6-christian-nationalism.html.

27. Fea, "The Fear Sweepstakes," 23.

28. Ibid., 25.

29. "America's Changing Religious Landscape," Pew Research Center, 2014, https://www.pewresearch.org/religion/wp-content/uploads/sites/7/2015/05/RLS-08-26-full-report.pdf.

30. Hannah Hartig, "Republicans Turn More Negative toward Refugees as Number Admitted to U.S. Plummets," Pew Research Ctr., May 24, 2018, https://www.pewresearch.org/short-reads/2018/05/24/republicans-turn-more-negative-toward-refugees-as-number-admitted-to-u-s-plummets/.

31. Melissa Deckman, Dan Cox, Robert Jones, and Betsy Cooper, "Faith and the Free Market: Evangelicals, the Tea Party, and Economic Attitudes," *Politics and Religion* 10 (2017): 82–110.

32. Ibid., 99.

33. Ibid., 106.

34. Ibid., 100.

35. An excellent article explaining the range of views is David Geselbracht, "For Some Evangelical Christians, Climate Action Is a God-Given Mandate," *Grist*, June 23, 2021, https://grist.org/politics/evangelical-christians-climate-action-god-mandate-bible/. For a thoughtful story on the punishment of Richard Cizik, top lobbyist for the National Association of Evangelicals, who was driven out of the organization over his progressive position on climate change, see Gregory Warner and Jess Jiang, "The Loneliness of the Climate Change Christian," NPR, October 14, 2020, https://www.npr.org/2020/10/14/923715751/the-loneliness-of-the-climate-change-christian.

36. Pew Research Center, "Religion and Views on Climate and Energy Issues," October 22, 2015, https://www.pewresearch.org/science/2015/10/22/religion-and-views-on-climate-and-energy-issues/.

37. Dobbs v. Jackson Women's Health Organization, 142 S. Ct. 2228 (2022).

38. Adam Liptak, "An Extraordinary Winning Streak for Religion at the Supreme Court," *New York Times*, April 5, 2021, https://www.nytimes.com/2021/04/05/us/politics/supreme-court-religion.html.

39. Bostock v. Clayton County, Georgia, 140 S. Ct. 1731 (2020).

40. 303 Creative LLC v. Elenis, 143 S. Ct. 2298 (2023).

41. 26 U.S.C. § 501(c)(3).

42. Rebecca Speare-Cole, "Franklin Graham Says Trump 'Will Go Down in History as One of the Great Presidents," *Newsweek*, December 16, 2020, https://www.newsweek.com/franklin-graham-election-donald-trump-great-president-1555090.

43. Jeffrey Martin, "Franklin Graham Compares 10 Republicans Who Voted to Impeach Trump to Betrayal of Christ," *Newsweek*, January 14, 2021, https://www.newsweek.com/franklin-graham-compares-10-republicans-who-voted-impeach-trump-betrayal-christ-1561809.

44. The motto of Capitol Ministries, the group featured in this portion of the book, can be found at https://capmin.org/.

45. Margaret Talbot, "Are Evangelical Leaders Saving Scott Pruitt's Job?" *New*

Yorker, June 8, 2018, https://www.newyorker.com/news/daily-comment/are-evangelical-leaders-saving-scott-pruitts-job.

46. Ralph Drollinger, "God's Design for a Societal Safety Net," Capitol Ministries, September 25, 2017, https://capmin.org/gods-design-societal-safety-net/. Emphasis in original.

47. Ralph Drollinger, "Coming to Grips with the Religion of Environmentalism," Capitol Ministries, April 2, 2018, https://capmin.org/coming-to-grips-with-the-religion-of-environmentalism/. Emphasis in original. This study was re-posted in February 2022.

48. Pew Research Center, "Members of the Southern Baptist Convention," in *Religious Landscape Study*, (2014), https://www.pewresearch.org/religion/religious-landscape-study/religious-denomination/southern-baptist-convention/#racial-and-ethnic-composition; Dalia Fahmy, "7 Facts about Southern Baptists," Pew Research Center, June 7, 2019, https://www.pewresearch.org/short-reads/2019/06/07/7-facts-about-southern-baptists/.

49. Ruth Graham and Elizabeth Dias, "'Take the Ship': Conservatives Aim to Commandeer Southern Baptists," *New York Times*, June 12, 2021, https://www.nytimes.com/2021/06/12/us/southern-baptists-conservatives.html.

50. Eliza Griswold, "The Fight for the Heart of the Southern Baptist Convention," *New Yorker*, June 10, 2021, https://www.newyorker.com/news/on-religion/the-fight-for-the-heart-of-the-southern-baptist-convention.

51. Ruth Graham, "Southern Baptists Narrowly Head Off Ultraconservative Takeover," *New York Times*, June 15, 2921, https://www.nytimes.com/2021/06/15/us/southern-baptist-convention-president-ed-litton.html.

52. Guidepost Solutions LLC, *Report of the Independent Investigation: The Southern Baptist Convention Executive Committee's Response to Sexual Abuse Allegations and an Audit of the Procedures and Actions of the Credentials Committee* (May 15, 2022), https://www.sataskforce.net/s/Guidepost-Solutions-Independent-Investigation-Report___.pdf.

53. Liam Adams, "Southern Baptist Abuse Reform Task Force Starts Work: What to Know," *The Tennessean*, September 16, 2022, https://www.tennessean.com/story/news/religion/2022/09/16/southern-baptist-abuse-reform-task-force-what-to-know/69498393007/.

54. "Update from the Abuse Reform Implementation Task Force," September 16, 2022, https://www.abusereformtaskforce.net/updates/update-from-the-abuse-reform-implementation-task-force.

55. Boto quoted in Guidepost Solutions LLC, *Report of the Independent Investigation*, 6.

56. Peter Wehner, "The Evangelical Church Is Breaking Apart," *The Atlantic*, October 24, 2021, https://www.theatlantic.com/ideas/archive/2021/10/evangelical-trump-christians-politics/620469/.

57. Wehner, "The Evangelical Church."

58. Wehner, "The Evangelical Church."

59. Jones, *White Too Long.*

60. Michael Gerson, "The Last Temptation," *The Atlantic*, April 2018, https://www.theatlantic.com/magazine/archive/2018/04/the-last-temptation/554066/.

61. Robert P. Jones, "White Evangelicals Can't Quit Donald Trump," *The Atlantic*, April 20, 2018, https://www.theatlantic.com/politics/archive/2018/04/white-evangelicals-cant-quit-donald-trump/558461/.

62. Russell Moore, "The Roman Road from Insurrection," blog, January 11, 2021, https://www.russellmoore.com/2021/01/11/the-roman-road-from-insurrection/.

63. Andrew Seidel et al., *Christian Nationalism and the January 6, 2021, Insurrection*, Baptist Joint Committee for Religious Liberty, February 10, 2022, 10, https://bjconline.org/wp-content/uploads/2022/02/Christian_Nationalism_and_the_Jan6_Insurrection-2-9-22.pdf.

64. Baptist Joint Committee for Religious Liberty, "Religious Liberty for All," https://bjconline.org/mission-history/, accessed November. 21, 2023.

65. Freedom from Religion Foundation, "Who We Are," https://ffrf.org/about.

66. Amanda Tyler, "Introduction," in Seidel et al., *Christian Nationalism.*

67. Paul A. Djupe and Jacob Dennen, "Christian Nationalists and QAnon Followers Tend to Be Anti-Semitic," *Washington Post*, January 26, 2021, https://www.washingtonpost.com/politics/2021/01/26/christian-nationalists-qanon-followers-tend-be-anti-semitic-that-was-visible-capitol-attack/.

68. Andrew Whitehead and Samuel Perry, "What Is Christian Nationalism?," in Seidel et al., *Christian Nationalism*, 2. See also Andrew Whitehead and Samuel Perry, *Taking America Back for God* (New York: Oxford University Press, 2020).

69. Ibid., 3.

70. Andrew Seidel, "Events, People, and Networks Leading Up to January 6," in Seidel et al., *Christian Nationalism*, 15.

71. Ibid., 16–17.

72. Ibid., 23.

73. Michael Luo, "The Wasting of the Evangelical Mind," *The New Yorker*, March 4, 2021, https://www.newyorker.com/news/daily-comment/the-wasting-of-the-evangelical-mind

74. Juliana Kim, "U.S. Capitol rioter the 'QAnon Sham'is released early from federal prison," NPR, March 31, 2023, https://www.npr.org/2023/03/31/1167319814/qanon-shaman-jacob-chansley-capitol-riot-early-release-reentry.

CHAPTER 7

1. Potok's comments are made on the video that accompanies Clyde Haberman, "Memories of Waco Siege Continue to Fuel Far-Right Groups," *New York Times*, July 13, 2015, https://www.nytimes.com/2015/07/13/us/memories-of-waco-siege-continue-to-fuel-far-right-groups.html.

2. Cassandra Vinograd, "Oath Keepers Turn Up at Michael Brown Protests in Ferguson, Missouri," *NBC News*, August 11, 2015, https://www.nbcnews.com/storyline/michael-brown-shooting/oath-keepers-turn-michael-brown-protests-ferguson-missouri-n407696.

3. Kathleen Gray, "In Michigan, a Dress Rehearsal for the Chaos at the Capitol on Wednesday," *New York Times*, January 9, 2021, https://www.nytimes.com/2021/01/09/us/politics/michigan-state-capitol.html.

4. Constitutional Sheriffs & Peace Officers Association, "Statement of Positions," https://cspoa.org/statement-of-positions/, accessed August 3, 2023.

5. Stephanie Mencimer, "He Was a Board Member of the Oath Keepers. Now He's Holding State-Approved Trainings for Law Enforcement in Texas," *Mother Jones*, October 29, 2021, https://www.motherjones.com/politics/2021/10/oath-keepers-texas-richard-mack-profile-sheriff/.

6. Protect America Now, https://protectamericanow.com/stand-together/, accessed August 3, 2023.

7. Julia Harte and R. Jeffrey Smith, "'The Army to Set Our Nation Free,'" Center for Public Integrity, April 18, 2016, https://publicintegrity.org/national-security/the-army-to-set-our-nation-free/.

8. Sheera Frenkel and Annie Karni, "Proud Boys Celebrate Trump's 'Stand By' Remark about Them at the Debate," *New York Times*, September 29, 2020, https://www.nytimes.com/2020/09/29/us/trump-proud-boys-biden.html.

9. See, e.g., Anti-Defamation League, "Backgrounder: Sovereign Citizen Movement," February 6, 2017, https://www.adl.org/resources/backgrounders/sovereign-citizen-movement.

10. People's Rights, "Your Rights," https://www.peoplesrights.org/your-rights, accessed July 27, 2023.

11. Ammon Bundy for Governor, "Keep Idaho Plan," section 15 (abortion), 2022, https://www.votebundy.com/about/keep-idaho-idaho-plan/?4.15.

12. Sam Jackson, "Conspiracy Theories in the Patriot/Militia Movement," presented at George Washington University Program on Extremism, May 2017, 13–14, https://extremism.gwu.edu/sites/g/files/zaxdzs2191/f/downloads/Jackson%2C%20Conspiracy%20Theories%20Final.pdf.

13. Brady Act, Pub. L. No. 103-159, 107 Stat. 1536 (1993). The assault weapons ban was imposed under the Public Safety and Recreational Firearms Use Protec-

tion Act of 1994. Pub. L. No. 103-322, Title XI, subtitle A, 108 Stat. 1796 (1996). It lapsed on September 13, 2004.

14. Manny Fernandez, "Conspiracy Theories over Jade Helm Training Exercise Get Some Traction in Texas," *New York Times*, May 6, 2015, https://www.nytimes.com/2015/05/07/us/conspiracy-theories-over-jade-helm-get-some-traction-in-texas.html.

15. Jackson, "Conspiracy Theories," 9.

16. Robert Downen and William Melhado, "Trump Vows Retribution at Waco Rally: 'I Am Your Warrior, I Am Your Justice,'" *Texas Tribune*, March 25, 2023, https://www.texastribune.org/2023/03/25/donald-trump-waco-rally-retribution-justice/.

17. Kathleen Belew, *Bring the War Home: The White Power Movement and Paramilitary America* (Cambridge, MA: Harvard University Press, 2018), 19–32.

18. Ibid., 3.

19. See, e.g., Peter B. Kraska and Louis J. Cubellis, "Militarizing Mayberry and Beyond: Making Sense of American Paramilitary Policing," *Justice Quarterly* 14 (1997): 607–629.

20. The best book on Ruby Ridge was written by Jess Walter, a journalist who covered the events as they unfolded. Jess Walter, *Ruby Ridge: The Truth & Tragedy of the Randy Weaver Family* (New York: ReganBooks, 2002) (previously published as *Every Knee Shall Bow: The Truth & Tragedy of Ruby Ridge and the Randy Weaver Family*).

21. Ibid., 185.

22. Ibid., 186.

23. The PBS program *American Experience* produced a documentary on the incident. Barak Goodman, dir., "Ruby Ridge: Every Knee Shall Bow," *American Experience*, 2021, https://www.pbs.org/wgbh/americanexperience/films/ruby-ridge/.

24. U.S. Department of Justice, *Report of the Ruby Ridge Task Force to the Office of Professional Responsibility of Investigation of Allegations of Improper Governmental Conduct in the Investigation, Apprehension and Prosecution of Randall C. Weaver and Kevin L. Harris*, June 10, 1994, https://www.justice.gov/sites/default/files/opr/legacy/2006/11/09/rubyreportcover_39.pdf.

25. "How What Happened 25 Years Ago at Ruby Ridge Still Matters Today," *All Things Considered*, NPR, August 18, 2017, https://www.npr.org/2017/08/18/544523302/how-what-happened-25-years-ago-at-ruby-ridge-still-matters-today.

26. Ibid.

27. Ibid.

28. Auntie Side Eye, "David Koresh Home Video," YouTube, March 8, 1993, https://www.youtube.com/watch?v=_bkoUoZUPWY.

29. Malcolm Gladwell, "Sacred and Profane: How Not to Negotiate with

Believers," *New Yorker*, March 24, 2014, https://www.newyorker.com/magazine/2014/03/31/sacred-and-profane-4.

30. Ibid.

31. Ibid.

32. Ibid.

33. For an excellent description of Janet Reno's professional circumstances at the time, see Jane Mayer, "Janet Reno, Alone," *New Yorker*, November 23, 1997, https://www.newyorker.com/magazine/1997/12/01/janet-reno-alone. Reno was incensed when she realized she had been misled by the FBI regarding the potential lethality of the tear gas. Edward Walsh and Richard Leiby, "Reno, Angry, Vows to Press FBI on Waco," *Washington Post*, August 27, 1999, https://www.washingtonpost.com/wp-srv/national/daily/aug99/reno27.htm.

34. Clyde Haberman, "Memories of Waco Siege Continue to Fuel Far-Right Groups," *New York Times*, July 12, 2015, https://www.nytimes.com/2015/07/13/us/memories-of-waco-siege-continue-to-fuel-far-right-groups.html, and accompanying video, *The Shadow of Waco, RetroReport*, prod. Liam Dalzell, ed. Bret Sigler, and narr. Zachary Green. I rearranged the comments from their order in the video but did not change their content in any way.

35. Aaron Brilbeck, "Michigan Militia Group Had Ties to Timothy McVeigh," *News9*, October 9, 2020, https://www.news9.com/story/5f80fb1f1f327834b9461b18/michigan-militia-group-had-ties-to-timothy-mcveigh.

36. Mitch Smith, "Man Receives Nearly 20 Years in Prison for Plot to Kidnap Gov. Gretchen Whitmer," *New York Times*, December 28, 2022, https://www.nytimes.com/2022/12/28/us/barry-croft-michigan-sentencing.html.

37. For an analysis of these developments, see "The Second Wave, Return of the Militias," Southern Poverty Law Center, August 2009, https://www.splcenter.org/sites/default/files/d6_legacy_files/downloads/The_Second_Wave.pdf.

38. Sergio Olmos, "Why U.S. Far-Right Groups Are Shifting Their Focus to Local Communities," *The Guardian*, December 22, 2021, https://www.theguardian.com/world/2021/dec/22/us-far-right-groups-local-impacts.

39. Ibid.

40. Mike Baker and Danielle Ivory, "Why Public Health Faces a Crisis across the U.S.," *New York Times*, October 18, 2021. The quote used as the heading for this section comes from this article.

41. Michelle Mello, Jeremy Green, and Joshua Sharfstein, "Attacks on Public Health Officials during COVID-19," *JAMA* 324 (2020): 741–742.

42. Baker and Ivory, "Why Public Health Faces a Crisis across the U.S." The quote used as the heading for this section comes from this article.

43. Ibid.

44. Ibid.

45. Jessica Pishko, "He Calls Himself the 'American Sheriff.' Whose Law Is He Following?" *Politico*, October 15, 2021, https://www.politico.com/news/magazine/2021/10/15/mark-lamb-arizona-constitutional-sheriff-elections-republicans-514781.

46. Ibid.

47. Lou Marzeles, "Songer Statement Sets Off Backlash," *The Goldendale Sentinel*, June 30, 2021, https://www.goldendalesentinel.com/news/songer-statement-sets-off-backlash/article_0ed968b8-d9c1-11eb-9851-27951a6e3ab1.html.

48. Ibid.

49. Jacob Bertram, "Songer Speaks at 'We the People' Rally," *Columbia Gorge News*, July 29, 2020, https://www.columbiagorgenews.com/free_news/songer-speaks-at-we-the-people-rally/article_211cbe56-18bb-571d-8a30-81e5448e4db9.html.

50. Kathleen Gray, "In Michigan, a Dress Rehearsal for the Chaos at the Capitol on Wednesday," *New York Times*, January 9, 2021, https://www.nytimes.com/2021/01/09/us/politics/michigan-state-capitol.html.

51. "US: Armed Protesters Demand End to Michigan Coronavirus Lockdown," *Al Jazeera*, April 30, 2020, https://www.aljazeera.com/news/2020/4/30/us-armed-protesters-demand-end-to-michigan-coronavirus-lockdown.

52. Michael Ames, "How Ammon Bundy Helped Foment an Anti-Masker Rebellion in Idaho," *New Yorker*, December 21, 2020, https://www.newyorker.com/news/us-journal/how-ammon-bundy-helped-foment-an-anti-masker-rebellion-in-idaho.

53. Ibid.

54. Jane Hu, "When Public Health Becomes the Public Enemy," *High Country News*, September 24, 2021, https://www.hcn.org/issues/53.10/north-extremism-when-public-health-becomes-the-public-enemy-community.

55. Ian Max Stevenson, "Ammon Bundy Arrested in Trespassing Case at St. Luke's after Police Take 10-Month-Old," *Idaho Statesman*, March 12, 2022, https://www.eastidahonews.com/2022/03/ammon-bundy-arrested-in-trespassing-case-at-st-lukes-after-police-take-10-month-old/.

56. Ian Max Stevenson, "Boise Hospital Sues Ammon Bundy, Others Involved in Protests over Child Welfare Case," *East Idaho News*, May 11, 2022, https://www.eastidahonews.com/2022/05/boise-hospital-sues-ammon-bundy-others-involved-in-protests-over-child-welfare-case/.

57. Giffords Law Center to Prevent Gun Violence, "Guns in Public, Open Carry," https://giffords.org/lawcenter/gun-laws/policy-areas/guns-in-public/open-carry/, accessed August 3, 2023.

58. Rachel Monroe, "Free Country, Permitless Carry and the New Gun-Rights Extremism," *Harper's Magazine*, November 2021, https://harpers.org/archive/2022/02/free-country-permitless-carry-new-guns-rights-extremism/.

59. Mathew Miller, Wilson Zhang, and Deborah Azrael, "Firearm Purchasing During the COVID-19 Pandemic: Results from the 2021 National Firearms Survey," *Annals of Internal Medicine*, February 2022, https://doi.org/10.7326/M21-3423.

60. N.Y. State Rifle and Pistol Association v. Bruen, 142 S. Ct. 2111 (2022).

61. See, e.g., Jacob D. Charles, "Are Gun Laws Constitutional? Courts Must Now Look at History to Decide," *Washington Post*, June 30, 2022, https://www.washingtonpost.com/politics/2022/06/30/bruen-clarence-thomas-supreme-court-second-amendment/.

62. Ed Yong, "We're Already Barreling toward the Next Pandemic," *The Atlantic*, September 29, 2021; Ed Yong, "The Pandemic's Legacy Is Already Clear," *The Atlantic*, September 30, 2022.

63. Oath Keepers, "By-Laws," § 8.05, https://web.archive.org/web/20211112000100/https://oathkeepers.org/bylaws/#article-viii.

64. Indiana Oath Keepers, http://www.indianaoathkeepers.org/membership.html, accessed August 3, 2023.

65. 10 U.S.C. § 502.

66. Anti-Defamation League, *The Oath Keepers, Anti-Government Extremists Recruiting Military and Police*, 2015, https://www.adl.org/sites/default/files/documents/assets/pdf/combating-hate/The-Oath-Keepers-ADL-Report.pdf.

67. Sam Jackson, *Oath Keepers: Patriotism and the Edge of Violence in a Right-Wing Antigovernment Group* (New York: Columbia University Press, 2020).

68. Eric McQueen, "Blog Post, Examining Extremism: The Oath Keepers," Center for Strategic & International Studies, June 17, 2021, https://www.csis.org/blogs/examining-extremism/examining-extremism-oath-keepers.

69. Mike Giglio, "A Pro-Trump Militant Group Has Recruited Thousands of Police, Soldiers, and Veterans," *The Atlantic*, November 2020, https://www.theatlantic.com/magazine/archive/2020/11/right-wing-militias-civil-war/616473/.

70. Ibid.

71. Anti-Defamation League, "Backgrounder: The Oath Keepers," November 3, 2020, updated January 13, 2022, https://www.adl.org/resources/backgrounders/oath-keepers.

72. Southern Poverty Law Center, "Oath Keepers," https://www.splcenter.org/fighting-hate/extremist-files/group/oath-keepers, accessed December 28, 2022.

73. Brian Heffernan, "In Ferguson, Oath Keepers Draw Both Suspicion and Gratitude," *Al Jazeera America*, December 14, 2014, http://america.aljazeera.com/articles/2014/12/14/oath-keepers-fergusonprotests.html.

74. Southern Poverty Law Center, "Oath Keepers."

75. Erica Chenoweth and Jeremy Pressman, "This Summer's Black Lives Matter Protesters Were Overwhelmingly Peaceful, Our Research Finds," *Washington Post*, October 16, 2020, https://www.washingtonpost.com/politics/2020/10/16/

this-summers-black-lives-matter-protesters-were-overwhelming-peaceful-our-research-finds/.

76. District of Columbia U.S. Attorney's Office, "34 Months Since the Jan. 6 Attack on the Capitol," U.S. Department of Justice, November 6, 2023, https://www.justice.gov/usao-dc/33-months-jan-6-attack-capitol-0.

77. Department of Justice, "Attorney General Merrick B. Garland Delivers Remarks on the First Anniversary of the Attack on the Capitol," press release, January 5, 2022, https://www.justice.gov/opa/gallery/attorney-general-merrick-b-garland-delivers-remarks-first-anniversary-attack-capitol.

78. Ibid.

79. Ibid.

80. 18 U.S.C. § 2384.

81. Alan Feuer, "Stewart Rhodes Is Not the Only Oath Keeper on Trial," *New York Times*, October 10, 2022.

82. Indictment at 10, United States of America v. Elmer Stewart Rhodes, Kelly Meggs, Jessica Watkins, Joshua James, Roberto Minuta, Joseph Hackett, David Moerschel, Brian Ulrich, Thomas Caldwell, and Edward Vallejo (D.D.C. January 12, 2022), https://www.justice.gov/opa/press-release/file/1462481/download.

83. Ibid.

84. Ibid., 13.

85. Ibid., 14.

86. 10 U.S.C. § 252, which reads: "Whenever the President considers that unlawful obstructions, combinations, or assemblages, or rebellion against the authority of the United States, make it impracticable to enforce the laws of the United States in any State by the ordinary course of judicial proceedings, he may call into Federal service such of the militia of any State, and use such of the armed forces, as he considers necessary to enforce those laws or to suppress the rebellion."

87. Matt Zapotsky, "Trump Threatens Military Action to Quell Protests, and the Law Would Let Him Do It," *Washington Post*, June 1, 2020, https://www.washingtonpost.com/national-security/can-trump-use-military-to-stop-protests-insurrection-act/2020/06/01/c3724380-a46b-11ea-b473-04905b1af82b_story.html.

88. Zachary Cohen, "Top US General Rejected Trump Suggestions Military Should 'Crack Skulls' during Protests Last Year, New Book Claims," CNN, June 24, 2021, https://www.cnn.com/2021/06/24/politics/bender-book-trump-milley-protests/index.html.

89. Indictment at 18, United States v. Rhodes et al.

90. Jan Wolfe, "Oath Keeper Stewart Rhodes Says Member Were 'Stupid' to Enter Capitol on Jan. 6," *Wall Street Journal*, November 7, 2022.

91. Government's Omnibus Sentencing Memorandum and Motion for Upward Departure at 101, United States v. Rhodes et al., No. 22-cr-15-APM (D.D.C.

May 5, 2023), https://s3.documentcloud.org/documents/23807561/565-usa-omnibus-sentencing-memo.pdf.

92. Kyle Cheney, "Oath Keepers Founder Stewart Rhodes Gets 18 Years for Jan. 6 Seditious Conspiracy," *Politico*, May 25, 2023, https://www.politico.com/news/2023/05/25/oath-keepers-founder-stewart-rhodes-gets-18-years-for-jan-6-seditious-conspiracy-00098822.

93. Luke Mogelson, "How Trump Supporters Came to Hate the Police," *New Yorker*, September 10, 2022.

94. Jeffrey Goldberg, "James Mattis Denounces President Trump, Describes Him as a Threat to the Constitution," *The Atlantic*, June 3, 2020, https://www.theatlantic.com/politics/archive/2020/06/james-mattis-denounces-trump-protests-militarization/612640/.

CHAPTER 8

1. Rafe Pomerance, "The Dangers from Climate Warming: A Public Awakening," in *The Challenge of Global Warming*, ed. Dean Edwin Abrahamson (Washington, D.C.: Island Press, 1989), 259–269.

2. Naomi Oreskes, Erik M. Conway, and Matthew Shindell, "From Chicken Little to Dr. Pangloss: William Nierenberg, Global Warming, and the Social Deconstruction of Scientific Knowledge," *Historical Studies in the Natural Sciences* 38 (2008): 109–152. Emphasis in original.

3. This point has been made in several good books, including Thomas McGarity and Wendy Wagner, *Bending Science: How Special Interests Corrupt Public Health Research* (Cambridge, MA: Harvard University Press, 2008); and Naomi Oreskes and Erik Conway, *Merchants of Doubt: How a Handful of Scientists Obscured the Truth on Issues from Tobacco Smoke to Climate Change* (New York: Bloomsbury Press, 2011).

4. *Greenhouse Effect and Global Climate Change, Part 2: Hearing before the S. Comm. on Energy and Natural Resources*, 100th Cong., 1st Sess. 39 (1988), statement of Dr. James Hansen, director, NASA Goddard Institute for Space Studies.

5. Ibid., 34.

6. Andrew C. Revkin, "Strong Action Urged to Curb Warming," *New York Times*, June 11, 2008, https://www.nytimes.com/2008/06/11/world/11climate.html. See also Joint Science Academies Statement, "Climate Change Adaptation and the Transition to a Low Carbon Society," June 2008, http://insaindia.res.in/pdf/Climate_05.08_W.pdf.

7. IPCC, *Climate Change 2014 Synthesis Report, Summary for Policymakers* (2014), 4, 16, 17, https://www.ipcc.ch/site/assets/uploads/2018/02/AR5_SYR_FINAL_SPM.pdf ("high confidence" is IPCC-speak for conclusions that are so strongly supported by available research that the group regards them as dispositive).

8. IPCC, *Global Warming of 1.5°C* (2018), 4, https://www.ipcc.ch/sr15/. See also Coral Davenport "Major Climate Report Describes a Strong Risk of Crisis as Early as 2040," *New York Times*, October 7, 2018, https://www.nytimes.com/2018/10/07/climate/ipcc-climate-report-2040.html.

9. USGCRP, *Fourth National Climate Assessment*, Volume 2: *Impacts, Risks, and Adaptation in the United States: Report-in-Brief*, ed. D. R. Reidmiller et al. (Washington, D.C.: U.S. Global Climate Change Research Program, 2018), https://nca2018.globalchange.gov/.

10. USGCRP, *Fifth National Climate Assessment*, ed. Allison R. Crimmins et al. (Washington, D.C.: U.S. Global Climate Change Research Program, 2023), https://www.globalchange.gov/our-work/national-climate-assessment. For an excellent summary of the report and its implications, see Marianne Lavelle, Katie Surman, Kiley Price, and Nicholas Kusnetz, "Report Charts Climate Change's Growing Impact in the US While Stressing Benefits of Action," Inside Climate News, November 14, 2023, https://insideclimatenews.org/news/14112023/biden-national-cliimate-assessment/.

11. Elizabeth Kolbert, "The U.N.'s Terrifying Climate Report," *New Yorker*, August 15, 2021, https://www.newyorker.com/magazine/2021/08/23/the-uns-terrifying-climate-report.

12. Ibid.

13. James Hansen, "G-8 Failure Reflects U.S. Failure on Climate Change," *HuffPost*, August 9, 2009, https://www.huffpost.com/entry/g-8-failure-reflects-us-f_b_228597.

14. Gretchen Goldman and Paul Rogerson, "Assessing Trade and Business Groups' Position on Climate Change," Center for Science and Democracy at the Union of Concerned Scientists, February 2013, 6, https://www.ucsusa.org/sites/default/files/2019-09/trade-and-business-groups-climate-change.pdf.

15. For more information on where Krupp stood entering the climate change fight, see James Verini, "The Devil's Advocate," *The New Republic*, September 24, 2007, https://newrepublic.com/article/62836/devils-advocate.

16. Petra Bartosiewicz and Marissa Miley, *The Too Polite Revolution: Why the Recent Campaign to Pass Comprehensive Climate Legislation in the United States Failed*, January 2013, 30–31, https://papers.ssrn.com/sol3/papers.cfm?abstract_id=2200690. The report was commissioned by the Rockefeller Family Fund in conjunction with the Columbia University Graduate School of Journalism.

17. Ibid.

18. Theda Skocpol, *Naming the Problem: What It Will Take to Counter Extremism and Engage Americans in the Fight against Global Warming*, January 2011, https://scholars.org/sites/scholars/files/skocpol_captrade_report_january_2013_0.pdf.

19. Ibid., 9–11.

20. Pub. L. No. 118-148, 124 Stat. 119.

21. Skocpol, *Naming the Problem*, 35.

22. Ibid.

23. Pub. L. No. 111-203, Title X, 124 Stat. 1376, 1955 (2010).

24. S. 2877, Carbon Limits and Energy for America's Renewal (CLEAR) Act, 111th Congress (2009), https://www.congress.gov/111/bills/s2877/BILLS-111s2877is.pdf.

25. Skocpol, *Naming the Problem*, 125.

26. Ibid., 126.

27. Ibid., 127.

28. Joseph Romm, "The Problem Wasn't the Green Groups: What Skocpol Gets Wrong about the Climate Bill Fight," *Grist*, January 19, 2013, https://grist.org/politics/the-problem-wasnt-the-green-groups-what-skocpol-gets-wrong-about-the-climate-bill-fight/.

29. Ibid.

30. Ibid.

31. Ibid.

32. Ibid.

33. Joe Romm, "The Failed Presidency of Barack Obama, Part 2," *ThinkProgress*, November 4, 2010, https://archive.thinkprogress.org/the-failed-presidency-of-barack-obama-part-2-8ac8253e600d/.

34. Bill McKibben, "Beyond Baby Steps: Analyzing the Cap-and-Trade Flop," *Grist*, January 14, 2013, https://grist.org/climate-energy/beyond-baby-steps-analyzing-the-cap-and-trade-flop/.

35. Eric Tucker and Ben Fox, "FBI Director Says Antifa Is an Ideology, Not an Organization," *Washington Post*, September 17, 2020.

36. Congressional Research Service, "Antifa—Background," March 1, 2018, https://crsreports.congress.gov/product/pdf/IF/IF10839/2.

37. Mark Bray, *Antifa: The Antifascist Handbook* (Brooklyn, NY: Melville House, 2017), xii.

38. Ibid., xxiv.

39. Derek Hawkins, "A Dartmouth Antifa Expert Was Disavowed by His College President for 'Supporting Violent Protest,' Angering Many Faculty," *Washington Post*, August 29, 2017, https://www.washingtonpost.com/news/morning-mix/wp/2017/08/28/a-dartmouth-antifa-expert-was-disavowed-by-his-college-president-for-supporting-violent-protest-angering-many-faculty/.

40. Philip Hanlon, Statement on Lecturer in History Mark Bray, posted on Aug. 21, 2017, by the Office of the President, Dartmouth, https://president.dartmouth.edu/news/2017/08/statement-lecturer-history-mark-bray.

41. Hawkins, "A Dartmouth Antifa Expert."

42. Bray, *Antifa*, xv.

43. Ibid., xiii; Robert O. Paxton, *The Anatomy of Fascism* (New York: Vintage, 2004), 17.

44. Bray, *Antifa*, xiii.

45. Ibid., xv.

46. Yaron Steinbuch, "Milo Yiannopoulos Says He Is 'Ex-Gay,' Wants to Rehabilitate Conversion Therapy," *New York Post*, March 10, 2021, https://nypost.com/2021/03/10/milo-yiannopoulos-announces-he-is-ex-gay-and-sodomy-free/.

47. Allum Bokhari and Milo Yiannopoulos, "An Establishment Conservative's Guide to the Alt-Right," Breitbart, March 29, 2016.

48. Ibid.

49. Ibid.

50. Anti-Defamation League, "Backgrounder: From Alt Right to Alt Lite: Naming the Hate," July 12, 2017, https://www.adl.org/resources/backgrounders/from-alt-right-to-alt-lite-naming-the-hate.

51. Kimberly Hefling, "Universities Fear a Violent 2018," *Politico*, December 26, 2017, https://www.politico.com/story/2017/12/26/white-nationalists-antifa-university-violence-305014.

52. Nicole Hensley, "Video Shared ahead of CPAC Shows Milo Yiannopoulos Appearing to Speak Fondly of Relationships between Men and 'Young Boys,'" *Daily News*, February 20, 2017, https://www.nydailynews.com/news/national/video-shows-milo-yiannopoulos-speaking-fondly-pedophilia-article-1.2977071.

53. Anti-Defamation League, "Milo Yiannopoulos: Five Things to Know," March 10, 2017, https://www.adl.org/resources/backgrounders/milo-yiannopoulos-five-things-to-know.

54. Jelani Cobb, "The Mistake the Berkeley Protesters Made about Milo Yiannopoulos," *New Yorker*, February 15, 2017, https://www.newyorker.com/news/daily-comment/the-mistake-the-berkeley-protesters-made-about-milo-yiannopoulos.

55. Erica Chenoweth and Jeremy Pressman, "This Summer's Black Lives Matter Protesters Were Overwhelmingly Peaceful, Our Research Finds," *Washington Post*, October 16, 2020, https://www.washingtonpost.com/politics/2020/10/16/this-summers-black-lives-matter-protesters-were-overwhelming-peaceful-our-research-finds/.

56. *The Oregonian* published an informative story about this history and its long-lasting effects. Kristen de Leon and Mark Friesen, "Is Portland Still the Whitest Big City in America?," *The Oregonian*, October 2, 2022, https://www.oregonlive.com/data/2022/10/is-portland-still-the-whitest-big-city-in-america.html.

57. U.S. Department of Justice, Civil Rights Division, "Civil Rights Division Highlights: 2009–2017: Fulfilling America's Promise of Equal Justice and Equal Opportunity for All," January 2017, 29, https://www.justice.gov/crt/page/file/923096/download; U.S. Department of Justice, "Court Approves Police Re-

form Agreement in Portland, Oregon," press release, August 29, 2014, https://perma.cc/9ZNS-JF5G.

58. Jonathan Levinson, Conrad Wilson, James Doubek, and Suzanne Nuyen, "America Reckons with Racial Injustice: Federal Officers Use Unmarked Vehicles to Grab People in Portland, DHS Confirms," *All Things Considered*, NPR, July 17, 2020, https://www.npr.org/2020/07/17/892277592/federal-officers-use-unmarked-vehicles-to-grab-protesters-in-portland.

59. Adam Goldman, Katie Benner, and Zolan Kanno-Youngs, "How Trump's Focus on Antifa Distracted Attention from the Far-Right Threat," *New York Times*, January 30, 2021, https://www.nytimes.com/2021/01/30/us/politics/trump-right-wing-domestic-terrorism.html.

60. Hallie Golden, Mike Baker and Adam Goldman, "Suspect in Fatal Portland Shooting Is Killed by Officers during Arrest," *New York Times*, September 3, 2020, updated April 12, 2021, https://www.nytimes.com/2020/09/03/us/michael-reinoehl-arrest-portland-shooting.html.

61. Ibid.

62. Neil MacFarquhar, "Suspect in Kenosha Killings Lionized the Police," *New York Times*, August 27, 2020, updated October 31, 2021, https://www.nytimes.com/2020/08/27/us/kyle-rittenhouse-kenosha.html.

63. Meg Kelly and Elyse Samuels, "Who Caused the Violence at Protests? It Wasn't Antifa," *Washington Post*, June 22, 2020, https://www.washingtonpost.com/politics/2020/06/22/who-caused-violence-protests-its-not-antifa/.

64. Maggie Haberman and Charlie Savage, "Trump, Lacking Clear Authority, Says U.S. Will Declare Antifa a Terrorist Group," *New York Times*, May 31, 2020, updated June 10, 2020, https://www.nytimes.com/2020/05/31/us/politics/trump-antifa-terrorist-group.html.

65. Ibid.

66. "Remarks on the Nationwide Demonstrations and Civil Unrest following the Death of George Floyd in Minneapolis, Minnesota," *Daily Compilation of Presidential Documents*, June 1, 2020.

67. Kerby Goff and John McCarthy, "No, Antifa Didn't 'Infiltrate' Black Lives Matter during the 2020 Protests. But Did It Increase Violence?" *Washington Post*, February 8, 2022, https://www.washingtonpost.com/politics/2022/02/08/antifa-blm-extremism-violence/.

68. Chenoweth and Pressman, "This Summer's Black Lives Matter Protests."

69. Brittany Bernstein, "Biden Says Antifa Is 'An Idea, Not an Organization' during Presidential Debate," *National Review*, September 29, 2020, https://www.nationalreview.com/news/biden-says-antifa-is-an-idea-not-an-organization-during-presidential-debate/.

70. Ibid.

71. Luke Mogelson, "In the Streets with Antifa," *New Yorker*, October 25,

2020, https://www.newyorker.com/magazine/2020/11/02/trump-antifa-movement-portland.

72. Jerry Zremski, "Trump Tweet on Gugino Sparks Bipartisan Outrage," *The Buffalo News*, June 9, 2020, https://buffalonews.com/news/local/trump-tweet-on-gugino-sparks-bipartisan-outrage/article_0baee8ec-6f55-5b1e-912f-77f7e9462ecc.html.

73. Jaclyn Peiser, "'Their Tactics Are Fascistic': Barr Slams Black Lives Matter, Accuses the Left of 'Tearing Down the System,'" *Washington Post*, August 10, 2020, https://www.washingtonpost.com/nation/2020/08/10/barr-fox-antifa-blm/.

74. Allan Smith, "Justice Department Deems New York City, Portland and Seattle 'Anarchist Jurisdictions,'" *NBC News*, September 21, 2020, updated Sept. 22, 2020, https://www.nbcnews.com/politics/justice-department/justice-dept-deems-new-york-city-portland-seattle-anarchist-jurisdictions-n1240600.

75. Seth Jones, Catrina Doxsee, and Nicholas Harrington, "The Escalating Terrorism Problem in the United States," Center for Strategic and International Studies, June 2020, https://csis-website-prod.s3.amazonaws.com/s3fs-public/publication/200612_Jones_DomesticTerrorism_v6.pdf.

76. University of Maryland START, Global Terrorism Database, https://www.start.umd.edu/gtd/, accessed August 4, 2023.

77. Jones, Doxsee, and Harrington, "The Escalating Terrorism Problem." START, "Global Terrorism Database."

78. Davey Alba, "Antifa Falsehood Tops List of Misinformation after Capitol Rampage," *New York Times*, January 8, 2021, https://www.nytimes.com/2021/01/08/technology/antifa-falsehood-tops-list-of-misinformation-after-capitol-rampage.html.

CHAPTER 9

1. Byron Tau, "Obama: Republican 'Fever' Will Break after the Election," *Politico44 Blog*, June 6, 2012, https://www.politico.com/blogs/politico44/2012/06/obama-republican-fever-will-break-after-the-election-125059. Obama's full comment was "I believe that if we're successful in this election, when we're successful in this election, that the fever may break, because there's a tradition in the Republican Party of more common sense than that. My hope, my expectation, is that after the election, now that it turns out that the goal of beating Obama doesn't make much sense because I'm not running again, that we can start getting some cooperation again."

2. Citizens United v. FEC, 588 U.S. 310 (2010).

3. The relevant provision was 2 U.S.C. § 441b (recodified at 52 U.S.C. § 30118).

4. McConnell v. FEC, 540 U.S. 93 (2003). The case concluded that the Bipartisan Campaign Reform Act was constitutional.

5. 558 U.S. 310, 329 (2010).

6. Ibid., 359–360.

7. Ibid., 370–371.

8. Ibid., 371.

9. Austin v. Michigan Chamber of Commerce, 494 U.S. 652 (1990).

10. Ibid., 660.

11. Ibid., 669.

12. *Citizens United*, 558 U.S. 310, 399.

13. Ibid., 394.

14. Citations supporting the statements made in the remainder of this paragraph may be found at 558 U.S. 419–422.

15. Ibid., 447–448.

16. Ibid., 475.

17. SpeechNow.org v. FEC, 599 F.3d 686 (D.C. Cir. 2010).

18. McCutcheon v. FEC, 572 U.S. 180 (2014).

19. Megan Brenan, "Americans Most Satisfied with Nation's Military, Security," Gallup, January 28, 2019, https://news.gallup.com/poll/246254/americans-satisfied-nation-military-security.aspx.

20. Scott Rasmussen, "Voters Rate Political Corruption as America's Biggest Crisis," RealClear Politics, April 25, 2019, https://www.realclearpolitics.com/articles/2019/04/25/voters_rate_political_corruption_as_americas_biggest_crisis_140156.html.

21. The phrase "we the corporations" is borrowed from Adam Winkler's terrific book on the history of how corporations conducted a lengthy battle to vindicate their constitutional rights. Adam Winkler, *We the Corporations: How American Businesses Won Their Civil Rights* (New York: Liveright, 2018).

22. Ibid.

23. 118 U.S. 394 (1886).

24. Winkler, *We the Corporations*, xv.

25. Ibid.

26. Ibid., 369.

27. Barack Obama, "Address before a Joint Session of Congress on the State of the Union," *Public Papers of the Presidents of the United States*, book 1 (January 27, 2010), 75, 81, https://www.govinfo.gov/app/collection/ppp/president-44_Obama,%20Barack%20H./2010/01%21A%21January%201%20to%20June%2030%2C%202010.

28. Martin Kady, "Justice Alito Mouths 'Not True,'" *Politico Now Blog*, January 27, 2010, https://www.politico.com/blogs/politico-now/2010/01/justice-alito-mouths-not-true-024608.

29. Ariane Vogue, "Chief Justice Roberts 'Troubled' by Scene at the State of the Union Address," *ABC News*, March 10, 2020, https://abcnews.go.com/Politics/chief-justice-roberts-troubled-scene-state-union/story?id=10063937.

30. Ibid.

31. Jim Leach, "*Citizens United*: Robbing America of Its Democratic Idealism," *Daedalus* 142, no. 2 (2013): 95–101, 96–97. Emphasis in original.

32. This vivid phrase is borrowed from a paper authored by Thomas Mann and E.J. Dionne under the auspices of the Brookings Institution. Thomas Mann and E.J. Dionne, "The Futility of Nostalgia and the Romanticism of the New Political Realists," Brookings, June 17, 2015, https://www.brookings.edu/research/the-futility-of-nostalgia-and-the-romanticism-of-the-new-political-realists/.

33. The group defines itself as "nonpartisan, independent, and nonprofit, OpenSecrets is the nation's premier research group tracking money in U.S. politics and its effect on elections and public policy. Our mission is to track the flow of money in American politics and provide the data and analysis to strengthen democracy." OpenSecrets, https://www.opensecrets.org/, accessed August 7, 2023.

34. Shane Goldmacher, "The Little Red Boxes Making a Mockery of Campaign Finance Laws," *New York Times*, May 16, 2022, https://www.nytimes.com/2022/05/16/us/politics/red-boxes-campaign-finance-democrats.html.

35. Ibid.

36. J. D. Vance, *Hillbilly Elegy: A Memoir of a Family and Culture in Crisis* (New York: Harper, 2018).

37. 17 U.S.C. §504(c)(3).

38. OpenSecrets, "Super PACs," https://www.opensecrets.org/political-action-committees-pacs/super-pacs/2022, accessed November 7, 2024.

39. OpenSecrets, "2022 Outside Spending, by Super PACs," https://www.opensecrets.org/outside-spending/super_pacs, accessed November 7, 2023.

40. Anna Massoglia & Karl Evers-Hillstrom, "'Dark Money' Topped $1 Billion in 2020, Largely Boosting Democrats," OpenSecrets, March 17, 2021, https://www.opensecrets.org/news/2021/03/one-billion-dark-money-2020-electioncycle/.

41. Krumholz quoted in Jonathan Weisman and Rachel Shorey, "Fueled by Billionaires, Political Spending Shatters Record Again," *New York Times*, November 3, 2022, https://www.nytimes.com/2022/11/03/us/politics/midterm-money-billionaires.html.

42. Amisa Ratliff, "Seven Numbers to Know about the Campaign Money That Flowed to House and Senate Members in 2020," Issue One, December 17, 2020, https://issueone.org/articles/seven-numbers-to-know-about-the-campaign-money-that-flowed-to-house-and-senate-members-in-2020/.

43. Michael Beckel and Meredith McGehee, "The Price of Power," Issue One, 2017, https://issueone.org/wp-content/uploads/2017/05/price-of-power-final.pdf.

44. Ibid., 10–17.

45. Norah O'Donnell, "Are Members of Congress Becoming Telemarketers?" *Sixty Minutes*, April 24, 2016, https://www.cbsnews.com/news/60-minutes-are-members-of-congress-becoming-telemarketers/.

46. Ibid.

47. Jacob Grumbach, Alexander Sahn, and Sarah Staszak, "Gender, Race, and Intersectionality in Campaign Finance," *Political Behavior* 44 (2022): 319–340.

48. Democracy in Color, "About Us," https://democracyincolor.com/aboutus1, accessed August 7, 2023. See Democracy in Color, *Democratic SuperPACs 2020 Report Card: The Good, the Bad, and the Wasteful*, September 3, 2020, https://democracyincolor.com/2020-report-cards.

49. U.S. Const. art. V.

50. U.S. Const. art. V.

51. For an overview of this debate, see Congressional Research Service, *The Article V Convention to Propose Constitutional Amendments: Contemporary Issues for Congress*, Report No. R42589, updated March 29, 2016, https://crsreports.congress.gov/product/pdf/R/R42589.

52. Ibid., 15–16.

53. S.1, For the People Act of 2021, 117th Cong. (2021) (Sponsor Sen. Jeff Merkley [D-ME]), https://www.congress.gov/bill/117th-congress/senate-bill/1; H.R.1, For the People Act of 2021, 117th Cong. (2021) (Sponsor Rep. John P. Sarbanes [D-MD-3]), https://www.congress.gov/bill/117th-congress/house-bill/1. For a quick summary, see Congressional Research Service, "H.R. 1 and S. 1: Overview and Related CRS Products," May 17, 2021, https://crsreports.congress.gov/product/pdf/IF/IF11097.

54. OpenSecrets, "Top 10 Dark Money Spenders (2008-2014)," https://www.opensecrets.org/dark-money/shadow-infographic, accessed August 7, 2023.

55. Jane Mayer, "Inside the Koch-Backed Effort to Block the Largest Election-Reform Bill in Half a Century," *New Yorker*, March 29, 2021, https://www.newyorker.com/news/news-desk/inside-the-koch-backed-effort-to-block-the-largest-election-reform-bill-in-half-a-century.

56. Ibid.

57. Ibid.

58. Ibid.

59. Ibid.

60. Ibid.

61. H.R. 1, Subtitle A, § 5001(5).

62. Adam Skaggs and Fred Wertheimer, "Empowering Small Donors in Federal Elections," Brennan Center for Justice, 2012, 10, https://www.brennancenter.org/publication/empowering-small-donors-federal-elections.

63. Libby Watson, "Why Did Only 1 Presidential Candidate Take Public Financing?" Sunlight Foundation, January 27, 2016, https://sunlightfoundation.com/2016/01/27/why-did-only-1-presidential-candidate-take-public-financing/.

64. Michael Li and Chris Leaverton, "After Redistricting, Here's How Each Party Could Win the House," Brennan Center for Justice, August 3, 2022, https://

www.brennancenter.org/our-work/analysis-opinion/after-redistricting-heres-how-each-party-could-win-house.

65. Hearing on S. 1, The For the People Act, U.S. Senate Committee on Rules and Administration, 117th Cong. 130 (March 24, 2021) (Testimony of Michael Waldman, President, the Brennan Center for Justice at NYU Law School), https://www.govinfo.gov/content/pkg/CHRG-117shrg44074/pdf/CHRG-117shrg44074.pdf.

66. Campaign Legal Ctr., "H.R. 1/S. 1 Disclosure Provisions: How the For the People Act Would Fix American Democracy's Dark Money Problem," March 2021, at 5, https://campaignlegal.org/sites/default/files/2021-03/Disclosure%20Report%203.23_1030.pdf.

67. Ibid.

68. Ibid.

69. H.R. 1 § 4111, S. 1 § 4111 (to be codified at 52 U.S.C. § 30126(a)(1)-(2), (d)(1)(B)).

70. Wendy Weiser, Daniel I. Weiner, and Dominique Erney, "Congress Must Pass the 'For the People Act,'" Brennan Center for Justice, April 1, 2021, https://www.brennancenter.org/our-work/policy-solutions/congress-must-pass-people-act.

71. H.R. 1 § 4111, S. 1 § 4111 (to be codified at 52 U.S.C. § 30126(a)(1)-(3)).

72. H.R. 1 § 4111, S. 1§ 4111 (to be codified at 52 U.S.C. § 30126(a)-(f)). See also Campaign Legal Center, "H.R. 1/S. 1 Disclosure Provisions," 14. For an explanation of how such practices work, see Andy Kroll, "The Secrets of a Right-Wing Dark-Money Juggernaut—Revealed," *Rolling Stone*, October 29, 2019, https://www.rollingstone.com/politics/politics-features/dark-money-republican-party-americans-for-job-security-peter-thiel-devos-904900/.

73. 26 U.S.C. §501(c)(4)(A).

74. Ibid.

75. Brian Schwartz, "Pro-Trump Dark Money Groups Organized the Rally That Led to Deadly Capitol Hill Riot," CNBC, January 9, 2021, https://www.cnbc.com/2021/01/09/pro-trump-dark-money-groups-organized-the-rally-that-led-to-deadly-capitol-hill-riot.html.

76. Jonathan Weisman and Michael D. Shear, "I.R.S. Scandal: Questions and Answers," *New York Times*, May 20, 2013, https://www.nytimes.com/2013/05/21/us/politics/irs-scandal-questions-and-answers.html.

77. Government Accountability Office, "Campaign Finance: Federal Framework, Agency Roles and Responsibilities, and Perspectives," No. GAO-20-66R, February 3, 2020, 40–42, https://www.gao.gov/assets/gao-20-66r.pdf.

78. 26 U.S.C. §501(c)(3).

79. Brian Faler, "The $80 Billion Question: What Will the IRS Do with

All Its New Money?" *Politico*, August 16, 2022, https://www.politico.com/news/2022/08/16/irs-spending-new-money-00051523.

80. Charles Homans, "Mitch McConnell Got Everything He Wanted. But at What Cost?" *New York Times Magazine*, January 22, 2019, https://www.nytimes.com/2019/01/22/magazine/mcconnell-senate-trump.html.

81. McConnell v. FEC, 540 U.S. 93 (2003).

82. Ibid.

83. Dave Levinthal, "How Washington Starves Its Election Watchdog," Center for Public Integrity, May 4, 2016, https://publicintegrity.org/politics/how-washington-starves-its-election-watchdog/.

84. Nicholas Confessore, "Election Panel Enacts Policy by Not Acting," *New York Times*, August 25, 2014, https://www.nytimes.com/2014/08/26/us/politics/election-panel-enacts-policies-by-not-acting.html.

85. Anthony Herman, "The FEC: Where a 'Tie' Can Be (Almost) a 'Win,'" Covington, March 20, 2014, https://www.insidepoliticallaw.com/2014/03/20/the-fec-where-a-tie-can-be-almost-a-win/.

86. Ann Ravel, *Dysfunction and Deadlock: The Enforcement Crisis at the Federal Election Commission Reveals the Unlikelihood of Draining the Swamp*, Office of Commissioner Ann M. Ravel, February 2017, https://shpr.legislature.ca.gov/sites/shpr.legislature.ca.gov/files/Ravel%20-%20FEC%20Dysfunction.pdf.

87. Ann Ravel, "Dysfunction and Deadlock at the Federal Election Commission," *New York Times*, February 20, 2017, https://www.nytimes.com/2017/02/20/opinion/dysfunction-and-deadlock-at-the-federal-election-commission.html.

88. U.S. House Committee on Administration to FEC, letter, April 1, 2019, https://www.fec.gov/documents/1429/House_Admin_Letter_to_FEC.pdf; FEC to U.S. House Committee on Administration, response letter, May 1, 2019, https://www.fec.gov/about/committee-on-house-administration-april-2019-questions/.

89. H.R. 1 § 6002, S. 1 § 6002 (to be codified at 52 U.S.C. § 30106(a)(1)-(3), (5),(c), (e), and (f)).

90. H.R. 1 § 6004, S. 1 § 6004 (to be codified at 52 U.S.C. § 30109(a)).

BIBLIOGRAPHY

Alemany, Jacqueline, Emma Brown, Tom Hamburger, and Jon Swaine. "Ahead of Jan. 6, Willard Hotel in Downtown D.C. Was a Trump Team 'Command Center' for Effort to Deny Biden Presidency." *Washington Post* (October 23, 2021).

Amann, Diane Marie. "John Paul Stevens and Equally Impartial Government." 43 *U.C. Davis Law Review* 885 (2010).

Anderson, Carol. *The Second: Race and Guns in a Fatally Unequal America* (New York: Bloomsbury, 2021).

Baldwin, James. *The Fire Next Time* (New York: Vintage International, 1963).

Ball, Howard. *A Defiant Life: Thurgood Marshall and the Persistence of Racism* (New York: Crown, 1999).

Barnes, Robert. "Supreme Court Takes Modest but Historic Step with Teleconference Hearings." *Washington Post* (May 4, 2020).

Baugh, Joyce A. *The Detroit School Busing Case* (Lawrence: University Press of Kansas, 2011).

Berry, Christopher R. "School Consolidation and Inequality (September 2006)." *ResearchGate* (January 2007). Accessed July 21, 2022. https://www.researchgate.net/profile/Christopher-Berry-8/publication/5091300_School_Consolidation_and_Inequality/links/54d243bb0cf25017917da65d/School-Consolidation-and-Inequality.pdf

Billington, Monroe. "Public School Integration in Missouri, 1954–64." 35(3) *Journal of Negro Education* 252 (Summer 1966).

"Biographical Directory of Article III Federal Judges, 1789–Present." *Federal Judicial Center*. Accessed July 7, 2022. https://www.fjc.gov/history/judges/search/advanced-search

Biskupic, Joan. "Clarence Thomas Has Found His Moment." *CNN* (May 11, 2020).

"Black Judges and Lawyers: Arbiters and Advocates for Human Rights, Civil Justice and Economic Power" (Preliminary Agenda of the Judicial Council for the National Bar Association, August 7–11, 1988). *Digital Collection, National Bar Association Archives at Drake University.* Accessed July 7, 2022. http://content.library.drake.edu/digital/collection/p16331coll9/id/2065

Blight, David D. *Frederick Douglass* (New York: Simon & Schuster, 2018).

Bloch, Susan Low. "Celebrating Thurgood Marshall: The Prophetic Dissenter." 52 *Howard Law Journal* 667 (2009).

Bork, Robert. "Neutral Principles and Some First Amendment Problems." 47 *Indiana Law Journal* 1 (1971).

Brady, Diane. *Fraternity* (New York: Spiegel & Grau, 2012).

Branch, Taylor. *Parting the Waters: America in the King Years, 1954–63* (New York: Simon & Schuster, 1988).

Brands, H. W. *Heirs of the Founders* (New York: Doubleday, 2018).

Brennan, William. "Speech to the Text and Teaching Symposium." *Georgetown University* (October 12, 1985). Accessed July 7, 2022. https://fedsoc.org/commentary/publications/the-great-debate-justice-william-j-brennan-jr-october-12-1985

Brief for the United States as Amicus Curiae Supporting Petitioners, *Wygant v. Jackson Board of Education*, 1985 WL 669739 (1985).

Brief of the National Medical Association, et al., *Bakke v. Regents of the Univ. of California*, 1977 WL 189515 (1977).

Brown, Emma. "Ginni Thomas, Wife of Supreme Court Justice, Pressed Ariz. Lawmakers to Help Reverse Trump's Loss, Emails Show." *Washington Post* (May 20, 2022).

Brown-Nagin, Tomiko. *Civil Rights Queen: Constance Baker Motley and the Struggle for Equality* (New York: Pantheon, 2022).

———. *Courage to Dissent* (Oxford: Oxford University Press, 2011).

Brown-Scott, Wendy. "Justice Thurgood Marshall and the Integrative Ideal." 26 *Arizona State Law Journal* 535 (1994).

Buccola, Nicholas. *The Fire Is Upon Us* (Princeton: Princeton University Press, 2019).

Burgess, Katherine. "Shelby County District Attorney Abandons Pursuit of Death Penalty in Pervis Payne Case." *The Commercial Appeal* (November 18, 2021).

Burns, Cynthia. "The Fading of the *Brown* Objective: A Historical Perspective of the Marshall Legacy in Education." 35 *Howard Law Journal* 95 (1991).

Cameron, Chris. "These Are the People Who Died in Connection with the Capitol Riot." *New York Times* (January 5, 2022).

Camia, Catalina. "Congressman Stands by Calling Clarence Thomas 'Uncle Tom.'" *USA Today* (April 30, 2014).

Cannon, Lou. "Reagan Pledges He Would Name a Woman to the Supreme Court." *Washington Post* (October 15, 1980).

Carter, Robert. *A Matter of Law* (New York: New Press, 2005).

Cashin, Sheryll. "Justice Thurgood Marshall: A Race Man's Race-Transcending Jurisprudence." 52 *Howard Law Journal* 507 (2009).

Chabot, Christine Kexel, and Benjamin Remy Chabot. "Mavericks, Moderates, or Drifters? Supreme Court Voting Alignments, 1838–2018." 76 *Missouri Law Review* 999 (2011).

Chambers, Julius. "Thurgood Marshall's Legacy." 44 *Stanford Law Review* 1249 (1992).

Chernow, Ron. *Grant* (New York: Penguin, 2017).

Cimbala, Paul, and Randall Miller, eds. *The Freedmen's Bureau and Reconstruction: Reconstructing America* (New York: Fordham University Press, 1999).

Civil Rights Act of 1964 §7, 42 U.S.C. §2000e et seq. (1964).

Clemon, U. W., and Stephanie Y. Moore. "Justice Clarence Thomas: The Burning of Civil Rights Bridges." 1 *Alabama Civil Rights and Civil Liberties Law Review* 49 (2011).

Cohen, Adam. *Supreme Inequality: The Supreme Court's Fifty-Year Battle for a More Unjust America* (New York: Penguin, 2020).

Coltharp, Donna. "Writing in the Margins: Brennan, Marshall, and the Inherent Weakness of Liberal Judicial Decision-Making." 29 *St. Mary's Law Journal* 1 (1997).

Columbia Oral History Project. "The Reminiscences of Thurgood Marshall." In *Thurgood Marshall: His Speeches, Writings, Arguments, Opinions, and Reminiscences*, ed. Mark Tushnet (Chicago: Lawrence Hill Books, 2001), 413.

Congressional Record, 84th Congress Second Session. Vol. 102, part 4 (March 12, 1956) 4459–4460 ("Southern Manifesto").

"Congress Names Building for Thurgood Marshall in Record Two Days." *Jet* (February 22, 1993).

Consovoy, William S., and Nicole Stelle Garnett. "'To Help, Not to Hurt': Justice Thomas's Equality Canon." 127 *Yale Law Journal Forum* 221 (2017).

Cook Jr., Julian Abele. "Thurgood Marshall and Clarence Thomas: A Glance at Their Philosophies." 73 *Michigan Bar Journal* 298 (1994).

Davies, Gareth. *See Government Grow: Education Politics from Johnson to Reagan* (Lawrence: University Press of Kansas, 2007).

De Tocqueville, Alexis. *Democracy in America*, trans. George Lawrence (New York: Perennial Classics, 2000).

Dreyfuss, Joel, and Charles Lawrence III. *The Bakke Case: The Politics of Inequality* (New York: Harcourt, 1979).

Driver, Justin. *The School House Gate: Public Education, the Supreme Court, and the Battle for the American Mind* (New York: Pantheon, 2018).

Du Bois, W. E. B. "Does the Negro Need Separate Schools?" 4 *Journal of Negro Education* 328 (1935).

———. *The Souls of Black Folk* (New York: Bantam Classic, 1989).

Entin, Jonathan L. "Justice Thomas, Race, and the Constitution Through the Lens of Booker T. Washington and W. E. B. Du Bois." 88 *University of Detroit Mercy Law Review* 755 (2011).

Feldman, Noah. *The Three Lives of James Madison* (New York: Picador, 2017).

"Florance Street School." *Historical Marker Database.* Accessed July 7, 2022. https://www.hmdb.org/marker.asp?marker=12088

Ford, Matt. "Thurgood Marshall's Patient but Relentless War." *The Atlantic* (September 6, 2007).

"Freedmen's Bureau Acts of 1865 and 1866." *U.S. Senate.* Accessed July 7, 2022. https://www.senate.gov/artandhistory/history/common/generic/Freedmens-Bureau.htm

Garnett, Nicole Stelle. "'But for the Grace of God Go I': Justice Thomas and the Little Guy." 4 *New York University Journal of Law and Liberty* 626 (2009).

"General Convention." *Journal of the General Convention of . . . the Episcopal Church, Anaheim, 2009.* Accessed July 7, 2022. https://episcopalarchives.org/cgi-bin/acts/acts_resolution.pl?resolution=2009-B020

Gerber, Scott D. "Justice for Clarence Thomas: An Intellectual History of Justice Thomas's Twenty Years on the Supreme Court." 88 *University of Detroit Mercy Law Review* 667 (2011).

Gerhardt, Michael J. "Divided Justice: A Commentary on the Nomination and Confirmation of Justice Thomas." 60 *George Washington Law Review* 969 (1992).

Gerstein, Josh. "Clarence Thomas Defends Silence in Supreme Court Health Care Arguments." *Politico* (April 6, 2012).

Gilkes, Erwin, and Robert Bork. "Address: Erosion of the President's Power in Foreign Affairs." 68 *Washington University Law Quarterly* 693 (1990).

Gotham, Kevin Fox. "Missed Opportunities, Enduring Legacies: Segregation and Desegregation in Kansas City, Missouri." 43(2) *American Studies* 5 (Summer 2002).

Graetz, Michael, and Linda Greenhouse. *The Burger Court and the Rise of the Judicial Right* (New York: Simon & Schuster, 2016).

Green, Emma. "The Clarence Thomas Effect." *The Atlantic* (July 10, 2019).

Greenhouse, Linda. *Becoming Justice Blackmun* (New York: Times, 2005).

Hamilton, Alexander. "No. 78: The Judiciary Department." In *The Federalist Papers,* ed. Charles R. Kesler (New York: Signet Classic, 1961), 463.

Hansberry, Lorraine. *A Raisin in the Sun* (New York: Vintage, 1958).

Harvey, William B., Adia M. Harvey, and Mark King. "The Impact of the Brown v.

Board of Education Decision on Postsecondary Participation of African Americans." 73(3) *The Journal of Negro Education* 328 (2004).

Haygood, Wil. *Showdown: Thurgood Marshall and the Supreme Court Nomination That Changed America* (New York: Knopf, 2015).

Heck, Edward V. "Justice Brennan and the Heyday of Warren Court Liberalism." 20 *Santa Clara Law Review* 841 (1980).

Higginbotham Jr., A. Leon. "Clarence Thomas in Retrospect." 45 *Hastings Law Journal* 1405 (1993).

"High Tech Lynching: Thomas Denies Anita Hill Harassment Allegations." *Washington Post* (October 11, 1991). Accessed July 7, 2022. https://www.washingtonpost.com/video/politics/high-tech-lynching-thomas-denies-anita-hill-harassment-allegations/2018/09/18/370097aa-bbae-11e8-adb8-01125416c102_video.html

Hill, Ruth Johnson. "Mr. Justice Thurgood Marshall 1908–1993: A Bio-Bibliographic Research Guide." 20 *Southern University Law Review* 113 (1993).

Hirshman, Linda. *Sisters in Law: How Sandra Day O'Connor and Ruth Bader Ginsburg Went to the Supreme Court and Changed the World* (New York: Harper Perennial, 2016).

"History." *National Bar Association. Accessed July 14, 2022.* https://www.nationalbar.org/NBA/History.aspx

Jackson Jr., Kennell. "Review: *Black Education: Myths and Tragedies.*" 5(7) *Change* 58 (September 1973).

Jackson, Ketanji Brown. "Opening Statement for Supreme Court Hearings." *Politico* (March 21, 2022). Accessed July 7, 2022. https://www.politico.com/news/2022/03/21/kentaji-brown-jackson-opening-statement-supreme-court-00018980

———. "Supreme Court Nominee Judge Ketanji Brown Jackson Statement." *C-SPAN* (February 25, 2022). Accessed July 7, 2022. https://www.c-span.org/video/?c5003288/supreme-court-nominee-judge-ketanji-brown-jackson-statement

James Jr., Rawn. *Root and Branch: Charles Hamilton Houston, Thurgood Marshall, and the Struggle to End Segregation* (New York: Bloomsbury, 2010).

Johnson, Lyndon B. "Commencement Address at Howard University: 'To Fulfill These Rights' (June 4, 1965)." *Teaching American History.* Accessed July 7, 2022. https://teachingamericanhistory.org/library/document/commencement-address-at-howard-university-to-fulfill-these-rights/

———. "Signing of the Elementary and Secondary Education Act, 4/11/1965." *LBJ Library.* Accessed July 7, 2022. https://www.youtube.com/watch?v=QQzCV1UdPLc

"Junction School." Lyndon B. Johnson National Historical Park Texas. *National Park Service. Accessed July 7, 2022.* https://www.nps.gov/lyjo/planyourvisit/junctionschool.htm

"Justice Marshall Receives National Bar Association Award." *C-SPAN* (August

10, 1988). Accessed July 7, 2022. https://www.c-span.org/video/?3962-1/justice-marshall-receives-national-bar-association-award

Kaczynski, Andrew. "Democratic Congressman Makes Shocking Racial Comments About Republicans, Clarence Thomas, Mitch McConnell." *BuzzFeed.News* (April 29, 2014). Accessed July 7, 2022. https://www.buzzfeednews.com/article/andrewkaczynski/democratic-congressman-makes-shocking-racial-comments-about

Keiser, Gretchen. "Photo Inspires Look Back at Era When Catholic Schools Segregated." *Georgia Bulletin* (January 9, 2014).

Kennedy, Randall. *Sellout: The Politics of Racial Betrayal* (New York: Pantheon, 2008).

Kiel, Daniel. "Accepting Justice Kennedy's Dare." 78 *Fordham Law Review* 2873 (2010).

———. "Avoiding *Atkins*: How Tennessee Is on the Verge of Unconstitutionally Executing an Individual with Intellectual Disabilities." *Law and Inequality (Inequality Inquiry)* (2020). Accessed July 7, 2022. https://lawandinequality.org/2020/11/18/avoiding-atkins-how-tennessee-is-on-the-verge-of-unconstitutionally-executing-an-individual-with-intellectual-disabilities/#

———. "A Bolt of Lightning: Measuring the Impact of Modern Transitions on the Supreme Court." 42 *Cardozo Law Review* 2813~~, 2828~~ (2021).

King, Gilbert. *Devil in the Grove* (New York: Perennial, 2012).

King Jr., Martin Luther. "Our God Is Marching On." In *A Testament of Hope*, ed. James M. Washington (San Francisco: Harper, 1986), 227.

Kluger, Richard. *Simple Justice* (New York: Vintage, 1975).

Kotz, Nick. *Judgment Days: Lyndon Baines Johnson, Martin Luther King Jr., and the Laws That Changed America* (New York: Houghton Mifflin, 2005).

Kroft, Steve. "Clarence Thomas: The Justice Nobody Knows." *CBS News: 60 Minutes* (September 27, 2007).

Lackey, Michael. "A Brief History of the Haverford Group." In *The Haverford Discussions: A Black Integrationist Manifesto for Racial Justice*, ed. Michael Lackey (Charlottesville: University of Virginia Press, 2013), xi.

Lee, Gary. "Black Lawyers' Group Divided on Thomas." *Washington Post* (August 5, 1991).

Lemann, Nicholas. "Hating on Herbert Hoover." *The New Yorker* (October 16, 2017).

Lewis, David Levering. *W. E. B. Du Bois: The Fight for Equality and the American Century, 1919–1963* (New York: Henry Holt, 2000).

Lewis, John. *Walking with the Wind* (New York: Harcourt Brace, 1998).

Lewis, Neil A. "Invitation to Justice Thomas Creates Furor." *New York Times* (May 29, 1998).

———. "Justice Thomas Declines to Drop Speech to Bar." *New York Times* (June 17, 1998).

Liptak, Adam. "Clarence Thomas Breaks 10 Years of Silence at Supreme Court." *New York Times* (February 29, 2016).

———. "Justice Clarence Thomas Breaks His Silence." *New York Times* (January 14, 2013).

———. "The Same Words, but Differing Views." *New York Times* (June 29, 2007).

Lithwick, Dahlia. "Hands Off Thomas." *Slate* (May 30, 2009).

Lithwick, Dahlia, and Mark Joseph Stern. "The Clarence Thomas Takeover." *Slate* (August 2, 2017).

Lovett, Bobby L. *America's Historically Black Colleges and Universities: A Narrative History* (Atlanta: Mercer University Press, 2015).

Marcus, Marcia L. "Learning Together: Justice Marshall's Desegregation Opinions." 61 *Fordham Law Review* 69 (1992).

Marshall, Thurgood. "Reflections on the Bicentennial of the United States Constitution." In *Thurgood Marshall: His Speeches, Writings, Arguments, Opinions, and Reminiscences*, ed. Mark Tushnet (Chicago: Lawrence Hill, 2001), 281.

———. "Remarks at the Annual Conference of the Second Circuit, Sept. 8, 1989." In *Thurgood Marshall: His Speeches, Writings, Arguments, Opinions, and Reminiscences*, ed. Mark Tushnet (Chicago: Lawrence Hill, 2001), 217.

Martin, Andrew D., and Kevin M. Quinn. "Dynamic Ideal Point Estimation via Markov Chain Monte Carlo for the U.S. Supreme Court, 1953–1999." 10 *Political Analysis* 134 (2002).

Mayer, Jane. "Is Ginni Thomas a Threat to the Supreme Court?" *The New Yorker* (January 21, 2022).

Mazzei, Patricia. "How a High School Debate Team Shaped Ketanji Brown Jackson." *New York Times* (February 26, 2022).

McDonogh, Gary. *Black and Catholic in Savannah, Georgia* (Knoxville: University of Tennessee Press, 1993).

McFadden, Robert D. "Damon Keith, Federal Judge Who Championed Civil Rights, Dies at 96." *New York Times* (April 28, 2019).

McGregor, Jena. "Justice Thomas's Supreme Silence." *Washington Post* (January 17, 2013).

McNeil, Genna Rae. *Groundwork: Charles Hamilton Houston and the Struggle for Civil Rights* (Philadelphia: University of Pennsylvania Press, 1983).

"Measures." *Martin-Quinn Scores*. Accessed July 7, 2022. https://perma.cc/DMB5-4P6N

Meese, Edwin. "A Jurisprudence of Original Attention." *American Bar Association* (July 9, 1985). Accessed July 7, 2022. https://www.justice.gov/sites/default/files/ag/legacy/2011/08/23/07-09-1985.pdf

———. "The Law of the Constitution." *Tulane University* (October 21, 1986). Accessed July 7, 2022. https://www.justice.gov/sites/default/files/ag/legacy/2011/08/23/10-21-1986.pdf

Merida, Kevin, and Michael Fletcher. *Supreme Discomfort: The Divided Soul of Clarence Thomas* (New York: Broadway, 2007).

Moore, Gary A., and Michael K. Braswell. "Quotas and the Codification of the Disparate Impact Theory: What Did *Griggs* Really Say and Not Say?" 55 *Albany Law Review* 459 (1991).

Morris, Jerome. "Malcolm X's Critique of the Education of Black People." 25(2) *The Western Journal of Black Studies* 126 (2001).

NAACP. "Editorial." *The Crisis* (January 1917).

"National Bar Association (1925–)." *BlackPast. Accessed July 14, 2022. https://www.blackpast.org/african-american-history/national-bar-association-1925/*

"1952 Argument: Briggs v. Elliott." In *Brown v. Board: The Landmark Oral Argument Before the Supreme Court*, ed. Leon Friedman (New York: New Press, 2004), 36.

"1953 Argument: Briggs v. Elliott." In *Brown v. Board: The Landmark Oral Argument Before the Supreme Court*, ed. Leon Friedman (New York: New Press, 2004), 179.

Onwuachi-Willig, Angela. "Just Another Brother on the SCT?: What Justice Clarence Thomas Teaches Us About the Influence of Racial Identity." 90 *Iowa Law Review* 931 (2004).

———. "Using the Master's 'Tool' to Dismantle His House: Why Justice Clarence Thomas Makes the Case for Affirmative Action." 47 *Arizona Law Review* 113 (2005).

"Old Frederick Douglass High School (1924)." *Baltimore Places.* Accessed July 7, 2022. http://places.baltimoreheritage.org/old-douglass-high-school/

"Oral Argument: Cooper *v.* Aaron." *Oyez* Accessed July 7, 2022. https://www.oyez.org/cases/1957/1_misc

"Oral Argument: Green *v.* County School Board of New Kent County." *Oyez.* Accessed July 7, 2022. https://www.oyez.org/cases/1967/695

"Oral Argument: Regents of the University of California *v.* Bakke." *Oyez.* Accessed July 7, 2022. https://www.oyez.org/cases/1979/76-811

"Oral Argument: Voisine *v.* United States." *Oyez.* Accessed July 7, 2022. https://www.oyez.org/cases/2015/14-10154

"Oral Argument: Wygant *v.* Jackson Board of Education." *Oyez.* Accessed July 7, 2022. https://www.oyez.org/cases/1985/84-1340

Ossei-Owusu, Shaun. "Racial Revisionism." 119 *Michigan Law Review* 1165 (2021).

Page, Clarence. "Thomas' Sister Gives Lie to Welfare Fable." *Chicago Tribune* (July 24, 1991).

Parker, Wendy. "The Story of *Grutter v. Bollinger*: Affirmative Action Wins." *Wake Forest Legal Studies Research Paper* (2006). Accessed July 7, 2022. http://users.wfu.edu/mcclanas/bookchapter.pdf

Paul, John Richard. *Without Precedent: Chief Justice John Marshall and His Times* (New York: Riverhead, 2018).

Powell, Cedric Merlin. "Justice Thomas, Brown, and Post-Racial Determinism." 53 *Washburn Law Journal* 451 (2014).

"Public School No. 103." *Explore Baltimore Heritage. Accessed July 7, 2022.* https://explore.baltimoreheritage.org/items/show/75

Reagan, Ronald. "Address Before a Joint Session of Congress on the State of the Union—1987." *Ronald Reagan Presidential Library and Museum.* Accessed August 24, 2022. https://www.reaganlibrary.gov/archives/speech/address-joint-session-congress-state-union-1987

———. "Inaugural Address (January 20, 1981)." *Ronald Reagan: Presidential Foundation and Institute.* Accessed July 7, 2022. https://www.reaganfoundation.org/ronald-reagan/reagan-quotes-speeches/inaugural-address-2/

———. "A Time for Choosing (October 27, 1964)." *Ronald Reagan Presidential Library and Foundation.* Accessed July 7, 2022. https://www.youtube.com/watch?v=qXBswFfh6AY

"Retirement of Justice Marshall." *C-SPAN* (June 28, 1991). Accessed July 7, 2022. https://www.c-span.org/video/?18679-1/retirement-justice-marshall

Richardson, Jeanita W., and J. John Harris III. "*Brown* and Historically Black Colleges and Universities (HBCUs): A Paradox of Desegregation Policy." 73(3) *Journal of Negro Education* 365 (2004).

Rickford, Russell. *We Are an African People: Independent Education, Black Power, and the Radical Imagination* (Oxford: Oxford University Press, 2016).

Roberts, Gene, and Hank Klibanoff. *The Race Beat: The Press, the Civil Rights Struggle, and the Awakening of a Nation* (New York: Knopf, 2007).

Robin, Corey. *The Enigma of Clarence Thomas* (New York: Metropolitan, 2019).

Rothstein, Richard. *The Color of Law* (New York: Livewright, 2017).

Rowan, Carl. "Thomas Is Far from 'Home.'" *Chicago Sun-Times* (July 4, 1993).

Ryan, James. *"Schools, Race, and Money."* 109 *Yale Law Journal* 249 (1999).

Schwartz, Ian. "Pence on Gorsuch: We Want to Give Clarence Thomas an Aid in His Lonely Fight." *Real Clear Politics* (February 5, 2017).

Scott, Eugene. "Trump Hits Scalia over Comments on Black Students." *CNN* (December 13, 2015).

Segedy, Andria. "St. Pius X History: Savannah Churches, Community Opened Doors to Classical Education During Segregation." *Savannah Morning News* (September 15, 2018).

Selmi, Michael. "The Life of *Bakke*: An Affirmative Action Retrospective." 87 *Georgetown Law Journal* 981 (1998).

Shear, Michael. "Biden Made a Campaign Pledge to Put a Black Woman on the Supreme Court." *New York Times (*January 26, 2022).

Skutch, Jan. "1963, Desegregation Changed the Lives of 19 Savannah Teens, Society." *Savannah Morning News* (August 18, 2013).

Slotkin, Jason. "Protesters Swarm Michigan Capitol amid Showdown over Governor's Emergency Powers." *NPR* (May 1, 2020).

Solum, Lawrence B. "What Is Originalism? The Evolution of Contemporary Originalist Theory." *Georgetown University Law Center* (2011). Accessed July 7, 2022. https://scholarship.law.georgetown.edu/cgi/viewcontent.cgi?article=2362&context=facpub

Sotomayor, Sonia. *My Beloved World* (New York: Knopf, 2013).

Sowell, Thomas. *Black Education: Myths and Tragedies* (New York: McKay, 1972).

———. *Race and Economics* (New York: McKay, 1975).

Sracic, Paul A. *San Antonio v. Rodriguez and the Pursuit of Equal Education* (Lawrence: University Press of Kansas, 2006).

Starkey, Brando Simeo. "Uncle Tom and Justice Clarence Thomas: Is the Abuse Defensible?" 4 *Georgetown Journal of Law and Modern Critical Race Perspectives* 101 (2012).

Sullivan, Patricia. "A Small, Mostly White Virginia Town Put up a 'Black Lives Matter' Banner. Ginni Thomas Denounced It." *Washington Post* (July 10, 2020).

"Supreme Court Nomination Announcement." *C-SPAN* (July 1, 1991). Accessed July 7, 2022. https://www.c-span.org/video/?18649-1/supreme-court-nomination-announcemen

"Supreme Court Nominations (1789–Present)." *U.S. Senate*. Accessed July 7, 2022. https://www.senate.gov/legislative/nominations/SupremeCourtNominations1789present.htm

Suskind, Ron. *A Hope in the Unseen: An American Odyssey from the Inner City to the Ivy League* (New York: Broadway, 1998).

Swire, Sonnet, and Veronica Stracqualursi. "GOP Senator Says Black Woman Supreme Court Pick Would Be 'Beneficiary' of Affirmative Action." *CNN* (January 29, 2022).

Taylor Jr., Stuart. "Marshall Sounds Critical Note on Bicentennial." *New York Times* (May 7, 1987).

Tensley, Brandon. "The Many Joys of Ketanji Brown Jackson's Historic Confirmation." *CNN* (April 7, 2022).

Thomas, Clarence. "Affirmative Action Goals and Timetables: Too Tough? Not Tough Enough!" 5 *Yale Law & Policy Review* 402 (1987).

———. "Be Not Afraid." *American Enterprise Institute* (February 13, 2001). Accessed July 7, 2022. https://www.aei.org/research-products/speech/be-not-afraid/

———. "Freedom: A Responsibility, Not a Right." 21 *Ohio Northern University Law Review* 5 (1994).

———. *My Grandfather's Son* (New York: Perennial, 2007).

———. "Supreme Court Justice Speech." *C-SPAN* (July 29, 1998). Accessed July 7, 2022. https://www.c-span.org/video/?109490-1/supreme-court-justice-speech

Totenburg, Nina. "Justice Scalia, the Great Dissenter, Opens Up." *NPR: Morning Edition* (April 28, 2008).

Tumulty, Karen. "Sister of High Court Nominee Traveled Different Road." *Los Angeles Times* (July 5, 1991).

Tushnet, Mark V. "The Jurisprudence of Thurgood Marshall." 1996 *University of Illinois Law Review* 1129 (1996).

———. "The Supreme Court and Race Discrimination, 1967–1991: The View from the Marshall Papers." 36 *William and Mary Law Review* 473 (1995).

U.S. Commission on the Bicentennial of the U.S. Constitution. "We the People" (1976).

U.S. Constitution.

U.S. Department of Justice. "National Advisory Commission on Civil Disorders, Report" (1967). Accessed on July 7, 2022. https://www.ncjrs.gov/pdffiles1/Digitization/8073NCJRS.pdf

U.S. Supreme Court. "Press Release" (March 16, 2020). Accessed July 7, 2022. https://www.supremecourt.gov/publicinfo/press/pressreleases/pr_03-16-20

———. "Press Release" (April 3, 2020). Accessed July 7, 2022. https://www.supremecourt.gov/publicinfo/press/pressreleases/pr_04-03-20

Van Patten, Jonathan K. "The Partisan Battle over the Constitution: Meese's Jurisprudence of Original Intention and Brennan's Theory of Contemporary Ratification." 70 *Marquette Law Review* 389 (1987).

Weisberg, Jessica. "*Remembering Ruth Bader Ginsburg in Her Own Words.*" *Elle* (September 21, 2020).

Welch, William M. "Thomas Presided over Shift in Policy at EEOC, Records Show." *Associated Press* (July 25, 1991).

White, Adam. "Just, Wise, and Constitutional: Justice Thomas's Legacy in Law and Politics." *Law & Liberty* (April 17, 2014).

Whitford, Emma. "College Urged to Strip Clarence Thomas's Name from Building." *Inside Higher Ed* (October 15, 2018). Accessed July 14, 2022. https://www.insidehighered.com/quicktakes/2018/10/15/college-urged-strip-clarence-thomass-name-building

Wilkerson, Isabel. *The Warmth of Other Suns* (New York: Vintage, 2010).

Williams, Heather Andrea. *Self-Taught: African American Education in Slavery and Freedom* (Chapel Hill: University of North Carolina Press, 2005).

Williams, Juan. "Black Conservatives, Center Stage." *Washington Post* (December 16, 1980).

———. "A Question of Fairness." *The Atlantic* (February 1987).

———. *Thurgood Marshall: American Revolutionary* (New York: Three Rivers, 1998).

Williams, Pete. "Supreme Court Makes History with Oral Arguments by Phone. But It's Business as Usual for the Justices." *NBC News (*May 4, 2020).

"William T. Coleman, Jr." *The History Makers*. Accessed July 7, 2022. https://www.thehistorymakers.org/biography/william-t-coleman-jr

Wing, Nick. "Clarence Thomas: Obama Only President Because He's What Elites Expect from a Black Person." *Huffington Post* (May 3, 2013).

Woodward, Bob, and Scott Armstrong. *The Brethren: Inside the Supreme Court* (New York: Simon & Shuster, 1979).

Woodward, Bob, and Robert Costa, "Virginia Thomas Urged White House Chief to Pursue Unrelenting Efforts to Overturn the 2020 Election, Texts Show." *Washington Post* (March 24, 2022).

CASES

Aaron v. McKinley, 173 F.Supp. 944 (E.D. Ark. 1959)

Abrams v. U.S., 250 U.S. 616 (1919)

Adams v. United States, 319 U.S. 312 (1943)

Adarand Constructors, Inc. v. Pena, 515 U.S. 200 (1995)

Alexander v. Holmes County Board of Education, 396 U.S. 1218 (1969)

Allen v. State Board of Elections, 393 U.S. 544 (1969)

Atkins v. Virginia, 536 U.S. 304 (2002)

Baxter v. Bracey, 590 U.S. ___, 140 S.Ct. 1862 (2020)

Beer v. U.S., 425 U.S. 130 (1976)

Board of Education of Oklahoma City v. Dowell, 498 U.S. 237 (1991)

Dowell v. Okla City Bd of Educ, 778 F.Supp. 1144 (W.D. Okla. 1991)

Box v. Planned Parenthood of Indiana and Kentucky, 587 U.S. ___, 139 S.Ct. 1780 (2019)

Briggs v. Elliott, 342 U.S. 350 (1952)

Briggs v. Elliott, 98 F.Supp. 529 (E.D. S.C. 1951)

Briggs v. Elliott, 103 F.Supp. 920 (E.D. S.C. 1952)

Briggs v. Elliott, 132 F.Supp. 776 (E.D. S.C. 1955)

Brnovich v. DNC, 594 U.S. ___, 141 S.Ct. 2321 (2021)

Brown v. Board of Education, 347 U.S. 483 (1954)

Brown v. Board of Education, 98 F.Supp. 797 (D. Kan. 1951)

Brown v. Board of Education, 349 U.S. 294 (1955)

Calvary Chapel Dayton Valley v. Sisolak, 591 U.S. ___, 140 S.Ct. 2603 (2020)

City of Los Angeles v. Lyons, 461 U.S. 95 (1983)

City of Mobile v. Bolden, 446 U.S. 55 (1980)

City of Richmond v. J.A. Croson, Co., 488 U.S. 469 (1989)

City of Richmond v. U.S., 429 U.S. 358 (1975)

City of Rome v. U.S., 446 U.S. 156 (1980)
Civil Rights Cases, 109 U.S. 3 (1883)
Connecticut v. Teal, 457 U.S. 440 (1982)
Cooper v. Aaron, 358 U.S. 1 (1958)
Aaron v. Cooper, 163 F.Supp. 13 (E.D. Ark. 1958)
Aaron v. Cooper, 257 F.2d 33 (8th Cir. 1958)
DeFunis v. Odegaard, 416 U.S. 312 (1974)
Dred Scott v. Sandford, 60 U.S. 393 (1857)
Scott v. Emerson, 15 Mo. 576 (Mo. 1852)
Dunn v. Blumstein, 405 U.S. 330 (1972)
Evenwel v. Abbott, 578 U.S. 54 (2016)
Fair v. Meredith, 371 U.S. 828 (1962) (denying cert)
Meredith v. Fair, 83 S.Ct. 10 (1962) (vacating stay)
Meredith v. Fair, 305 F.2d 343 (5th Cir. 1962)
Fisher v. University of Texas, 570 U.S. 297 (2013)
Flowers v. Mississippi, 588 U.S. ___, 139 S.Ct. 2228 (2019)
Foster v. Chatman, 578 U.S. 488 (2016)
Freeman v. Pitts, 503 U.S. 467 (1992)
Fullilove v. Klutznick, 448 U.S. 448 (1980)
Furman v. Georgia, 408 U.S. 238 (1972)
Gamble v. U.S., 587 U.S. ___, 139 S.Ct. 1960 (2019)
Georgia v. McCollum, 505 U.S. 42 (1992)
Gratz v. Bollinger, 539 U.S. 244 (2003)
Green v. County School Board of New Kent County, 391 U.S. 430 (1968)
Griggs v. Duke Power, 401 U.S. 424 (1971)
Griswold v. Connecticut, 381 U.S. 479 (1965)
Grutter v. Bollinger, 539 U.S. 306 (2003)
Hammer v. Dagenhart, 247 U.S. 251 (1918)
Hampton v. Jefferson County Board of Education, 102 F.Supp.2d 358 (W.D. Ky. 2000)
Harrison v. Day, 106 S.E.2d 636 (Va. 1959)
Heyward v. Public Housing Administration, 238 F.2d 689 (5th Cir. 1956)
Holder v. Hall, 512 U.S. 874 (1994)
Keyes v. Denver School District, No. 1, 413 U.S. 189 (1973)
Korematsu v. U.S., 323 U.S. 214 (1944)
Lyons v. Oklahoma, 322 U.S. 596 (1944)
Mahanoy Area School District v. B.L., 594 U.S. __, 141 S.Ct. 2038 (2021)
McKesson v. Doe, 592 U.S. ___, 141 S.Ct. 48 (2020)
McLaurin v. Okla State Board of Regents, 339 U.S. 637 (1950)
Metro Broadcasting, Inc. v. FCC, 497 U.S. 547 (1990)
Milliken v. Bradley, 418 U.S. 717 (1974)
Bradley v. Milliken, 338 F.Supp. 582 (E.D. Mich. 1971)

Bradley v. Milliken, 345 F.Supp. 914 (E.D. Mich. 1972)
Milliken v. Bradley, 433 U.S. 267 (1977)
Mississippi v. Flowers, 588 U.S. ___, 139 S.Ct. 2228 (2019)
Missouri ex rel Gaines v. Canada, 305 U.S. 337 (1938)
Missouri v. Jenkins, 495 U.S. 33 (1990)
Jenkins v. Missouri, 593 F.Supp. 1485 (W.D. Mo. 1984)
Jenkins v. Missouri, 639 F.Supp. 19 (W.D. Mo. 1985)
Missouri v. Jenkins, 515 U.S. 70 (1995)
Murray v. Pearson, 182 A. 590 (Md. 1935)
Northwest Austin Municipal District v. Holder, 557 U.S. 193 (2009)
Patton v. Mississippi, 332 U.S. 463 (1947)
Payne v. Tennessee, 501 U.S. 808 (1991)
Payne v. State, 2007 WL 4258178 (Tenn. Ct. Crim. App. 2007) (denying DNA petition)
Tennessee v. Payne, Nos. 87-04409 & 87-04410, Order (Tenn. Sup. Ct. Feb. 24, 2020) (setting execution date)
PICS v. Seattle School District, 551 U.S. 701 (2007)
Plessy v. Ferguson, 163 U.S. 537 (1896)
Reed v. Rhodes, 179 F.3d 453 (6th Cir. 1999)
Reed v. Rhodes, 422 F.Supp. 708 (N.D. Ohio 1976)
Reed v. Rhodes, 934 F.Supp. 1533 (N.D. Ohio 1996)
Regents of the Univ. of California v. Bakke, 438 U.S. 265 (1978)
Bakke v. Regents of the Univ. of California, 553 P.2d 1152 (Cal. 1976)
Republican Party of Pennsylvania v. Boockvar, 592 U.S. ___, 141 S.Ct. 643 (2020)
Republican Party of Pennsylvania v. Degraffenreid, 592 U.S. ___, 141 S.Ct. 732 (2021)
Ricci v. Destefano, 557 U.S. 557 (2009)
Roe v. Wade, 410 U.S. 113 (1973)
Roman Catholic Diocese of Brooklyn v. Cuomo, 592 U.S. ___, 141 S.Ct. 63 (2020)
San Antonio ISD v. Rodriguez, 411 U.S. 1 (1973)
Rodriguez v. San Antonio ISD, 337 F.Supp. 280 (W.D. Tex.1971)
Shelby County v. Holder, 570 U.S. 529 (2013)
Shelley v. Kraemer, 334 U.S. 1 (1948)
Sipes v. McGhee, 316 Mich. 614 (1947)
Sipuel v. Bd of Regents of Univ of Oklahoma, 332 U.S. 631 (1948)
Smith v. Allwright, 321 U.S. 649 (1944)
Snyder v. Louisiana, 552 U.S. 472 (2008)
South Bay United Pentecostal Church v. Newsom, 590 U.S. ___, 140 S.Ct. 1613 (2020)
South Carolina v. Katzenbach, 383 U.S. 301 (1966)
Stell v. Savannah-Chatham County Board of Education, 220 F. Supp. 667 (1963)

Swann v. Charlotte-Mecklenburg Board of Education, 402 U.S. 1 (1971)
Swann v. Charlotte-Mecklenburg Board of Education, 306 F.Supp. 1299 (W.D. N.C. 1969)
Sweatt v. Painter, 339 U.S. 629 (1950)
Taylor v. Alabama, 335 U.S. 252 (1948)
Texas v. Pennsylvania, 592 U.S. ___, 141 S.Ct. 1230 (2020)
Tinsley v. City of Richmond, 368 U.S. 18 (1961)
Trump v. Thompson, 595 U.S. ___, 142 S.Ct. 680 (2022)
U.S. v. Carolene Products, 304 U.S. 144 (1938)
U.S. v. Darby, 312 U.S. 100 (1941)
U.S. v. Fordice, 505 U.S. 717 (1992)
Ayers v. Allain, 674 F.Supp. 1523 (N.D. Miss. 1987)
Ayers v. Allain, 914 F.2d 676 (5th Cir. 1990)
U.S. v. Lopez, 514 U.S. 549 (1995)
U.S. v. Missouri, 515 F.2d 1365 (8th Cir. 1975)
Village of Arlington Heights v. Metropolitan Housing Corp., 429 U.S. 252 (1977)
Voisine v. U.S., 579 U.S. 686 (2016)
Wards Cove Packing Co. v. Atonio, 490 U.S. 642 (1989)
Washington v. Davis, 426 U.S. 229 (1976)
Watson v. Fort Worth Bank and Trust, 487 U.S. 977 (1988)
Watts v. Indiana, 338 U.S. 49 (1949)
Wygant v. Jackson Board of Education, 476 U.S. 267 (1986).
Wygant v. Jackson Board of Education, 546 F.Supp. 1195 (E.D. Mich. 1982)
Zelman v. Simmons-Harris, 536 U.S. 639 (2002)
Ziglar v. Abbasi, 582 U.S. ___, 137 S.Ct. 1843 (2017)

INDEX